THE EUROPEAN UNDERSTANDING OF INDIA

General Editors of the Series

K. A. BALLHATCHET

P. J. MARSHALL

D. F. POCOCK

European attempts to understand India have been pursued in a variety of fields. Many of the books and articles that resulted are still of great historical importance. Not only do they provide valuable information about the India of the time; they are also of significance in the intellectual history of Europe. Each volume in the present series has been edited by a scholar who is concerned to elucidate both its Indian and its European relevance.

The British Discovery of Hinduism in the Eighteenth Century

The British
Discovery of Hinduism in the
Eighteenth Century

Edited by
P. J. MARSHALL
Lecturer in History, King's College, London

CAMBRIDGE
AT THE UNIVERSITY PRESS
1970

Published by the Syndics of the Cambridge University Press
Bentley House, 200 Euston Road, London N.W.1
American Branch: 32 East 57th Street, New York, N.Y.10022

Selection and editorial material © Cambridge University Press 1970

Library of Congress Catalogue Card Number: 73-111132

Standard Book Number: 521 07737 0

Printed in Great Britain
at the University Printing House, Cambridge
(Brooke Crutchley, University Printer)

Contents

Plate

Text illustrations

These illustrations are a selection from those included by Jones in his 'Essay on the Gods of Greece, Italy and India' and are reproduced by courtesy of the Secretary of State for Foreign and Commonwealth Affairs.

Preface

Since the sixteenth century large parts of the world have been subjected not only to the political, military or economic power of Europe, but to the power of European ideas as well. But if the Europeans have exported more than they imported, the intellectual exchange has not been all one way; the conquerors have not been entirely uninfluenced by the conquered. This book will attempt to show how increasing knowledge of one alien civilisation forced Europeans to reconsider and even to modify certain widely accepted ideas.

In the second half of the eighteenth century the triumph of British arms in India gave Europeans new opportunities for studying Indian civilisation. It is hardly surprising that many of those who took advantage of these new opportunities should have been British or that Indian religion should have been the main object of their inquiries. Religion was still the major preoccupation of the intellectual life of eighteenth-century Europe, even for those who rejected its formal claims, and religion seemed to be the key for understanding all things Indian. Nearly all investigators were drawn to Hinduism, rather than to Islam, with which they believed themselves to be already familiar, or to Buddhism, which most Europeans could not identify with certainty. A selection from what seem to be the most significant accounts of Hinduism written in English in the second half of the eighteenth century are here reproduced.

It must be stressed that this book is intended to be a study of Europeans and their beliefs, not of Hinduism. The accounts in it seem to me to be interesting not for the information which they give or fail to give about Hinduism, but for what they reveal of the authors and their contemporaries. The purpose of the Introduction and the notes is therefore to try to show something of the assumptions with which Europeans approached Hinduism, of the sources available to them, of the interpretations they put on what they had learnt, and of how their discoveries were received by a

vii

Preface

wider public. The notes do not attempt to correct misapprehensions, inaccuracies or distortions.

My deficiencies, which include a total ignorance of Indian languages and a knowledge of Hinduism which is limited and superficial, have made me heavily dependent on the expertise of others, and I have received unfailing generosity from all those to whom I have turned for help. I would like particularly to thank Professor K. A. Ballhatchet, the General Editor of this series, for much helpful advice. Mr J. B. Harrison and Dr Geoffrey Parrinder read drafts of the Introduction and suggested valuable amendments to it. Mr Edward Courtney resolved many of the problems raised by Sir William Jones's classical allusions. Dr Wendy O'Flaherty and Mrs Marta Guha devoted a great deal of time and effort to the Glossary and I am deeply in their debt. They are in no way responsible for any inaccuracies and inconsistencies that may remain in it. Many of the identifications in the Glossary are due to the resourcefulness of Professor Ashin Das Gupta, Dr Uma Das Gupta and Mr Ranajit Guha. Mr Simon Digby also gave me much help with the Glossary.

I have omitted the majority of illustrations which accompanied the texts and have in some instances deleted sentences which directed the reader's attention to illustrations not reproduced. Phonetic renderings of long passages of Sanskrit in Halhed's Preface have also been omitted. The original spelling has been preserved throughout, but capitalisation has been modernised and italics have been more sparingly used. The only accents and diacritical marks used in transcriptions of words from Asian languages are those of the original authors.

Sir William Jones's transcriptions present few problems for modern readers, since his principles of transcription are not very different from those generally in use at the present time. But it is often extremely difficult to identify the original behind attempts made by Holwell, Dow or Halhed to reproduce phonetically the sounds made to them by their *pandits*. Modern transcriptions (often very tentative ones) are provided either in the notes or in a Glossary at the end of the book.

As this book is about the British discovery of Hinduism, it

viii

Preface

seemed appropriate to refer in the notes and the Introduction to contemporary English translations of books originally written in other European languages, where these are available.

The place of publication for all books cited is London, unless otherwise indicated.

P. J. M.

Textual Note

The sources for the texts are as follows:

1 *Interesting Historical Events relative to the Provinces of Bengal and the Empire of Indostan*, vol. ii, 1767
2 *The History of Hindostan*, vol. i, 1768
3 *A Code of Gentoo Laws, or Ordinations of the Pundits*, 1776
4 and 5 *The Bhăgvăt-Gēētā, or Dialogues of Krĕĕshnă and Ărjŏŏn*, 1785
6 *Asiatick Researches*, vol. i, chapter IX, 1789 (First written in 1784, revised for publication)
7 *Asiatick Researches*, vol. i, chapter XXV, 1789 (The third anniversary discourse, delivered 2 February 1786)
8 *Asiatick Researches*, vol. ii, chapter VII, 1790 (Written in January 1788)

Note on Footnotes

The original footnotes of the authors are indicated by numerals; additional footnotes inserted by the editor are indicated by letters. Where both types of note occur on the same page, the author's note is invariably given first.

Introduction

The great wave of exploration, trade and conquest which began in the late fifteenth century inevitably brought Europeans into much closer contact with non-European peoples. Over the next two centuries information about the peoples of Asia, Africa and America was gradually amassed and disseminated among the European reading public. Knowledge of other civilisations invited comparisons with that of Europe itself, comparisons which by the mid-eighteenth century had become highly flattering to the Europeans. Europeans had proved their military prowess over and over again; western European living standards were markedly higher than any outside Europe; the superiority of European scientific knowledge and technical accomplishments was hardly open to question; western Europeans were able to contrast their own political and legal systems with what they called 'Asiatic despotism'; and since most Europeans could not conceive of criteria for judging works of art which were different from their own, they had no hesitation in disparaging the cultural achievements of others.

The apparently unsophisticated societies of North America or Africa, the extinct civilisations of the Near East, or those which had disintegrated before the onslaught of the Spaniards in South and Central America did little to weaken European self-confidence. However superficially and myopically they may have judged, most eighteenth-century Europeans were prepared to dismiss Islam as recent, derivative and anyway in retreat. There remained, however, the civilisations of China and India, which did not fit so easily into a pattern of European supremacy. By the middle of the eighteenth century there was enough information available to indicate their great age, their continuing vitality, and their practical achievements; and there were also Europeans willing to exploit this information. Criticism of certain aspects of European society commonly took the form of unfavourable comparisons with China or less frequently with India. While this combination of increased awareness of the rest of the world and increased self-criticism did not effectively dent eighteenth-century complacency, it did provoke a debate in which European values were for the first time seriously called in question. The controversies were fiercest over China. High claims were made for the Chinese system of government, for Chinese art, and above all for Confucianism (Buddhism being generally ignored or disparaged).[1] Since the late seventeenth century, opponents of Christianity had been setting themselves the task of demolishing its claims to be the unique vehicle of God's purposes on earth by showing that Old Testament history was a corruption of more ancient religions and that other faiths were preferable to Christianity in their ethical teaching. Confucianism seemed to be an admirable candidate on both counts; disputes about the nature of Confucianism and the implications for Christianity if the more favourable accounts of it could be accepted dominated the European debate on China.[2]

Widespread European discussion of India took place rather later, mostly occurring in the second half of the eighteenth century, but here too religious controversies overshadowed other issues. Although a number of published accounts of India had appeared in Europe during the sixteenth and seventeenth centuries, perhaps because they lacked the powerful advocacy of the great Jesuit works on China, they do not seem to have received very much public notice. In the eighteenth century, however, European rivalries attracted attention to India and European conquests gave new facilities for gathering information. From the 1760s books on India began to multiply. Readers of these books would have been reassured that in general Europe had little to fear from comparisons with India. With the Mughal empire collapsing and most of the successor states in disorder, few argued that India had anything to teach the West politically.

[1] G. R. Welbon, *The Buddhist Nirvana and its Western Interpreters* (Chicago, 1968), pp. 18–22.

[2] For a brief outline of these controversies see R. Shackleton, 'Asia as seen by the French Enlightenment', R. Iyer ed., *The Glass Curtain between Asia and Europe* (Oxford, 1965); for a fuller account, B. Guy, *The French Image of China before and after Voltaire* (*Studies on Voltaire and the Eighteenth century*, xxi) (Geneva, 1963); also L. Dermigny, *La Chine et l'Occident. Le Commerce à Canton au xviiie siècle* (Paris, 1964), i, 17 ff.

Introduction

Indian literature not written in Persian remained largely inaccessible to Europeans until they could master Sanskrit. Indian Islamic architecture and the 'pagodas' and sculpture of south India were well known, while the cave temples of Ellora, Elephanta and Salsette were periodically visited and described by travellers, but it would require a major change in aesthetic standards before 'proportions and forms, so different from Grecian rules' or 'grotesque and fanciful' sculpture would be admired.[1] For all their great reputation with antiquity, Indian philosophy and science, with the possible exception of astronomy, now seemed to have very little to offer. Indeed, most Europeans believed that India was in a state of intellectual stagnation. Nothing seemed to have changed since the Greeks wrote their accounts. Indian learning appeared to have degenerated into the uncomprehending repetition of time-honoured formulae. Speculation and endeavour were thought to have been stifled by an enervating climate, political despotism, a fertile soil producing the necessaries of life without any stimulus to effort, and a religious system which forbade change in any aspect of its believers' lives.[2] Yet in spite of much adverse comment on its effects on Indian society, Hinduism found its champions in Europe. The debate set off by Confucianism was revived. Another candidate was put into the field against Christianity and its historical claims and the purity of its doctrines were asserted.

The debate on China had been largely confined to continental Europe and above all to France. In spite of their military débâcle in India, the achievement of the French in exploring Indian civilisation and in analysing and publicising the latest findings is remarkable. In the early eighteenth century the Jesuit series of *Lettres édifiantes et curieuses* contained much material on Hinduism, some of it of high quality, written by French members of the south Indian missions.[3] The precocious Abraham Anquetil

---

[1] An article on Elephanta by Lt.-Col. Barry, *Annual Register* (1784–5), II, 90–1.

[2] A few examples of this kind of explanation are: J. L. Niecamp, *Histoire de la Mission Danoise dans les Indes Orientales* (Geneva, 1745), I, 84 ff.; Robert Orme, 'Effeminacy of the Inhabitants of Indostan', India Office Library, Orme MSS, I, 121–37; J. Rennell, *Memoir of a Map of Hindoostan*, 2nd ed. (1792), pp. xxi ff.

[3] Some of these were translated into English by J. Lockman, *Travels of the Jesuits, into various parts of the World*, 2nd ed. (1762), 2 vols.

I-2

Duperron launched his deciphering of Avestan in 1771 in a book which also contained much on Indian subjects.[1] Pierre Sonnerat included a comprehensive survey of Hinduism in his *Voyage aux Indes Orientales* published in 1782; and Guillaume Le Gentil de La Galaisière provided the fullest of the early accounts of Indian astronomy.[2] Their material and that of other travellers was sifted from an orthodox point of view in articles, such as those by Etienne Mignot and Joseph de Guignes, in the *Mémoires de l'Académie royale des Inscriptions et Belles Lettres*,[3] and from an unorthodox point of view most obviously by Voltaire, the Abbé Raynal, and the future mayor of revolutionary Paris, Jean-Sylvain Bailly. Much information on India also came to eighteenth-century Europe from Danish sources. The Danish Lutheran mission, established like the Jesuits on the Coromandel Coast, provided a stream of letters published in various collections[4] and in the annual *Account of the Origins and Designs* of the British Society for Promoting Christian Knowledge, who contributed to subsidising them. But once the British began their conquests in the second half of the century, Europe came more and more to see India through British eyes. Although the Church of England and other British Christian bodies had largely kept aloof from the controversies stirred up by Confucianism, they could not ignore the controversies about Hinduism; the case for the prosecution against Christianity was still largely argued from across the Channel, but much of the evidence was being provided by Englishmen and many English Christians spoke for the defence.

The pieces included in this book have been chosen to represent the major British contributions to European understanding of Hinduism in the second half of the eighteenth century. They

[1] *Zend-Avesta, ouvrage de Zoroastre* (Paris, 1771), 3 vols.

[2] In two articles in *Mémoires de l'Académie royale des Sciences* for 1772, part ii, see below, p. 32.

[3] Mignot published five *mémoires* 'Sur les anciens philosophes de l'Inde' in tome xxxi (1761–3); de Guignes wrote three entitled 'Recherches historiques sur la religion Indienne' xl (1773–6), 'Reflexions sur un livre Indien intitulé Bagavadam', xxxviii (1770–2), and 'Observations historiques et géographiques sur le récit de Pline concernant l'origine, l'antiquité des Indiens', xlv (1780–4).

[4] A number of these appeared in English, e.g., *Propagation of the Gospel in the East*, 2 parts (1710); *Several Letters relating to the Protestant Danish Mission at Tranquebar in the East Indies* (1720); *An Account of the Religion, Manners and Learning of the People of Malabar*, trans. J. T. Philipps (1717).

Introduction

begin with chapters on 'The Religious Tenets of the Gentoos' taken from the second part of John Zephaniah Holwell's *Interesting Historical Events relative to the Provinces of Bengal and the Empire of Indostan*, published in 1767, and 'A Dissertation concerning the Customs, Manners, Language, Religion and Philosophy of the Hindoos' from the first volume of Alexander Dow's *History of Hindostan*, published in 1768. Neither work shows any major advance in knowledge over previous accounts of Hinduism, and in places Holwell suggests that he was either remarkably credulous or remarkably inventive, but the manner in which both were written and the time at which they appeared won them a public attention not given to earlier offerings. The next two items show much greater insight into their subject. Nathaniel Brassey Halhed's Preface to his translation of *A Code of Gentoo Laws*, issued in 1776, reveals some acquaintance with a wide range of important sources. Charles Wilkins's *The Bhăgvăt-Geetā, or Dialogues of Krĕĕshnă and Ărjŏŏn* (of which Wilkins's own Preface and an introductory letter by Warren Hastings are here given) appeared in 1785, and was the first published translation into a European language of any major Sanskrit work. Finally, three essays by Sir William Jones, 'on the Hindus', 'on the Gods of Greece, Italy and India' and 'on the Chronology of the Hindus', are included. These appeared in the first two numbers of *Asiatick Researches*, the journal of the Bengal Asiatic Society, which were published in 1789 and 1790. Jones's contemporaries regarded his essays as the final and definitive statement of the claims and nature of Hinduism. Later research has inevitably shown the limitations in Jones's approach and the gaps in his knowledge, but to appreciate his quality it is only necessary to read his essays in conjunction with those of Dow and Holwell written no more than twenty years earlier. His studies and translations reached a very wide European audience and created an awareness of Hinduism that was almost entirely new.[1]

Holwell was born in Dublin in 1711.[2] He was given what seems to have been a conventional merchant's training, but became a

---

[1] R. Schwab, *La Renaissance Orientale* (Paris, 1950), pp. 59–71.

[2] The chief source for information on him is H. E. Busteed, *Echoes from Old Calcutta*, 4th ed. (1908), pp. 47–52.

surgeon, first on an East Indiaman and later in the East India Company's service in Bengal. He had a highly contentious career, becoming *zamindar* of Calcutta, being incarcerated in the Black Hole, and eventually succeeding to the Governorship of Bengal for a brief period in 1760 before he left India. He lived in retirement in England for another thirty-eight years, dying in 1798. Although he had made many enemies during his active career, his obituary described him as a person 'in whom brilliancy of talents, benignity of spirit, social vivacity, and suavity of manners were so eminently united, as to render him the most amiable of men'.[1] It is clear that he did not know Sanskrit, but it is likely that he had a good knowledge of some other Asian languages. Long service on the Calcutta Mayor's Court and the Calcutta *Zamindar's* Court must have given him some grasp of Hindustani and Bengali and he apparently also knew Arabic. His books suggest that he had strong and increasingly eccentric opinions, a ready pen, and an alert if disorderly mind. Apart from various personal polemics, he published in 1765 the first part of a disjointed and inchoate work largely concerned with Hinduism, to which he gave the appropriately rambling title of *Interesting Historical Events, relative to the Provinces of Bengal and the Empire of Indostan...As also the Mythology and Cosmogony, Fasts and Festivals of the Gentoos, followers of the Shastah, and a Dissertation on the Metempsychosis, commonly, though erroneously, called the Pythagorean doctrine*. In 1767 he added a second part, and in 1771 a third. In 1779 he reissued parts two and three, with the altered title of *A Review of the Original Principles, religious and moral, of the Ancient Bramins*. Finally, in 1786 he brought out a tract called *Dissertation on the Origin, Nature, and Pursuits of Intelligent Beings, and on Divine Providence, Religion and Religious Worship*, which to an even greater degree than his earlier books is as much a statement of personal beliefs as an exposition of Hinduism.

Very little can be ascertained about Alexander Dow and unfortunately nothing at all is known about his education. He was born in Scotland, probably in 1735 or 1736, and is reported to have run away from an apprenticeship to go to the East Indies as a sailor. In 1760 he was appointed an Ensign in the Company's

---

[1] *Gentleman's Magazine*, LXVIII (1798), pt. ii, 999.

Introduction

Bengal Army and had risen to the rank of Colonel by the time he died in India in 1779. By normal eighteenth-century standards he was much more accomplished than Holwell. His views on moral, religious and political questions were conventionally 'enlightened'.[1] Reviewers found that he talked 'like a sensible, rational man',[2] which is more than they found in Holwell. He wrote two plays, called *Zingis* and *Sethona*, both of which were staged at the Drury Lane theatre. He undertook two major Persian translations, though his reputation as a Persian scholar was said to have been 'far from high in Bengal'.[3] In 1769 he published *Tales translated from the Persian of Inatulla*, and in the previous year the first two volumes of his *History of Hindostan* appeared. They purported to be a translation of the seventeenth-century historian, Firishta, but have been described as 'an interpretation in which there is little to distinguish a very free translation from Dow's own glosses'.[4] A third volume was added to the *History of Hindostan* in 1772. The Dissertation on the Hindus appeared in the first volume, more dissertations being added in the third. Dow admitted that he had been unable to learn Sanskrit and that he had been forced to rely for his knowledge of Hinduism on translations into Persian and into 'the vulgar tongue of the Hindoos'.[5]

The importance of Dow and Holwell lies less in the novelty of what they said than in the audience that they reached. Both authors were widely reviewed and discussed in Britain. A notice in the *Annual Register*, possibly written by Burke, called Holwell's account of Hinduism 'a very curious and important acquisition to the general stock of literature in Europe',[6] while Dow was said by a reviewer to be better informed on Hinduism 'than any preceding writer'.[7] Holwell was translated into German in 1767,[8]

---

[1] See R. Guha, *A Rule of Property for Bengal* (Paris and The Hague, 1963), pp. 21–41.

[2] *Critical Review*, XXVI (1768), 81.

[3] Lord Teignmouth, *Memoir of the Correspondence of John Lord Teignmouth* (1843), I, 105–6.

[4] P. Hardy, 'Firishta', *Encyclopaedia of Islam*, new edn. (Leiden and London, 1960–), II, 923; also J. S. Grewal, 'British Historical Writing from Alexander Dow to Mountstuart Elphinstone on Muslim India', London Ph.D. thesis, 1963.

[5] See below, p. 108.   [6] *Annual Register* (1766), II, 307.

[7] *Monthly Review*, XXXIX (1768), 387.

[8] By E. Thiel in J. T. Koehler, *Sammlung neuer Reisebeschreibungen aus fremden Sprachen* (Göttingen and Gotha, 1767–9), I.

7

and into French in 1768.[1] Dow's Dissertation on the Hindus appeared in French in 1769,[2] and was reproduced again, with much additional material of his own, in a French version by the Swiss savant Jean-Rodolphe Sinner.[3] Voltaire had read Holwell in English by December 1767;[4] he also read Dow and a rather earlier English account by Luke Scrafton, called *Reflections on the Government of Indostan*, which first appeared in 1763. He was lavish in his praise of all three authors, particularly of Holwell and Dow, making extensive use of them in his correspondence and in his published works, and writing 'C'est surtout chez MM Holwell et Dow qu'il faut s'instruire'.[5] Voltaire had been attracted to Hinduism in 1760 when he was presented with a manuscript called the 'Ezour Vedam', or commentary on the Hindu scriptures, now known with a beautiful appropriateness to have been a forgery perpetrated by his great antagonists the Society of Jesus.[6] Holwell and Dow abundantly confirmed the favourable impression created by the 'Ezour Vedam', and praises of Hinduism frequently occur in his later writings.

While Dow was probably a typical product of an eighteenth-century Scottish education, Nathaniel Brassey Halhed, the son of a Director of the Bank of England, had undergone the full rigours of an upper-class English one at Harrow and Christ Church.[7] Although he later complained that his Greek had suffered from 'the levity of youth and the dissipation of Xt Church',[8] he reflects credit on both institutions. His writings show that as well as a conventional classical grounding, he had read very widely at an

---

[1] *Evénements historiques, intéressants, relatifs aux provinces de Bengale* (Amsterdam, 1768).

[2] *Dissertation sur les Moeurs, les Usages, le Langage, la Religion et la Philosophie des Hindous* (Paris, 1769).

[3] *Essai sur les Dogmes de la Metempsychose et du Purgatoire enseignés par les Bramins de l'Indostan* (Berne, 1771).

[4] *Voltaire's Correspondence*, ed., T. Besterman (Geneva, 1953–65), LXVII, 210, 217–8.

[5] *Oeuvres complètes de Voltaire* (Paris, 1877–85), XXIX, 166. Large borrowings from Holwell and Dow can be found in *Fragments historiques sur l'Inde, Lettres à M. Pauw, Précis du siècle de Louis XV, Dieu et les Hommes, Essai sur les Moeurs.*

[6] *Voltaire's Correspondence*, XLIV, 254, XLVII, 72; A. Debidour, 'L'Indianisme de Voltaire', *Revue de Littérature Comparée*, IV (1924), 29–30.

[7] The main source for the following paragraph is an anonymous article 'Warren Hastings in Slippers', *Calcutta Review*, XXVI (1856).

[8] Letter to G. Costard, 1779, British Museum, Stowe MS, 757, f. 23.

Introduction

early age. A later acquaintance recalled that he had 'seldom met a man who knew so much of so many things, or who had so ready a command of all he knew'.[1] He went to India in 1771 as a Writer in the Company's Bengal service, publishing his *Gentoo Code* in 1776 and a *Grammar of the Bengal Language* in 1778. He left India with Warren Hastings in 1785, apparently intending to lead 'the easy life of an independent gentleman' and to devote his talents to Oriental scholarship. Though he lived for another forty-five years, he produced nothing to compare with the two books he had written in his twenties. Two events seem to have wrecked his career. In 1790 he lost a large part of his fortune invested in France, and in 1795 he committed what appears on the surface to be a wholly inexplicable aberration, from which he seems never to have recovered. An M.P. since 1791, he became in 1795 the advocate both in the House of Commons and in the press of the self-styled prophet Richard Brothers, who had announced that he was shortly to be 'revealed' as the ruler of the world. There were rumours that Halhed would be confined for lunacy, and in fact he lived in seclusion until 1809, when, as an act of charity, he was appointed a Chief Assistant to the Examiner of Correspondence at East India House.

Halhed was clearly an excellent linguist with a serious interest in the development of language. He had learnt enough Persian in four years to be able to put the Persian version of the Sanskrit original of the Code into English, and his papers contain many Persian translations which he made later.[2] He also learnt Bengali quickly and claimed to be the first European who had ever been able to conduct the Company's Bengali correspondence,[3] as well as being the first European to see the connexion between Bengali and Sanskrit.[4] His knowledge of Bengali and its literature has been called 'astounding for the day' by a modern Bengali scholar.[5] Precisely how much Sanskrit he knew is a matter of doubt. He gave a brief account of Sanskrit grammar and prosody,

[1] E. B. Impey, *Memoirs of Sir Elijah Impey* (1846), p. 355.
[2] B. M. Add. MSS 5657, 5658.
[3] Memorial to the Company, 18 Nov. 1783, National Library of Scotland, MS 1072, f. 96.
[4] *Grammar of the Bengal Language* (Hooghli, 1778), p. xix.
[5] S. Sen, *History of Bengali Literature* (New Delhi, 1960), p. 178.

and quoted widely from Sanskrit literature in the Preface to the Code, as well as making a large collection of Sanskrit manuscripts, many of which were specially copied for him. But all the translations surviving in his papers are from Persian versions. In the Preface to the Code he admitted that he only had 'slender information' about Sanskrit at his disposal and had as yet found no *pandit* willing to teach him, though he had high hopes of one of 'more liberal sentiments'.[1] When he wrote the Preface to the Bengali Grammar some three years later it would seem that his *pandit* had still only 'imparted a small portion of his language', even if 'he readily displayed the principles of his grammar'.[2] In 1779 Halhed was lamenting the death of his *pandit*.[3] Whatever may have been the limits of Halhed's knowledge of Sanskrit, his study of it did enable him to formulate theories about its relationship to other languages which Sir William Jones was later to develop. In the Preface to the Bengali Grammar Halhed wrote that he had been 'astonished to find the similitude of Shanscrit words with those of Persian and Arabic, and even of Latin and Greek'.[4] He developed these ideas further in a manuscript written in 1779. He found in Sanskrit

every part of speech, and every distinction which is to be found in either Greek or Latin, and that in some particulars it is more copious than either ...I do not attempt to ascertain as a fact, that either Greek or Latin are derived from this language; but I give a few reasons wherein such a conjecture might be founded: and I am sure that it has a better claim to the honour of a parent than, Phoenician or Hebrew.[5]

The *Gentoo Code* had been commissioned by Warren Hastings. In 1772 the Company had taken the decision that it should 'stand forth as dewan' and assume direct responsibility for the administration of civil justice in Bengal. This meant that Europeans were frequently called upon to act as judges in cases to be decided according to Hindu law. Hastings hoped to be able to provide them with a clear and undisputed corpus of law which would replace the conflicting sources and rival interpretations quoted by the *pandits*. Eleven *pandits* were instructed to draw on the best

---

[1] See below, p. 157.   [2] *Bengal Grammar*, pp. x–xi.
[3] Letter to G. Costard, 1779, B. M. Stowe MS, 757, f. 12.
[4] *Op. cit.* p. iii.
[5] Letter to G. Costard, 1779, B. M. Stowe MS, 757, ff. 25–6.

Introduction

authorities and to lay down the law once and for all on certain disputed points. The Sanskrit code which they produced was then translated into Persian and rendered from Persian into English by Halhed, who added to his own Preface ('planned and executed ... within the space of a fortnight'),[1] partly to explain the Code and partly to give information about the Hindus and their religion. The work was completed in 1775 and published in England the following year.[2] From a practical point of view the Code was a failure. It did not inspire complete confidence and was never accepted as a final authority; it merely provided the *pandits* with another source to interpret.[3] But it was a great success as a literary curiosity. William Robertson, the historian, called it 'undoubtedly the most valuable and authentic elucidation of Indian policy and manners that has been hitherto communicated to Europe',[4] and Burke referred to it as 'This ancient book, probably a compilation of the most ancient laws in the world'.[5] It too was translated into French[6] and into German,[7] and Bentham contemplated publishing a digest of it.[8]

Comparatively little is known about the early career of Charles Wilkins. He too went to Bengal as a Writer at the age of twenty, where he became a close friend of Halhed. With the sole assistance of Indian craftsmen he personally made 'every tool necessary for forming the punches and matrices, and casting a complete fount of Bengal characters' for Halhed's Grammar.[9] He himself said that it was Halhed who first persuaded him to take up Sanskrit in 1778.[10] He began work on a translation of the *Mahabharata* and was given leave of absence from his duties by Hastings to continue it at Benares, where he attended public recitals of

[1] Letter to G. Costard, 1779, B. M. Stowe MS, 757, f. 10.
[2] The MS is in the India Office Library, MSS Eur. B.11, 12.
[3] J. D. M. Derrett, 'Sanskrit legal treatises compiled at the instance of the British', *Zeitschrift für vergleichende Rechtswissenschaft*, LXIII (1961), 77–88.
[4] *An Historical Disquisition concerning the Knowledge which the Ancients had of India* (London, Edinburgh, 1791), p. 273.
[5] E. A. Bond ed., *Speeches of the Managers and Counsel in the Trial of Warren Hastings* (1859–61), IV, 363.
[6] By J. B. R. Robinet, *Code des Loix des Gentoux* (Paris, 1778).
[7] By R. E. Raspe, *Gesetzbuche der Gentoo's* (Hamburg, 1778).
[8] *The Correspondence of Jeremy Bentham*, ed., T. L. S. Sprigge (1963), II, 62–3.
[9] J. Nichols, *Literary Anecdotes of the Eighteenth Century* (1812–15), VI, 638.
[10] *A Grammar of the Sanskrita Language* (1808), p. viii.

'those wonderful poems denominated *Purans*',[1] and found that his house became 'the resort of the learned men of Kasee'.[2] When Hastings visited Benares in the autumn of 1784 he evidently encouraged Wilkins to publish the *Bhagavad Gita* separately. The translation appeared in print in Britain the following year, and in 1787 Wilkins published a translation of the *Hitopadesha*, a version of the famous *Panchatantra* fables, already known in Europe from Persian sources as 'the Fables of Pilpai'.[3] Wilkins left India in 1786. He later became Librarian to the Company and Examiner at the Company's College at Haileybury.

Although the *Gita* was rendered into French[4] and 'Mr Wilkin translating the Geeta' was to be the subject of a drawing by William Blake entitled 'The Bramins',[5] Wilkins's work seems to have had comparatively little immediate public impact: it did not appear startlingly new to those who had read Holwell, Dow or Halhed, and in popular estimation it was soon overshadowed by Jones. But Jones himself was in no doubt as to the magnitude of Wilkins's achievement. He advised those who wished to 'form a correct idea of Indian religion and literature' to begin by forgetting 'all that has been written on the subject, by ancients or moderns, before the publication of the *Gita*'.[6] Halhed may have known more Sanskrit than his English predecessors, but while he did not succeed in making any extended translation from it, Wilkins did. Wilkins was certainly the first Englishman to do so and was probably the first European to have done so for several generations. In two papers, later published in *Asiatick Researches*, he also showed that he was the first European to have succeeded in deciphering Sanskrit-based inscriptions of any antiquity.[7]

Both Halhed and Wilkins paid what are quite obviously sin-

[1] Letter to J. Sullivan, 25 Aug. 1813, B. M. Add. MS 29234, f. 207.

[2] Letter to Hastings, 11 Apr. 1784, B. M. Add. MS 29163, f. 112; see also an undated letter, *ibid.* 29167, ff. 296–7.

[3] *The Hĕĕtōpădēs of Vĕĕshnŏŏ-Sărmā* (Bath, 1787).

[4] M. Parraud, *Le Bhaguat-Geeta* (Paris, 1787).

[5] The drawing, now lost, is described in 'A Descriptive Catalogue of Pictures' exhibited by Blake in 1809 (*The Complete Writings of William Blake*, ed., G. Keynes (1966), p. 583). I owe this information to the kindness of Mr David Bindman of Westfield College.

[6] *The Works of Sir William Jones* (1799), I, 363.

[7] *Asiatick Researches*, I, 123–30, II, 167–9; S. N. Mukherjee, *Sir William Jones* (Cambridge, 1968), pp. 77–8.

Introduction

cere and deeply-felt tributes to Warren Hastings's patronage. The marked advance made during his administration in Indian studies, Islamic, as in the case of Francis Gladwin,[1] William Davy,[2] and Jonathan Scott,[3] as well as Hindu, owed much to his prompting and encouragement. Indian scholars benefited as well as Europeans. *Pandit* Radhakanta, who was to give Jones so much assistance, wrote his *Puranaprakasha* at Hastings's request,[4] and the Calcutta *Madrasa* was founded in 1781 on his initiative. There was certainly a practical motive for this patronage: Hastings believed that even if the Company accepted full responsibility for the government of Bengal and placed some of its European servants in the most important administrative posts, it should still govern in ways familiar to the mass of the population and should apply Hindu and Muslim law with only limited innovation. If the Company was to govern in accordance with Indian traditions, it must find out what these traditions were. But Hastings's Oriental interests went far beyond the utilitarian. He was not the 'unlettered man' which he professed himself to be. He had absorbed the values of the classical education that he had received at Westminster and believed that the study of literature diffused a 'generosity of sentiment' and a disdain for 'meaner occupations'.[5] Persian and Sanskrit literature should be studied for their own sake. His own versifying included versions of Wilkins's translations[6] as well as innumerable Latin 'imitations'. He did not know Sanskrit, but he was said to be familiar with 'the common dialects of Bengal' and to be 'proficient' in Persian.[7]

There is neither space nor need to attempt to review the career of William Jones in any detail.[8] Educated at Harrow and

[1] See *The Ayeen Akbery* (Calcutta, 1783–6), I, ix–xi.
[2] Davy, translator of *Institutes political and military...By the Great Timour* (Oxford, 1783), was Hastings's Persian secretary.
[3] See the Dedication to *A Translation of the Memoirs of Eradut Khan* (1786), p. iii.
[4] See below, p. 268.   [5] See below, p. 189.
[6] B. M. Add. MS 29235, ff. 50–66.
[7] Lord Teignmouth, *Memoirs of the Life, Writings, and Correspondence of Sir William Jones*, 2nd ed. (1807), p. 297.
[8] Teignmouth's *Memoir* was first published in 1804. More recently there have appeared a collection of essays in the *Bulletin of the School of Oriental and African Studies*, XI (1946), A. J. Arberry, *Asiatic Jones* (1946); G. H. Cannon, *Oriental Jones* (1964); and S. N. Mukherjee's admirable *Sir William Jones* (Cambridge, 1968), on which I have drawn heavily.

University College, Oxford, he quickly distinguished himself as a poet, critic and linguist, built up a successful practice as a barrister and made a name as a radical pamphleteer. He was a man of very great personal charm and remarkable intellectual versatility. His contribution to the understanding of Hinduism and Sanskrit literature only represents a part of his work as an Orientalist, and his achievement as an Orientalist is only a part of his wider scholarly interests: he was also a classical scholar of very high standing, a historian, and a distinguished academic lawyer, as well as being able to write with authority on astronomy, botany and the theory of music. He was an exceptionally gifted linguist, who mastered both European and Asian languages with great facility. He learnt Arabic and Persian while at Oxford and made his early reputation as an Orientalist with a Persian grammar, essays on Persian and Arabic literature and adaptations from Persian and Arabic poetry. In 1783 after much solicitation he was appointed a puisne judge of the Supreme Court at Calcutta, and went to India for the first time. He dominated the intellectual life of the British community in India, founding the Asiatic Society of Bengal, which from 1784 coordinated the efforts of individual scholars, and organising the publication of *Asiatick Researches*, which was to make their findings known all over Europe.

When Jones arrived in India he knew comparatively little about either Hinduism or Sanskrit. Some years previously with quite uncharacteristic philistinism he had even asked Anquetil Duperron how 'un homme né dans ce siècle' could 's'enfatuer des fables Indiennes' and had begged him 'pour l'amour de vousmême, et pour celui du public' not to trouble the world with translations from the books of these 'Linganistes'.[1] But he was quickly drawn to Sanskrit. He was able to enlist the help of an increasing number of *pandits* and by September 1785 he reported that he was proceeding 'slowly, but surely'; by May 1786 he had begun to make his first translation with the aid of 'a loose Persian paraphrase'; and in September 1786 he described himself as 'tolerably strong in Sanscrit'.[2] He continued to make translations and to write studies based on Sanskrit sources until his death in Calcutta in 1794.

---

[1] *Jones Works*, IV, 612. [2] Teignmouth, *Jones Memoirs*, pp. 330, 344, 352.

Introduction

Within a few months of taking up the study of Sanskrit Jones came to the same conclusion as Halhed about the similarities between Sanskrit, Latin and Greek, although, unlike Halhed, he did not try to show that the other two were derived from Sanskrit. He found the resemblances

so strong indeed, that no philologer could examine them all three, without believing them to have sprung from some common source, which, perhaps, no longer exists: there is a similar reason, though not quite so forcible, for supposing that both the Gothick and the Celtick, though blended with a very different idiom, had the same origin with the Sanscrit; and the old Persian might be added to the same family...[1]

From similarity of languages Jones assumed similarity of origin for the peoples who spoke these languages. In a paper 'on the Origin and Families of Nations' he argued that there was 'incontestable proof' 'that the first race of Persians and Indians, to whom we may add the Romans and Greeks, the Goths, and the old Egyptians or Ethiops, originally spoke the same language and professed the same popular faith', and he suggested Iran as the common place of origin.[2]

Jones's work has been taken as the starting point for the modern study of the Indo-European family of languages and of the migration of peoples. A more realistic assessment would probably be that his theories were in a well established tradition of inquiry and that, while they were usually founded on more solid knowledge and worked out with more precision than those of his contemporaries, he was to some extent developing and publicising the ideas of others, who lacked either Jones's world-wide reputation or his literary ability.[3] There is no clear evidence as to how he reached his conclusions, and assumptions that his approach to the problems of language and history was more 'scientific' than that of his contemporaries cannot be substantiated.[4] His work cannot be understood outside the context of eighteenth-century disputes about the authority of Moses, Jones believing that his

---

[1] See below, pp. 252–3.   [2] *Jones Works*, i, 129–32.
[3] Mukherjee, *Jones*, chap. vi. For a recent exposition of the opposite view see H. Aarsleff, *The Study of Language in England, 1780–1860* (Princeton, 1967), pp. 124 ff.
[4] The description of how Jones came to reach his conclusions in Cannon, *Oriental Jones*, pp. 140–1 seems to be largely conjectural.

15

discovery of a common place of origin for the human race somewhere in the Middle East was a clear vindication of *Genesis*.

Jones was the heir to over a century of speculation about migrations from Asia into Europe. Scythia had many supporters as the original home of the European peoples,[1] and both Boxhorn, the seventeenth-century Dutch philologist, and Leibnitz had tried to establish connexions between Scythian and European languages.[2] More recently Jean-Sylvain Bailly had suggested that the civilisations of Asia and Europe had originated in some now extinct source in Central Asia. In his opinion the original Brahmins had come out of Central Asia bringing their skills and learning with them, and he entered into controversy with Voltaire, who argued, largely on the strength of Holwell, that India had been the cradle of civilisation.[3] With his knowledge of Sanskrit Jones was able to bring a new element of precision to these speculations. But even here he had his precursors. He knew more Sanskrit than Halhed and could argue with more confidence about Sanskrit's connexion with other languages than Halhed had done; but both Halhed and a French Jesuit[4] had been working towards the same conclusion.

Jones's Indian writings reflect the extraordinary range of his mind. One of his major translations was the *Institutes of Hindi Law; or, the Ordinances of Menu*, the other Kalidasa's play *Sacontala, or the Fatal Ring*. Apart from studying language, history and religion, he wrote on literature and music, analysed the Hindu philosophical schools, and showed some acquaintance with Indian science. In his portrayal of Indian civilisation Jones never tried to deny European superiority. But he insisted that if the achievement of Europe was 'transcendently majestick', Asia had 'many beauties, and some advantages peculiar to herself'.[5] His advocacy of these beauties and advantages was conspicuously successful. His articles in the *Asiatick Researches*, and his version of

---

[1] E.g. Paul Pezron's *The Antiquities of Nations*, trans. D. Jones (1706).

[2] G. Bonfante, 'Ideas on the Kinship of European Languages from 1200–1800', *Cahiers d'Histoire mondiale*, I (1954), 691–5.

[3] *Lettres sur l'Origine des Sciences, et sur celle des peuples de l'Asie* (Paris and London, 1777); *Voltaire's Correspondence*, XCIII, 9–10; E. B. Smith, *Jean-Sylvain Bailly, Astronomer, Mystic, Revolutionary* (*Transactions of the American Philosophical Society* XLIV, pt. IV) (Philadelphia, 1954).

[4] Mukherjee, *Jones*, pp. 95–6.   [5] *Jones Works*, I, 10.

Shakuntala were frequently to be translated, and the list of his European admirers is an impressive one, including Goethe, Herder, Friedrich Schlegel, Chateaubriand, Quinet, Michelet, Hugo, Lamartine, de Maistre and Lamennais.[1] His success was no doubt largely due to his powers of presentation, but it also owed something to changes in European taste, which are already apparent in Jones's own work. He defies classification as either a rationalist or a romantic,[2] but there are passages in his writings which show a concern for feeling and emotion alien to earlier writers on Hinduism. In quoting from the *Upanishads*, Halhed found it necessary to apologise for including what was 'the very acme and enthusiasm of allegory', and he looked for 'lively and pleasing' images, 'elegant and concise' diction and 'metre not inharmonious' in Sanskrit poetry.[3] Hastings warned readers of Wilkins's *Gita* that they were likely to find some passages in it 'cloathed with ornaments of fancy unsuited to our taste' and others 'elevated to a track of sublimity into which our habits of judgement will find it difficult to pursue them'.[4] Jones remained loyal to the canons of the European classics, but he also found the Hindu epics 'magnificent and sublime in the highest degree',[5] and he admired the emotional fervour of what he called 'the mystical poetry of the Persians and Hindus': 'the raptures of the Masnavi, and the mysteries of the Bhagavat'.[6] He was evidently stirred by 'the wild musick of Cali's priests at one of her festivals' as he had been stirred by 'the Scythian measures of Diana's adorers in the splendid opera of Iphigenia in Tauris'.[7]

Serious study of Hinduism obviously depended on mastery of Sanskrit, but it also required knowledge of texts and access to them. Since the sixteenth century European travellers had reported the existence of Hindu sacred books, which they called 'Beths', 'Beds', 'Bedas', or 'the Vedam', as well as various 'Shasters'. By the end of the seventeenth century Hindu manuscripts were beginning to accumulate in European libraries, although for the most part they remained undeciphered. In 1698,

---

[1] Schwab, *Renaissance Orientale*, pp. 59–71; R. Taylor, 'The East and German Romanticism', Iyer, ed., *The Glass Curtain*, pp. 188–200.

[2] Mukherjee, *Jones*, pp. 111–12.   [3] See below, pp. 149, 153.

[4] See below, p. 186.   [5] See below, p. 259.

[6] *Jones Works*, I, 445–8.   [7] See below, p. 237.

for instance, a 'Ramainum or History of Ram, in the Sanscreet language' together with some translations into 'Tulinga' and books in the ' Malabar language' were shown to the Royal Society on their way to the Bodleian.[1] Vigorous efforts were made in the 1730s to collect manuscripts for the Bibliothèque Royale.[2] A manuscript translation of part of the *Gita* into Portuguese had been made in the sixteenth century,[3] but the earliest published translation of any significance seems to have been Abraham Roger's 'hundred proverbs' attributed to Bhartrihari, appearing in Dutch in 1651 and later in French.[4] Roger's example in presenting authentic texts had few imitators. Some account of the Hindu scriptures was, however, made available to the European reading public in the letters written in the first half of the eighteenth century by the Jesuits in south India, the most notable being a survey sent home in 1740 by Jean-François Pons. Unlike his famous predecessor de Nobili, Pons did not know Sanskrit, but he had some idea of the scope and nature of the *Vedas*, he could give an outline of the philosophical schools, and he was able to discuss a fairly wide range of Hindu literature.[5] Duperron collected Sanskrit dictionaries on his Indian journey from 1755–61, in addition to his Zoroastrian manuscripts.[6]

Neither Holwell or Dow seems to have been acquainted with the latest French knowledge of Hindu sources. Holwell reproduced long extracts from what he called 'the Shastah', based on manuscripts which he had lost in the sack of Calcutta in 1756.[7] He believed that his 'Shastah' was the oldest and purest source of Hinduism; he had been told that it was at least 4,866 years old and he accepted that it was the most ancient statement of religious belief in the world. In making his translation Holwell seems so to have distorted his original by imposing Christian terminology and Christian concepts on it that identification is impossible. He had presumably acquired a devotional text of some kind.

[1] *Philosophical Transactions of the Royal Society*, xx (1698), 421–4.
[2] *Lettres édifiantes et curieuses*, xxi (1734), 455–6.
[3] D. F. Lach, *Asia in the Making of Europe* (Chicago, 1965), i, 280.
[4] As *La Porte ouverte pour parvenir à la Connoissance du Paganisme caché* (Amsterdam, 1670), pp. 293 ff.
[5] *Lettres édifiantes et curieuses*, xxvi (1743), 233 ff.
[6] See the translation of his paper to the Académie des Sciences in the *Annual Register* (1762), ii, 109.   [7] See below, p. 46.

Introduction

The texts which Dow introduced into his Dissertation appear to be more authentic. Two of the four passages which he quoted at length were, he claimed, from a commentary on the *Vedas* called the 'Bedang Shaster'.[1] 'Bedang' seems to be a corruption of *Vedanta*, but the texts are clearly Puranic in origin and in fact have reasonably close similarities to passages in the *Bhagavat Purana*.[2] The third passage, from the so-called 'Dirm Shaster', with its mention of Krishna as 'the giver of bliss',[3] was probably also derived from the same source. Dow stated that he had deposited the manuscript from which he had drawn his last and longest extract, the 'Neadirsin Shaster', in the British Museum. What he deposited has, in fact, no relation to the translation;[4] but the 'Neadirsin Shaster' is clearly, as its name implies, an exposition of the *Nyaya* philosophical system, very much studied in eighteenth-century Bengal.[5]

Halhed's Preface shows that his knowledge of Hindu literature was much more extensive than that of either Holwell or Dow. His collection of manuscripts bought by the British Museum in 1796 is an impressive one. Twenty legal treatises, with the *Law of Manu* heading the list, were consulted for the Code.[6] He had explored grammars and collections of *kavya* poetry. A copy of the *Mahabharata* in eight volumes was made for him at Benares,[7] and he quoted from the *Bhagavad Gita* in his Preface.[8] He also quoted from the *Bhagavat Purana*, unlike Dow, identifying his source;[9] he was later to make a translation from a Persian version of its famous tenth book on the life of Krishna and from Persian copies of two other *Puranas*.[10] He referred to Dara Shukoh's version of the *Upanishads* in Persian in the Preface,[11] and later translated that as well.[12] The pride of his collection must have been a fragment of the Black *Yajurveda*.[13] Full versions of the *Vedas* were not, however, to become available to Europeans until rather later, and were not to be effectively studied until Henry Thomas Colebrooke

[1] See below, p. 119.
[2] See below, pp. 119–20.
[3] See below, p. 128.
[4] See below, p. 131.
[5] See below, p. 130.
[6] Listed in the *Code of Gentoo Laws*, pp. 26–8.
[7] B. M. Add. MSS 5569–76.
[8] See below, p. 163.
[9] See below, p. 162.
[10] B. M. Add. MS 5657.
[11] See below, p. 148.
[12] B. M. Add. MS 5658.
[13] B. M. Add. MS 5660E.

published his paper 'on the *Vedas* or Sacred Writings of the Hindus' in the *Asiatick Researches* of 1805. European study of the *Vedas* was made possible by the purchase of a copy at Jaipur by Colonel Antoine Polier, who deposited it in the British Museum in 1789 after letting Jones see it in India. The judge Sir Robert Chambers also acquired a copy of the *Rig Veda* and parts of the other *Vedas*.[1] Once inquirers had obtained the proficiency in Sanskrit enjoyed by Wilkins and Jones and once Europeans had gained access to the most carefully guarded of all texts, the full range of Hindu literature was open to them. But there still remained the problems of selecting from what Jones called 'the infinity' of Hindu sources[2] and of interpretation.

English writers in the second half of the eighteenth century were the heirs to over two hundred years of attempts by Europeans to interpret Hinduism. Interpretations had generally followed the same lines: comparatively soon Europeans had begun to make the distinction, which was to have so long a life, between what they regarded as 'popular' Hinduism and 'philosophical' Hinduism. Popular cults were described to be condemned or ridiculed, but most writers were also prepared to admit the existence of metaphysical assumptions and ethical doctrines in Hinduism of which they could approve because they seemed to be similar to western concepts, although the similarities which they found now seem to depend largely on the inability of Europeans to describe a religious system except in Christian terms.

Even if some intellectual curiosity about Hinduism was aroused, the attitude of the great mass of Europeans who came into contact with it was always either ridicule or disgust. Books were filled with accounts of a multiplicity of deities, repellent images and barbarous customs. Most early travellers concluded that the Hindus were no more than idolaters, worshipping images or natural objects. This was the theme of the first Portuguese accounts from the Malabar Coast.[3] The seventeenth-century English traveller, William Bruton, described the Bengalis as

---

[1] B. M. Add. MS 29233, ff. 279–80.
[2] *Jones Works*, I, 362–3.
[3] Lach, *Asia in the Making of Europe*, I, 353–4.

Introduction

'barbarous and idolatrous people', who worshipped the sun and the moon, animals and plants.[1] Even in the early eighteenth century the Jesuit Pierre Martin told his correspondents: '. . . you wou'd scarce believe me, shou'd I name the vile and infamous creatures to which they pay divine honours. 'Tis my opinion, that no idolatry among the antients was ever more gross, or more horrid, than that of these Indians'.[2] But it became more common to believe that some idea of a supreme God had been implanted in all peoples and that, however much this original insight had been later overlaid, complete idolatry, or for that matter atheism, was impossible.[3] As Europeans became aware of the existence of a single Hindu religious entity, they almost invariably described it as a theistic God, since they could conceive of it in no other terms. Henry Lord, the English chaplain at Surat in the early seventeenth century, reported that though their ceremonies were 'a may-game of superstition', the Hindus did 'give worshippe to God'.[4] At Benares François Bernier met 'the chief of the Pandets', who told him that God alone was 'absolute, and the only omnipotent lord and master'.[5] Both the Danish missionaries and most of the Jesuits agreed that, whatever might be its practice, the theory of Hinduism implied worship of a single supreme being. Christians also found some similarities in Hinduism to their concept of the immortality of the soul, even if they were contaminated from their point of view with unacceptable beliefs in transmigration or in the individual soul as an emanation of *brahman* seeking unity with *brahman*, proof to Bernier that 'there are no opinions so ridiculous or extravagant, of which the mind of man is not capable'.[6] The conduct of Hindus was often pictured as deplorable, but Hindu moral teaching was sometimes commended. Captain Hamilton had known 'many of them practise very much holiness in their lives by the help of morality'.[7] Pons called the

---

[1] 'News from the East Indies; or a Voyage to Bengalla', *A Complete Collection of Voyages and Travels*, published T. Osborn (1745), II, 278–9.

[2] Lockman, *Travels of the Jesuits*, II, 416.

[3] E.g. P. Baldaeus, 'A True and Exact Description o fthe most celebrated East India Coasts', A. and J. Churchill, *A Collection of Voyages and Travels*, 3rd ed. (1744–6), III, 73.

[4] 'A Display of two Forraign Sects in the East-Indies', *ibid.* VI, 331–2.

[5] 'Mr F. Bernier's Voyage to Surat', *Voyages and Travels*, Osborn, II, 209–10.

[6] *Ibid.* II, 211. [7] *A New Account of the East Indies* (Edinburgh, 1727), I, xxii.

Nitishastra 'une très belle...science morale';[1] and some Danish writers were also sympathetic.[2]

For most European authors any good points in Hinduism were still outweighed by its vices, and in any case were as nothing compared with the Hindu rejection of Christianity. But even the smallest particles of grain in a welter of pagan chaff required explanation. This was a perennial problem for Christians, by no means confined to Hinduism; it presented itself most obviously in the Christian response to the philosophy of Greece and Rome.[3] Explanations tended to fall into two categories, natural or historical. Some Christians argued that pagans had stumbled on intimations of truth through the use of God-given reason or through the contemplation of a divinely ordered universe. Thomas La Grue in his 'Avis au lecteur', added in 1670 to the French translation of Abraham Roger's book on Hinduism, wrote that God had left the Hindus in ignorance because of their sins, 'mais il ne s'est toutesfois laissé inconnu parmy eux; ils ont peu facilement trouver le Dieu invisible par les choses visibles et par leurs causes' as Aristotle had done.[4] The simplest of the historical explanations, and one that was accepted by virtually all Christians throughout the eighteenth century, was that the Hindus and all other pagans had been part of a single undivided human race until the building of the Tower of Babel, when the peoples of the earth had been scattered. Until the dispersion, all the human race had accepted the simple truth of the unity of God; after the dispersion, the Jews alone remained faithful, but any traces of monotheism in others could be attributed to distant recollections of the remote past. The translation of the Abbé Guyon's *History of the East Indies Ancient and Modern*, which appeared in 1757, is an example of this type of explanation. 'Altho' the Indians are descended from Shem, whose posterity preserved the memory of the true God for a longer time than those of Ham and Japhet, yet the darkness which spread itself over every human mind effaced the idea which the Creator had imprinted there; and they transferred their homage to the sun, the moon, to trees, and other

---

[1] *Lettres édifiantes et curieuses*, XXVI, 237–8.
[2] Niecamp, *Histoire de la Mission Danoise*, I, 87.
[3] E. C. Dewick, *The Christian Attitude to other Religions* (Cambridge, 1953).
[4] *La Porte ouverte*, the 'avis' is unpaginated.

sensible objects.' But 'whether from the remains of tradition, or the light of nature alone', they continued to acknowledge 'one God creator of the universe'.[1]

More elaborate historical arguments were also used to explain the existence of elements in Hinduism which could be commended from a Christian point of view. Some Christians maintained that after the dispersal of the peoples Hinduism had come under the influence of Jewish beliefs or even of Christian ones. The theory that all that was best in the ancient world could be traced to Jewish origins was commonplace in the late seventeenth century. Bossuet thought that the Greeks had been granted 'a kind of preparation to the knowledge of the truth', which had come 'from the place where the Jews had been dispersed'.[2] The French historian, André Dacier, whose life of Pythagoras was translated into English, argued that Plato and Aristotle inherited the knowledge of Pythagoras, who in his turn had picked up his learning in Egypt. 'But how came the Egyptians by these sublime sciences...? Doubtless from the correspondence those people had with the people of God, from the time they had been captives in Egypt'.[3] La Grue thought that the Greeks had been taught philosophy by the Brahmins rather than by the Egyptians, but again he insisted that the ultimate source of knowledge was the Jews, who had taught the Brahmins. Even among modern Hindus there was evidence 'pour prouver que leurs predecesseurs ayant veu et entendu plusieurs choses des Juifs, en retiennent encore quelque chose'. La Grue also discussed the possibility, raised even in the sixteenth century by Portuguese who noted that Brahmins revered a god in three persons,[4] that Hinduism had been influenced by Christianity. He pointed out that the Apostle Thomas had carried the Gospel to the East, and he repeated the story of the mission of Pantaenus of Alexandria to announce Jesus Christ to the Brahmins.[5]

Theories that Hinduism might contain in it traces of Jewish and Christian influence were of particular interest to missionaries,

[1] Vol. I, 13, 28–9.
[2] *An Universal History...of M. Bossuet* (1778), p. 243.
[3] *The Life of Pythagoras with his Symbols and Golden Verses* (1707), p. 2.
[4] Lach, *Asia in the Making of Europe*, I, 401.
[5] *La Porte ouverte*, 'avis', unpaginated.

although one Danish account tried to turn the tables and suggest that far from the Hindus having borrowed from Christianity, 'the original of divers ceremonies, and pompous superstitions falsely call'd Christian and receiv'd into the Romish Church' were to be found in Hinduism.[1] The most extreme claims for a connexion between Hinduism and the Old Testament or Christianity were put forward in the early eighteenth century by members of the Jesuit missions, notably by Jean Bouchet. Bouchet unequivocally stated his purpose as being

to prove that the Indians borrowed their religion from the books of Moses and the prophets: that notwithstanding various fictions with which their books are interspersed, they yet cannot quite eclipse the truths concealed under them. Finally, that, abstracted from the religion of the Hebrews, which they learnt (at least in part) by their correspondence with the Jews and the Egyptians; we likewise discover among them, some evident footsteps of the Christian religion, which had been preached to them by the Apostle St Thomas, by Pantaenus and several other eminent personages in the first ages of the Church.

He pointed out supposed resemblances between Abraham and Brahma and Krishna and Moses, as well as the Hindus' 'confused idea' of the Trinity.[2] In trying to prove these connexions, the Jesuits were retreading the perilous paths they had already trod over Confucianism, and they were under the same pressure to do so. To improve their chances of making conversions the Jesuits in China had made some (to them superficial) compromises with Confucianism. When these 'Chinese rites' were attacked in Europe, they had defended themselves by trying to minimise the gap between Confucianism and Christianity. Concessions were also made in south India to meet Hindu scruples: child marriage, Hindu insigniae and names, and caste segregation were all given some degree of toleration. The 'Malabar rites' came under attack in their turn: a controversy began in 1703 and lasted until 1744. Once again the Jesuits were obliged to defend themselves by defending Hinduism in a rather oblique way.[3]

Explanations of the existence of elements in Hinduism of

---

[1] *An Account of the Religion of Malabar*, trans. Philipps, preface.
[2] Lockman, *Travels of the Jesuits*, II, 241, 272.
[3] For a brief account see K. S. Latourette, *A History of the Expansion of Christianity* (1939–55), III, 269–71.

which Europeans could approve either in historical terms or in terms of the light of nature had originally been formulated by Christians. But the problem could be approached from other points of view; and the Christian explanations could be turned against their users. The argument that all the peoples of the earth had some intimations of divine truth through God-given reason and the contemplation of a rational universe was a particularly vulnerable one. If 'reason' was to be interpreted in a secular rather than in a Christian way, as a fact of human nature not as a gift of God, any similarity between Hinduism and the Jewish or Christian faiths could become a source of embarrassment for Christians. It could be argued that these similarities merely showed that it was 'natural' for all men to believe in a single supreme being, in the immortality of the soul, and in certain basic principles of morality. Instead of being the model of which other beliefs were pale imitations, Christianity could be portrayed as just one offshoot of a universal 'natural' religion, any dogmas beyond these simple truths being mere excrescences and later accumulations. This was, of course, the basic position of late seventeenth- and early eighteenth-century deists. When the Jesuits stressed the similarities between Confucianism or Hinduism and Christianity they were putting ammunition into the deist armoury.

Historical explanations of what Europeans regarded as the commendable aspects of Hinduism could also be taken over by the opponents of Christianity. Chronology was the vital issue. If the religions of Egypt, China or India could be shown to be similar to that of the Jews but to have been in existence before the time when Moses was conventionally believed to have drawn up the Law and written the history of the world in the Pentateuch, or if the apparently Christian aspects of Confucianism or Hinduism could be shown to have been established before the birth of Christ, then the disaffected believed that victory would be theirs. Both the Christian and the Jewish faiths would have been proved to have been derived from older religions, and their claims to be the unique instrument of God's providence would, it was thought, have been refuted. By the time the Hindus were pressed into service against Christianity the Egyptians and the Chinese had already served their turn, and so the positions that both sides would take up were already known in advance. The more intrepid Christians, like Sir Isaac Newton in his *Chronology of Ancient Kingdoms Amended*, insisted that no civilisation was earlier than the Jewish one.[1] The more circumspect, like William Warburton in the *Divine Legation of Moses*, conceded the greater age of the Egyptians at least, but denied that they had significantly influenced either the Mosaic Law or the inspired history recorded by Moses in *Genesis*. The anti-Christian case received its most abrasive statement in Voltaire's *Philosophie de l'histoire*, first published in 1765. Voltaire asked whether the Jews had taught other nations or whether they had been taught by them and he left his readers in no doubt as to the answer: other peoples had both older and more refined civilisations. Voltaire had hesitated in the past between the claims of India and China, but the 'Ezour Vedam' seems finally to have convinced him that the Indians were the most ancient people on earth.[2]

The claims which Voltaire made on behalf of the Hindus were to be fully upheld by Holwell and Dow, and to receive some support from Halhed. Holwell and Dow both wrote from a position very close to deism, even though Holwell was undoubtedly a Christian, if of a very eccentric kind, and Dow's reference to 'revelation'[3] suggests that he too was at least nominally Christian. Holwell's deistic leanings are very apparent in the chapters reproduced here, and they become even more pronounced in his later writings. He maintains that all religions have 'ancient fundamental tenets', which are 'short, pure, simple and uniform' but degenerate into 'ceremonials, and complicated modes of worship';[4] and he detests 'priestcraft' and 'sacerdotal slavery'.[5] In the *Dissertation on the Metempsychosis*, which he added in 1771 as a third part of his *Interesting Historical Events*, he openly stated that all the world's religions rested on the same 'primitive truths revealed by a gracious God to man'.[6] This was orthodox deism, but his list of

---

[1] See F. Manuel, *Isaac Newton, Historian* (Cambridge, 1963).

[2] There is a valuable Introduction and Commentary to J. H. Brumfitt's edition of *La Philosophie de l'histoire* (*Studies on Voltaire and the Eighteenth century*, XXVIII) (Geneva, 1963).   [3] See below, p. 139.   [4] See below, p. 51.

[5] See below, p. 59.   [6] pp. 4–5.

Introduction

'primitive truths' was far from orthodox, including belief in fallen angels and in metempsychosis. He was particularly hostile to the Christian doctrine of the Trinity and to the existing structure of the Church of England; he was also an enthusiastic advocate of vegetarianism. Dow was much more conventional. He believed that: 'To attentive inquirers into the human mind, it will appear, that common sense, upon the affairs of religion, is pretty equally divided among all nations',[1] and that 'whatever the external ceremonies of religion may be, the self-same infinite being is the object of universal adoration'.[2]

Writing from a deist point of view, Holwell and Dow gave the opponents of Christianity what they were looking for: a religion based on monotheism with a concept of the immortality of the soul and an acceptable moral code, which owed nothing to contact with either Jews or Christians, Holwell being particularly severe on attempts to make Hinduism derivative from Christianity.[3] Holwell stated that belief in 'one God, eternal, omnific, omnipotent and omniscient' was fundamental to Hinduism; the deities of the pantheon were 'to be taken only in a figurative sense'.[4] Dow agreed that Brahmins 'invariably believe in the unity, eternity, omniscience and omnipotence of God: ... the polytheism of which they have been accused, is no more than the symbolical worship of the divine attributes'.[5] Both Holwell and Dow showed that the doctrine of the immortality of the soul was clearly present in Hinduism, even if in the form of transmigration (which greatly attracted Holwell) with a belief in a plurality of hells and heavens. Holwell found from practical experience that modern Hindus were as 'degenerate, crafty, superstitious, litigious and wicked a people, as any race of beings in the known world'; but he regarded the teaching of the 'Shastah' on the origins of moral evil as 'rational and sublime',[6] while the few Brahmins who actually lived by the code of the 'Shastah' were 'the purest models of genuine piety that now exist, or can be found on the face of the earth'.[7] Dow again concurred: 'The Hindu doctrine... while it teaches the purest morals... is systematically formed on

---

[1] See below, p. 139. [2] *History of Hindostan*, I, lxxvi.
[3] See below, p. 67. [4] See below, pp. 77, 101.
[5] See below, p. 138. [6] See below, p. 70.
[7] *Interesting Historical Events*, II, 152.

philosophical opinions.'[1] The existence of a pure ethical code in a non-Christian society was a point which unbelievers were very anxious to establish. The mild, benevolent Brahmin was an answer to exhortations to 'have done with this groundless commendation of natural law . . . ; examine its influence over the pagans of our own times, over the sensual inhabitants of Ottaheitè, over the cannibals of New Zealand, or the remorseless savages of America'.[2]

The attractions of Holwell's and Dow's picture of Hinduism were greatly enhanced for non-Christians by the fact that Holwell, at least, gave them reason to believe that these excellences had been in existence long before the Mosaic Dispensation, and, moreover, that the history of the Hindus would upset the Biblical history of the world. Hindu claims to a history of some million years were already known in Europe, and Dow did no more than restate a version of Hindu chronology.[3] Holwell, on the other hand, gave Hindu chronology qualified support. He had been told that his 'Shastah' had been put into writing 4,866 years ago, that is 650 years before the Flood and over 1,500 years before Moses wrote his history, according to orthodox dating.[4] Holwell did not insist on this date for the 'Shastah', but he did believe that 'the original tenets of Bramah are most ancient' and were not derived from any other source. Indeed, in his opinion, the religions of Egypt and Persia were derived from India, and the mythology of the ancient European world from the later perversions of Hinduism.[5] Although Holwell had suggested in part two of *Interesting Historical Events* that all the world's religions were versions of an Indian original, he had not specifically included the Jewish. In part three he abandoned caution. He described the teaching of 'Bramah' as 'to a moral certainty the original doctrines, and terms of restoration, delivered by God himself from the mouth of his first created Birmah to mankind at his first creation in the form of man'. Christ's teaching was merely a restatement of this doctrine. In fact, Christ and 'Birmah' were probably separate

[1] *History of Hindostan*, I, lxxvi.
[2] R. Watson, *An Apology for Christianity*, 2nd ed. (Cambridge, 1777), p. 212.
[3] See below, p. 124.
[4] John Blair, *The Chronology and History of the World* (1754).
[5] See below, pp. 61–4.

appearances on earth of the same person with the same message. The Mosaic Dispensation fitted rather awkwardly in between them.[1]

The portrayal of Hinduism in Wilkins's writings would on some points have confirmed impressions already given by Holwell and Dow. There is no clear evidence about his religious beliefs, but he too seems to have had deist leanings. In a note to his translation of the *Gita* he compared Hindu commentators with 'those of more enlightened nations, who for ages have been labouring to entangle the plain unerring clew of our holy religion'.[2] He thought that the purpose of the *Gita* was to set up 'the doctrine of the unity of the Godhead, in opposition to idolatrous sacrifices, and the worship of images', and that 'the most learned Brahmans of the present times' were 'unitarians'.[3] He wrote a most beguiling account of the Sikhs: their religion commanded a belief 'in one God, omnipotent and omnipresent...; that there will be a day of retribution, when virtue will be rewarded and vice punished...; and inculcates the practice of all virtues, but particularly an universal philantrophy...'.[4]

Loyal Anglican though he seems to have been, Halhed did not write his Preface to give comfort either to Christian apologists or to their opponents. He declined to try to fit the Hindus into either of the two moulds into which they had invariably been forced in the past. He did not side with the orthodox and argue that the Hindus had deviated from divine truths instilled into them before the dispersal of the human race or by contact with Jews or Christians, nor could he accept the deist contention that they had deviated from the pure light of reason and natural religion. Although he makes no reference to Hume in his writings, his scepticism about both points of view is akin to Hume's. He doubted whether 'human nature... be really so much the same as is commonly asserted'.[5] He was not convinced by theories that primitive peoples held primitive truths, from whatever source they may have derived them. It should be borne in mind, he

---

[1] *Interesting Historical Events*, III, 71 ff.
[2] *The Bhăgvăt-Gēētā*, p. 154.   [3] See below, pp. 193–4.
[4] 'Observations and Inquiries concerning the Seeks and their College, at Patna', *Asiatick Researches*, I, 292.
[5] Letter to G. Costard, 1779, B. M. Stowe MS, 757, f. 7.

wrote, that 'the institution of a religion has been in every country the first step towards an emersion from savage barbarism...; [and] that the human mind at that period...has by no means acquired that facility of invention, and those profound habits of thinking, which are necessary to strike out, to arrange, and to complete a connected, consistent chain of abstruse allegory'. It was, therefore, pointless to foist 'allegorical constructions, and forced allusions to a mystic morality' onto 'the plain and literal context of every pagan mythology'.[1] There is very little in the Preface about monotheism, free will or the origins of moral evil. The scepticism of the Preface did not survive Halhed's later study of the *Upanishads* in Dara Shukoh's Persian version. The *Upanishads* no doubt gave him a fuller appreciation of Hinduism, but unhappily they also gave him insights of another kind; he began to see 'personifications of matter space and time' in the 'three great angels' of Hinduism.[2] This sort of speculation finally led to his catastrophic intervention in the affairs of Richard Brothers. In one of his publications he announced that having by 'unwearied attention' been enabled to discover 'the true meaning couched under the Hindu triad of energies or powers', he had turned to the Bible, and 'fortified...with this pre-acquired aptitude for such studies' he had seen the truth of Richard Brothers's prophecies.[3]

If Halhed did not give the unbelievers a portrayal of Hinduism of which they could make much use, he was a valuable ally over matters of chronology. He set out the Hindu theory of the four *yugas*, giving them a total of about eight million years, and quoted examples of works purporting to have been composed at the beginning of the first *yuga* and early in the second. He made it clear that he was not prepared to dismiss these claims out of hand, however irreconcilable they might be with a Christian view of the world's history. He also added that there was no mention of a flood in the Hindu scriptures (an astonishing statement from someone who claimed some acquaintance with the *Puranas*), apparently further proof of their great age. Aware of the conclusions

---

[1] See below, p. 145.
[2] Preface to an unpublished translation, dated May 1787, B. M. Add. MS 5658, f. 19.
[3] *Testimony to the Authenticity of the Prophecies of Richard Brothers* (1795), p. 10.

which might be drawn from what he had written, Halhed sought refuge in circumlocution.

Great surely and inexplicable must be the doubts of mere human reason upon such a dilemma when unassisted and uninformed by divine revelation; but while we admit the former in our argument, we profess a most un-shaken reliance upon the latter, before which every suspicion must subside, and scepticism be absorbed in conviction: yet from the premises already established, this conclusion at least may fairly be deduced, that the world does not now contain annals of more indisputable antiquity than those delivered down by the ancient Bramins.[1]

In a letter to one of his critics he admitted that his arguments 'in Rabelais's phrase began to smell of the faggot', again professed his orthodoxy, but stuck to his guns:

how any of the descendants of Noah could so totally lose every trace of the language, the manners and religion of their general parent, as well as by what means there should have proceeded from three persons so many differ-ent species of human creatures, while not one single addition has been made to the number of those species since the invention and use of history, are difficult questions, and tho' connected with our subject, not necessarily requiring a discussion: and as I think, should be simply referred to the general rule I ventured to adopt in my Preface:—*That a man may propose doubts as a philosopher, without being called to account for them as a Christian*; for if we are forbidden to consider any cause where revelation has already pronounced upon the effect, the world might still have persisted in believing that the sun and moon suspended by Joshua were absolute and not relative —real as well as apparent.[2]

Holwell's and Dow's conclusions were accepted without reser-vation by Voltaire. He called Holwell's 'Shastah' the oldest homage to God on earth, and Dow's 'catechism' the most beauti-ful monument of all antiquity.[3] Indians were clearly monotheists and had taught monotheism to the Chinese;[4] they had invented the concepts of a soul distinct from the body and of the immor-tality of the soul.[5] The Abbé Raynal was less enthusiastic about some of the beliefs described by Holwell, but he accepted that 'amidst a variety of absurd superstitions, puerile and extrava-gant customs, strange ceremonies and prejudices, we may also discover the traces of sublime morality, deep philosophy and

[1] See below, p. 162.
[2] Letter to G. Costard, 1779, B. M. Stowe MS, 757, ff. 8–9.
[3] *Oeuvres*, xxix, 167, 183.
[4] *Ibid.* xxix, 167.   [5] *Ibid.* xxviii, 140.

refined policy'.[1] Jean Bailly especially admired the opening section of Holwell's 'Shastah': 'Cette idée très belle et très philosophique que l'Etre suprême est incompréhensible, que son essence est impénétrable et qu'il est insensé à l'homme d'entreprendre de la sonder'; that was something that not even Newton or Leibnitz had recognized.[2] Holwell's chronology was eagerly seized upon. Voltaire had no doubt that the 'Shastah' was over 5,000 years old, and that it showed that the 'Brachmanes' were older by several centuries than the Chinese, who were themselves older than the rest of mankind.[3] To Raynal, India, not the Middle East, was the earliest inhabited part of the globe and the Indians were 'the first who received the rudiments of science, and the polish of civilisation'.[4] Bailly also thought that India had instructed the rest of the world, although in his opinion India had itself been colonised from further north.[5] Bailly tried to bring a new precision into chronological discussions by using astronomical calculations on lines first attempted by Newton when he had dated the expedition of the Argonauts by the observations on Chiron's sphere.[6] Indian astronomical skill had long been known and some of their tables for calculating eclipses had been brought back to Europe. Very detailed tables had recently been made available by the astronomer Le Gentil de La Galaisière, who had spent some time on the Coromandel Coast studying Indian techniques at first hand.[7] Le Gentil's tables contained observations purporting to go back to the beginning of the last Hindu *yuga*, or to 3102 B.C. In his *Histoire de l'Astronomie ancienne*, published in 1775, Bailly announced that the tables were probably 5,000 to 6,000 years old.[8] Twelve years later he published a more detailed account, verifying the data in the tables and explaining why he believed that it could only have been obtained by actual observations and not by retrospective calculation.[9] By orthodox dating 3102 B.C. was

[1] *A Philosophical and Political History of the Settlements and Trade of the Europeans in the East and West Indies*, trans. J. Justamond (1777), I, 38.
[2] *Voltaire's Correspondence*, XCIII, 9.   [3] *Oeuvres*, XXIX, 479.
[4] *History of the Indies*, I, 35, 38.   [5] *Lettres sur l'Origine des Sciences*.
[6] See below, p. 289; and Manuel, *Newton, Historian*, pp. 65 ff.
[7] See his two 'Mémoires sur l'Inde', *Mémoires de l'Académie royale des sciences* (1772), II.   [8] p. 114.
[9] *Traité de l'Astronomie Indienne et Orientale* (Paris, 1787); Smith, *Jean-Sylvain Bailly*, pp. 498–500.

some 650 years before the flood. Bailly tried to soften the blow by suggesting that Hindu chronology was compatible with the dating of the flood derived from the Greek Septuagint, which put it back by an extra nine hundred years;[1] but his conclusions caused grave misgivings to orthodox Christians, who hoped that they would be disproved.[2]

Voltaire seems to have been in some confusion of mind as to how to use to the best advantage the new weapon against Christianity which the English had put into his hands. His first reaction was to exult that the Old Testament and Christianity could now definitely be shown to be derivative. He reflected that 'la foi peut être un peu ébranlée' when it was appreciated that the first man according to the Hindus was called Adimo and that Abraham and Brahma were really the same.[3] He assured Frederick the Great 'que notre sainte religion Chrétienne est uniquement fondée sur l'antique religion de Brama'.[4] But he also felt that the pretensions of the children of Israel could be exposed by showing that not only were they a people of recent origin, but that their history had been ignored by all other peoples with any claim to antiquity. Indian history showed not 'la moindre trace de l'histoire sacrée judaique, qui est notre histoire sacrée. Pas un seul mot de Noé...; pas un seul mot d'Adam...Pourquoi tant d'antiques nations les ont-elles ignorés, et pourquoi un petit peuple nouveau les a-t-il connus?'[5] Hinduism was still being used as a stick to beat Christianity during the French Revolution. Louis Langlès of the Bibliothèque Nationale, described Hinduism as the basis of all the world's religions, including Christianity; the Pentateuch was an abridgement of Egyptian books which originated in India.[6] Volney suggested that Christ was no more than an embodiment of a common eastern tradition, including the 'Hindoo god, Chris-en, or Christna'.[7]

English reactions to the findings of Holwell, Dow or Halhed mostly showed an orthodox Christian point of view. Gibbon, the

---

[1] *Traité*, p. cxxv.
[2] E.g. Robertson, *Historical Disquisitions*, pp. 360–2.
[3] *Voltaire's Correspondence*, LXVII, 255–6.
[4] *Ibid.* XCII, 182.   [5] *Oeuvres*, XXIX, 110–11.
[6] *Fables et Contes Indiens* (Paris, 1790), pp. x–xiii.
[7] *The Ruins: or a Survey of the Revolutions of Empires*, 3rd ed. (1796), pp. 292–3.

most obvious Englishman to have exploited them in the manner of Voltaire, was evidently not much interested in investigations into the origins of peoples or religions, which could produce no result except 'toilsome and disappointed efforts'. He contented himself with witticisms about 'antiquarians of profound learning and easy faith, who . . . conducted the great grandchildren of Noah from the Tower of Babel to the extremities of the Globe'.[1] The English literary public in general seem to have been willing to accept a sympathetic portrayal of Hinduism, but they were not prepared to accept claims for its antiquity which could be subversive to Christianity; there was no disposition to accept Holwell's or Halhed's chronology. While there was considerable flexibility about dating and no rigid adherence to Ussher's system,[2] the essentials of the Biblical version of creation and of the world's history were not seriously questioned in eighteenth-century England.[3] Joseph Priestley, the greatest scientist of the late eighteenth century, came to the defence of Moses,[4] as Newton had done at the beginning of the century. Comments on Holwell varied from the *Annual Register's* restrained 'the arguments brought by Mr Holwell to prove the antiquity and originality of the Gentoo scriptures, are not so clear and conclusive as might be wished',[5] to the belligerence of the *Critical Review*: ' . . . the credit of this same Chartah Bhade Shastah, of Bruma, Bramma, Burma, Brumma, Birma, Bramah, or the Lord knows who, rests upon no other authority than the implicit veneration of the illiterate and credulous Gentoos, and the eminently *discerning* Mr Holwell.'[6] The *Gentleman's Magazine* regarded Halhed's eight million years for the four Hindu *yugas* as 'rather too much for an European to digest readily'.[7] An Anglican clergyman published an open letter to Halhed, telling him that Hindu chronology was 'fictitious and absurd' and that no Hindu scripture could be older than the handing down of the Law to Moses on Sinai, since 'the forming of an

[1] *The Decline and Fall of the Roman Empire*, ed. J. B. Bury (1896–1900), i, 217.

[2] Blair, *Chronology and History*, preface, unpaginated.

[3] R. N. Stromberg, *Religious Liberalism in Eighteenth-century England* (Oxford, 1954), pp. 26–7.

[4] *A Comparison of the Institutions of Moses with those of the Hindoos* (Northumberland, 1799).   [5] *Annual Register* (1766), ii, 309.

[6] xxxii (1771), 131.   [7] xlvii (1777), 636.

alphabet seems a work beyond human invention', which could only have been taught by God.[1] The most open-minded reaction seems to have been that of Richard Watson, later bishop of Llandaff. In a Discourse to the Clergy of Ely he suggested that Hindu chronology was probably 'a mere fable' and that it was unlikely that the Hindus did not have a tradition of the flood, which was common to most ancient civilisations, yet he still believed that these questions should be examined; 'the consequences of truth...can never be injurious to the rights, or well founded expectations of the human race' and 'no faith can be acceptable to God, which is not grounded upon reason'.[2]

To his contemporaries, faith and reason seemed to coincide admirably in Sir William Jones. His own religious views, though unequivocally Christian, may, in fact, have been less straightforward than was generally supposed. He thought that there was a wide gap between the Church of England and 'the religion of the Gospel' and he also disliked the Christian view of eternal punishment, regarding the Hindu doctrine of transmigration as 'incomparably more rational, more pious and more likely to deter men from vice'.[3] But little of this appeared in his publications. He announced at the beginning of his essay 'on the Chronology of the Hindus' that all truths must be open to inquiry and that he would reject the Mosaic history if it could be disproved,[4] but he also committed himself in the essay 'on the Gods of Greece, Italy and India' to the proposition that 'Either the first eleven chapters of Genesis, all due allowances being made for a figurative Eastern style, are true, or the whole fabrick of our national religion is false.'[5] Perhaps not surprisingly, his researches ended in the vindication of Moses. He found that 'the adamantine pillars of our Christian faith' could not be shaken by 'any inquiries into the Indian theology'.[6] He told the Asiatic Society in his anniversary discourse of 1793 that ten years of study in India had only confirmed in his mind 'the Mosaick accounts of the primitive world'.[7] In his essay on Chronology he set to work to cut the

[1] G. Costard, *A Letter to Nathaniel Brassey Halhed* (Oxford, 1778), pp. 15–16.
[2] Reprinted in the *Asiatick Miscellany*, I (1785), 9–11.
[3] Mukherjee, *Jones*, pp. 118–19.
[4] See below, p. 262.   [5] See below, p. 200.
[6] See below, p. 243.   [7] *Jones Works*, I, 145.

ground from under the feet of Voltaire, Raynal and Bailly and to bring the Indians into the fold of the Old Testament dating by showing that claims that India was the oldest inhabited part of the earth, or that it had a civilisation, including written records, going back to before 3000 B.C. were untenable, whatever Holwell or Halhed may have thought to the contrary notwithstanding. His method was to reconstruct the Indian tradition by assembling the Puranic king lists supplied to him by Radhakanta,[1] and to try to fix points in them by the use of outside evidence. The most promising piece of outside evidence, already used by the French historian de Guignes,[2] seemed to be the Chinese traditions which missionaries had been publishing in Europe. Chinese sources gave Jones a dating for the Buddha at about 1000 B.C., and he arranged the Puranic kings each side of this date.[3] By modern estimates he conceded more than he need have done; the dating of his later figures can probably be halved.[4] But he had done enough to set the minds of most Christians at rest. He had shown that the Indian historic period could not have begun much before 2000 B.C. at the earliest, safely after the dispersal of the peoples in *Genesis*, and that the first Indian writings were later than the conventional dating for Moses's activities as a historian, which was 1452 B.C. although this was a point on which Jones subsequently revised his opinion; his colleague in the Asiatic Society, Samuel Davis, suggested astronomical calculations which made it necessary for him to put the composition of the *Vedas* back to 1580 B.C.[5] All Indian history before approximately 2000 B.C. could be dismissed as 'chiefly mythological', founded either 'on the dark enigmas of their astronomers' or 'on the heroick fictions of their poets', but he pointed out very strong similarities between parts of this mythology and the early chapters of *Genesis*.[6] In a supplement to the essay on Chronology he became more dogmatic: there could be no doubt that some Hindu myths were versions of *Genesis*.[7]

Jones was aware that he was treading on dangerous ground and

[1] See below, p. 268.
[2] 'Recherches historiques sur la religion Indienne', *Mémoires de l'Académie royale des Inscriptions et des Belles Lettres*, XL (1773–6), 196–7.
[3] See below, p. 273.
[4] See below, p. 287.   [5] *Jones Works*, III, 54–6.
[6] See below, p. 286.   [7] *Jones Works*, I, 326–7.

that it might be concluded that Moses had merely repeated Egyptian or Indian mythology. But he emphatically rejected any such conclusion.[1] His own explanation for the similarities was the simplest of the historical explanations habitually used by Christians. The peoples of the earth had all originated, as *Genesis* explained, in a single place, where they had all practised the 'rational adoration of the only true God' before their dispersal.[2] The Indians preserved memories of this period of their history in the legends of the first and second Manus, who could be identified with Adam and Noah. While accepting the simplest of the Christian interpretations, Jones would have nothing to do with the more elaborate ones. He refused to try to find either Jewish or Christian influence in Hinduism; the Christian Trinity 'cannot without profaneness be compared with that of the Hindus'.[3] In his essay 'on the Gods of Greece, Italy and India' he tried to show that Indian and European mythology was basically the same and to prove that these similarities arose not because the myths had spread from one country to another, but because Europeans and Asians shared a common past, from which similarity of language and even of philosophical schools also sprang. Like other eighteenth-century students of mythology, he traced its origins to the deeds of heroes, to the worship of natural phenomena, especially the sun, and to allegory.[4]

Jones's chronology was warmly welcomed by English Christians. In 1788 Richard Watson reissued his Discourse to the Clergy of Ely with a note that Jones had now proved the existence of the flood in Hindu traditions.[5] Joseph Priestley used Jones's dating in his defence of Moses.[6] By far the most elaborate use of him was by Thomas Maurice. Maurice compiled two works, outdoing even Holwell's *Interesting Historical Events* in length, discursiveness and lack of organisation, which he called *The History of Hindostan*[7] and *Indian Antiquities*.[8] He described India 'as the

---

[1] See below, pp. 242–3.   [2] See below, p. 196.
[3] See below, p. 243.
[4] F. Manuel, *The Eighteenth Century confronts the Gods* (Cambridge, Mass., 1959).
[5] *Sermons on Public Occasions, and Tracts on Religious Subjects* (Cambridge, 1788), p. 221.
[6] *A Comparison of the Institutions of Moses*, pp. 7–15.
[7] 2 vols (1795–8).   [8] 7 vols (1793–1800).

debateable ground on which the fury of Jacobin hostility had reared her most triumphant banners' and he set out to rout 'the whole host of infidel writers'.[1] With the aid of Jones he accomplished this task to his own satisfaction. He believed that when the similarities with Christian belief are recognised in Hinduism, and when it is appreciated that these similarities did not arise through any connexion between Jews and Indians, 'the result...must be an increased confidence in the great truths of revelation; and thus the *Indian Antiquities* cannot fail of being considered of national benefit'.[2]

If British public opinion was not prepared to accept a chronology which would be damaging to orthodox Christian belief, it seems to have been willing to give a generally sympathetic hearing to the other claims made for Hinduism by Holwell, Dow, Wilkins or Warren Hastings. The deism of Holwell and Dow may have been too extreme for most of their readers, but there was still common ground between the authors and their public. Beneath the luxurious foliage of Hinduism, Holwell, Dow and Wilkins had all perceived a few simple truths about the unity of God, the immortality of the soul and moral conduct. These were the main preoccupations of many eighteenth-century Christians. The views of 'liberal' Anglicans have been described as the 'reduction of necessary beliefs to a few fundamentals, and a tendency towards moralism'.[3] Religious experience, or dogma received less attention. A religion that seemed to share this concern with simple truth and personal conduct was likely to be treated with sympathy and respect.

Holwell brought the worst out of reviewers, but otherwise critics were generally well disposed. The *Critical Review* found Hinduism as displayed by Holwell 'such a continued series of nonsense, rhapsody, and absurdity, that the quoting it must insult the common understanding',[4] but it detected some 'true philosophy', mixed with 'Pythagorism, debased Christianity' and 'materialism' in Dow's account.[5] The *Monthly Review* accepted that Dow had proved that Brahmins believed 'in the unity, eter-

---

[1] *Memoirs of the Author of Indian Antiquities* (1819–20), I, 102.
[2] *Indian Antiquities*, IV, preface.
[3] Stromberg, *Religious Liberalism*, p. 92.
[4] XXII (1766), 343.   [5] XXVI (1768), 83.

nity, omniscience and omnipotence of God'.[1] In discussing Halhed's Preface the reviewer for the *Gentleman's Magazine* concluded that 'the Beids' contained 'speculative divinity. . .without any mixture of idolatry'.[2] The proposition that Hindus were basically monotheists was usually accepted. In a sermon in other respects hostile to Hinduism, Joseph White, Professor of Arabic at Oxford, conceded that 'the idea of one supreme God' was a part of Hindu belief.[3] William Robertson thought that Hindu monotheism had been conclusively proved.[4]

Hindu morals and manners as exhibited in Halhed's Code were commended by most commentators, although there were exceptions, like the astronomer George Costard, who found 'many of these Gentoo laws frivolous' and others '*absurd* and *cruel*'.[5] An M.P. told the House of Commons that 'their similarity in many cases to the Mosaic Law, proved both their antiquity and wisdom'.[6] Edmund Burke, who, according to Fox, habitually 'spoke of the piety of the Hindoos with admiration, and of their holy religion and sacred functions with an awe bordering on devotion',[7] studied the Code with the care 'that such an extraordinary view of human affairs and human constitutions deserves'.[8] He considered the Hindus to be 'the most benevolent' of people, who 'extend their benevolence to the whole animal creation' (unlike that 'Protestant sect called Mahometanism. . .that has for one of its dogmas, the servitude of all mankind that do not belong to it').[9] 'Wherever the Hindu religion has been established, that country has been flourishing.'[10] Robertson saw the Code as being founded 'upon the great and immutable principles of justice which the human mind acknowledges and respects, in every age, and in all parts of the earth'.[11] Halhed had included with his Preface a

---

[1] xxxix (1768), 386. [2] xlvii (1777), 524.

[3] *A Sermon. . .on the duty of attempting the Propagation of the Gospel among our Mahometan and Gentoo Subjects in India* (1785), p. 42.

[4] *Historical Disquisitions*, pp. 325–6.

[5] *Letter to Halhed*, p. 4.

[6] Speech of John Courtenay, 27 June 1781. *Parliamentary History of England, from the earliest period to the year 1803*, xxii, 559.

[7] Lord Holland, *Memoirs of the Whig Party during my time* (1852–4), i, 6.

[8] Bond, *Speeches in the Trial of Hastings*, iv, 363.

[9] *Correspondence of Edmund Burke* (Cambridge, 1958–), vii, eds., P. J. Marshall and J. A. Woods, 118.

[10] Bond, *Speeches*, i, 33–4. [11] *Historical Disquisitions*, p. 275

short Preliminary Discourse by the *pandits* who had compiled the Code.[1] The *pandits* had risen to the occasion and produced a moving appeal for universal religious toleration. 'Few Christians', Halhed wrote, 'would have expressed themselves with a more becoming reverence for the grand and impartial designs of providence in all its works, or with a more extensive charity towards all their fellow creatures of every profession.'[2] The *pandits'* discourse was well received in Britain. The *Critical Review* described it as 'a most sublime performance. . . We are persuaded that even this enlightened quarter of the world cannot boast any thing that soars so completely above the narrow, vulgar, sphere of prejudice and priestcraft. The most amiable part of modern philosophy is hardly upon a level with the extensive charity, the comprehensive benevolence, of a few rude, untutored, Hindoo Bramins'.[3]

Jones's portrayal of Hinduism was not in essence different from that of earlier English writers. He too was primarily interested in fundamental religious truths and in ethics, and he found both in Hinduism. He added his testimony that 'the omnipresence, wisdom and goodness of God' was 'the basis of Indian philosophy', and he insisted that the ethical teaching of Christianity could be found in Hinduism, and indeed in other Asian religions; he was one of the comparatively small number of Europeans who tried to obtain a fair hearing for Islam.[4] But partly because Jones knew more about Hinduism than his predecessors and partly because his sympathies seem to have been wider than theirs, his picture was a rather fuller one. He was able to give a favourable account of what Christians have traditionally found to be the most intractable aspect of Hindu theology, the doctrine of monism, that is of the unity between the individual soul and *brahman*, as expounded in the *Upanishads* and in the writings of the *Vedanta* school.[5] Monism had been a stumbling block to both Christians and non-Christians. The Jesuit Pons admired the concept of an eternal, immaterial, infinite *atma*, but he thought that anyone who accepted it was bound also, 'avec un orgueil plus

---

[1] See below, pp. 182–3. [2] See below, pp. 164–5.
[3] XLIV (1777), 178. [4] *Jones Works*, i, 166, 168–9.
[5] G. Parrinder, *Upanishads, Gita and Bible* (1962), pp. 34–45.

outré que celui de Lucifer', to accept the proposition 'Je suis l'Etre suprême'.[1] The Abbé Mignot made the same point: Christians must reject a doctrine that allowed man to believe that he was God.[2] From a secular point of view, Bailly thought that the distinction between *atma* and *maya* was crude and false.[3] But Jones was prepared to keep an open mind. He thought that human reason could neither 'fully demonstrate, nor fully disprove' the teaching of the Vedantists, but that 'nothing can be farther removed from impiety'.[4] Jones was also better equipped to come to terms with the popular cults of Hinduism than many of his contemporaries. Like them, his ideal was a sober, 'rational' piety, but he was not repelled by 'a figurative mode of expressing the fervour of devotion, or the ardent love of created spirits towards their beneficent Creator'.[5] He admired Hindu devotional literature, such as the *Bhagavat Purana* and the *Gita Govinda*, from which he made translations, and he was even reconciled to apparent eroticism, which was 'no proof of depravity in their morals'.[6]

Jones's favourable verdict on Hinduism was repeated by writers in Britain, as those of Holwell, Dow and Halhed had been. In the 1790s Thomas Maurice still felt it fitting to follow Jones's example and to launch 'forth into the warmest strains of admiration on the survey of the virtues, learning, fortitude, and industry of this innocent and secluded race of men'.[7] But there are signs that opinion was beginning to harden against Hinduism. This was most obviously so among committed Christians. More and more members of the Church of England were turning against 'the cult of "mere morality"' and 'the encroachment of natural on supernatural religion',[8] and were asserting what they believed to be the great fundamental of Protestant Christianity, man's total depravity and the utter impossibility of salvation without Christ. For Evangelicals there could be no common ground with

---

[1] *Lettres édifiantes*, xxvi, 248–51.

[2] 'Mémoires sur les anciens philosophes de l'Inde', *Mémoires de l'Académie royale des Inscriptions et Belles Lettres*, xxxi (1761–3), 320.

[3] *Lettres sur l'Origine des Sciences*, p. 53.

[4] *Jones Works*, i, 166.   [5] *Ibid.* i, 445.

[6] See below, p. 226.   [7] *Indian Antiquities*, i, lxiii.

[8] J. D. Walsh, 'Origins of the Evangelical Revival' in Walsh and G. V. Bennett, eds., *Essays in Modern English Church History* (1966), pp. 148–50.

non-Christian beliefs; monotheism and high ethical standards counted for nothing. To tolerate such beliefs and thus to leave their adherents in darkness was a vice not a virtue. Although the Society for Promoting Christian Knowledge had been supporting the Danish mission since 1710, there had been no attempt to follow up British conquests with a missionary campaign. A sermon preached at Oxford in 1784 on *The Duty of attempting the Propagation of the Gospel among our Mahometan and Gentoo Subjects in India* was an isolated event.[1] But calls to action were coming from India itself. In the 1760s and 1770s liberal Christians in India had written indulgent accounts of Hinduism which had found favour with liberal Christians at home; by the 1780s Evangelicals in India were beginning to write harsh condemnations of Hinduism to stir Evangelicals at home. Charles Grant is the most famous example of Evangelical zeal in India. In 1785 he wrote of the Hindus to the Methodist Thomas Coke: 'It is hardly possible to conceive any people more completely enchained than they are by their superstition.'[2] He and others drafted a proposal for launching missions in 1787 which stated: 'In fact the people are universally and wholly corrupt, they are as depraved as they are blind, and as wretched as they are depraved.'[3] In 1792 he composed his famous 'Observations on the State of Society among the Asiatic Subjects of Great Britain'. Halhed's Code was summarised to show 'the immorality, the injustice and the cruelty' of Hindu customs. Hindus were once again classified as idolaters. Grant conceded that there might be some element of the worship of a supreme being in Hinduism, but Dow was castigated for implying that 'the speculative admission of one or more important truths' might prove the rightness of a religion; 'so latitudinarian an opinion' fell 'below even the creed of deism'.[4] In the debate on the clause to sanction missionaries in the Charter Bill of 1793, 'Resorting to history, and to extracts from the letters of several of the more eminent servants of the Company', William Wilberforce 'inferred that the natives of India, and more particularly the

[1] By Joseph White, published 1785.
[2] *The Life of the Rev. Thomas Coke, LL.D.* (Leeds, 1815), p. 201.
[3] H. Morris, *The Life of Charles Grant* (1904), p. 111.
[4] *Parliamentary Papers, House of Commons* (1812–13), x, 76–88, 103.

Brahmins, were sunk into the most abject ignorance and vice.'[1]
The House of Commons was to hear much language of this kind
in the years ahead.

Hostility to Hinduism in the 1790s extended beyond Evangelical circles, although the reasons for it are less tangible. It may
reflect greater confidence in the superiority of all things European
being generated by the widening gap between Asian and European standards which industrialisation and scientific knowledge
were bringing about. Joseph Priestley had a low opinion of
Hinduism. He thought that comparisons between the Old Testament and Hindu scripture provided the strongest possible argument for the divine inspiration of Moses. Jones might write of the
'sublime devotion' of the Hindus; in Priestley's opinion, 'the
general character of the devotion of the Hindoos is that of a debas-
ing superstition'.[2] Within a few years James Mill was to begin
work on the great philippic against Hinduism and its European
admirers contained in the first chapter of his *History of British
India.*

The pieces that follow will show the limitations of their authors
only too clearly. With the possible exception of Jones, they did
not try to understand what Hinduism meant to millions of
Indians. They invariably made a distinction between 'popular'
Hinduism, which they did not deem worthy of study, and 'philosophical' Hinduism, which they tried to define as a set of hard and
fast doctrinal propositions and to place in current theories about
the nature and history of religion. All of them wrote with contemporary European controversies and their own religious preoccupations very much in mind. As Europeans have always tended
to do, they created Hinduism in their own image. Halhed perhaps
apart, they believed that certain basic truths and certain moral
principles were common to all religions, although present in their
most refined form in Protestant Christianity. Their study of
Hinduism confirmed their beliefs, and Hindus emerged from
their work as adhering to something akin to undogmatic Protest-
antism. Later generations of Europeans, interested themselves in

---

[1] *The Parliamentary Register*, 2nd series, xxxv, 583.
[2] *Comparison of the Institutions of Moses*, pp. 6–7.

mysticism, were able to portray the Hindus as mystics. But for all their limitations, the authors represented in this book show an attractive generosity towards their subject. They wished to make the best case they could for the Hindus, even if they could not conceive of a case in other than European terms. Holwell set out to rescue 'those most venerable sages the Bramins' from their detractors.[1] Dow tried to counter those who by a 'very unfair account, have thrown disgrace upon a system of religion and philosophy, which they did by no means investigate'.[2] Halhed found the *pandits* who had helped him 'truly elevated above the mean and selfish principles of priestcraft'.[3] Hastings believed that the Hindu scriptures would 'survive when the British dominion in India shall have long ceased to exist, and when the sources which it once yielded of wealth and power are lost to remembrance'.[4] In his opening discourse to the newly-founded Asiatic Society, Jones had spoken of the 'inexpressable pleasure' which he had felt as his ship crossed the Indian Ocean and he found himself 'in the midst of so noble an amphitheatre, almost surrounded by the vast regions of Asia'.[5] This sense of delight is present in all his Indian writings. Generosity and goodwill were not always to be the most notable features of later interpretations of Hinduism.

[1] See below, p. 48.
[2] See below, p. 108.
[3] See below, p. 164.
[4] See below, p. 189.
[5] *Jones Works*, I, 1–2.

1

John Zephaniah Holwell, chapters on 'The Religious Tenets of the Gentoos'

To the Public

PRELIMINARY DISCOURSE

When a man, excited by an irresistable and laudable impulse for the good of his country, first speaks before an august assembly; he feels a certain kind of dread, awe, and trepidation, which he finds himself unable immediately to conquer; especially if he has not been much used to speak in public, or perchance possesses some share of modesty in his composition. Thus, I conceive, it fares with every considerate author, on his first appearance before that august assembly the public.

In this plight I felt myself in the year 1758, when I exhibited to you a scene of unparalleled horror and distress, which I judged not unworthy a place in our annals;[a] justice, and the necessity of the times, lately urged my second appearance, and obliged me to draw my pen in defence of injured worth and character:[b] but now, by use and indulgence grown bolder, (a very common case) I present myself before you of my own voluntary choice.

Independency, and a pleasing retirement, however delectable in themselves, have yet their seasons of vacancy and leisure, that may want filling up. And happy ought that man to esteem himself, who can employ those voids and blanks in time to the emolument, or even literary amusement of mankind.

[a] *A Genuine Narrative of the Deplorable Deaths of the English Gentlemen and others, who were suffocated in the Black Hole* (1758).

[b] Two tracts written by Holwell had appeared in 1764: *An Address to the Proprietors of East India Stock setting forth...the necessity and the real motives for the Revolution in Bengal in 1760* and *Important Facts regarding the East India Company's affairs in Bengal from 1752 to 1760.*

Such is my situation, and such are my motives, for taking up the pen again; motives, so laudable in themselves, will, I trust, engage the candor and indulgence of my readers for any defects in the following performance.

The East-Indies, and particularly Bengall, are now become so important an object and concern to Great Britain, that every elucidation thereof, must, I think, be acceptable, that is founded on facts, just observations, and faithful recitals.

Through a course of thirty years residence in Bengall, my leisure hours were employed in collecting materials relative to the transactions, revolutions and occurrences of that invaluable country; and the religious tenets of its inhabitants, natives of Indostan; which I flattered myself, when reduced to form and order, might prove worthy your attention.

It is well known that at the capture of Calcutta, A.D. 1756, I lost many curious Gentoo manuscripts, and among them two very correct and valuable copies of the Gentoo *Shastah.*[a] They were procured by me with so much trouble and expence, that even the commissioners of restitution, though not at all disposed to favour me, allowed me two thousand Madras rupees in recompence for this particular loss; but the most irreparable damage I suffered under this head of grievances, was a translation I made of a considerable part of the *Shastah*, which had cost me eighteen months hard labour:[b] as that work opened upon me, I distinctly saw, that the mythology, as well as the cosmogony of the Egyptians, Greeks and Romans, were borrowed from the doctrines of the Bramins; contained in this book; even to the copying their exteriors of worship, and the distribution of their idols, though grossly mutilated and adulterated. But more of this in the course of my present work.

I should in the compass of one year more, with the close application, I intended bestowing on it, have accomplished a complete translation of the whole *Shastah*; that would, I flattered myself, have been a valuable acquisition to the learned world; had not the fatal catastrophe of fifty-six put it totally out of my power ever to attempt it again.

[a] The original of Holwell's 'Shastah' cannot be identified.
[b] Judging by the words which he reproduces, Holwell must have made his translation out of a Hindustani version.

John Zephaniah Holwell

From that change in our affairs abroad, a new chain of pursuits engrossed my time and attention; so that I could no longer devote either, to the studies I had before so much at heart. However, during the last eight months of my residence in Bengall, being freed from the plagues of government, (thanks to my very honourable masters for it)[a] I reassumed my researches with tolerable success; which, joined to some manuscripts recovered by an unforeseen and extraordinary event (that possibly I may hereafter recite) enables me to undertake the task I now assign myself.

It is true I intended a much nobler entertainment for my readers; but as that is now irrecoverably beyond my reach, without once more doubling the Cape of Good Hope, (to which I feel not the least inclination) we must content ourselves with the homely fare we have before us, ranged in the best manner our straitened circumstances will admit of—as it is essentially necessary at this interesting period, that we should be able to form some clearer ideas of a people, with whom we have had such important transactions; and of whom so little is truely known.[1]

Having studiously perused all that has been written of the empire of Indostan, both as to its ancient, as well as more modern state; as also the various accounts transmitted to us, by authors in almost all ages (from Arrian,[b] down to the Abbé de Guyon)[c] concerning the Hindoos, and the religious tenets of the Bramins, I venture to pronounce them all very defective, fallacious, and unsatisfactory to an inquisitive searcher after truth; and only tending to convey a very imperfect and injurious resemblance of a people, who from the earliest times have been an ornament to the creation—if so much can with propriety be said of any known people upon earth.

[1] Here I would be understood to mean the Gentoos only, now labouring under Mahometan tyranny, but fated, I hope, soon to feel the blessings of a mild British government.

[a] Holwell had succeeded to the Governorship of Fort William in February 1760, but he was replaced in July by Henry Vansittart (1732–70).

[b] Flavius Arrianus (c. A.D. 96–180), author of the *Anabasis*, or history of Alexander.

[c] A translation of the *Histoire des Indes* (Paris, 1744), by Claude-Marie Guyon (1699–1771) had appeared in English in 1757 as *A New History of the East-Indies, Ancient and Modern*, 2 vols.

British Discovery of Hinduism

All the modern writers represent the Hindoos as a race of stupid and gross idolaters: from the ancients indeed these people met with better treatment; although they too, as well as the others, were equally ignorant in the subjects they treated of.

The modern authors who have wrote on the principles and worship of the Hindoos, are chiefly of the Romish communion; therefore we need wonder the less that they (from a superstitious zeal inseparable from that communion) should depreciate and traduce the mythology of the venerable ancient Bramins, on so slender a foundation as a few insignificant literal translations of the *Viedam*; and these, not made from the book itself, but from unconnected scraps and bits, picked up here and there by hearsay from Hindoos, probably as ignorant as themselves.[a]

From such weak grounds and evidence as this, and by the help of a few exhibitions of the seemingly monstrous idols of the Hindoos, the Popish authors hesitate not to stigmatize those most venerable sages the Bramins, as having instituted doctrines and worship, which if believed, would reduce them below the level of the brute creation; as every reader must have observed, who has misspent his time in the perusal of them. In the way of their proper calling and function, they were however right; as having been appointed to propagate their own system of theology abroad; though strictly speaking, their own tenets were more idolatrous than the system they travelled so far to stigmatize. On this mistaken method and false zeal of propagating any faith at any rate, I beg to be indulged in making the following general reflections, which naturally arise from the subject before us.

In the first place, I observe, ignorance, superstition and partiality to ourselves, are too commonly the cause of presumption and contempt of others. Secondly, that those whose knowledge of states and kingdoms extends no further than the limits of their native land, often imagine all, beyond it, scarce worth their thoughts; or at least greatly inferior in comparison with their

[a] Many of Guyon's most offensive comments on Hinduism were based on the *Naauwkeurige beschrijvinge van Malabar en Choromandel* (Amsterdam, 1672) (trans. in A. and J. Churchill, *A Collection of Voyages and Travels,* 3rd ed. (1744–5), vol. III), by the Dutch chaplain Philippus Baldaeus (1631–71). Although Baldaeus mentions 'the Vedam' (the Tamil name for the *Vedas*), he never claimed that his account was a translation of it.

own; a conclusion natural, though absurd. Thirdly, if from clime and country, we proceed to individuals; we shall see the same unwarrantable prepossession, and preference to self take place; and proceeding still further in our reflections, we may observe, the same confined way of thinking and judging, leads the multitude (and I wish I could say the multitude only) of every nation and sect, to arraign and have in utter detestation and contempt, the religious principles and worship of all that happen to be out of the pale of their own church, or mode of faith.

That every nation and sect should have a high and even superior opinion of the religious principles, under which they were born and educated, is extremely natural and just; provided they do not, from an intemperate zeal of religious vanity (now so much the fashion) presume to condemn, depreciate or invade the religious principles of others—this condemning spirit can proceed only from one of the three following causes; a defect in understanding; a want of knowledge of the world (in men and things); or a bad (and restless) heart. The salvation of mankind, so much pretended, has no place in the wishes or labours of these zealots; or they would not go about seeking whom they can confound in spirit, destroying the peace and tranquility of their poor fellow christians.

Men who have been conversant with foreign countries, and made proper and benevolent remarks on the manners and principles of their inhabitants; will not despise or condemn the different ways by which they approach the Deity; but revere it still as a divine worship, though they may piously lament it deviates so much from their own.

To rescue distant nations from the gross conceptions entertained of them by the multitude, of all other persuasions, is the true business and indispensable duty of a traveller; or else his travels and remarks, can only amuse his readers, without conveying to them any useful instruction or solid satisfaction.

A mere description of the exterior manners and religion of a people, will no more give us a true idea of them; than a geographical description of a country can convey a just conception of their laws and government. The traveller must sink deeper in his researches, would he feast the mind of an understanding reader.

His telling us such and such a people, in the East or West-Indies, worship this stock, or that stone, or monstrous idol; only serves to reduce in our esteem, our fellow creatures, to the most abject and despicable point of light. Whereas, was he skilled in the language of the people he describes, sufficiently to trace the etymology of their words and phrases, and capable of diving into the mysteries of their theology; he would probably be able to evince us, that such seemingly preposterous worship, had the most sublime rational source and foundation.

The traveller, who without these essential requisites, (as well as industry and a clear understanding) pretends to describe and fix the religious tenets of any nation whatever, dishonestly imposes his own reveries on the world; and does the greatest injury and violence to letters, and the cause of humanity. How far the productions of most travellers may justly fall under this censure, I submit to the public.

To the want of this attention and capacity in the traveller, we may ascribe in a great measure, the despicable, and I dare say unworthy notion, we too aptly entertain of most nations very remote from us; whereas were we better informed, we should find our minds opened; our understandings enlarged; and ourselves inspired with that benevolence for our species; without which, the human form becomes rather a disgrace than ornament.

I am sorry to say, that in general the accounts published of the manners and religious principles of the East and West-Indies, have been in the light and superficial way before objected to: but as my knowledge extends only to the former, I shall confine my remarks to them; and endeavour to extricate them in some degree from the gross absurdities we have conceived of them: confessing myself amazed that we should so readily believe the people of Indostan a race of stupid idolaters; when, to our cost, in a political and commercial view, we have found them superior to us.

Having transiently mentioned the *Viedam* and *Shastah*, (the Gentoos' scriptures) it is necessary, I should inform you: the book first named, is followed by the Gentoos of the Mallabar and Cormandel coasts; and also by those of the Island of Ceylon. The *Shastah* is followed by the Gentoos of the provinces of Bengall; and by all the Gentoos of the rest of India, commonly called India proper; that is to say—the greatest part of Orissa, Bengall proper, Bahar, Banaras, Oud, Eleabas,[a] Agra, Delhy, &c. all along the course of the rivers Ganges, and Jumna, to the Indus.[b]

Both these books contain the institutes of their respective religion and worship; often couched under allegory and fable; as well as the history of their ancient Rajahs and princes—their antiquity is contended for by the partisans of each—but the similitude of their names, idols, and great part of their worship, leaves little room to doubt, nay plainly evinces, that both these scriptures were originally *one*. And if we compare the great purity and chaste manners of the *Shastah*, with the great absurdities and impurities of the *Viedam*;[c] we need not hesitate to pronounce, the latter a corruption of the former. All that I need add here, is, that my remarks follow the *Shastah* only.

Chapter IV

The Religious Tenets of the Gentoos, followers of the Shastah of Bramah.

INTRODUCTION

We have already premised, that in the prosecution of this our fourth general head, we should touch only on the original principal tenets of these antient people the Gentoos; for were we to penetrate into, and discuss the whole of their modern ceremonials, and complicated modes of worship; our labor would be without end: these are as diffuse, as the ancient fundamental tenets of Bramah are short, pure, simple and uniform; in this predicament the Gentoos are not singular, as the original text of every

[a] Allahabad.

[b] Dow also believed that Hindus in northern and southern India belonged to different 'sects', a distinction which Holwell later elaborated (see below, pp. 57–8). It is not clear whether they were drawing a contrast between the *shaivite* south and the *vaishnavite* Bengal, or, as Dow seems to be doing (see below, p. 130), between the predominance of the *Vedanta* in the south and the *Nyaya* in Bengal.

[c] Holwell's knowledge of what he supposed to be the 'Viedam' was presumably derived from Baldaeus's account (see above, p. 48), in fact largely a narrative of the incarnations of Vishnu.

theological system, has, we presume, from a similar cause, unhappily undergone the same fate; though at first promulged as a divine institution.

We shall not say much regarding the antiquity of these people; nor shall we amuse ourselves with the reveries of chronologers and historians; who have labored to fix with precision (though not two of them agree in opinion) the various migrations after the flood; it shall suffice for our purpose, that by their own shewing, Indostan was as early peopled, as most other parts of the known world.

The first invaders of this empire, found the inhabitants a potent, opulent, civilized, wise, and learned people; united under one head, and one uniform profession of divine worship; by the fundamental principles of which, they were precluded communication, and social converse, with the rest of mankind; and these invasions first made them a warlike people also.

Alexander the Great, invaded them in later times, and found them in the same state; and though it should seem, from Arrian's[a] and Quintus Curtius's[b] history of that prince's expeditions, that the different principalities he conquered, were independant kingdoms, and governed by independant kings and princes; yet the Gentoo records of Bindoobund[c] and Banaras shew, that at that period, and much later, all the principalities of this empire, were in subjection to, and owned allegiance to one head, stiled the Mhaahah Rajah of Indostan; a prince of the Succadit[d] family, said to be lineally descended from their great prince and legislator Bramah; and that it was not until after the extinction of this sacred family (as the Gentoos call it) that the Rajahs assumed an independency.

But it did not sufficiently sooth the vanity of Alexander, nor that of his historians, to record his conquests of a few petty Rajahs and governors of provinces; and though we do not contest the fact of that invasion, yet we think ourselves justified in concluding the greatest part of its history is fabulous; yet, that it claims

---

[a] See above, p. 47.

[b] Quintus Curtius Rufus wrote his *Historiae Alexandri Magni* in the first century B.C.

[c] Brindaban, centre of Krishna cults.

[d] Presumably Shaka, see below, p. 59.

greater credit and belief, than those of Bacchus[a] and Sesostris:[b] the Greek and Latin construction and termination of the names, and places, of the princes and kingdoms of Indostan, said by Alexander's historians to be conquered by him; bear not the least analogy or idiom of the Gentoo language, either ancient or modern; as any one the least conversant in it can testify; and although the ground work of their history was founded on fact, yet the superstructure carries strongly the semblance of invention and romance: and he who is acquainted with this empire, and can give full credit to those legends, may upon as just a foundation believe Alexander to have been the son of Jupiter Ammon,[c] or, with Q. Curtius, that the Ganges opened into the Rea Sea.[d]

The annals of the Gentoos, give testimony of Alexander's invasion; where he is recorded under the epithets, of *Mhaahah Dukkoyt, é Kooneah*, a most mighty robber and murderer,[e] but they make not any mention of a Porus,[f] nor of any name that has the smallest allusion or likeness to it; and yet the action between Alexander and this imaginary King Porus, has been pompously exhibited by the historians of the former, and has happily afforded subject matter for representations, that do the highest honour to the art and genius of man.

The liberty we have taken with these so long celebrated historians, may seem to our readers to be foreign to our subject, but in the end we hope it will appear otherwise; when they find that these authors have (either from their own fertile inventions, or from mis-information, or rather from want of a competent knowledge in the language of the nation) mis-represented, or to speak more favorably, mis-conceived their religious tenets as much as they have the genius and state of their government.

The space of time employed in Alexander's expedition in this empire, did not afford a possibility of acquiring any adequate knowledge of a language in itself so highly difficult to attain in

[a] In Greek tradition Dionysus had conquered India. Alexander's soldiers claimed to find his cult well established there.
[b] Sesostris was a legendary king of Egypt, believed by the Greeks to have made large conquests in Asia.
[c] A legend current in Alexander's own lifetime.
[d] *Historiae Alexandri*, book VIII, chap. IX.
[e] Maha dakait e kunia. The 'annals' cannot be identified.
[f] The name given to the ruler of a region in north-western India by the Greeks.

the smallest degree of perfection, even from many years residence and intimate converse with the natives; can it be possibly believed then, that any of Alexander's followers could in this short space acquire such perfection in the Gentoo language as could enable them justly to transmit down the religious system of a nation, with whom they can scarcely be said to have had any communication?

Touching the antiquity of the scriptures, we are treating of, we have much more to say, in support of our conjecture and belief, that the *Shastah* of Bramah, is as ancient, at least, as any written body of divinity that was ever produced to the world. But it is previously necessary, that we explain the word Bramah, which has been variously wrote, and indiscriminately applied by many authors, and particularly by Baldeus, who confounds Birmah and Bramah as being the same person, though nothing in nature can be more different.[a] This could proceed only, from the specific meaning and origin of those words not being clearly understood; and this we conceive has led many other writers into the same error: our present disquisition therefore calls, not only for the explanation of these words, but also of the other two supposed primary created beings Bistnoo, and Sieb. For unless these three persons Birmah, Bistnoo,[b] and Sieb,[c] are distinctly comprehended, and held in remembrance, a considerable portion of the allegorical part of the *Shastah* of Bramah, will appear utterly unintelligible.

Different authors stile him, Bruma, Bramma, Burma, Brumma, Birmah, Bramah; and although they write him thus variously, they are unanimous in thinking him the same person, and give him the same attributes. They are all, it is true, derivatives from the same root, Brum, or Bram (for these are synonimous in the *Shastah*) but none of all the above appellatives are to be found in the *Shastah*, but Birmah and Bramah. They are all compounded of *brum* or *bram*, a spirit, or essence, and *mah*, mighty; *brum*, in an absolute and simple sense signifies the spirit or essence of God, and is but upon one occasion mentioned as a person, and that is when *brum* is represented with the habiliments and four arms of Birmah, floating on a leaf, upon the face of a troubled chaos,

---

[a] Churchill, *Collection of Voyages*, III, 783.   [b] Vishnu.   [c] Shiva.

immediately preceding the act of the creation of the universe. Birmah is understood in an absolute personal sense, and in a figurative one; in the former as the first of the three primary created angelic beings—in this sense the word signifies litterally the mighty second. For though Birmah is the first of the three prime beings, he is stiled second in power to God only, and sometimes in the *Shastah* has the name of Birmahah, the most mighty second. In the figurative sense the word Birmah means creation, created, and sometimes creator, and represents what the Bramins call, the first great attribute of God, his power of creation.

Bramah is the title solely appropriated to the promulger of the *Shastah*, and implies the spirituality and divinity of his mission and doctrines; hence it is, that his successors assumed the name of Bramins, supposing themselves to inherit the same divine spirit.

As the word Birmah, is used in a personal, and figurative sense, so is Bistnoo and Sieb; personally, as being the second and third of the first created angelic beings, who had pre-eminence in heaven, the word Bistnoo, litterally signifies a cherisher, a preserver, a comforter; and Sieb, a destroyer, an avenger, a mutilator, a punisher; and these three persons, when figuratively applied in the *Shastah* (as they frequently are) represent what the Bramins call the three first and great attributes of God, his power to create, his power to preserve, and his power to change or destroy. And we shall see that in the distribution of the Almighty's commands to these primary persons, tasks are assigned to each, of a very different nature; to Birmah, works of power, government and glory; to Bistnoo, works of tenderness and benevolence; and to Sieb, works of terror, severity and destruction. This last mentioned person is the object of great dismay and terror to the Gentoos, but modern expounders of Bramah's *Shastah* have softened the rigor of his character by giving him names and attributes of a very different nature from that of Sieb. They call him Moisoor (a contraction of Mahahsoor, the most mighty destroyer of evil) and under this soothing title he is worshipped, not as Sieb the destroyer, but as the destroyer of evil. The other epithet they have given to him is Moideb, (a contraction of Mahahdebtah, the most mighty angel) in this sense he is worshipped as the averter of evil, and under this character he has the most altars erected to him.

This necessary interpretation and explanation premised, we proceed to the *Shastah* itself; and shall faithfully give a detail of the origin of this book; and the several innovations and changes it has suffered: a detail—which although known by all the learned amongst the Bramins, is yet confessed but by a few, and those only, whose purity of principle and manners, and zeal for the primitive doctrines of Bramah's *Shastah*, sets them above disguising the truth; from many of these, we have had the following recital.

That, when part of the angelic bands rebelled, and were driven from the face of God, and expelled from the heavenly regions; God doomed them in his wrath, to eternal punishment and banishment; but, that by the intercession of the faithful remaining bands, he was at length inclined to mercy, and to soften the rigor of their sentence, by instituting a course only, of punishment, purgation, and purification; through which, by due submission, they might work out a restoration to the seats they had lost by their disobedience.

That God in full assembly of the faithful bands specified their course of punishment, purgation and purification; registered, and declared his decree, immutable, and irrevocable; and commanded Birmah, to descend to the banished delinquents and signify unto them the mercy and determination of their creator.

That Birmah fulfilled God's command, descended to the delinquent angels, and made known unto them the mercy and immutable sentence, that God their creator had pronounced and registered against them.

That the great and unexpected mercy of God, at first made a deep impression upon all the delinquents, except on the leaders of their rebellion; these in process of time, regained their influence, and confirmed most of the delinquents in their disobedience, and thereby the merciful intentions of their creator, became in a great measure frustrated.

That about the beginning of the present age (i.e. 4866 years ago) the three primary created beings and the rest of the faithful angelic host, feeling the deepest anguish for the exalted wickedness of their delinquent brethren, concluded it could only proceed, from their having by time, forgot the terms of their salvation; which had been only verbally delivered to them by Birmah: they therefore petitioned the Almighty, that he would be pleased to suffer his sentence, and the conditions of their restoration, to be digested into a body of written laws for their guidance; and that some of the angelic beings, might have permission to descend to the delinquents, to promulge and preach this written body of laws unto them, that they might thereby be left without excuse, or the plea of ignorance, for their continuance in disobedience.

That God assented, to the petitions of the angelic bands; when they, one and all, offered to undertake this mission, but God selected from amongst them those whom he deemed most proper for this work of salvation; who were appointed to descend to the different regions of the habitable universe. That a being from the first rank of angels was destined for the eastern part of this globe, whom God dignified with the name of Bramah, in allusion to the divinity of the doctrine and mission he had in charge.

That Birmah by the command of God dictated to Bramah and the other deputed angels, the terms and conditions, which had been primarily delivered to the delinquents, by the mouth of Birmah; that Bramah received, and entered the laws of God in Debtah Nagur, (literally, the language of angels) and that when Bramah descended at the beginning of the present age, and assumed the human form and government of Indostan, he translated them into the Sanscrît, a language then universally known throughout Indostan; and called the body of laws *the Chatah Bhade*[1] *Shastah* of Bramah (literally, the four scriptures of divine words of the mighty spirit)[a] which he promulged, and preached to the delinquents, as the only terms of their salvation and restoration.

That for the space of a thousand years, the doctrines of the *Chatah Bhade*, were preached and propagated, without variation or innovation; and many of the delinquents benefited from them and were saved: but that about the close of this period, some Goseyns[2] and Battezaaz[3] Brahmins, combining together, wrote a paraphrase on the *Chatah Bhade*, which they called the *Chatah*[4] *Bhade* of Brahmah[5] or the six scriptures of the mighty spirit;[b] in this work the original text of Bramah's *Chatah Bhade* was still preserved. About this period also it was, that the Goseyns and Battezaaz Bramins, began to appropriate to themselves the use of the Sanscrît character, and instituted in the place of it the common Indostan character in use at this day: it was now also that they first began to veil in mysteries, the simple doctrines of Bramah.

That, about five hundred years later, that is, fifteen hundred years from the first promulgation of Bramah's *Shastah*; the Goseyns, and Battezaaz Bramins, published a second exposition, or commentary on the *Chatah Bhade*; which swelled the Gentoo scriptures to eighteen books: these the commentators entitled the *Aughtorrah Bhade Shastah*, or the eighteen books of divine words,[c] it was drawn up in a compound character, of the common Indostan, and Sanscrît; the original text of the *Chatah Bhade*, was in a manner sunk and alluded to only; the histories of their Rajahs and country,

---

[1] A written book.   [2] Gentoo Bishops.

[3] Expounders of the *Shastah*.   [4] Six.

[5] From the promulging this *Bhade*, the polytheism of the Gentoos took its rise.

[a] The Hindi 'fourth' and 'sixth' (*chautah* and *chhatah*) look very much the same in English transcription. Holwell normally writes 'chartah' for four and 'chatah' for six; but, as on this occasion, he is not always consistent.

[b] The six books next in sanctity to the *Vedas* may be a confused reference to the six *Vedangas* or possibly to the six philosophical schools.

[c] Presumably the eighteen *Puranas*.

were introduced under figures and symbols, and made a part of their religious worship, and a multitude of ceremonials, and exteriour modes of worship, were instituted; which the commentators said were implied in Bramah's *Chatah Bhade*, although not expressly directed therein, by him; and the whole enveloped in impenetrable obscurity by allegory and fable, beyond the comprehension even of the common tribe of Bramins themselves; the laity being thus precluded from the knowledge of their original scriptures had a new system of faith broached unto them, which their ancestors were utterly strangers to.

That this innovation of the *Aughtorrah Bhade* produced a schism amongst the Gentoos, who until this period had followed one prosession of faith throughout the vast empire of Indostan; for the Bramins of Cormandell and Mallabar finding their brethren upon the course of the Ganges had taken this bold step to inslave the laity, set up for themselves, and formed a scripture of their own, founded as they said upon the *Chatah Bhade* of Bramah; this they called the *Viedam*[1] of Brummah, or divine words of the mighty spirit; these commentators, by the example of their brethren, interspersed in their new religious system, the histories of their governors, and country, under various symbols and allegories, but departed from that chastity of manners, which was still preserved in the *Aughtorrah Bhade Shastah*.

Thus, the original, plain, pure, and simple tenets of the *Chatah Bhade* of Bramah (fifteen hundred years after its first promulgation) became by degrees utterly lost; except, to three or four Goseyn families, who at this day are only capable of reading, and expounding it, from the Sanscrît character; to these may be added a few others of the tribe of Batteezaaz Bramins, who can read and expound from the *Chatah Bhade*, which still preserved the text of the original, as before remarked.

How much soever the primitive religion of the Gentoos suffered by these innovations; their government underwent no change for many centuries after, all acknowledging allegiance to one universal Rajah of the Succadit family,[a] lineally descended from their prince and lawgiver Bramah. The princes of this line opposed the innovations made in their primitive faith, with a fruitless opposition, which endangered the existence of their own government; so that at length they were reduced to the necessity of subscribing, first to the *Chatah Bhade*, and subsequently to the *Aughtorrah Bhade*; although their wisdom foresaw, and foretold, the fatal consequences these innovations would have on the state and the nation: but the Goseyns and Bramins, having tasted the sweets of priestly power by the first of these *Bhades*, determined to enlarge, and establish it, by the promulgation of the last; for in this the exterior modes of worship were so multiplied, and such a numerous train of new divinities created, which the people never before

---

[1] *Viedam* in the Mallabar language signifies the same as *Shastah* in the Sanscrît, viz. divine words—and sometimes, the words of God.

[a] See below, p. 59.

had heard or dreamed of, and both the one and the other were so enveloped by the Goseyns and Bramins in darkness, penetrable to themselves only, that those professors of divinity, became of new and great importance, for the daily obligations of religious duties, which were by these new institutes imposed on every Gentoo, from the highest to the lowest rank of the people, were of so intricate and alarming a nature, as to require a Bramin to be at hand, to explain and officiate, in the performance of them: they had however the address to captivate the minds of the vulgar, by introducing show and parade into all their principal religious feasts, as well as fasts; and by a new single political institution, to wit, the preservation of their cast or tribe, the whole nation was reduced to sacerdotal slavery.

From the period that the *Aughtorrah Bhade* was published as the rule of the Gentoo faith and worship, superstition, the sure support of priestcraft, took fast possession of the people; and their consciences, actions, and conduct, in spirituals and temporals, were lodged in the breasts of their household Bramins, and at their disposal; for every head of a family was obliged to have one of those ghostly fathers at his elbow, and in fact the people became in general mere machines, actuated and moved, as either the good or evil intentions of their household tyrant dictated.

The *Aughtorrah Bhade Shastah*, has been invariably followed by the Gentoos inhabiting from the mouth of the Ganges to the Indus, for the last three thousand three hundred and sixty-six years. This precisely fixes the commencement of the Gentoo mythology, which, until the publication of that *Bhade*, had no existence amongst them: every Gentoo of rank or wealth, has a copy of this scripture in his possession; under the care and inspection of his domestic Bramin; who every day reads and expounds a portion of it to the family.

Sixteen hundred and seventy-nine years, from the promulgation of the *Aughtorrah Bhade Shastah*, the sacred line of Bramah became extinct, in the person of Succadit, the last Mahahmahah Rajah; (most mighty king) he reigned over all Indostan, sixty years; his decease caused a general lamentation amongst the people; and from his death, a new Gentoo epocha took place, called the Æra of Succadit; and the present year (A.D. 1766) is the year of Succadit, sixteen hundred eighty-seven.[a]

The death of Succadit, became not only remarkable for a new epocha of time, but also for another signal event in the Gentoo annals; namely, a total revolution of their government: the royal and sacred line being extinct, the vice-roys of this extensive empire (who had been for some years strengthening themselves in their respective governments, and preparing for this expected event) on the demise of Succadit, set up a claim of independency, to the lands over which they had ruled under the emperor: they all assumed the title of Rajah, a distinction which, before this memorable period, had been only given to four or five of the first officers of the state; who also

[a] That is A.D. 79. The Hindu Shaka era began in A.D. 78 Cf. Holwell's 'Succadit' with Jones's 'Saca' (see below, p. 290).

generally filled the chief governments of the empire. Confusion followed. Those commanders who found themselves invested with greater force and power, attacked, conquered, and joined to their governments, the territories of those who lay contiguous to them; whilst others who lay more distant preserved their independency: and thus the empire was divided into as many kindgoms, as there had been vice-royships and governments. Between these Rajahs, there subsisted a continual warfare. From an empire thus divided against itself, what could be expected, but that which, in a few centuries, consequently and naturally followed.

For the simple and intelligible tenets and religious duties, enjoined by the *Chartah Bhade*, being thus absorbed and lost, in the attention and adherence, paid to the extravagant, absurd, and unintelligible non-essentials of worship, instituted by the *Aughtorrah Bhade*; laid the foundation of the miseries, with which in succeeding times, Indostan was visited; and the merciful intention of God, for the redemption of the delinquent angels, (destined to inhabit this part of the earthly globe) was rendered fruitless. The holy tribe of Bramins, who were chosen and appointed by Bramah himself, to preach the word of God, and labor the salvation of the delinquents; in process of time lost sight of their divine original, and in its place substituted new and strange doctrines; that had no tendency, but to the establishing their own power: the people hearkened unto them, and their minds were subdued and enslaved; their ancient military genius, and spirit of liberty was debilitated; discord and dissention arose amongst the rulers of the land, and the state grew ripe for falling at the first convulsion; and in the end suffered an utter subversion, under the yoke of Mahommeden tyranny; as a just punishment inflicted on them by God, for their neglect of his laws, commands and promises, promulged to them, by his great and favored angel Bramah, in the *Chartah Bhade Shastah*.

The foregoing detail, contains the genuine conceptions and belief, which the Bramins themselves entertain of the antiquity of their scriptures, and of the two remarkable innovations they have undergone; particulars which we have had repeatedly confirmed to us, in various conferences with many of the most learned and ingenuous, amongst the laity of the Koyt[1], and other casts,[a] who are often better versed in the doctrines of their *Shastah* than the common run of the Bramins themselves.

We hope it will not be displeasing to our readers, if from the foregoing recital, we reduce into a narrow compass, and into one

---

[1] The tribe of writers.

[a] The term 'caste' was firmly established in English usage by this time. It is used by all the authors reproduced in this book. The word is derived from the Portuguese 'casta' (H. Yule and A. C. Burnell, *Hobson-Jobson* (reprinted 1968), pp. 170–1).

view, the stedfast faith of the Gentoos. Touching the antiquity of their scriptures; (the point now only under our consideration) it appears therefore that they date the birth of the tenets and doctrines of the *Shastah*, from the expulsion of the angelic beings from the heavenly regions; that those tenets were reduced into a written body of laws, four thousand eight hundred and sixty-six years ago, and then by God's permission were promulged and preached to the inhabitants of Indostan. That these original scriptures underwent a remarkable change or innovation a thousand years after the mission of their prophet and law-giver Bramah, in the publication of the *Chatah Bhade Shastah*; and that three thousand three hundred and sixty-six years past, these original scriptures suffered a second and last change or innovation, in the publication of the *Aughtorrah Bhade Shastah*; which occasioned the first and only schism amongst the Gentoos, that subsists to this day, namely between the followers of the *Aughtorrah Bhade Shastah*, and the followers of the *Viedam*.

Without reposing an implicit confidence in the relations the Bramins give of the antiquity of their scriptures; we will with our readers' indulgence, humbly offer a few conjectures that have swayed us into a belief and conclusion, that the original tenets of Bramah are most ancient; that they are truly original, and not copied from any system of theology, that has ever been promulged to, or obtruded upon the belief of mankind: what weight our conjectures may have with the curious, or how far it may rather appear in the prosecution of our work, that other theological systems have been framed from this, we readily submit to those, whose genius, learning and capacity in researches of this kind, are much superior to our own.

It has been without reserve asserted, that the Gentoos received their doctrines and worship, from the Persees or Egyptians; but without (as we conceive) any degree of probability, or grounds, for the foundation of this opinion:[a] reason and facts, seeming to us, to be on the side of the very contrary opinion.

That there was a very early communication between the

---

[a] The most confident statement that Hinduism was an offshoot from Egypt had been made by Mathurin Veyssière de La Croze, *Histoire du Christianisme des Indes*, 2nd ed. (The Hague, 1758), ii, 222–35, 239–40.

empires of Persia, Egypt and Indostan, is beyond controversy; the former lay contiguous to Indostan; and although Egypt lay more remote from it, there still was an easy passage open between them, by the navigation from the Red-Sea, to the Indus: therefore it will appear no strained conclusion, if we say; it is most likely there had been frequent intercourse between the learned Magi of both those nations, and the Bramins, long before the last mentioned sages were visited by Zoroaster and Pythagoras.

It is necessary to remark that the Bramins did not, indeed could not, seek this intercourse, for the principles of their religion forbad their travelling, or mixing with other nations; but so famed were they in the earliest known times for the purity of their manners, and the sublimity of their wisdom and doctrines, that their converse was sought after, and solicited universally by the philosophers, and searchers after wisdom and truth. For this character of them, we have the concurring testimony of all antiquity.

At what period of time, Indostan was visited by Zoroaster and Pythagoras, is not clearly determined by the learned; we will suppose it, with the generality of writers, to have been about the time of Romulus. That these sages travelled, not to instruct, but, to be instructed; is a fact that may be determined with more precision; as well as, that they were not in Indostan together. As they both made a long residence with the Bramins North West of the Ganges (for the name of *Zardhurst*, and *Pythagore* retain a place in the Gentoo annals 'as travellers in search of wisdom') it is reasonable to conclude they might in some degree be instructed in the Sanscrît character, and consequently, in the doctrines and worship instituted by the *Chatah* and *Aughtorrah Bhades*.[a]

It is worthy notice that the metempsychosis as well as the three grand principles taught in the greater Eleusinian mysteries;

[a] The 'Gentoo annals' cannot be identified. There was no agreement among eighteenth-century scholars about the dating of Zoroaster, but a number of traditions linked him with Pythagoras (J. Duchesne-Guillemin, *The Western Response to Zoroaster* (Oxford, 1958), pp. 1–5). Pythagoras was traditionally believed to have been responsible for the introduction into Greek thought of doctrines such as the unity of God and the immortality of the soul, which he had learnt in the East. Some Greek and Latin sources suggested that he had visited India (E. Mignot, 'Mémoires sur les anciens philosophes de l'Inde', *Mémoires de l'Académie royale des Inscriptions et Belles Lettres*, xxxı (1761–3), 90–2), but these suggestions do not seem to have been taken very seriously.

namely, the unity of the godhead, his general providence over all creation, and a future state of rewards and punishments; were fundamental doctrines of Bramah's *Chartah Bhade Shastah*, and were preached by the Bramins, from time immemorial to this day, throughout Indostan: not as mysteries, but as religious tenets, publicly known and received; by every Gentoo, of the meanest capacity; this is a truth, which, we conceive, was unknown to the learned investigator of the Eleusinian mysteries; or it is probable he would, with more caution, have asserted, that the Eastern nations received their doctrines from the Egyptians.[a]

Although the polytheism of the Gentoos had its origin from the first promulgation of the *Chatah Bhade Shastah*, and their mythology from the publication of the *Aughtorrah Bhade*; yet the above mentioned theological dogmas remained inviolable and unchanged: and as these, with the firm persuasion of the prae-existent state of the spirit, or soul, have ever been, and still are, the very basis of all the Gentoo worship; it appears to us most probable, (from the early communication before remarked, and the reasons before given) that the Egyptians borrowed these tenets from the Bramins.

That Pythagoras took the doctrine of the metempsychosis, from the Bramins, is not disputed: yet future times erroneously stiled it Pythagorean; an egregious mistake, which could proceed only from ignorance of its original.

Whatever may have been the period, that Indostan was visited by the two travelling sages abovementioned; it is acknowledged that Pythagoras undertook that journey, some years later than Zoroaster:—when Pythagoras left India, he went into Persia, where he conversed with the Magi of that country, and was instructed in their mysteries; and is said (with probability of truth) to have held many conferences with Zoroaster, on the doctrines of the Bramins.[b] They had both been initiated in all the mysteries,

[a] Holwell is referring to William Warburton (1698–1779), Bishop of Gloucester, who had included a long section on the Eleusinian mysteries, celebrated by the Athenians, in his *Divine Legation of Moses* (4th ed. (1755–88), I, 141–210). Warburton was an author whom Holwell felt it particularly necessary to refute, since 'the superior antiquity of the Egyptians' was a main plank of the *Divine Legation*.

[b] Contemporaries were more inclined to accept that Pythagoras had visited Persia than that he had visited India (A. Dacier, *The Life of Pythagoras with his Symbols and Golden Verses* (1707), p. 13).

and learning, of the Egyptians; and Pythagoras, in his second visit to Egypt, before his return to Greece, probably repaid the debt of wisdom he had received from the Magi, by giving them new, and stronger lights, into the theology, cosmogony and mythology of the Bramins, from their *Chatah*, and *Aughtorrah Bhades*.

The moral institutes, of Zoroaster, and Pythagoras; inculcated and taught by the one to the Persians; and by the other, to the Greeks; truely bore the stamp of divine, but their system of theology, surely that of madness. They had so long, and intensely thought, and reasoned on the divine nature, and the cause of evil; that the portion of divine nature they possessed, seemed utterly impaired, and bewildered, as soon as they began to form their crude principles into a system; they appear to have preserved the basis and out-lines of Bramah's *Shastah*, on which (probably in conjunction with the Persian and Egyptian Magi) they raised an aerial superstructure, wild and incomprehensible and labored to propagate an unintelligible jargon of divinity, which neither themselves, nor any mortal since their time, could explain, or reduce to the level of human understanding.[a]

How far, on a comparison between the modes of worship, instituted by the *Chatah* and *Aughtorrah Bhades*, and those of the antient Egyptians, Greeks and Romans, it may appear that those of the Bramins are originals, and those of the latter copies only, we submit to the enquiry of the learned into those intricate studies, when in the course of our work we exhibit to the reader some specimens of the Gentoo mythology, and an account of their fasts and festivals.

By the fundamental doctrines and laws of the Gentoos, they cannot admit of proselytes or converts, to their faith or worship; nor receive them into the pale of their communion, without the loss

---

[a] Thomas Hyde's *Historia Religionis veterum Persarum* (Oxford, 1700), was the principal source of European knowledge for Persian religion. But Holwell was probably also aware of the findings of the French traveller Abraham Anquetil Duperron, who had recently acquired both manuscripts of the *Zend Avesta* and the skill to decipher them. One of his papers had appeared in translation in the *Annual Register* for 1762, which admitted (pt. II, p. 103) that the manuscripts 'appear at first view little better than a heap of idle tales, calculated to amuse a barbarous people'. Collections of 'Symbols' and 'Golden Verses' (translated in Dacier, *Life of Pythagoras*, pp. 97–134, 151–65) were attributed to Pythagoras in the eighteenth century.

of their cast, or tribe; a disgrace, which every Gentoo would rather suffer death than incur: and although this religious prohibition, in its consequences, reduced the people to a slavish dependence on their Bramins; yet it proved the cement of their union as a nation; which to this day remains unmixed with any other race of people. These are circumstances which, to the best of our knowledge, remembrance, and reading; peculiarly distinguish the Gentoos, from all the nations of the known world, and plead strongly in favor of the great antiquity of this people, as well as the originality of their scriptures.

Another consideration, to the same purpose, claims our notice; namely the perpetuity of the Gentoo doctrines, which through a succession of so many ages, have still remained unchanged, in their fundamental tenets; for although the *Chatah* and *Aughtorrah Bhades*, enlarged the exteriors of their worship, yet these derive their authority and essence, in the bosom of every Gentoo, from the *Chartah Bhade* of Bramah: and it is no uncommon thing, for a Gentoo, upon any point of conscience, or any important emergency in his affairs or conduct, to reject the decision of the *Chatah* and *Aughtorrah Bhades*, and to procure, no matter at what expence, the decision of the *Chartah Bhade*, expounded from the Sanscrît.

Enough has been said, to shew that the genuine tenets of Bramah, are to be found only in the *Chartah Bhade*; and as all who have wrote on this subject, have received their information from crude, inconsistent reports, chiefly taken from the *Aughtorrah Bhade*, and the *Viedam*; it is no wonder that the religion of the Gentoos has been traduced, by some, as utterly unintelligible; and by others, as monstrous, absurd, and disgraceful to humanity: our design is to rescue these ancient people, from those imputations; in order to which we shall proceed, without further introduction or preface, to investigate their original scriptures, as contained in the *Chartah Bhade*; at the close of each section we shall subjoin, such remarks, and explanations, as may appear to us necessary and pertinent to our subject.

For the greater perspicuity, we will present to our readers the fundamental doctrines of the Bramins, under five distinct sections; as they are ranged in the first book of this *Shastah*: viz.

I.   Of God and his Attributes.
II. The creation of Angelic Beings.
III. The Lapse of part of those Beings.
IV. Their Punishment.
V.   The mitigation of that Punishment, and their final Sentence.

SECTION I.

Of God and his Attributes. God is One.[1] Creator of all that is. God is like a perfect sphere, without beginning or end. God rules and governs all creation by a general providence resulting from first determined and fixed principles. Thou shalt not make enquiry into the essence and nature of the existence of the Eternal One, nor, by what laws he governs. An enquiry into either, is vain, and criminal. It is enough, that day by day, and night by night, thou seest in his works; his wisdom, power, and his mercy. Benefit thereby.

REMARKS

The foregoing simple and sublime description of the Supreme Being, constitutes the first chapter, or section of the *Shastah*. The Bramins of the *Aughtorrah Bhade* teach, that there originally existed a chapter of the *Shastah*, which explained and solely treated of the divine nature and essence; but that it was soon irrecoverably lost, and never transmitted to posterity by Bramah, who tore it out of his *Chartah Bhade*.

Baldeus, who resided thirty years on the Island of Ceylon, and has given a laborious translation of the *Viedam*; recites a similar anecdote from those scriptures, and says, 'that the lost part treated of God, and the origin of the universe, or visible worlds, the loss of which is highly lamented by the Bramins'.[a] In which this author seems to have plunged into a double error; first, in alleging the part lost, treated of the origin of the universe; whereas both the *Viedam*, and *Shastah*, are elaborate on the subject; and fix not only the period of its creation, but also its precise age, and term of duration, (as we shall shew hereafter); consequently and secondly, they could not properly be said to lament a loss they never sustained. But in truth, the whole of this matter is

[1] *Ekhummesha*, litterally, the one that ever was; which we translate, the eternal one.
[a] Churchill, *Collection of Voyages*, III, 783.

allegorical, a circumstance, which Baldeus, it seems, never adverted to.

In various discourses we have had, with some learned Bramins, on the above cited passage of the *Aughtorrah Bhade*, they were all unanimous in their sense and interpretation of it: namely, that to man was given for the exercise of his reason, and virtue, the contemplation of the visible wonders of the creation; but, that the Eternal One had precluded all enquiry into his origin, nature and essence, and the laws by which he governs; as subjects inexplicable to, and beyond the limited powers of created beings; therefore it is emphatically said, that Bramah tore out that part, implying the prohibition of such enquiries, as useless and presumptuous.

Had one tythe of the time and trouble, which the just mentioned ecclesiastic bestowed in rendering a literal translation of the *Viedam*, been employed in attempting an explanation of its mysteries; his labors might have proved worthy the attention of the learned; whereas, by contenting himself with a bare version, without aiming at the interpretation of the allegorical parts of those scriptures, his toils, which must have been great and intense, have only produced a monster, that shocks reason and probability. They are mis-representations like these, which we have lamented in the preliminary discourse, to the first part of this our work, as injurious to human nature; various and enormous are the mistakes, which this author has fallen into from the above cause, through the whole of his voluminous work, which might be proved in a multitude of instances; but one shall suffice as a specimen of the whole, which nothing but the mistaken zeal of a christian can excuse.

The *Viedam* (according to Baldeus) gives the same place and power to Birmah or Bramah (for he erroneously makes these names synonimous) as the *Shastah* does; and as the Mallabars acknowledge Bramah to be the son of God, and supreme governor of angels; nay even ascribe to him a human form: *so it is evident, that these attributes, must have their origin from what they have heard, though perhaps confusedly, of Jesus Christ the Son of God.*[a]

[a] Churchill, *Collection of Voyages*, iii, 783.

SECTION II

The Creation of Angelic Beings. The Eternal One, absorbed in the contemplation of his own existence; in the fullness of time, resolved to participate his glory and essence with beings capable of feeling, and sharing his beatitude, and of administering to his glory. These beings then were not. The Eternal One willed. And they were. He formed them in part of his own essence; capable of perfection, but with the powers of imperfection; both depending on their voluntary election. The Eternal One first created Birmah, Bistnoo, and Sieb; then Moisasoor,[a] and all the Debtah-Logue.[1] The Eternal One gave pre-eminence to Birmah, Bistnoo and Sieb. He appointed Birmah, Prince of the Debtah-Logue, and put the Debtah under subjection to him; he also constituted him his vicegerent in heaven, and Bistnoo and Sieb, were established his co-adjutors.

The Eternal One divided the Debtah into different bands, and ranks, and placed a leader or chief over each. These worshipped round the throne of the Eternal One according to their degree, and harmony was in heaven. Moisasoor, chief of the first angelic band, led the celestial song of praise and adoration to the Creator, and the song of obedience to Birmah his first created. And the Eternal One rejoiced in his new creation.

REMARKS

Mankind in general of every denomination, and religious profession, have subscribed to the opinion of the existence of angelic beings; and have each formed their crude, peculiar, and imaginary conceptions of their origin and destination. Crude and imaginary indeed must be the best human construction, on so marvellous a subject. The simple, rational, and sublime cause, assigned by Bramah, for this act of creation; is most worthy a great and benign being, and conveys a striking and interesting impression, not only of his power, but of his benevolence.

Bramah, in the opening of this section, seems to place the Eternal One, in the situation of an absolute, good, and powerful monarch, without subjects; which in fact is being no monarch at all: for however happy, or blessed such a being may be, in the contemplation of his own sole existence and almighty power; yet he cannot (say the Bramins) be completely so, without partakers in his glory and beatitude; who should also, be conscious of the

---

[1] *Debtah*, angels; *Logue*, a people, multitude, or congregation; *Debtah-Logue*, the angelic host.

[a] Presumably Mahishasura, the great demon of the *Mahabharata*, or the buffalo demon killed by Durga.

tenure of their own existence, as well as of the power, and benevolent intentions of their creator, and worship him, accordingly.

But a blind and necessary obedience and worship, from any new
creation of rational beings, (which must have followed had they
been created perfect) would have fallen short of their Creator's
purpose; therefore Bramah says, the Eternal One, formed them
'capable of perfection, but with the powers of imperfection';
without subjecting them to either, that their adoration and obedience should be the result of their own free-will; the worship
alone worthy his acceptance.

From the doctrine contained in this section it appears, that the
powers of perfection and imperfection, (or in other words the
powers of good and evil) were coeval in the formation of the first
created beings: the Bramins in their paraphrase on this chapter,
reconcile the supposed incompatibility of the existence of moral
evil, consistently with the justice, power, and goodness of the
supreme being, by alleging, 'that as the Debtah were invested
with the absolute powers of perfection, their lapse from that state,
cannot impeach either the power, justice, or goodness of the
Eternal One; whose motives for their creation were benevolent;
and the duty enjoined them light and easy. To chaunt forth for
ever, the praises of their Creator, to bless him for their creation,
and to acknowledge, and be obedient to Birmah, and his two co-
adjutors Bistnoo and Sieb.'

Human penal laws, which have their existence in every well
regulated government of the world; always pre-suppose that the
individuals subjected to those laws, are invested with full powers
and capacity of paying obedience to them; otherwise, their imposition becomes an act of tyranny; but the premises granted, then
the breach and violation of them is criminal, and justly punishable,
without an imputation of injustice in the institutor. Shall man
then appear scrupulously cautious in his institutes and laws, not to
offend against reason and justice, and yet dare to doubt of, or
arraign the justice of his Creator?

Whence the origin, and existence of moral evil? Is a question
that has puzzled, and exercised the imagination, and understanding of the learned and speculative in all ages. We confess we
have hitherto met with no solution of this interesting enquiry, so

satisfactory, conclusive, and rational as flows from the doctrine before us. Authors have been driven to very strange conclusions on this subject, nay some have thought it necessary to form an apology in defence of their Creator, for the admission of moral evil into the world; and assert, 'That God was necessitated to admit moral evil in created beings, from the nature of the materials he had to work with; that God would have made all things perfect, but that there was in matter an evil bias, repugnant to his benevolence, which drew another way; whence arose all manner of evils': and that, therefore, 'to endue created beings with perfection; that is to produce good exclusive of evil, is one of those impossibilities, which even infinite power cannot accomplish'. And consequently that from this apologetical cause only, 'the wickedness and miseries of God's creatures can be fairly reconciled, with his infinite power and goodness'.

Interesting as this subject is, and must be, to every thinking being, our best conceptions of it, must fall far short of certainty; it is however surely encumbent on us to adopt such sentiments (more especially when we resolve to broach them to the world) as will appear most worthy infinite power and infinite goodness. How far this consideration has been regarded in the reveries cited in the preceding paragraph, we submit to our readers; in our own conceptions we cannot help saying those authors appear to us to have left the argument in a much worse state than they found it; and in place of a rational apology for their Creator, seem the rather tacitly to impeach his power, in the first and greatest of his attributes; his power of creation: for God is not only the creator of angels and men; but creator of matter also; and could have made that perfect, had he so willed. Whether God could endue created beings with perfection, or produce good exclusive of evil, we conceive is not the question; (although a doubt of it is highly presumptuous, if not impious) but the quære is whether God could create a race of beings, endued with the powers of absolute free agency; on the certainty of which position, the possibility of sin in created beings absolutely, and necessarily depends.

How much more rational and sublime the text of Bramah, which supposes the Deity's voluntary creation, or permission of evil; for the exaltation of a race of beings, whose goodness as free agents could not have existed without being endued with the contrasted, or opposite powers of doing evil.

SECTION III

The Lapse of Part of the Angelic Band. From the creation of the Debtah Logue, joy and harmony encompassed the throne of the Eternal One, for the space of Hazaar par Hazaar Munnuntur;[1] and would have continued to the end of time, had not envy and jealousy took possession of Moisasoor, and other leaders of the angelic bands; amongst whom was Rhaabon,[a] the next in dignity to Moisasoor; they, unmindful of the blessing of their creation, and the duties enjoined them, reject the powers of perfection, which the Eternal One had graciously bestowed upon them, exerted their powers of imperfection, and did evil in the sight of the Eternal One. They withheld their obedience from him, and denied submission to his vicegerent, and his coadjutors, Bistnoo, and Sieb, and said to themselves—We will rule —And fearless of the omnipotence, and anger of their Creator, they spread their evil imaginations amongst the angelic host, deceived them, and drew a large portion of them from their allegiance. And there was a separation from the throne of the Eternal One. Sorrow seized the faithful angelic spirits, and anguish was now first known in heaven.

SECTION IV

The Punishment of the Delinquent Debtah. The Eternal One, whose omniscience, prescience and influence, extended to all things, except the actions of beings, which he had created free; beheld with grief and anger, the defection of Moisasoor, Rhaabon, and the other angelic leaders and spirits. Merciful in his wrath, he sent Birmah, Bistnoo and Sieb, to admonish them of their crime, and to perswade them to return to their duty; but they exulting in the imagination of their independence, continued in disobedience. The Eternal One then commanded Sieb,[2] to go armed with his omnipotence, to drive them from the Mahah Surgo,[3] and plunge them into the Onderah,[4] there doomed to suffer unceasing sorrows, for Hazaar par Hazaar Munnunturs.[5]

[1] A phrase often made use of in the *Shastah* to express infinite extension or duration of time; the word *Munnuntur* in its absolute and literal sense will be subsequently explained; the word *Hazaar*, literally signifies a thousand; *Hazaar par Hazaar*, thousands upon thousands.

[2] Why Sieb was sent on this command has been already explained in our introduction.

[3] Supreme heaven, litterally the great eminence, from *Mahah*, great; and *Surgo,* high; eminent in a local sense, the firmament being commonly distinguished, by the Gentoos, by the name of Surgo.   [4] *Onder*, dark; *Onderah*, intense darkness.

[5] In this place the expression (which we have explained in a preceding note) means everlasting.

[a] Ravana.

REMARKS

That there was a defection or rebellion in heaven, the records of antiquity, sacred and prophane, bear allusive testimony of; we will not aver, that this opinion took its rise from the doctrines of the Bramins, though it is most probable it did; be this as it may, we cannot help concluding, that the conceptions conveyed by the *Shastah*, of this extraordinary event, are more consistent with, and do greater honor to the dignity of an omnipotent being, than those handed down to us in fables of the sages, poets and philosophers of Egypt, Greece and Rome. From these our Milton copied, with extravagance of genius and invention. They all, without exception, unworthily impeach God's omnipotence by the powers of contention given to the apostate angels, to oppose their Creator in arms and battle; and although sacred writ[1] seems to countenance this warfare in heaven, it can only allude to the act of expulsion of the delinquents, as any other interpretation would lessen omnipotence.

The *Shastah* opens this section by denying the prescience of God touching the actions of free agents; the Bramins defend this dogma by alleging, his prescience in this case, is utterly repugnant and contradictory to the very nature and essence of free agency, which on such terms could not have existed.

SECTION V

The Mitigation of the Punishment of the delinquent Debtah, and their final sentence. The rebellious Debtah groaned under the displeasure of their Creator in the Onderah, for the space of one Munnuntur; during which period, Birmah, Bistnoo and Sieb, and the rest of the faithful Debtah, never ceased imploring the Eternal One, for their pardon and restoration. The Eternal One, by their intercession at length relented, and although he could not foresee the effect of his mercy on the future conduct of the delinquents: yet unwilling to relinquish the hopes of their repentance, he declared his will. That they should be released from the Onderah, and be placed in such a state of tryal and probation, that they shall still have power, to work out their own salvation. The Eternal One then promulged his gracious intentions, and delegating the power and government of the Mahah Surgo, to Birmah; he retired into himself, and became invisible to all the angelic host, for the space of

[1] Revelations, chap. xii. ver. 7.

five thousand years. At the end of this period he manifested himself again, resumed the throne of light, and appeared in his glory. And the faithful angelic bands, celebrated his return in songs of gladness.

When all was hushed, the Eternal One said, let the Dunneahoudah[1] of the fifteen Boboons[2] of purgation and purification appear, for the residence of the rebellious Debtah.[a] And it instantly appeared.

And the Eternal One said, let Bistnoo,[3] armed with my power, descend to the new creation of the Dunneahoudah, and release the rebellious Debtah from the Onderah, and place them in the lowest of the fifteen Boboons.

Bistnoo stood before the throne and said, Eternal One, I have done as thou hast commanded. And all the faithful angelic host, stood with astonishment, and beheld the wonders, and splendor of the new creation of the Dunneahoudah.

And the Eternal One spake again unto Bistnoo and said: I will form bodies for each of the delinquent Debtah, which shall for a space be their prison and habitation; in the confines of which, they shall be subject to natural evils, in proportion to the degree of their original guilt. Do thou go, and command them to hold themselves prepared to enter therein, and they shall obey thee.

And Bistnoo stood again before the throne, and bowed and said, Eternal One, thy commands are fulfilled. And the faithful angelic host, stood again astonished, at the wonders they heard, and sung forth the praise and mercy of the Eternal One.

When all was hushed, the Eternal One said again unto Bistnoo, the bodies which I will prepare for the reception of the rebellious Debtah, shall be subject to change, decay, death, and renewal, from the principles wherewith I shall form them; and through these mortal bodies, shall the delinquent Debtah undergo alternately eighty-seven changes, or transmigrations; subject more or less, to the consequences of natural and moral evil, in a just proportion to the degree of their original guilt, and as their actions through those successive forms, shall correspond with the limited powers which I shall annex to each; and this shall be their state of punishment and purgation.

And it shall be, that when the rebellious Debtah shall have accomplished and passed through the eighty-seven transmigrations—they shall from my abundant favor, animate a new form, and thou Bistnoo shalt call it Ghoij.[4]

And it shall be, that when the mortal body of the Ghoij shall by a natural decay, become inanimate, the delinquent Debtah shall, from my more abundant favor, animate the form of Mhurd,[5] and in this form I will enlarge their intellectual powers, even as when I first created them free; and in this form shall be their chief state of their trial and probation.

[1] *Dooneah*, or *dunneah*, the world, *Dunneahoudah*, the worlds, or the universe.
[2] *Boboons*, regions or planets.
[3] Why Bistnoo was sent on this service we have already explained in our introduction.   [4] *Ghoij*, the cow; *Ghoijal*, cows; *Goijalbarry*, a cow-house.
[5] *Mhurd*, the common name of man, from *Murto*, matter, or earth.
[a] This seems to be a version of the doctrine of the seven *lokas*, or heavens, and the seven *patalas*, or hells.

The Ghoij shall be by the delinquent Debtah, deemed sacred and holy, for it shall yield them a new and more delectable food, and ease them of part of the labor, to which I have doomed them. And they shall not eat of the Ghoij, nor of the flesh of any of the mortal bodies, which I shall prepare for their habitation, whether it creepeth on Murto, or swimmeth in Jhoale,[1] or flyeth in Oustmaan,[2] for their food shall be the milk of the Ghoij, and the fruits of Murto.

The mortal forms wherewith I shall encompass the delinquent Debtah are the work of my hand, they shall not be destroyed, but left to their natural decay; therefore whichsoever of the Debtah, shall by designed violence bring about the dissolution of the mortal forms, animated by their delinquent brethren, thou Sieb, shalt plunge the offending spirit into the Onderah, for a space, and he shall be doomed to pass again the eighty-nine transmigrations, whatsoever stage he may be arrived to, at the time of such his offence. But whosoever of the delinquent Debtah, shall dare to free himself by violence, from the mortal form, wherewith I shall inclose him, thou Sieb shalt plunge him into the Onderah for ever. He shall not again have the benefit of the fifteen Boboons of purgation, probation, and purification.

And I will distinguish by tribes and kinds, the mortal bodies which I have destined for the punishment of the delinquent Debtah, and to these bodies I will give different forms, qualities and faculties, and they shall unite and propagate each other in their tribe and kind, according to a natural impulse which I will implant in them; and from this natural union, there shall proceed a succession of forms; each in his kind and tribe, that the progressive transmigrations of the delinquent spirits, may not cease.

But whosoever of the delinquent Debtah shall unite with any form out of his own tribe and kind; thou Sieb shalt plunge the offending spirit into the Onderah, for a space, and he shall be doomed to pass through the eighty-nine transmigrations, at whatsoever stage he may be arrived, at the time he committed such offence.

And if any of the delinquent Debtah shall (contrary to the natural impulse which I shall implant in the forms which they shall animate) dare to unite in such unnatural wise, as may frustrate the increase of his tribe and kind; thou Sieb shalt plunge them into the Onderah for ever. And they shall not again be entitled to the benefit of the fifteen Boboons of purgation, probation and purification.

The delinquent and unhappy Debtah, shall yet have it in their power, to lessen and soften their pains and punishment, by the sweet intercourse of social compacts; and if they love and cherish one another, and do mutual good offices, and assist and encourage each other in the work of repentance for their crime of disobedience; I will strengthen their good intentions, and they shall find favor. But if they persecute one another, I will comfort the persecuted, and the persecutors shall never enter the ninth Boboon, even the first Boboon of purification.

---

[1] *Jhoale*, water, fluid.   [2] The air.

John Zephaniah Holwell

And it shall be, that if the Debtah benefit themselves of my favor in their eighty-ninth transmigration of Mhurd, by repentance and good works, thou Bistnoo shalt receive them into thy bosom and convey them to the second Boboon of punishment and purgation, and in this wise shalt thou do, until they have passed progressively the eight Boboons of punishment, purgation and probation, when their punishment shall cease, and thou shalt convey them to the ninth; even the first Boboon of purification.

But it shall be, that if the rebellious Debtah, do not benefit of my favor in the eighty-ninth transmigration of Mhurd, according to the powers, wherewith I will invest them; thou Sieb, shalt return them for a space into the Onderah, and from thence after a time which I shall appoint, Bistnoo shall replace them in the lowest Boboon of punishment and purgation for a second trial; and in this wise shall they suffer, until by their repentance and perseverance in good works, during their eighty-ninth mortal transmigration of Mhurd, they shall attain the ninth Boboon, even the first of the seven Boboons of purification. For it is decreed that the rebellious Debtah shall not enter the Mahah Surgo, nor behold my face, until they have passed the eight Boboons of punishment, and the seven Boboons of purification.

When the angelic faithful host, heard all that the Eternal One had spoken, and decreed, concerning the rebellious Debtah; they sung forth his praise, his power, and justice.

When all was hushed, the Eternal One said to the angelic host, I will extend my grace to the rebellious Debtah, for a certain space, which I will divide into four Jogues.[1] In the first of the four Jogues, I will, that the term of their probation in the eighty-ninth transmigration of Mhurd, shall extend to 100,000 years—in the second of the four Jogues, their term of their probation in Mhurd, shall be abridged to 10,000 years—in the third of the four Jogues, it shall be yet abridged to 1000 years—and in the fourth Jogue to 100 years only. And the angelic host, celebrated in shouts of joy, the mercy and forbearance of God.

When all was hushed, the Eternal One said, It shall be, that when the space of time, which I have decreed for the duration of the Dunneahoudah, and the space which my mercy has allotted for the probation of the fallen Debtah, shall be accomplished, by the revolutions of the four Jogues, in that day, should there be any of them who remaining reprobate, have not passed the eighth Boboon of punishment and probation, and have not entered the ninth Boboon, even the first Boboon of purification; thou Sieb shalt, armed with my power, cast them into the Onderah for ever. And thou shalt then destroy the eight Boboons of punishment, purgation and probation, and they shall be no more. And thou Bistnoo shalt yet for a space preserve the seven Boboons of purification, until the Debtah, who have benefited of my grace and mercy, have by thee been purified from their sin: and in the day when that shall be accomplished, and they are restored to their state, and admitted to my presence, thou Sieb shalt then destroy the seven Boboons of purification, and they shall be no more.

[1] *Jogues*, ages, precise periods of time.

And the angelic faithful host trembled at the power, and words of the Eternal One.

The Eternal One, spoke again and said: I have not withheld my mercy from Moisasoor, Rhaboon, and the rest of the leaders of the rebellious Debtah; but as they thirsted for power, I will enlarge their powers of evil; they shall have liberty to pervade, and enter into the eight Boboons of purgation and probation, and the delinquent Debtah, shall be exposed and open to the same temptations, that first instigated their revolt: but the exertion of those enlarged powers, which I will give to the rebellious leaders, shall be to them, the source of aggravated guilt, and punishment; and the resistance made to their temptations, by the perverted Debtah; shall be to me the great proof, of the sincerity of their sorrow and repentance.

The Eternal One ceased. And the faithful host shouted forth songs of praise and adoration, mixed with grief, and lamentation for the fate of their lapsed brethren. They communed amongst themselves, and with one voice by the mouth of Bistnoo, besought the Eternal One, that they might have permission to descend occasionally to the eight Boboons of punishment, and purgation, to assume the form of Mhurd, and by their presence, council and example, guard the unhappy and perverted Debtah, against the further temptations of Moisasoor, and the rebellious leaders. The Eternal One assented, and the faithful heavenly bands, shouted their songs of gladness and thanksgiving.

When all was hushed, the Eternal One spake again and said, Do thou Birmah, arrayed in my glory, and armed with my power, descend to the lowest Boboon of punishment and purgation, and make known to the rebellious Debtah, the words that I have uttered, and the decrees which I have pronounced against them, and see they enter into the bodies, which I have prepared for them.

And Birmah stood before the throne, and said, Eternal One I have done as thou hast commanded. The delinquent Debtah rejoice in thy mercy, confess the justice of thy decrees, avow their sorrow and repentance, and have entered into the mortal bodies which thou hast prepared for them.

REMARKS

The foregoing is almost a litteral translation from the *Chartah Bhade* of Bramah, as we despaired of reaching the sublime stile and diction of the original; it will not we hope be displeasing to our reader, if we assist his memory and recollection by a recapitulation of the ground work of these doctrines, presented to him in one connected view; the more especially, as we shall also be thereby the better enabled to form our necessary explanatory remarks.

We have seen that the original divine institutes of Bramah are simple and sublime, comprehending the whole compass of all that is; God, angels, the visible and invisible worlds, man and beasts; and is comprized under the following articles of the Gentoo Creed. To wit—

That there is one God, eternal, omnific, omnipotent, and omniscient, in all things excepting a prescience of the future actions of free agents. That God from an impulse of divine love and goodness, first created three angelic persons to whom he gave precedence, though not in equal degree. That he afterwards from the same impulse created an angelic host, whom he placed in subjection to Birmah his first created, and to Bistnoo and Sieb, as coadjutors to Birmah. That God created them all free, and intended they should all be partakers of his glory and beatitude, on the easy conditions of their acknowledging him their Creator, and paying obedience to him, and to the three primary created personages, whom he had put over them. That, in process of time, a large portion of the angelic host at the instigation of Moisasoor and others of their chief leaders, rebelled and denied the supremacy of their Creator, and refused obedience to his commands. That in consequence the rebels were excluded heaven, and the sight of their Creator, and doomed to languish for ever in sorrow and darkness. That, after a time, by the intercession of the three primary, and the rest of the faithful angelic beings, God relented, and placed the delinquents in a more sufferable state of punishment and probation, with powers to gain their lost happy situation. That for that purpose a new creation of the visible and invisible worlds instantaneously took place, destined for the delinquents. That the new creation consisted of fifteen regions, seven below, and seven above this terraqueous globe, and that this globe and the seven regions below it are stages of punishment and purgation, and the seven above stages of purification, and consequently that this globe is the eighth, last and chief stage of punishment, purgation and trial. That mortal bodies were prepared by God, for the rebel angels, in which they were for a space to be imprisoned, and subject to natural and moral evils, more or less painful in proportion to their original guilt, and through which they were doomed to transmigrate under eighty-nine different forms, the last into that of man, when the powers of the animating rebel spirits, are supposed to be enlarged equal to the state of their first creation. That under this form God rests his chief expectations of their repentance and restoration, and if they fail, and continue reprobate under this form, they are returned to the lowest region, and sentenced to go through the same course of punishment, until they reach the ninth region, or first stage of purification, where although they cease from punishment, and gain remission and forgiveness of their guilt of rebellion; yet, they are not permitted to enter heaven, nor behold their Creator, before they have passed the seven regions of purification. That the rebel leaders had power given them by God, to enter the eight regions of punishment and probation, and that the faithful angelic spirits, had permission occasionally to descend to those regions, to guard the delinquents against the future attempts of their leaders. And that, consequently, the souls, or spirits which animate every mortal form, are delinquent angels in a state of punishment, for a lapse from innocence, in a pre-existent state.

We will presume to say, that the difference between the doctrines hitherto imputed, to these ancient people, when compared with the original tenets of the *Chartah Bhade*, will now appear so obvious to the learned and curious reader, that a further discussion of this point, is we conceive needless, and would in truth be a tacit reflection upon his understanding. Yet we are far from condemning the authors, who have treated on this subject; they took their information from the best lights they had; it is only to be regretted, that in place of drinking at the fountain head, they have swallowed the muddy streams which flowed from the *Chatah* and *Aughtorrah Bhades*. The author on his departure from Bengal in the year 1750, imagined himself well informed in the Gentoo religion, his knowledge had been acquired by conversations with the Bramins of those *Bhades* who were near, as little acquainted with the *Chartah Bhade* of Bramah, as he was himself, and he had then thoughts of obtruding his crude notions on the public, had not a different necessary application of his time luckily prevented him.

When we peruse some portions of Milton's account of the rebellion and expulsion of the angels, we are almost led to imagine, on comparison, that Bramah and he were both instructed by the same spirit; had not the soaring, ungovernable, inventive genius of the latter, instigated him to illustrate his poem with scenes too gross and ludicrous, as well as manifestly repugnant to, and inconsistent with, sentiments we ought to entertain of an omnipotent being (as before remarked) in which we rather fear he was inspired by one of these malignant spirits (alluded to in the *Shastah* and elsewhere) who have from their original defection, been the declared enemies of God and man. For however we are astonished and admire the sublimity of Milton's genius, we can hardly sometimes avoid concluding his conceits truely diabolical. But this by the by.

Our readers are now possessed for the first time of a faithful account of the metempsychosis of the Bramins—commonly called the transmigration of souls, a term hitherto we believe little understood, that this doctrine was originally peculiar to the Gentoos, will not admit of doubt, although in after times it was embraced by the Egyptian Magi,[a] and by some sects amongst the Chinese and Tartars.[b] Pythagoras, who favored this doctrine, and was a convert to it, labored to introduce it amongst his countrymen the Greeks, but failed in the attempt. He succeeded better with them, in the theogony, cosmogony and mythology of the Bramins' *Aughtorrah Bhade Shastah*, although these constituted no part of the original theology of Bramah.

As we have reserved a part expressly for a dissertation on the doctrine of the metempsychosis,[c] we will avoid further mention of it here; but as the Bramins of the *Chatah* and *Aughtorrah Bhades*, inculcate and teach many corollary branches of doctrine which spring from this root, it is necessary that we recite a few of the most established ones.

When the delinquent Debtah, by the mediation of Birmah, Bistnoo and Moisoor, and the faithful angelic host, were released from the Onderah; all, except Moisasoor, Rhaabon, and the rest of the rebel leaders, were so struck with the goodness and mercy of the Eternal One, that they persevered in a pious resignation and true penitence, during the first of the four Jogues, and multitudes ascended, and passed through the fifteen Boboons, and regained their forfeited estate. This period of time is called in the *Shastah* the Suttee Jogue, when the term of the spirits' probation in Mhurd, was extended to one hundred thousand years.

In the second of the four Jogues, Moisasoor and the rebel leaders so effectually exerted their influence over the delinquent Debtah, that they soon began to forget their crime and disregard their punishment in the Onderah; they rejected the councils and examples of the guardian Debtah, and stood a second time in defiance of their Creator; and Moisasoor drew over one third of the remaining unpurified spirits. This period is distinguished in the *Shastah*, by the name of the Tirtah Jogue, in which the Eternal One retrenched the term of the spirits' probation in Mhurd, to ten thousand years. In this Jogue however, many persevered in goodness, ascended through the fifteen Boboons, and regained the Mahah Surgo.

In the third of the four Jogues, Moisasoor's influence increased, and he drew over half of the remaining unpurified spirits, in each of the eight

[a] According to the Greeks (Herodotus, 'Histories', II, 123).

[b] Belief in transmigration was attributed to the Chinese adherents of 'Fo', i.e. to Buddhists (*The General History of China . . . Done from the French of P. Du Halde* (1736), III, 39–42).

[c] Chap. viii of *Interesting Historical Events*, published in the 3rd part, 1771.

Boboons of punishment and probation. This period is called in the *Shastah*, the Duapaar, or Dwapaar Jogue, in which the term of probation in Mhurd, was reduced to one thousand years; yet in this Jogue there were many who ascended and regained the Mahah Surgo.

In the fourth Jogue, Moisasoor acquired as full possession of the hearts of the remaining delinquent Debtah as when they first rose in rebellion with him, with very few exceptions; this period in the *Shastah* is called the Kolee Jogue, in which the term of probation in Mhurd is limited to one hundred years only. Yet even this Jogue affords some instances of the delinquent spirits surmounting the eight lower Boboons, by penitence and good works; notwithstanding the unwearied diligence of Moisasoor, Rhaaboon, and the rest of the rebellious leaders, and delinquent Debtah, who had a second time fallen under his influence.

The four Jogues or ages having been so frequently mentioned in the last paragraphs, we cannot do better than explain their meaning here, as such explanation would prove too long for a note, it may be remembered, they are called the Suttee Jogue, the Tirtah Jogue, the Dupaar Jogue, and the Kolee Jogue; we will speak to each in their order.

The Suttee Jogue, or the first age, literally the age of truth, figuratively the age of goodness; in this age Endeer is fabled to be born, according to the *Aughtorrah Bhade*; and appointed King of the Universe—the word Endeer[a] literally signifies good, and is in that *Shastah* opposed to Moisasoor or evil, and the various battles said to be fought between this rebel angel and Endeer, and their descendants in every Jogue, allegorically exhibit the conflicts and progress of good and evil in the universe; Endeer's being appointed universal monarch in the Suttee Jogue, alludes to the state of the delinquent Debtah in this age, upon their emerging from the Onderah, when the impression of God's mercy acted so powerfully on their hearts, as to preserve them in penitence and purity, during this age, notwithstanding the utmost efforts of Moisasoor (or evil) and his adherents, to engage them in a second defection. From the word *Suttee* (truth) the word *Sansah* in Bengals, and *Sutch*, in the Moors are derived, any one acquainted in the least degree with those tongues, knows that the phrase *Sansah Kotah*, in the one, and *Sutch Bhaat*, in the other, is commonly used to assert the verity of any thing advanced, and simply signifies, words of truth.

[a] Indra.

John Zephaniah Holwell

The Tirtah Jogue, or second age. By the term prefixed to this age, the order of the Jogues should seem inverted, as the word in its simple construction signifies third. The words, *teen*, *tarah*, *tise*, *trese*, and *tetrese*, which express the numbers three, thirteen, twenty-three, thirty and thirty-three, are all derivatives from the Sanscrît, *Tirtah*; or *Tirtea*, as it is sometimes wrote, and means the third, but oftener the third part, as in the present instance, where the term Tirtah Jogue given to the second age, is allusive to the second defection of one third of the remaining unpurified delinquent spirits, from that penitence and purity which governed them in the Suttee Jogue. In this age Rhaam[a] is fabled to be born for the protection of the delinquent Debtah, against the snares and attempts of Moisasoor and his adherents. The word Rhaam in the Sanscrît, literally signifies protector, but in many parts of the *Aughtorrah Bhade* this personage is mentioned in a more extended sense, as the protector of kingdoms, states and property. *Rhaam! Rhaam!* is used as a pious salutation, between two Gentoos when they meet in the morning, thereby recommending each other's person and property to the protection of this Demi-god.

The Duapaar Jogue, or third age. This term prefixed to the third age, alludes to the second defection from penitence and goodness of one half of the remaining unpurified Debtah—*dua*, or *dwa* simply signifies, two, or the second, but here by the addition of *paar*, it means the half; thus *duapaar deen*, expresses half the day, and *duapaar rhaat* half the night, that is if the phrase issues from the mouth of a polite Gentoo—but the vulgar would say *adah deen* and *adah rhaat*, *adah* being the common Bengal word for half. In the beginning of this Jogue the *Aughtorrah Bhade* fixes the birth of Kissen Taghoor.[b] The word *kissen* in the Sanscrît signifies a scourge, and this being is in that *Bhade* frequently distinguished as the scourge of tyrants and tyranny. *Tagoor* literally means revered, respected, and is a common appellation given to Bramins.

The Kolee Jogue, or the fourth and present age. *Kolee* in the Sanscrît signifies corruption, pollution, impurity, consequently Kolee Jogue means the age of pollution. In this age (say the Bramins) children shall bear false witness against their parents, and before the expiration of it—the stature of the Mhurd by the

---

[a] Rama.   [b] Krishna.

wickedness of the rebellious Debtah that animates it, shall be so reduced, that he will not be able to pluck a Bygon (berengelah)[1] without the help of a hooked stick. We have often, whilst at the head of the judicial court of Cutcherry at Calcutta, heard the most atrocious murders and crimes confessed, and an extenuation of them attempted, by pleading, it was the Kolee Jogue. How far the poetical conceits of Ovid, and others, touching the golden, &c. ages, have been framed from Bramah's four Jogues, we leave to the investigation of the curious.

It is an established doctrine of the *Aughtorrah Bhade*, that the three primary created personages, as well as the rest of the heavenly angelic faithful spirits, have from time to time according to the permission given them by God, descended to the eight Boboons of punishment, and have voluntarily subjected themselves to the feelings of natural and moral evil, for the sake of their brethren, the delinquent Debtah. And to this end, have undergone the eighty-nine transmigrations;[2] and that it is those benevolent spirits, who have at different times appeared on this earthly region, under the mortal forms and names of Endeer, Bramah, Jaggernaut, Kissen Tagoor, Rhaam, Luccon, Kalkee (or Kallee), Sursuttee, Gunnis, Kartic, &c.[a] that have opposed and fought against Moisasoor, Rhaabon, and their iniquitous adherents— and have proved themselves under the various characters of kings, generals, philosophers, lawgivers and prophets, shining examples to the delinquent Debtah, of stupendous courage, fortitude, purity and piety. That their visitations were frequent during the Tirtah, and Duapaar Jogues, but rare since the commencement of the Kolee Jogue, because in this age the delinquent Debtah in general are deemed utterly reprobate, and hardened in their wickedness beyond the powers of council or example; so that they are in a manner left, and given up to their own powers, and abandoned to the full influence of Moisasoor. But that there are still in every period of time some few instances of the delinquents' exer-

---

[1] The Egg Plant.

[2] Hence the Gentoos' dread of killing even by accident any thing that has life, as thereby they may not only dispossess the spirits of their allied Debtah, but also, those of the celestial Debtah, who are working for their redemption.

[a] Indra, Brahma, Jagannatha, Krishna, Rama, Lakshmana, Kalki, Sarasvati, Ganesha, Karttikeya.

tion of their own powers for their salvation, and that when this is manifested to God, he permits the celestial Debtah invisibly to aid, confirm, and support them.

Although the *Shastah* of Bramah denies the prescience of God respecting the actions of free-agents, yet the Bramins maintain that his knowledge extends to the thoughts of every created being, and that the moment a thought is conceived by the soul or spirit, it is sympathetically conveyed to God. It is upon this principle that the adorations, prayers, petitions and thanksgivings, which the Gentoos prefer to the Deity himself are offered in solemn silence; but it is not so with regard to the invocations and worship, instituted by the *Aughtorrah Bhade* to be paid to the subordinate celestial beings, for these are addressed in loud prayer, joined to the clang of various musical instruments.

We have already slightly touched on the religious veneration paid to the Ghoij in a particular district of Bengall, although it is beyond doubt, that their devotion to this animal was universal throughout Indostan in former times. The original source of this regard, was of a two fold nature, as a religious and political institution: first, in a religious sense; as holding in the rotation of the metempsychosis, the rank immediately preceding the human form; this conception is the true cause of that devout, and sometimes enthusiastic veneration paid to this animated form, for the Bramins inculcate that when the Ghoij suffers death by accident or violence, or through the neglect of the owner, it is a token of God's wrath against the wickedness of the spirit of the proprietor, who from thence is warned that at the dissolution of his human form, he will not be deemed worthy of entering the first Boboon of purification, but be again condemned to return to the lowest region of punishment: hence it is, that not only mourning and lamentation ensue on the violent death of either cow of calf—but the proprietor is frequently enjoined, and oftener voluntarily undertakes, a three years pilgrimage in expiation of his crime, forsaking his family, friends and relations, he subsists during his pilgrimage on charity and alms. It is worthy [of] remark, that the penitent thus circumstanced, ever meets with the deepest commiseration, as his state is deemed truely pitiable; two instances have fallen within our own knowledge where the penitents have devoted themselves to the service of God, and a pilgrimage during the term of their life.

Secondly, the Ghoij is venerated by the Gentoos in a political sense, as being the most useful and necessary of the whole animal creation, to a people forbid feeding on flesh, or on any thing that had breathed the breath of life; for it not only yielded to them delectable food, but was otherways essentially serviceable in the cultivation of their lands; on which depended their vegetable subsistence.

The Gentoos hold that the females of all animated forms are, more or less, favored of God, but more eminently in the form of Moiyah in the eighty-ninth transmigration; the word signifies excellent, and is applied to the female of Mhurd; Rhaan is the common name for woman, though it usually means a married Moiyah, and the Gentoo princesses have no higher title than Rhaanee. The female or Moiyah of Mhurd, is supposed to be animated by the most benign and least culpable of the apostate angels, and that from this form, in every period of the four Jogues, an infinitely greater number of the delinquent spirits, have entered the first region of purification, than from the form of Mhurd.

The sudden death of infants, the Bramins say, marks the spirit favored of God, and that it is immediately received into the bosom of Bistnoo, (the preserver) and conveyed to the first region of purification. The sudden death of adults, on the contrary, they pronounce a mark of God's wrath against the animating spirit, as its term of probation in Mhurd, is cut short. The great age of man, when it is accompanied with the enjoyments of his faculties and understanding, is pronounced by the Bramins to be the greatest blessing God can bestow upon this mortal state, as thereby the term of the spirit's probation is prolonged; adding that the limited space of one hundred years, decreed by God in the present Kolee Jogue, is full short for the works of repentance and goodness, and that when the life and understanding is preserved beyond that limited term, it ought to be deemed a signal mark of God's special grace and favor.

Longevity, in (what we call) the brute creation, is by the Bramins esteemed a mark of the great delinquency of the spirits which animate those tribes, because they are so long debarred and with-held from their great and chief state of probation in Mhurd. The Gentoos estimate the greater or lesser delinquency of the apostate spirits, by the class of mortal forms they are doomed to inhabit; thus, all voracious and unclean animals are supposed to be animated by the most malignant spirits; if a hog or dog touch a Gentoo, he is defiled, not from the animal form, but from the perswasion, that the Debtah animating that form, is a malignant spirit. Every voracious animal, that inhabits the earth, air and waters, and men whose lives and actions are publicly and atrociously wicked, come under that class of spirits. On the contrary, those spirits that animate the forms which subsist on vegetables, and do not prey upon each other, are pronounced favored of God.

The general warfare which is observed in the animal world, whereby the destruction of one species is the necessary support and subsistence of others, the Bramins assert is the lot of punishment decreed by God for the most guilty of the apostate angels, who are thereby made his instruments of punishment to each other, every of these tribes being a destined prey to one another. The natural enmity which some classes of animals bear to others, whereby they live in a continued state of war and contention, whenever they meet, although they do not subsist on each other, proceeds they say from the same cause; the delinquent Debtah being destined as a punishment, in those forms to exercise that propensity to hatred, envy, and animosity, on one another, which they had so impotently dared to exert against their Creator.

The rotation of animal forms destined for the habitation of the delinquent Debtah are not, say the Bramins, precisely the same, on repetition of the eighty-nine transmigrations; but are arbitrary and rest with the will of God; but it is their belief that the least guilty of the Debtah, transmigrate only through those forms which by their nature are destined to subsist on the vegetable creation; and that the three changes immediately preceding the spirits animating the Ghoij (that is the eighty-fifth, eighty-sixth, and eighty-seventh) are into the most innocent of the species of birds, the goat and the sheep, the animals most favored of God, next to the Ghoij and Mhurd. From hence the rigid Bramins execrate with bitterness, the cruelty of those nations, who wickedly and wantonly, select and slaughter the best beloved created forms of God, namely the birds, the goat, the sheep, and the cow, to satisfy their unnatural lust of appetite, in defiance not only to his express command and prohibition, but in opposition to the natural and obvious construction of the mouth and digestive faculties of Mhurd, which marks him, destined with other forms most favored of God, to feed and subsist on the fruits and produce of the earth with the additional blessing of the milk of the Ghoij, and of other animals. For this degeneracy, they account no otherwise, than piously lamenting the pitiable state of Mhurd, since the commencement of the Kolee Jogue, adding, that by just consequence the transgression carries its punishment along with it, for by this assemblage of unnatural and forbidden food, variety of diseases are entailed, which cut short the term of probation in Mhurd, by which the delinquent spirit robs himself of more than half of that space of indulgence and trial which his Creator has graciously bestowed upon him, and which he by a fresh instance of his disobedience, ungratefully rejects.

Ovid in his fifteenth book of Metamorphoses introduces Pythagoras dissuading mankind from killing and feeding on his fellow creatures. Our readers will excuse us, if we transcribe such parts of his pathetic arguments, as are strictly in point with the subject of the preceding paragraph.

> He first the taste of flesh, from tables drove,
> And argued well, if arguments could move.
> O mortals! from your fellows' blood abstain,
> Nor taint your bodies, with a food prophane;
> While corn and pulse by nature are bestow'd,
> And planted orchards bend their willing load;
> While labor'd gardens wholesome herbs produce,
> And teeming vines, afford their gen'rous juice;
> Nor tardier fruits of cruder kind are lost,
> But tam'd by fire or mellow'd by the frost;
> While kine to pails distended udders bring,
> And bees their honey, redolent of spring;
> While earth, not only can your needs supply,
> But lavish of her stores, provides for luxury;
> A guiltless feast, administers with ease,
> And without blood, is prodigal to please;
> Wild beasts their maws, with their slain breth'ren fill,

John Zephaniah Holwell

And yet not all,—for some refuse to kill;
Sheep, goats, and oxen, and the nobler steed,
On browse and corn, and flow'ry meadows feed;
Bears, tigers, wolves, the angry lion's brood,
Whom heaven endu'd with principles of blood,
He wisely sunder'd, from the rest to yell,
In forest, and in lonely caves to dwell;
Where stronger beasts, oppress the weak by night,
And all in prey, and purple feasts delight.

O impious use! to Nature's laws opposed,
Where bowels are, in others' bowels closed;
Where fatten'd, by their fellow's fat they thrive,
Maintain'd by murder, and by death, they live;
'Tis then for nought, that mother Earth provides
The stores of all she shows, and all she hides;
If men with fleshy morsels must be fed,
And chaw with bloody teeth the breathing bread;
What else is this, but to devour our guests,
And barb'rously renew Cyclopean feasts?
We by destroying life, our life sustain,
And gorge th' ungodly maw, with meats obscene.

Not so the golden age, who fed on fruit,
Nor durst with bloody meals their mouths pollute;
Then birds, in airy space, might safely move,
And tim'rous hares on heaths securely rove,
Nor needed fish the guileful hooks to fear,
For all was peaceful, and that peace sincere.
Whoever was the wretch, and curs'd be he,
That envy'd first, our food's simplicity;
The essay of bloody feasts, on brutes began,
And after forged the sword to murder man;
Had he the sharpened steel, alone employed
On beasts of prey, which other beasts destroyed,
Or man invaded, with their fangs and paws,
This had been justifyed by Nature's laws,
And self defence:—but who did feasts begin
Of flesh, he stretch'd necessity, to sin.
To kill man-killers, man has lawful power,
But not the extended licence to devour.

Ill habits gather, by unseen degrees,
As brooks make rivers, rivers run to seas;
The sow, with her broad snout, for rooting up,
Th' entrusted seed, was judg'd to spoil the crop;
And intercept the sweating farmer's hope.
The covetous churl, of unforgiving kind,

The offender of the bloody priest resign'd;
Her hunger was on plea, for that she dy'd;
The goat came next in order to be tried.
The goat had crop'd the tendrils of the vine,
In vengeance the laity, and clergy join,
Where one had lost his profit, one his wine.
Here was, at least, some shadow of offence,
The sheep was sacrificed, on no pretence,
But meek, and unresisting innocence.
A patient, useful creature, born to bear,
The warm and woolly fleece, that cloth'd her murderer;
And daily to give down the milk she bred,
A tribute for the grass on which she fed:
Living both food and raiment she supplies,
And is of least advantage, when she dies.
    How did the toiling ox, his death deserve,
A downright simple drudge, and born to serve?
O tyrant! with what justice can'st thou hope;
The promise of the year a plenteous crop,
When thou destroy'st thy lab'ring steer, who till'd
And plough'd with pain, thy else ungrateful field?
From his yet reeking neck, to draw the yoke,
That neck with which the surly clods he broke;
And to the hatchet, yield thy husband man,
Who finished autumn, and the spring began.
    Nor this alone! but heaven itself to bribe,
We to the gods, our impious acts ascribe;
First recompence with death, their creatures toil,
Then call the blest above to share the spoil.
The fairest victim, must the pow'rs appease
(So fatal 'tis sometimes too much to please)
A purple fillet his broad brow adorns,
With flow'ry garlands crown'd and gilded horns:
He hears the murd'rous prayer the priest prefers,
But understands not! 'tis his doom he hears:
Beholds the meal, betwixt his temples cast,
(The fruit and product of his labors past)!
And in the water, views perhaps the knife,
Uplifted to deprive him of his life;
Then broken up alive, his entrails sees
Torn out for priests t'inspect the gods' decrees.
    From whence, O mortal man! this gust of blood
Have you deriv'd? and interdicted food?
Be taught by me, this dire delight to shun,
Warn'd by my precepts, by my practice, won;

And when you eat the well-deserving beast,
Think, on the lab'rer of your field, you feast.

Then let not piety be put to flight,
To please the taste of glutton appetite;
But suffer inmate souls secure to dwell,
Lest from their seats your parents you expel;
With rabid hunger feed upon your kind,
Or from a beast dislodge a brother's mind.

That Pythagoras carried such sentiments from the Bramins, and labored to obtrude them upon his countrymen, is beyond controversy; the pathetic perswasives he urged to them in that age to abstain from the feeding on their brethren of the creation, proved however as ineffectual then, as we conceive it would be in the present, the more's the pity—for it is to be feared we shall to the end of the chapter—rise, kill and eat.[a]

Regarding the description (which Ovid puts in the mouth of Pythagoras) of the ancient religious sacrifices, we must in justice to the Bramins say he could not borrow it from them; in this particular the original religious tenets of the Gentoos differ from all the ancients, for they were strangers to those bloody sacrifices and offerings; neither of the Gentoo *Bhades* having the least allusion to that mode of worshipping the deity; and the Bramins say, nothing but Moisasoor himself could have invented so infatuated and cruel an institution, which is manifestly so repugnant to the true spirit of devotion, and abhorrent to the Eternal One.

That every animal form is endued, with cogitation, memory and reflection, is one of the most established tenets of the Bramins; indeed it must consequentially be so, on the supposed metempsychosis of the apostate spirits, through these mortal forms. Every state of the delinquent spirits' abode in the eight Boboons, they say, is a state of humiliation, punishment and purgation, that of Mhurd not excepted; and that the purpose of the Eternal One would be defeated by himself, had he not endued them with rationality and a consciousness of their situation. In the form of Mhurd alone, is the spirit's state of probation, because in this form only, he again becomes an absolute and free agent; and in this alone lies the difference between Mhurd, and the rest of

[a] Acts, x, 13.

the animal created forms, for in these, the spirit's intellectual faculties are circumscribed, more or less, by the varied construction of the forms, and limited within certain bounds, which they cannot exceed, that consciousness of those confined powers, and envy at the superiour state of Mhurd, constitutes their chief punishment; that this unceasing envy, and resentment of the usurped tryanny which Mhurd assumed over the animal creation (from the beginning of the Kolee Jogue) are the causes which made them in general shun his society, and live in a state of enmity with him, according to the force of the natural powers, which the Eternal One has endued them with; that where some of the species appear an exception to this general bent, it proceeds from the weakness of their natural powers; or the superiour craft and subtility of Mhurd, who first deceitfully allured them to slavery and destruction. That neither envy or enmity in the animal created forms, nor usurped tyranny on the part of Mhurd, had existence in the breasts of either, before the beginning of the Kolee Jogue, when a universal degeneracy of almost all the remaining unpurified Debtah prevailed through all their mortal forms—which until that period had lived in amity and harmony, as conscious of being involved under the same sentence and displeasure of their Creator; and lastly—that the usurped tyranny of Mhurd over the rest of the delinquent angels was displeasing to the Eternal One, and will be a charge exhibited against the spirit by Bistnoo at the dissolution of Mhurd, for that in place of cherishing the unhappy delinquents during their state of humiliation and punishment, they do, by the force of their tyrannic usurpation, labor to make their state more miserable, than the Eternal One intended it should be, in violation of his express injunction, that they should love one another.

The Bramins hold, that every distinct species of animal creation have a comprehensive mode of communicating their ideas, peculiar to themselves; and that the metempsychosis of the delinquent spirits extends through every organised body, even to the smallest insect and reptile; they highly venerate the bee, and some species of the ant, and conceive the spirits animating those forms are favored of God, and that its intellectual faculties, are more enlarged under them, than in most others.

John Zephaniah Holwell

Although we have already shewn that the bloody sacrifices of the ancients was no part of the Gentoo tenets, yet there subsists amongst them at this day, a voluntary sacrifice, of too singular a nature, to pass by us unnoticed; the rather as it has been frequently mentioned by various authors, without we conceive that knowledge and perspicuity which the matter calls for; the sacrifice we allude to, is the Gentoo wives burning with the bodies of their deceased husbands. We have taken no small pains to investigate this seeming cruel custom, and hope we shall be able to throw same satisfactory lights on this very extraordinary subject, which has hitherto been hid in obscurity; in order to which we will first remove one or two obstructions that lie in our way, and hinder our nearer and more perfect view of it.

The cause commonly assigned for the origin of this sacrifice (peculiar to the wives of this nation) is, that it was a law constituted to put a period to a wicked practice that the Gentoos' wives had of poisoning their husbands; for this assertion we cannot trace the smallest semblance of truth, and indeed the known fact, that the sacrifice must be voluntary, of its self refutes that common mistake. It also has been a received opinion, that if the wife refuses to burn, she loses her cast (or tribe) and is stamped with disgrace and infamy, an opinion equally void of foundation in fact as the other. The real state of this case is thus circumstanced. The first wife (for the Gentoo laws allow bigamy, although they frequently do not benefit themselves of the indulgence, if they have issue by the first) has it in her choice to burn, but is not permitted to declare her resolution before twenty-four hours after the decease of her husband; if she refuses, the right devolves to the second, if either, after the expiration of twenty-four hours, publicly declare, before the Bramins and witnesses, their resolution to burn, they cannot then retract. If they both refuse at the expiration of that term, the worst consequence that attends their refusal, is lying under the imputation of being wanting to their own honor, purification, and the prosperity of their family, for from their infancy, they are instructed by the household Bramin to look upon this catastrophe, as most glorious to themselves, and beneficial to their children: the truth is, that the children of the wife who burns, become thereby illustrious, and are sought after in marriage by the most opulent and honourable of their cast, and sometimes received into a cast superiour to their own.

That the Bramins take unwearied pains to encourage, promote, and confirm in the minds of the Gentoo wives, this spirit of burning, is certain (their motives for it, the penetration of our readers may by and by probably discover) and although they seldom lose their labor, yet instances happen, where fear, or love of life, sets at nought all their preaching; for it sometimes falls out that the first wife refuses, and the second burns; at others, they both refuse; and as but one can burn, it so happens, that when the second wife has issue by the deceased, and the first none, there commonly ensues a violent contention between them, which of the two shall make the sacrifice; but this dispute is generally determined by the Bramins, in favor of the first, unless she is prevailed on by perswasion, or other motives to wave her right, in favor of the second. Having elucidated these matters, we will proceed to give our readers the best account, we have been able to obtain of the origin of this remarkable custom.

At the demise of the mortal part of the Gentoos' great lawgiver and prophet Bramah, his wives, inconsolable for his loss, resolved not to survive him, and offered themselves voluntary victims on his funeral pile. The wives of the chief Rajahs, the first officers of the state, being unwilling to have it thought that they were deficient in fidelity and affection, followed the heroic example set them by the wives of Bramah; the Bramins (a tribe then newly constituted by their great legislator) pronounced and declared, that the delinquent spirits of those heroines, immediately ceased from their transmigrations, and had entered the first Boboon of purification—it followed, that their wives claimed a right of making the same sacrifice of their mortal forms to God, and the *manes* of their deceased husbands; the wives of every Gentoo caught the enthusiastic (now pious) flame. Thus the heroic acts of a few women brought about a general custom, the Bramins had given it the stamp of religion, they foisted it into the *Chatah* and *Aughtorrah Bhades*, and instituted the forms and ceremonials that were to accompany the sacrifice, strained some obscure passages of Bramah's *Chartah Bhade*, to countenance their declared sense of the action, and established it as a religious tenet throughout Indostan, subject to the restrictions before recited, which leaves it a voluntary act of glory, piety and fortitude. Whether the Bramins were sincere in their declared sense, and consecration of this act, or had a view to the securing the fidelity of their own wives, or were actuated by any other motives, we will not determine.

When people have lived together to an advanced age, in mutual acts of confidence, friendship and affection; the sacrifice a Gentoo widow makes of her person (under such an affecting circumstance as the loss of friend and husband) seems less an object of wonder; but when we see women in the bloom of youth, and beauty, in the calm possession of their reason and understanding, with astonishing fortitude, set at nought, the tender considerations of parents, children, friends, and the horror and torments of the death they court, we cannot resist viewing such an act, and such a victim, with tears of commiseration, awe and reverence.

We have been present at many of these sacrifices: in some of the victims, we have observed a pitiable dread, tremor, and reluctance, that strongly spoke repentance for their declared resolution; but it was now too late to retract, or retreat; Bistnoo was waiting for the spirit. If the self doomed victim discovers want of courage and fortitude, she is with gentle force obliged to ascend the pile, where she is held down with long poles, held by men on each side of the pile, until the flames reach her; her screams and cries, in the mean time, being drowned amidst the deafening noise of loud musick, and the acclamations of the multitude. Others we have seen go through this fiery trial, with most amazing steady, calm, resolution, and joyous fortitude. It will not we hope be unacceptable, if we present our readers with an instance of the latter, which happened some years past at the East India company's factory at Cossimbuzaar,[a] in the time of Sir Francis Russell's chiefship,[b] the author, and several other gentlemen of the factory were present, some of whom are now living: from a narrative, which the author then transmitted to England he is now enabled to give the particulars of this most remarkable proof of female fortitude, and constancy.

[a] Kasimbazar.
[b] Sir Francis Russell, 6th Baronet (d.1743).

At five of the clock on the morning of the 4th of February, 1742–3, died Rhaam Chund Pundit of the Mahahrattor[a] tribe, aged twenty-eight years; his widow (for he had but one wife) aged between seventeen and eighteen, as soon as he expired, disdaining to wait the term allowed her for reflection, immediately declared to the Bramins and witnesses present her resolution to burn; as the family was of no small consideration, all the merchants of Cossimbuzaar, and her relations, left no arguments unessayed to dissuade her from it—Lady Russell,[b] with the tenderest humanity, sent her several messages to the same purpose; the infant state of her children (two girls and a boy, the eldest not four years of age) and the terrors and pain of the death she sought, were painted to her in the strongest and most lively colouring—she was deaf to all, she gratefully thanked Lady Russell, and sent her word she had now nothing to live for, but recommended her children to her protection. When the torments of burning were urged in terrorem to her, she with a resolved and calm countenance, put her finger into the fire, and held it there a considerable time, she then with one hand put fire in the palm of the other, sprinkled incense on it, and fumigated the Bramins. The consideration of her children left destitute of a parent was again urged to her. She replied, he that made them, would take care of them. She was at last given to understand, she should not be permitted to burn;[1] this for a short space seemed to give her deep affliction, but soon recollecting herself, she told them, death was in her power, and that if she was not allowed to burn, according to the principles of her cast, she would starve herself. Her friends, finding her thus peremptory and resolved, were obliged at last to assent.

The body of the deceased was carried down to the water side, early the following morning, the widow followed about ten o'clock, accompanied by three very principal Bramins, her children, parents, and relations, and a numerous concourse of people. The order of leave for her burning did not arrive from Hosseyn Khan, Fouzdaar of Morshadabad,[c] until after one, and it was then brought by one of the Soubah's[d] own officers, who had orders to see that she burnt voluntarily. The time they waited for the order was employed in praying with the Bramins, and washing in the Ganges; as soon as it arrived, she retired and stayed for the space of half an hour in the midst of her female relations, amongst whom was her mother; she then divested herself of her bracelets, and other ornaments, and tyed them in a cloth, which hung like an apron before her, and was conducted by her female relations to one corner of the pile; on the pile was an arched arbor formed of dry sticks, boughs and leaves, open only at one end to admit her entrance; in this the body of the deceased was deposited, his head at the end opposite

---

[1] The Gentoos are not permitted to burn, without an order from the Mahommedan government, and this permission is commonly made a prequisite of.

[a] Presumably Maratha. [b] Anne, née Gee.

[c] The *faujdar*, local Governor, of Murshidabad, capital of Bengal.

[d] The *subah*, the Nawab of Bengal.

to the opening. At the corner of the pile, to which she had been conducted, the Bramin had made a small fire, round which she and the three Bramins sat for some minutes, one of them gave into her hand a leaf of the bale tree (the wood commonly consecrated to form part of the funeral pile) with sundry things on it, which she threw into the fire; one of the others gave her a second leaf, which she held over the flame, whilst he dropped three times some ghee on it, which melted, and fell into the fire (these two operations, were preparatory symbols of her approaching dissolution by fire) and whilst they were performing this, the third Bramin read to her some portions of the *Aughtorrah Bhade*, and asked her some questions, to which she answered with a steady, and serene countenance; but the noise was so great, we could not understand what she said, although we were within a yard of her. These over, she was led with great solemnity three times round the pile, the Bramins reading before her; when she came the third time to the small fire, she stopped, took her rings off her toes and fingers, and put them to her other ornaments; here she took a solemn majestic leave of her children, parents, and relations; after which, one of the Bramins dip'd a large wick of cotton in some ghee, and gave it ready lighted into her hand, and led her to the open side of the arbor; there, all the Bramins fell at her feet; after she had blessed them, they retired weeping; by two steps, she ascending the pile and entered the arbor; on her entrance, she made a profound reverence at the feet of the deceased, and advanced and seated herself by his head; she looked, in silent meditation on his face, for the space of a minute, then set fire to the arbor, in three places; observing that she had set fire to leeward, and that the flames blew from her, instantly seeing her error she rose, and set fire to windward, and resumed her station; ensign Daniel with his cane, separated the grass and leaves on the windward side, by which means we had a distinct view of her as she sat. With what dignity, and undaunted a countenance, she set fire to the pile the last time, and assumed her seat, can only be conceived, for words cannot convey a just idea of her. The pile being of combustible matters, the supporters of the roof were presently consumed, and it tumbled upon her.

We see our fair country-women shudder at an action, which we fear they will look upon, as a proof of the highest infatuation in their sex. Although it is not our intention here to defend the tenets of the Bramins, yet we may be allowed to offer some justification on behalf of the Gentoo women in the action before us. Let us view it (as we should every other action) without prejudice, and without keeping always in sight our own tenets and customs, and prepossessions that too generally result therefrom, to the injury of others; if we view these women in a just light, we shall think more candidly of them, and confess they act upon heroic, as well as rational and pious principles: in order to this we must consider them as a race of females trained from their infancy, in the full conviction of their celestial rank; and that this world, and the corporeal form that incloses them, is destined by God, the one as their place of punishment, the other as their prison. That their ideas are consequently raised to a soothing degree of dignity befiting angelic beings. They are nursed and instructed in the firm faith—that this voluntary sacrifice, is the most glorious period of their lives, and that thereby the celestial spirit is released from its transmigrations, and evils of a miserable existence, and flies to join the spirit of their departed husband, in a state of purification; add to this, the subordinate consideration of raising the lustre of their children, and of contributing by this action to their temporal prosperity; all these it must be owned are prevalent motives, for chearfully embracing death, and setting at nought every common attachment which the weakness of humanity urges, for a longer existence in a world of evil. Although these principles are in general so diametrically contrary to the prevailing spirit, and genius of our fair country-women, who (from a happy train of education) in captivating amusements and dissipation, find charms sufficient in this world, to engage their wishes for a perpetual residence in it; yet we will depend on their natural goodness of heart, generosity and candor, that they will in future look on these their Gentoo sisters of the creation, in a more favorable, and consistent light, than probably they have hitherto done; and not deem that action an infatuation, which results from principle. Let them also recollect that their own history affords illustrious examples in both sexes of voluntary sacrifices by fire, because they would not subscribe even to a different mode of professing the same faith. Besides—a contempt of death, is not peculiar to the women of India, it is the characteristic of the nation; every Gentoo meets that moment of dissolution, with a steady, noble, and philosophic resignation, flowing from the established principles of their faith.

Before we close this subject, we will mention one or two more particulars relative to it. It has been already remarked in a marginal note, that the Gentoo women are not allowed to burn, without an order of leave from the Mahommedan government; it is proper also to inform our readers this privilege is never withheld from them. There have been instances known, when the victim has, by Europeans, been forceably rescued from the pile; it is currently said and believed (how true we will not aver) that the wife of Mr Job Charnock*a* was by him snatched from this sacrifice; be this as it may, the outrage is considered by the Gentoos, an atrocious, and wicked violation of their sacred rites and privileges.

Having now brought our fourth general head to a conclusion, and faithfully, to the best of our knowledge (with the materials we are possessed of) exhibited the original tenets of the ancient Bramins, according to the first book of Bramah's *Chartah Bhade*; and having in our remarks given such elucidations as we thought our subject called for, we submit our imperfect work (for imperfect we must still call it) with all due deference to the public; hoping that some more capable head and hand, will be stimulated by our endeavours, to produce a more full, and satisfactory relation, of the rest of his doctrines. A large field is yet left open, for the exercise of industry and talents. Bramah's first section of his second book on the creation of this globe, will be the subject of our next general head. His third book directing the plain and simple modes of worship to be paid to God, and the three primary created beings, and his fourth sublime book, (which the Gentoos commonly call *Bramah Ka, Insoff Bhade*, or, Bramah's book of justice) wherein is expressly recited and enjoined, the duties and offices, which the delinquent Debtah shall observe and pay to each other; these two last mentioned books, and part of the second, we say, must lie in oblivion, until some one, blessed with opportunity, leisure, application, and genius, brings them to light.

a The founder of Calcutta, who died in 1693.

Chapter V

Of the Creation of the Worlds

INTRODUCTION

In the fifth section of our last general head, Bramah recites, that the Eternal One (after he had promulged his gracious intention, of mitigating the punishment of the fallen angels, at the intercession of the remaining faithful host), 'retired into himself, and became invisible to them, for the space of five thousand years.' In his introduction to the act of creation of the worlds in his second book, he takes again occasion to repeat the above mentioned passage, and explains it by an inference, that during that space, the Eternal One was employed in meditation on his intended new creation; and although it appears, from the same section, that this stupendous work, was produced by an instantaneous fiat of the Deity, yet Bramah, to display the infinite and amazing wisdom of his Creator, enters into a sublime, and philosophic disquisition and description, of his modes (if we may be allowed the expression) and manner of creation, in the marvellous construction of the fifteen Boboons, that constitute the Dunneahoudah, or universe; these descriptions, he couches under allegories, then commonly and familiarly understood, at which the reader will the less wonder, when he knows, that at this day it is the usual mode of conversing, amongst well educated Gentoos.

In this exhibition of infinite wisdom, Bramah gives a short, simple and elevated description, of each of the fifteen Boboons, their situation, their rank, and peculiar destination, with the appellations appropriated to the angelic inhabitants, in their progressive passage from one sphere to another. Our memory only supplies us with the names of the sojourners of the ninth, fifth, sixth and seventh, that is, the first, and three last of the seven regions of purification, to wit, the spheres of the Pereeth logue,[1] the Munnoo logue,[2] the Debtah logue,[3] and the Birmah

---

[1] *Logue*, literally people. *Pereeth logue*, purified people.

[2] *Munnoo logue*, people of contemplation, from *mun*, or *mon*, thought, reflection, alludes to God's being worshipped in this sphere in silent meditation.

[3] In this sphere the angels are first supposed to regain properly their title of Debtah.

logue;[1] in the last mentioned sphere, according to the Bramins' computation, a complete day is equal to twenty-eight Munnunturs of vulgar time. (Vid. sixth or next general head.)

On the foundation of Bramah's description of the fifteen Boboons, the compilers of the *Augotorrah Bhade* have raised an elaborate chimerical superstructure: that confounds the understanding.

As the Bramins' conceptions and calculation of the age and future duration of the universe, will be the subject of our next general head, we shall say nothing more of it here, than to remind our readers, that they date its existence from the rebellious angels being released from the Onderah.

We again lament the loss of our materials, which confines us to the eighth section of Bramah's second book that treats only of the creation of this terrestrial planet, to which we will now proceed, premising that it is distinguished by the title of the eighth Boboon of Murto, which literally signifies the region of earth.

Section VIII

Birmahah[2] or Creation. And it was—that when the Eternal One, resolved to form the new creation of the Dunneahoudah, he gave the rule of Mahah Surgo to his first created Birmah, and became invisible to the whole angelic host.

When the Eternal One, first began his intended new creation of the Dunneahoudah, he was opposed by two mighty Ossoors,[3] which proceeded from the wax of Brum's ear; and their names were Modoo[4] and Kytoo.[5]

And the Eternal One, contended and fought with Modoo and Kytoo,[a] five thousand years, and he smote them on his thigh,[6] and they were lost and assimilated with Murto.

And it was, that when Modoo and Kytoo were subdued, the Eternal One

[1] In this sphere the delinquents are supposed to be cleansed from the pollution of their sin, regenerated, and fit to enter again the Mahah Surgo, and to be readmitted to the presence of their Creator.

[2] This title is prefixed to every section of Bramah's second book, Birmah in the figurative sense (before explained) signifying creation.

[3] The common appellation given to giants, but is variously used in the *Shastah*, to express excrescence, excretion, and secretion.

[4] Discord, enmity.

[5] Confusion, tumult.

[6] Reduced them to subjection, or obedience: touching the thigh, amongst the ancient Gentoos, was a token of subjection.

[a] Madhu and Kaitabha.

7-2

emerged from his state of invisibility, and glory encompassed him on every side!

And the Eternal One spoke, and said, Thou Birmah[1] shalt create and form all things that shall be made in the new creation of the fifteen Boboons of punishment, and purification, according to the powers of the spirit, wherewith thou shalt be inspired. And thou, Bistnoo,[2] shalt superintend, cherish, and preserve all the things and forms which shall be created. And thou, Sieb,[3] shalt change, or destroy, all creation, according to the powers, wherewith I will invest thee.

And when Birmah, Bistnoo, and Sieb, had heard the words of the Eternal One, they all bowed obedience.[4]

The Eternal One spoke again, and said to Birmah, Do thou begin the creation and formation of the eighth Boboon, of punishment and probation, even the Boboon of Murto, according to the powers of the spirit wherewith I have endued thee, and do thou, Bistnoo, proceed to execute thy part.

And when Brum[5] heard the command, which the mouth of the Eternal One had uttered; he straightways formed a leaf of beetle, and he floated on the beetle leaf over the surface of the Jhoale; and the children[6] of Modo and Kytoo, fled before him, and vanished from his presence.

And when the agitation of the Jhoale had subsided, by the powers of the spirit of Brum, Bistnoo straightways transformed himself into a mighty boar,[7] and descending into the abyss of Jhoale, he brought up the Murto on his tusks. Then spontaneously issued from him, a mighty tortoise,[8] and a mighty snake.[9]

And Bistnoo put the snake erect upon the back of the tortoise, and placed Murto upon the head of the snake.

And all things were created and formed by Birmah in the eighth Boboon of punishment and probation, even the eighth of Murto, according to the powers of the spirit, wherewith the Eternal One had endued him.

And Bistnoo took upon him the superintendence and charge of all that was created, and formed, by Birmah in the eighth Boboon of Murto; and he cherished and preserved them, as the words of the Eternal One had directed, and commanded.

---

[1] Power of creation. Vid. introduction to the fourth chapter.

[2] Preserver. Vid. introduction to the fourth chapter.

[3] Mutilator, destroyer. Vid. introduction, &c.

[4] The foregoing exordium of the general act of creation of the Dunneahoudah, preceeds every one of the fifteen sections of Bramah's second book.

[5] Birmah and Brum, are, in the act of creation, synonimous terms.

[6] Supposed remains of discordant matter. The Bramins supposed the first principles of things prior to the creation of the universe, to have been in a fluid state.

[7] The Gentoos' symbol of strength, because, in proportion to his size, he is the strongest of all animals.

[8] The Gentoos' symbol of stability.

[9] The Gentoos' symbol of wisdom.

John Zephaniah Holwell

In the same sublime allegorical manner, has Bramah described the creation of Surjee,[1] and Chunder,[2] and the other twelve Boboons of the Dunneahoudah, without pretending, or aiming to dive into, and explain, the principles of matter, or the nature of those essential laws of motion by which the Deity guides and governs his creation; the wisdom of Bramah has elsewhere marked such fruitless enquiries, with the stamp of presumption and folly; and that the knowledge of these, and the mode of the existence of God, is concealed even from the three primary created beings themselves.

From the foregoing specimen of the creation of the eighth region, as well as from Bramah's historical discussion of the other fourteen, it is most obvious, that the personages which he introduces as actors in the work of that creation were intended by him to be taken only in a figurative sense, as expressive of the three supreme attributes of the Deity, his power to create, his power to preserve, and his power to change, or destroy, as before hinted.[3] For if they were to be understood in any other sense, it would expressly contradict his own text, where he represents the creation of the Dunneahoudah as proceeding from the instantaneous fiat of the Eternal One; and a further proof of Bramah's plain intention, results from his prefixing the same exordium to each of his sections of creation.

But as the real sense and meaning of the allegory (then clearly understood by all) was, in process of time, lost to the generality of the Gentoos; the compilers of the *Chatah* and *Aughtorrah Bhades*, took the advantage (which ignorance and time gave them) and not only realised Bramah's three mystical beings, but created also a multitude of subordinate actors, and made Demi-gods and divinities of them all, instituting particular days, fasts, and festivals, and other exterior worship, to each: thus Surjee and Chunder,[a] Modoo and Kytoo, and a race of their children and descendants, became Demi-gods and heroes; and scorning to confine themselves to the eighth Boboon, they ransacked the fourteen,

---

[1] The Sun.   [2] The Moon.
[3] Vid. Introduction to the fourth chapter.
[a] Surya and Chandra.

and framed divinities of the principal personages which their wild imagination supposed resident in each of them, and allotted to them peculiar divine worship, which subsists to this day.

It will not, we hope, be thought an improbable conjecture, if we say, that the allegorical parts of Bramah's *Chartah Bhade*, (which truely bears a divine semblance) being thus perverted or grossly mistaken by the very tribe, which he had instituted guardians over it, and being subsequently communicated to the Egyptian Magi, and by them circulated through the states of Greece, afforded them, as well as Rome and the whole Western world, those inexhaustible supplies of mythological systems, which held their existence and authority even long after the light of christianity had shone upon them. But to resume our more immediate subject.

The act of creation of the Boboon of Murto, is represented in the annexed plate No. 1. which (with others we shall have occasion to present to the reader) was drawn by the instructions, and under the eye of a judicious Bramin of the Battezaar tribe, the tribe, as before noticed, usually employed in expounding the *Shastahs*.

Brum[1] is represented lying and floating on a leaf of beetle[a], over the troubled surface of the abyss of Jhoale; the three primary beings appear before it, in the posture of adoration, Birmah on the right, Bistnoo in the middle, and Sieb on the left. On the right, above the abyss, is figured a huge boar, bearing on his tusks a lump of earth. On the left, above the abyss, is represented a tortoise, on which a snake rests his tail, bearing Murto (or the earth) on his head. Brum and Birmah are habited alike; and are each figured with four heads and four arms. The three primary beings, are supposed in the posture of adoration, to be receiving the commands of the Eternal One, touching his projected new creation; and the other figures express the three gradations of the work, namely the beginning, the progress, and completion.[2]

Notwithstanding the sagacious reader, by a bare reference to the marginal notes which we have affixed to the text of Bramah, will readily conceive the spirit of the allegory contained in it; yet

---

[1] Spirit or essence of the Eternal One: vide Introduction to the fourth chapter.
[2] Vide Plate No. i.
[a] Jones described this as 'manifestly intended by a bad painter for a lotos-leaf' (see below, p. 215).

Holwell's Hindu deities

John Zephaniah Holwell

as some passages of it require a further explanation than could be huddled into a note, we will add the whole interpretation of it under one connected view.

The Eternal One having determined on the creation of the universe, like a supreme wise architect, he retired for a space to project his stupendous plan, and prepare his materials. He was opposed in the operation by the discord, confusion and tumult of the elements that compose the abyss of Jhoale; he separated, subdued, brought them under subjection, and prepared them to receive his intended impressions. He exerts his three great attributes, to create, preserve, or destroy, which are figuratively represented by the three primary created beings. His spirit floats upon the surface of the abyss of Jhoale, or fluid matter. Creation takes place. Birmah (or Creation) is represented with four heads and four arms to denote the power of God in the act of creation. Bistnoo the preserver is transformed into a mighty boar, emblematically signifying the strength of God in the act of creation. The tortoise mystically denotes the stability and permanency of the foundation of the earth, and the snake the wisdom by which it is supported. These latter operations are given to Bistnoo, because the earth was the grand principle or parent, from whence he was to draw the means for the preservation of the future animal creation, destined for the prisons of the rebellious Debtah; a work which we may gather from Bramah's text, was reserved for the hand of God himself, as they were to be endued with rational powers. It may be asked why Brum, is represented floating, particularly on a beetle leaf? To this we can only reply, that the plant is deemed sacred amongst the Gentoos, its culture is made under the auspices of the *Shastah*, and instruction of the Bramins; unclean persons are prohibited entering into a beetle garden, as the approach of any impurity is pronounced fatal to the plant, in the infancy of its growth.[a]

To conclude this general head—how far Homer, Virgil, Lucretius, Ovid, Lucian, &c. have in their conceptions of the creation, (by means of the Egyptians) built on, and availed themselves of the simple cosmogony of Bramah, we leave the learned and curious to trace. Although in fact, it is obvious, that this ancient

[a] See Jones's comments, below, p. 216.

103

sage, aimed at no other solution of that stupendous and incomprehensible act, than to inculcate, that the universe was produced by the essence and voluntary power, strength and wisdom of God. That it is preserved and sustained by original constituent powers impressed on it by the Deity, and that it is liable to change and dissolution, at his divine pleasure and will.

Chapter VI

The Gentoo manner of computing Time, and their conception of the age of the universe, and the period of its dissolution.

[From Bramah's Chartah Bhade, in the supplement to his Birmahah.]

Sixty nimicks, or winks of the eye, make one pull.
Sixty pulls, make one gurree.
Sixty gurrees, make one complete day, or one day and one night.
Three hundred and sixty-five complete days and fifteen gurrees make one solar year.

The Gentoos divide the complete day into eight parts, to which they give the term *paar*, commencing their day at six in the morning; thus *ek paar dheen*[1] equals our nine in the morning; *duapaar dheen*, our noon; *teenpaar dheen*, our three afternoon; *chaarpaar dheen*, our six in the evening; the divisions of the night are distinguished by the word *rhaat* (night) in place of *dheen*, as *ek paar rhaat*, equals our nine at night; and so on.

It is the province of the Bramins in this country to keep the account of time, and there is no Gentoo of distinction but retains in his house and on his journeys one of these time keepers, whose intire business it is to regulate time, and strike the gurrees as they pass, on the Ghong, an extended sheet of copper, which yields the sound of a solemn bell.

Bramah measures space or duration of time, from the creation of the Dunneahoudah, or universe, by the revolutions of the four Jogues.

---

[1] Literally, one part of day.

John Zephaniah Holwell

	Years
The first age, or Suttee Jogue, contains thirty-two lac years of vulgar time, or	3,200,000
The second age, or Tirta Jogue, sixteen lac, or	1,600,000
The third age, or Dwapaar Jogue, eight lac, or	800,000
The fourth age, or Kolee Jogue, four lac, or	400,000
	6,000,000

Ekutter (seventy-one) revolutions of the four Jogues make one Munnuntur of vulgar time, or years 426,000,000.[a]

(The word Munnuntur, is in this place strictly applied by Bramah to space of time, but it is by him frequently used with a retrospect signification to the act of creation, and is sometimes given as an additional name to Birmah, as Birmah Munnuah, alluding to the creation being the result of thought and meditation; the word, as we before remarked in a marginal note, springs from Mon, or Mun, thought, reflection; Munnoo Logue, the people of thought, or contemplation. The compilers of the *Aughtorrah Bhade* derive the word Munnuntur from Munnuah or Munnooah, whom (by perverting the sense of Bramah) they make to be the fabulous personal offspring of Birmah, and report mighty feats of his prowess in war, against Moisasoor, and his adherents.)

When Bramah descended to promulge the written law and commands of the Eternal One to the Gentoos, he at the same time (namely, the beginning of the present Kolee Jogue)[1] declared, 'from the registers of Surgo, that the Dunneahoudah, was then entering into the eighth revolution of the four Jogues, in the second Munnuntur'; consequently, according to Bramah's account, (and if our calculation be right) the precise age of this, and the other fourteen planets of the universe, amounted to, at that period, four hundred and sixty eight millions of years. And if we substract the 4866 years, which have elapsed since the descent of Bramah, we shall find the remainder of the Kolee Jogue will be 359,134 years; at the expiration of which, Bramah pronounced and prophecied, that the patience and forbearance of the Eternal One would be withdrawn from the delinquent Debtah, and

[1] Vide Introduction to the fourth chapter.

[a] Varying accounts of the four *yugas*, or ages of the cosmos, were given by Holwell, Dow, Halhed and Jones (see below, pp. 124, 158, 263).

destruction by fire fall upon the eight regions of punishment, purgation and probation.[1]

In the supplement to his *Birmahah*, Bramah likewise taught, that the Boboon of Murto, had undergone three remarkable changes, and would undergo three more, before its final dissolution in common with the other seven Boboons; but he specifies not of what nature those changes were, or would be; he also declares, 'that after a long space, a second new creation will take place; but of what kind, or on what principles it would be constructed, was only known to the Eternal One.'

The cause of the superstitious veneration paid by the Gentoos to the numericals one and three has, we conceive, been obvious to the discerning reader as he travelled thro' these sheets. It is remarkable, that a Gentoo never gives or receives an obligation for an even sum; if he borrows or lends a hundred, a thousand, or ten thousand rupees, the obligation runs for a hundred and one, a thousand and one, ten thousand and one, &c. The Mahommedans, in conformity only, have generally adopted this custom; hence it was, that the revenues stipulated to be paid annually by Soujah Khan[a] into the royal treasury, were one khorore, one lac, one thousand, one hundred, and one rupee.[b]

[1] Vide towards the close of the fifth section.
[a] Suja Khan, Nawab of Bengal, 1727–39.
[b] I.e. 10,100,111.

2

Alexander Dow, 'A Dissertation concerning the Customs, Manners, Language, Religion and Philosophy of the Hindoos'

The learned of modern Europe have, with reason, complained that the writers of Greece and Rome did not extend their enquiries to the religion and philosophy of the Druids. Posterity will perhaps, in the same manner, find fault with the British for not investigating the learning and religious opinions, which prevail in those countries in Asia, into which either their commerce or their arms have penetrated. The Brahmins of the East possessed in antient times, some reputation for knowledge, but we have never had the curiosity to examine whether there was any truth in the reports of antiquity upon that head.

Excuses, however, may be formed for our ignorance concerning the learning, religion and philosophy of the Brahmins. Literary inquiries are by no means a capital object to many of our adventurers in Asia. The few who have a turn for researches of that kind, are discouraged by the very great difficulty in acquiring that language, in which the learning of the Hindoos is contained; or by that impenetrable veil of mystery with which the Brahmins industriously cover their religious tenets and philosophy.

These circumstances combining together, have opened an ample field for fiction. Modern travellers have accordingly indulged their talent for fable, upon the mysterious religion of Hindostan. Whether the ridiculous tales they relate, proceed from that common partiality which Europeans, as well as less enlightened nations, entertain for the religion and philosophy of their own country, or from a judgment formed upon some external ceremonies of the Hindoos, is very difficult to determine; but they have prejudiced Europe against the Brahmins, and by a very unfair account, have thrown disgrace upon a system of religion and philosophy, which they did by no means investigate.

The author of this dissertation must own, that he for a long time, suffered himself to be carried down in this stream of popular prejudice. The present decline of literature in Hindostan, served to confirm him in his belief of those legends which he read in Europe, concerning the Brahmins. But conversing by accident, one day, with a noble and learned Brahmin, he was not a little surprized to find him perfectly acquainted with those opinions, which, both in ancient and modern Europe, have employed the pens of the most celebrated moralists. This circumstance did not fail to excite his curiosity, and in the course of many subsequent conversations, he found that philosophy and the sciences had, in former ages, made a very considerable progress in the East.

Having then no intention to quit India for some time, he resolved to acquire some knowledge in the Shanscrita language; the grand repository of the religion, philosophy and history of the Hindoos. With this view, he prevailed upon his noble friend the Brahmin, to procure for him a Pundit, from the university of Benaris, well versed in the Shanscrita, and master of all the knowledge of that learned body. But before he had made any considerable progress in his studies, an unexpected change of affairs in Bengal, broke off all his literary schemes. He found that the time he had to remain in India would be too short to acquire the Shanscrita. He determined therefore, through the medium of the Persian language, and through the vulgar tongue of the Hindoos, to inform himself as much as possible, concerning the mythology and philosophy of the Brahmins. He, for this purpose, procured some of the principle Shasters, and his Pundit explained to him, as many passages of those curious books, as served to give him a general idea of the doctrine which they contain.

It is but justice to the Brahmins to confess that the author of this dissertation is very sensible of his own inability to illustrate, with that fullness and perspicuity which it deserves, that symbolical religion, which they are at so much pains to conceal from foreigners. He however can aver, that he has not misrepresented one single circumstance or tenet, though many may have escaped his observation.

The books which contain the religion and philosophy of the Hindoos, are distinguished by the name of Bedas. They are four in number, and like the sacred writings of other nations, are said to have been penned by the divinity. Beda in the Shanscrita, literally signifies Science: for these books not only treat of religious and moral duties, but of every branch of philosophical knowledge.

The Bedas are, by the Brahmins, held so sacred, that they permit no other sect to read them; and such is the influence of superstition and priest-craft over the minds of the other Casts in India, that they would deem it an unpardonable sin to satisfy their curiosity in that respect, were it even within the compass of their power. The Brahmins themselves are bound by such strong ties of religion, to confine those writings to their own tribe, that were any of them known to read them to others, he would be immediately excommunicated. This punishment is worse than even death itself among the Hindoos. The offender is not only thrown down from the noblest order to the most polluted Cast, but his posterity are rendered for ever incapable of being received into his former dignity.

All these things considered, we are not to wonder that the doctrine of the Bedas is so little known in Europe. Even the literary part of the Mahomedans of Asia, reckon it an abstruse and mysterious subject, and candidly confess, that it is covered with a veil of darkness, which they could never penetrate. Some have indeed supposed, that the learned Feizi,[a] brother to the celebrated Abul Fazil,[b] chief secretary to the Emperor Akbar,[c] had read the Bedas, and discovered the religious tenets contained in them to that renowned Prince. As the story of Feizi made a good deal of noise in the east, it may not be improper to give the particulars of it in this place.

Mahummud Akbar being a prince of elevated and extensive ideas, was totally divested of those prejudices for his own religion, which men of inferior parts not only imbibe with their mother's

[a] Faizi (1547–95). [b] Abu 'l Fazl Allami (1557–1602).
[c] Akbar (1542–1605) was Emperor from 1556.

milk, but retain throughout their lives. Though bred in all the strictness of the Mahommedan faith, his great soul in his riper years, broke those chains of superstition and credulity, with which his tutors had, in his early youth, fettered his mind. With a design to chuse his own religion, or rather from curiosity, he made it his business to enquire minutely into all the systems of divinity, which prevailed among mankind. The story of his being instructed in the christian tenets, by a missionary from Portugal, is too well known in Europe to require a place in this dissertation. As almost all religions admit of proselytes, Akbar had good success in his enquiries, till he came to his own subjects the Hindoos. Contrary to the practice of all other religious sects, they admit of no converts; but they allow that every one may go to heaven his own way, though they perhaps suppose, that theirs is the most expeditious method to obtain that important end. They chuse rather to make a mystery of their religion, than impose it upon the world, like the Mahommedans, with the sword, or by means of the stake, after the manner of some pious christians.

Not all the authority of Akbar could prevail with the Brahmins to reveal the principles of their faith. He was therefore obliged to have recourse to artifice to obtain the information which he so much desired. The Emperor, for this purpose, concerted a plan with his chief secretary, Abul Fazil, to impose Feizi, then a boy, upon the Brahmins, in the character of a poor orphan of their tribe. Feizi being instructed in his part, was privately sent to Benaris, the principal seat of learning among the Hindoos. In that city the fraud was practised on a learned Brahmin, who received the boy into his house, and educated him as his own son.

When Feizi, after ten years study, had acquired the Shanscrita language, and all the knowledge of which the learned of Benaris were possessed, proper measures were taken by the Emperor to secure his safe return. Feizi it seems, during his residence with his patron the Brahmin, was smitten with the beauty of his only daughter; and indeed the ladies of the Brahmin race are the handsomest in Hindostan. The old Brahmin saw the mutual passion of the young pair with pleasure, and as he loved Feizi for his uncommon abilities, he offered him his daughter in marriage. Feizi, perplexed between love and gratitude, at length discovered himself to the good old man, fell down at his feet, and grasping his knees, solicited with tears for forgiveness, for the great crime he had committed against his indulgent benefactor. The Brahmin, struck dumb with astonishment, uttered not one word of reproach. He drew a dagger, which he always carried on his girdle, and prepared to plunge it in his own breast. Feizi seized his hand, and conjured him, that if yet any atonement could be made for the injury he had done him, he himself would swear to deny him nothing. The Brahmin, bursting into tears, told him, that if Feizi should grant him two requests, he would forgive him, and consent to live. Feizi, without any hesitation, consented, and the Brahmin's requests were, that he should never translate the Bedas, nor repeat the creed of the Hindoos.

How far Feizi was bound by his oath not to reveal the doctrine of the Bedas to Akbar is uncertain; but that neither he, nor any other person, ever translated those books, is a truth beyond any dispute.[a] It is however well known, that the Emperor afterwards greatly favoured the Hindoo faith, and gave much offence to zealous Mahommedans, by practising some Indian customs which they thought savoured of idolatry. But the dispassionate part of mankind have always allowed, that Akbar was equally divested of all the follies of both the religious superstitions, which prevailed among his subjects.

To return from this digression, the Brahmins maintain, that the Bedas are the divine laws, which Brimha, at the creation of the world, delivered for the instruction of mankind. But they affirm that their meaning was perverted in the first age, by the ignorance and wickedness of some princes, whom they represent as evil spirits who then haunted the earth. They call those evil genii Dewtas, and tell many strange allegorical legends concerning them; such as, that the Bedas being lost, were afterwards recovered by Bishen, in the form of a fish, who brought them up from the bottom of the ocean, into which they were thrown by a Deo, or Demon.

[a] This story seems to have circulated widely. Anquetil Duperron (see above, pp. 3–4) heard that Faizi, after living three years at Benares 'habillé en Indou', had actually made a translation of the *Vedas* (*Zend-Avesta, ouvrage de Zoroastre* (Paris, 1771), I, cccxxxviii). One obvious difficulty about the story is that Faizi was in fact older than Abu 'l Fazl, although he did learn Sanskrit.

The first credible account we have of the Bedas, is, that about the commencement of the Cal Jug, of which æra the present year 1768, is the 4886th year, they were written, or rather collected by a great philosopher, and reputed prophet, called Beäss Muni, or Beäss the inspired. This learned man is otherwise called Krishen Basdeo, and is said to have lived in the reign of Judishter, in the city of Histanapore, upon the river Jumna, near the present city of Delhi.

The Brahmins do not give to Beäss Muni the merit of being the author of the Bedas. They however acknowledge, that he reduced them into the present form, dividing them into four distinct books, after having collected the detached pieces of which they are composed, from every part of India. It is, upon the whole, probable, that they are not the work of one man, on account of their immense bulk.

The Mahomedans of Asia, as well as some of the learned of Europe, have mistaken Brimha, an allegorical person, for some philosopher of repute in India, whom they distinguish by the disfigured names of Bruma, Burma, and Bramha, whom they suppose to have been the writer of the religious books of the Hindoos. Ferishta, in the history now given to the public, affirms, that Brimha was of the race of Bang, and flourished in the reign of Krishen, first monarch of Hindostan.[a] But the Brahmins deny, that any such person ever existed, which we have reason to believe is the truth; as Brimha in the Shanscrita language allegorically signifies Wisdom, one of the principal attributes of the supreme divinity.

The four Bedas contain 100,000 ashlogues or stanzas in verse, each of which consists of four lines. The first Beda is called Rug Beda, which signifies the science of divination, concerning which it principally treats. It also contains astrology, astronomy, natural philosophy, and a very particular account of the creation of matter, and the formation of the world.

The second Beda is distinguished by the name of Sheham. That word signifies piety or devotion, and this book accordingly treats of all religious and moral duties. It also contains many hymns in praise of the supreme being, as well as verses in honour of subaltern intelligences.

[a] *The History of Hindostan*, i, 10.

The third is the Judger Beda, which, as the word implies, comprehends the whole science of religious rites and ceremonies; such as fasts, festivals, purifications, penances, pilgrimages, sacrifices, prayers and offerings. They give the appellation of Obatar Bah to the fourth Beda. Obatar signifies in the Shanscrita, the being, or the essence, and Bah good; so that the Obatar Bah is literally the knowledge of the good being, and accordingly this book comprehends the whole science of theology and metaphysical philosophy.

The language of the Obatar Bah Beda is now become obsolete; so that very few Brahmins pretend to read it with propriety. Whether this proceeds from its great antiquity, or from its being wrote in an uncommon dialect of the Shanscrita, is hard to determine. We are inclined to believe that the first is the truth; for we can by no means agree with a late ingenious writer,[1] who affirms, that the Obatar Bah was written in a period posterior to the rest of the Bedas.[a]

It has been already observed, that the Bedas are written in the Shanscrita tongue. Whether the Shanscrita was, in any period of antiquity, the vulgar language of Hindostan, or was invented by the Brahmins, to be a mysterious repository for their religion and philosophy, is difficult to determine. All other languages, it is true, were casually invented by mankind, to express their ideas and wants; but the astonishing formation of the Shanscrita seems to be beyond the power of chance. In regularity of etymology and grammatical order, it far exceeds the Arabic. It, in short, bears evident marks, that it has been fixed upon rational principles, by a body of learned men, who studied regularity, harmony, and a wonderful simplicity and energy of expression.

Though the Shanscrita is amazingly copious, a very small grammar and vocabulary serve to illustrate the principles of the whole. In a treatise of a few pages,[b] the roots and primitives are all comprehended, and so uniform are the rules for derivations and inflections, that the etymon of every word is, with the greatest

---

[1] Mr Holwell: the author of the dissertation finds himself obliged to differ almost in every particular concerning the religion of the Hindoos, from that gentleman.

[a] See above, p. 59.

[b] Dow paid 60 rupees for a transcription of the *Mugdha-Bodha* grammar of Vopadeva, which he later presented to the British Museum (Add. MS 2831).

facility, at once investigated. The pronunciation is the greatest difficulty which attends the acquirement of the language to perfection. This is so quick and forcible, that a person, even before the years of puberty, must labour a long time before he can pronounce it with propriety; but when once that is attained to perfection, it strikes the ear with amazing boldness and harmony. The alphabet of the Shanscrita consists of fifty letters, but one half of these carry combined sounds, so that its characters in fact, do not exceed ours in number.

Before we shall proceed to the religion and philosophy of the Brahmins, it may not be improper to premise something concerning the most characteristical manners and customs of the Hindoos in general. The Hindoos are so called from Indoo or Hindoo, which, in the Shanscrita language, signifies the Moon; for from that luminary, and the sun, they deduce their fabulous origin. The author of the dissertation has in his possession, a long list of a dynasty of Kings, called Hindoo-buns or Chunder-buns, both of which words mean, the Children of the Moon. He also has a catalogue of the Surage-buns, or the Children of the Sun, from whom many of the Rajas of Hindostan pretend to derive their blood. Hindostan, the domestic appellation of India, is a composition of Hindoo, and Stan, a region; and the great river Indus takes its name from the people, and not the people from the river, as has been erroneously supposed in Europe.

The Hindoos have, from all antiquity, been divided into four great tribes, each of which comprehend a variety of inferior casts. These tribes do not intermarry, eat, drink, or in any manner associate with one another, except when they worship at the temple of Jagga-nat[1] in Orissa, where it is held a crime to make any distinction. The first and most noble tribe are the Brahmins, who alone can officiate in the priesthood, like the Levites among the Jews. They are not however excluded from government, trade, or agriculture, though they are strictly prohibited from all menial offices by their laws. They derive their name from Brimha,

---

[1] Jagga-nat signifies Lord of the creation. This is one of the names of Bishen and the Obatar, or Being, who is said to preside over the present period. He is represented under the figure of a fat man, sitting cross-legged, with his arms hanging down by his side as if they had no strength. This last circumstance alludes to the imbecility of this age. His temple is in the greatest repute of any now in India.

who they allegorically say, produced the Brahmins from his head, when he created the world.

The second in order is the Sittri tribe, who are sometimes distinguished by the name of Kittri or Koytri. They, according to their original institution, ought to be all military men; but they frequently follow other professions. Brimha is said to have produced the Kittri from his heart, as an emblem of that courage which warriors should possess.

The name of Beise or Bise is given to the third tribe. They are for the most part, merchants, bankers, and bunias or shopkeepers. These are figuratively said to have sprung from the belly of Brimha; the word Beish signifying a provider or nourisher. The fourth tribe is that of Sudder. They ought to be menial servants, and they are incapable to raise themselves to any superior rank. They are said to have proceeded from the feet of Brimha, in allusion to their low degree. But indeed it is contrary to the inviolable laws of the Hindoos, that any person should rise from an inferior cast into a higher tribe. If any therefore should be excommunicated from any of the four tribes, he and his posterity are forever shut out from society of every body in the nation, excepting that of the Harri cast,[a] who are held in utter detestation by all the other tribes, and are employed only in the meanest and vilest offices. This circumstance renders excommunication so dreadful, that any Hindoo will suffer the torture, and even death itself, rather than deviate from the article of his faith. This severity prevented all intermixture of blood between the tribes, so that, in their appearance, they seem rather four different nations, than members of the same community.

It is, as we have already observed, a principle peculiar to the Hindoo religion, not to admit of proselytes. Instead of being solicitous about gaining converts, they always make a mystery of their faith. Heaven, say they, is like a palace with many doors, and every one may enter in his own way. But this charitable disposition never encouraged other sects to settle among them, as they must have been excluded entirely from all the benefits of society.

[a] A scavenger caste (J. H. Hutton, *Caste in India*, 2nd ed. (Bombay, 1951), p. 280).

When a child is born, some of the Brahmins are called. They pretend, from the horoscope of his nativity, to foretel his future fortune, by means of some astrological tables, of which they are possessed. When this ceremony is over, they burn incense, and make an offering according to the circumstances of the parent; and without ever consulting them, tie the zinar[1] round the infant's neck, and impose a name upon him, according to their own fancy.

Between the age of seven and ten, the children are, by their parents, given away in marriage. The young pair are brought together, in order to contract an intimacy with one another. But when they approach to the years of puberty, they carefully separate them, till the female produces signs of womanhood. She then is taken from her parents to cohabit with her husband: nor is she ever after permitted to visit them. It is not lawful among the Hindoos to marry nearer than the eighth degree of kindred. Polygamy is permitted, but seldom practised; for they very rationally think, that one wife is sufficient for one man.

The extraordinary custom of the women burning themselves with their deceased husbands, has, for the most part, fallen into desuetude in India; nor was it ever reckoned a religious duty, as has been very erroneously supposed in the West.[a] This species of barbarity, like many others, rose originally from the foolish enthusiasm of feeble minds. In a text in the Bedas, conjugal affection and fidelity are thus figuratively inculcated: 'The woman, in short, who dies with her husband, shall enjoy life eternal with him in heaven.'[b] From this source the Brahmins themselves deduce this ridiculous custom, which is a more rational solution of it, than the story which prevails in Europe; that it was a political institution, made by one of the Emperors, to prevent wives from poisoning their husbands, a practice, in those days, common in Hindostan.

People of rank and those of the higher casts, burn their dead and throw some incense into the pile. Some throw the bodies of their friends into the Ganges, while others expose them on the

---

[1] A string which all the Hindoos wear, by way of charm or amulet.
[a] Cf. the opinions of Holwell (see above, p. 92) and Halhed (below, p. 179).
[b] This is not a Vedic text.

high ways, as a prey to vultures and wild beasts. There is one cast in the kingdom of Bengal, who barbarously expose their sick by the river's side to die there. They even sometimes choak them with mud, when they think them past hopes of recovery. They defend this inhuman custom by saying, that life is not an adequate recompence for the tortures of a lingering disease.

The Hindoos have a code of laws in the Nea Shaster.[a] Treason, incest, sacrilege, murder, adultery with the wife of a Brahmin, and theft, are capital crimes. Though the Brahmins were the authors of those laws, we do not find that they have exempted themselves from the punishment of death, when guilty of those crimes. This is one of those numerous fables, which modern travellers imported from the East. It is however certain, that the influence of the Brahmins is so great, and their characters as priests so sacred, that they escape in cases where no mercy would be shewn to the other tribes.

Petty offences are punished by temporary excommunications, pilgrimages, penances and fines, according to the degree of the crime, and the wealth of the guilty person. But as the Hindoos are now, for the most part, subject to the Mahommedans, they are governed by the laws of the Koran, or by the arbitrary will of the prince.

The Senasseys are a sect of mendicant philosophers, commonly known by the name of Fakiers, which literally signifies poor people. These idle and pretended devotees, assemble sometimes in armies of ten or twelve thousand, and, under a pretext of making pilgrimages to certain temples, lay whole countries under contribution. These saints wear no clothes, are generally very robust, and convert the wives of the less holy part of mankind to their own use, upon their religious progresses. They admit any man of parts into their number, and they take great care to instruct their disciples in every branch of knowledge, to make the order the more revered among the vulgar.

When this naked army of robust saints direct their march to any temple, the men of the provinces through which their road lies, very often fly before them, notwithstanding of the sanctified

---

[a] Dow seems to have derived this term from a misunderstanding of the etymology of the word *Nyaya*, see below, p. 130.

character of the Fakiers. But the women are in general more resolute, and not only remain in their dwellings, but apply frequently for the prayers of those holy persons, which are found to be most effectual in cases of sterility. When a Fakier is at prayers with the lady of the house, he leaves either his slipper or his staff at the door, which if seen by the husband, effectually prevents him from disturbing their devotion. But should he be so unfortunate as not to mind those signals, a sound drubbing is the inevitable consequence of his intrusion.

Though the Fakiers inforce with their arms, that reverence which the people of Hindostan have naturally for their order, they inflict voluntary penances of very extraordinary kinds upon themselves, to gain more respect. These fellows sometimes hold up one arm in a fixed position till it becomes stiff, and remains in that situation during the rest of their lives. Some clench their fists very hard, and keep them so till their nails grow into their palms, and appear through the back of their hands. Others turn their faces over one shoulder, and keep them in that situation, till they fix for ever their heads looking backward. Many turn their eyes to the point of their nose, till they have lost the power of looking in any other direction. These last, pretend sometimes to see what they call the sacred fire, which vision, no doubt, proceeds from some disorder arising from the distortion of the optic nerves.

It often appears to Europeans in India, a matter of some ridicule to converse with those distorted and naked philosophers; though their knowledge and external appearance, exhibit a very striking contrast. Some are really what they seem, enthusiasts; but others put on the character of sanctity, as a cloak for their pleasures. But what actually makes them a public nuisance, and the aversion of poor husbands, is, that the women think they derive some holiness to themselves, from an intimacy with a Fakier.

Many other foolish customs, besides those we have mentioned, are peculiar to those religious mendicants. But enthusiastic penances are not confined to them alone. Some of the vulgar, on the fast of Opposs, suspend themselves on iron hooks, by the flesh of the shoulder-blade, to the end of a beam. This beam turns round with great velocity, upon a pivot, on the head of a high pole.

The enthusiast not only seems insensible of pain, but very often blows a trumpet as he is whirled round above, and, at certain intervals, sings a song to the gaping multitude below; who very much admire his fortitude and devotion. This ridiculous custom is kept up to commemorate the sufferings of a martyr, who was in that manner, tortured for his faith.

To dwell longer upon the characteristical customs and manners of the Hindoos, would extend this dissertation too far. Some more particulars concerning that nation, will naturally arise from an investigation of their religion and philosophy. This last was the capital design of this introductory discourse; and we hope to be able to throw a new, if not a compleat light, on a subject hitherto little understood in the West. Some writers have very lately given to the world, an unintelligible system of the Brahmin religion; and they affirm, that they derived their information from the Hindoos themselves. This may be the case, but they certainly conversed upon that subject only with the inferior tribes, or with the unlearned part of the Brahmins: and it would be as ridiculous to hope for a true state of the religion and philosophy of the Hindoos from those illiterate casts, as it would be in a Mahommedan in London, to rely upon the accounts of a parish beadle, concerning the most abstruse points of the Christian faith; or, to form his opinion of the principles of the Newtonian philosophy, from a conversation with an English carman.

The Hindoos are divided into two great religious sects: the followers of the doctrine of the Bedang,[b] and those who adhere to the principles of the Neadirsin.[c] As the first are esteemed the most orthodox, as well as the most ancient, we shall begin to explain their opinions, by extracts literally translated from the original Shaster,[1] which goes by the name of Bedang.[d]

[1] Shaster literally signifies Knowledge: but it is commonly understood to mean a book which treats of divinity and the sciences. There are many Shasters among the Hindoos; so that those writers who affirmed, that there was but one Shaster in India, which, like the Bible of the Christians, or Koran of the followers of Mahommed, contained the first principles of the Brahmin faith, have deceived themselves and the public.[a]

[a] Dow is referring to Holwell.   [b] *Vedanta.*   [c] *Nyaya.*

[d] This extract and the one that follows it are typical accounts of the Creation as given in the *Puranas*. They seem to be based on passages in the *Bhagavat Purana* (cf. J. M. Sanyal, *The Srimad Bhagabatam* (Calcutta, 1952), book II, chap. v; book III, chap. XII). The immense popularity of the *Bhagavat Purana* and the frequency

Bedang, the title of the Shaster, or commentary upon the Bedas, concerning which we are about to treat, is a word compounded of Beda, *science*, and Ang, *body*. The name of this Shaster therefore, may be literally translated, the body of science. This book has, in Europe, been erroneously called Vedam;[a] and it is an exposition of the doctrine of the Bedas, by that great philosopher and prophet Beäss Muni, who, according to the Brahmins, flourished about four thousand years ago.[b] The Bedang is said to have been revised some ages after Beäss Muni, by one Sirrider Swami,[c] since which it has been reckoned sacred, and not subject to any further alterations. Almost all the Hindoos of the Decan, and those of the Malabar and Coromandel coasts, are of the sect of the Bedang.[d]

This commentary opens with a dialogue between Brimha,[1] the Wisdom of the Divinity; and Narud[2] or Reason, who is represen-

with which it was rendered into Indian vernaculars meant that it was widely encountered by Europeans. A French translation from a Tamil version was to arouse much comment (J. de Guignes, 'Reflexions sur un livre Indien intitulé Bagavadam', *Mémoires de l'Académie royale des Inscriptions et Belles Lettres*, XXXVIII (1770–2), 312 ff). It is not clear why Dow should have attached the term *Vedanta* to his extracts; the philosophical assumptions in them seem, in fact, to be those of the *Samkhya* school, as is characteristic of the *Puranas*.

[1] Brimha is the genitive case of Brimh, which is a primitive signifying God. He is called Brimha or Wisdom, the first attribute of the supreme divinity. The divine wisdom, under the name of Brimha, is figuratively represented with one head, having four faces, looking to the four quarters, alluding to his seeing all things. Upon the head of this figure is a crown, an emblem of power and dominion. He has four hands, implying, the omnipotence of divine wisdom. In the first hand he holds the four Bedas, as a symbol of knowledge, in the second a scepter, as a token of authority; and in the third a ring, or compleat circle, as an emblem of eternity. Brimha holds nothing in the fourth hand, which implies, that the Wisdom of God is always ready to lend his aid to his creatures. He is represented riding upon a goose, the emblem of simplicity among the Hindoos. The latter circumstance is intended to imply the simplicity of the operations of nature, which is but another name for the wisdom of the divinity. These explications of the insignia of Brimha, were given by the Brahmin, and are, by no means, conjectures of the author of this dissertation.

[2] Narud literally signifies Reason, emphatically called the son of the Wisdom of God. He is said to be the first-born of the Munis, of whom hereafter.

[a] This name, the Tamil equivalent of *Veda*, was indiscriminately applied in Europe to Hindu holy books (Yule and Burnell, *Hobson-Jobson*, pp. 962–3).

[b] All the *Puranas* were traditionally ascribed to Vyasa.

[c] The commentary on the *Bhagavat Purana* by Sridhara Swami was apparently well known in eighteenth-century Bengal (C. Wilkins, *A Catalogue of Sanscrita Manuscripts presented to the Royal Society by Sir William and Lady Jones* (1798), p. 5).

[d] The dominance of *Vedanta* thought in south India had been noted by Père Pons (see above, p. 18) in 1740 (*Lettres édifiantes et curieuses*, XXVI (1743), 247).

ted as the son of Brimha. Narud desires to be instructed by his father, and for that purpose, puts the following questions to him.

NARUD: O father! thou first of God,[1] thou art said to have created the world, and thy son Narud, astonished at what he beholds, is desirous to be instructed how all these things were made.

BRIMHA: Be not deceived, my son! Do not imagine that I was the creator of the world, independent of the divine mover,[2] who is the great original essence,[3] and creator of all things. Look, therefore, only upon me as the instrument of the great Will,[4] and a part of his being, whom he called forth to execute his eternal designs.

NARUD: What shall we think of God?

BRIMHA: Being immaterial,[5] he is above all conception; being invisible,[6] he can have no form;[7] but, from what we behold in his works, we may conclude that he is eternal,[8] omnipotent,[9] knowing all things,[10] and present every where.[11]

NARUD: How did God create the world?

BRIMHA: Affection,[12] dwelt with God, from all eternity. It was of three different kinds, the creative,[13] the preserving,[14] and the destructive.[15] This first is represented by Brimha, the second by Bishen,[16] and the third by Shibah.[17] You, O Narud! are taught to worship all the three, in various shapes and likenesses, as the creator,[18] the preserver,[19] and the destroyer.[20] The affection of God then produced power,[21] and power at a proper con-

---

[1] Brimh.   [2] The supreme divinity.

[3] Pirrim Purrus; from Pir first, and Purrus essence or being.

[4] Ish-Bur; from Ish will, and Bur great; commonly pronounced Ishur. This is one of the thousand names of God, which have so much perplexed the writers of Europe. In the answer of Brimha, mention is made of the first three great deities of the Hindoos; which three, however, they by no means worship as distinct beings from God, but only as his principal attributes.   [5] Nid-akar.

[6] Oderissa.   [7] Sirba-Sirrup.   [8] Nitteh.   [9] Ge-itcha.   [10] Subittera-dirsi.

[11] Surba-Birsi. These are the very terms used in the Bedang, in the definition of God, which we have literally translated in the text. Whether we, who profess christianity, and call the Hindoos by the detestable names of Pagans and Idolaters, have higher ideas of the supreme divinity, we shall leave to the unprejudiced reader to determine.

[12] Maiah, which signifies either affection or passion.

[13] Redjo-goon, the creative quality.

[14] Sittohgoon, the preserving quality.

[15] Timmugoon, the destructive quality.

[16] The preserver; Providence is personified under the name of Bishen.

[17] Shibah, the foe of good.

[18] Naat.   [19] Bishen.

[20] Shibah. The Hindoos worship the destructive attribute of the divinity, under the name of Shibah; but they do not mean evil by Shibah, for they affirm, that there is no such thing but what proceeds from the free agency of man.   [21] Jotna.

junction of time[1] and fate,[2] embraced goodness,[3] and produced matter.[4] The three qualities then acting upon matter, produced the universe in the following manner. From the opposite actions of the creative and destructive quality in matter, self-motion[5] first arose. Self-motion was of three kinds; the first inclining to plasticity,[6] the second to discord,[7] and the third to rest.[8] The discordant actions then produced the Akash,[9] which invisible element possessed the quality of conveying sound; it produced air,[10] a palpable element, fire,[11] a visible element, water,[12] a fluid element, and earth,[13] a solid element.

The Akash dispersed itself abroad. Air formed the atmosphere; fire, collecting itself, blazed forth in the host of heaven;[14] water rose to the surface of the earth, being forced from beneath by the gravity of the latter element. Thus broke forth the world from the veil of darkness, in which it was formerly comprehended by God. Order rose over the universe. The seven heavens were formed,[15] and the seven worlds were fixed in their places; there to remain till the great dissolution,[16] when all things shall be absorbed[17] into God.

God seeing the earth in full bloom, and that vegetation[18] was strong from its seeds, called forth for the first time, Intellect,[19] which he endued with various organs and shapes, to form a diversity of animals[20] upon the earth. He endued the animals with five senses, feeling, seeing, smelling, tasting, and hearing.[21] But to man he gave reflexion[22] to raise him above the beasts of the field.

---

[1] Kaal.   [2] Addaristo.

[3] Pir-kirti, from *Pir* good, and *Kirti* action. God's attribute of goodness, is worshipped as a Goddess, under the name of Pirkirti, and many other appellations, which comprehend all the virtues. It has been ridiculously supposed in Europe, that Purrus, and Pirkirti were the first man and woman, according to the system of the Hindoos; whereas by Purrus is meant God, or emphatically, *the Being*; and by Pirkirti, his attribute of goodness.

[4] Mohat. In other places of the Bedang, matter is distinguished by the name of Maha-tit, *the great substance.*   [5] Ahankar. The word literally signifies self-action.

[6] Rajas.   [7] Tamas.   [8] Satig.

[9] A kind of celestial element. The Bedang in another place, speaks of akash as a pure impalpable element, through which the planets move. This element, says the philosopher, makes no resistance, and therefore the planets continue their motion, from the first impulse which they received from the hand of Brimha or God; nor will they stop, says he, till he shall seize them in the midst of their course.

[10] Baiow.   [11] Tege.   [12] Joal.   [13] Prittavi.

[14] Dewta; of which Surage the Sun is first in rank.

[15] The names of the seven heavens are, Bu, Buba, Surg, Moha, Junnoh, Tapu, and Sutteh. The seven worlds are, Ottal, Bittal, Suttal, Joal, Tallattal, Rissatal, and Pattal. The author of the dissertation, by a negligence which he very much regrets, forgot to get the proper explanation of those names, or the uses to which the seven heavens were converted.   [16] Mah-pirly.   [17] Mucht.

[18] Birgalotta.   [19] Mun.   [20] Jount.

[21] The five senses are, Suppursina, Chowkowna, Nasiga, Rissina, Kurnowa.

[22] Manus.

The creatures were created male and female,[1] that they might propagate their species upon the earth. Every herb bore the seed of its kind, that the world might be cloathed with verdure, and all animals provided with food.

NARUD: What dost thou mean, O Father! by intellect?

BRIMHA: It is a portion of the Great Soul[2] of the universe, breathed into all creatures, to animate them for a certain time.

NARUD: What becomes of it after death?

BRIMHA: It animates other bodies, or returns like a drop into that unbounded ocean from which it first arose.

NARUD: Shall not then the souls of good men receive rewards? Nor the souls of the bad meet with punishment?

BRIMHA: The souls of men are distinguished from those of other animals; for the first are endued with reason[3] and with a consciousness of right and wrong. If therefore man shall adhere to the first, as far as his powers shall extend, his soul, when disengaged from the body by death, shall be absorbed into the divine essence, and shall never more re-animate flesh. But the souls of those who do evil,[4] are not, at death, disengaged from all the elements. They are immediately cloathed with a body of fire, air, and akash, in which they are, for a time, punished in hell.[5] After the season of their grief is over, they re-animate other bodies; but till they shall arrive at a state of purity, they can never be absorbed into God.

NARUD: What is the nature of that absorbed state[6] which the souls of good men enjoy after death?

BRIMHA: It is a participation of the divine nature, where all passions are utterly unknown, and where consciousness is lost in bliss.[7]

NARUD: Thou sayst, O Father! that unless the soul is perfectly pure, it cannot be absorbed into God: now, as the actions of the generality o men are partly good, and partly bad, whither are their spirits sent immediately after death?

[1] Nir and Madda signifies male and female.
[2] Purmattima literally signifies the *great soul*.
[3] Upiman.   [4] Mund.
[5] Nirick. The Hindoos reckon above eighty kinds of hells, each proportioned to the degree of the wickedness of the persons punished there. The Brahmins have no idea that all the sins that a man can commit in the short period of his life, can deserve eternal punishment; nor that all the virtues he can exercise, can merit perpetual felicity in heaven.
[6] Muchti.
[7] It is somewhat surprising, that a state of unconsciousness, which in fact is the same with annihilation, should be esteemed by the Hindoos as the supreme good; yet so it is, that they always represent the *absorbed state*, as a situation of perfect insensibility, equally destitute of pleasure and of pain. But Brimha seems here to imply, that it is a kind of delirium of joy.

B R I M H A : They must atone for their crimes in hell, where they must remain
for a space proportioned to the degree of their iniquities; then they rise
to heaven to be rewarded for a time for their virtues; and from thence
they will return to the world, to reanimate other bodies.

N A R U D : What is time?[1]

B R I M H A : Time existed from all eternity with God: but it can only be esti-
mated since motion was produced, and only be conceived by the mind,
from its own constant progress.

N A R U D : How long shall this world remain?

B R I M H A : Until the four jugs shall have revolved. Then Rudder[2] with the
ten spirits of dissolution shall roll a comet under the moon, that shall
involve all things in fire, and reduce the world into ashes. God shall
then exist alone, for matter will be totally annihilated.[3]

Here ends the first chapter of the Bedang. The second treats of
providence and free will; a subject so abstruse, that it was impossible to understand it, without a compleat knowledge of the
Shanscrita. The author of the Bedang, thinking perhaps, that the
philosophical catechism which we have translated above, was too
pure for narrow and superstitious minds, has inserted into his
work, a strange allegorical account of the creation, for the purposes of vulgar theology. In this tale, the attributes of God, the
human passions and faculties of the mind are personified, and

[1] Kaal. It may not be improper, in this place, to say something concerning the
Hindoo method of computing time. Their least subdivision of time is, the Nemish, or
twinkling of an eye. Three Nemishs make one Kaan, fifty Kaan one Ligger, ten
Liggers one Dind, two Dinds one Gurry, equal to forty-five of our minutes; four
Gurries one Pâr, eight Pârs one Dien or day, fifteen Diens one Packa, two Packas
one Mâsh, two Mâshes one Ribbi, three Ribbis one Aioon or year, which only consists of 360 days, but when the odd days, hours and minutes, wanting of a solar year,
amount to one revolution of the moon, an additional month is made to that year to
adjust the Callendar. A year of 360 days, they reckon but one day to the Dewtas or
host of heaven; and they say, that twelve thousand of those planetary years, make
one revolution of the four Jugs or periods, into which they divide the ages of the
world. The Sittoh Jug or age of truth contained, according to them, four thousand
planetary years. The Treta Jug, or age of three, contained three thousand years. The
Duapur Jug, or age of two, contained two thousand; and the Kalle Jug, or age of pollution, consists of only one thousand. To these they add two other periods, between the
dissolution and renovation of the world, which they call Sundeh, and Sundass, each of
a thousand planetary years; so that from one Maperly, or great dissolution of all
things, to another, there are 3,720,000 of our years. *a*

[2] The same with Shibah, the destroying quality of God.
Nisht.

a Cf. the versions given by Holwell (above, p. 105), Halhed and Jones (below
pp. 158, 263).

introduced upon the stage. As this allegory may afford matter of some curiosity to the public, we shall here translate it.

Brimh existed from all eternity, in a form of infinite dimensions. When it pleased him to create the world, he said, Rise up, O Brimha.[1] Immediately a spirit of the colour of flame issued from his navel, having four heads and four hands, Brimha gazing round, and seeing nothing but the immense image, out of which he had proceeded, he travelled a thousand years, to endeavour to comprehend its dimensions. But after all his toil, he found himself as much at a loss as before.

Lost in amazement, Brimha gave over his journey. He fell prostrate and praised what he saw, with his four mouths. The almighty, then, with a voice like ten thousand thunders, was pleased to say: Thou hast done well, O Brimha, for thou canst not comprehend me! Go and create the world. How can I create it? Ask of me, and power shall be given unto thee. O God, said Brimha, thou art almighty in power!

Brimha forthwith perceived the idea of things, as if floating before his eyes. He said, Let them be, and all that he saw became real before him. Then fear struck the frame of Brimha, lest those things should be annihilated. O immortal Brimh! he cried, who shall preserve those things which I behold? In the instant a spirit of a blue colour issued from Brimha's mouth, and said aloud, I will. Then shall thy name be Bishen,[2] because thou hast undertaken to preserve all things.

Brimha then commanded Bishen to go and create all animals, with vegetables for their subsistance, to possess that earth which he himself had made. Bishen forthwith created all manner of beasts, fish, foul, insects and reptiles. Trees and grass rose also beneath his hands, for Brimha had invested him with power. But man was still wanting to rule the whole: and Brimha commanded Bishen to form him. Bishen began the work, but the men he made were idiots with great bellies, for he could not inspire them with knowledge; so that in every thing but in shape, they resembled the beasts of the field. They had no passion but to satisfy their carnal appetites.

Brimha, offended at the men, destroyed them, and produced four persons from his own breath, whom he called by four different names. The name of the first was Sinnoc,[3] of the second, Sinnunda,[4] of the third, Sonnatin,[5] and of the fourth, Sonninkunar.[6] These four persons were ordered by Brimha, to rule over the creatures, and to possess for ever the world. But they refused to do anything but to praise God, having nothing of the destructive quality[7] in their composition.

Brimha, for this contempt of his orders, became angry, and lo! a brown spirit started from between his eyes. He sat down before Brimha, and began to weep: then lifting up his eyes, he asked him, ' Who am I, and where shall

[1] The wisdom of God.   [2] The providence of God.
[3] Body.   [4] Life.
[5] Permanency.   [6] Intellectual existence.
[7] Timmu-goon.

be the place of my abode?' Thy name shall be Rudder,[1] said Brimha, and all nature shall be the place of thine abode. But rise up, O Rudder! and form man to govern the world.

Rudder immediately obeyed the orders of Brimha. He began the work, but the men he made were fiercer than tigers, having nothing but the destructive quality in their compositions. They, however, soon destroyed one another, for anger was their only passion. Brimha, Bishen, and Rudder then joined their different powers. They created ten men, whose names were Narud, Dico, Bashista, Birga, Kirku, Pulla, Pulista, Ongira, Otteri and Murichi.[2] The general appellation of the whole, was the Munies.[3] Brimha then produced Dirmo[4] from his breast, Adirmo[5] from his back, Loab[6] from his lip, and Kam[7] from his heart. This last being a beautiful female, Brimha looked upon her with amorous eyes. But the Munies told him, that she was his own daughter; upon which he shrunk back, and produced a blushing virgin called Ludja.[8] Brimha thinking his body defiled by throwing his eyes upon Kam, changed it, and produced ten women, one of which was given to each of the Munies.

In this division of the Bedang Shaster, there is a long list of the Surage Buns, or children of the sun, who, it is said, ruled the world in the first periods. But as the whole is a mere dream of imagination, and scarcely the belief of the Hindoo children and women, we shall not trespass further on the patience of the public with these allegories. The Brahmins of former ages wrote many volumes of romances upon the lives and actions of those pretended kings, inculcating, after their manner, morality by fable. This was the grand fountain from which the religion of the vulgar in India was corrupted; if the vulgar of any country require any adventitious aid to corrupt their ideas, upon so mysterious a subject.

Upon the whole, the opinions of the author of the Bedang, upon the subject of religion, are not unphilosophical. He maintains that the world was created out of nothing by God, and that it will be again annihilated. The unity, infinity and omnipotence of the supreme divinity are inculcated by him: for though he presents us with a long list of inferior beings, it is plain that they are

---

[1] The weeper; because he was produced in tears. One of the names of Shibah, the destructive attribute of the Divinity.

[2] The significations of these ten names are in order, these: Reason, Ingenuity, Emulation, Humility, Piety, Pride, Patience, Charity, Deceit, Mortality.

[3] The Inspired.   [4] Fortune.

[5] Misfortune.   [6] Appetite.

[7] Love.   [8] Shame.

merely allegorical; and neither he nor the sensible part of his followers believe their actual existence. The more ignorant Hindoos, it cannot be denied, think that these subaltern divinities do exist, in the same manner, that Christians believe in angels: but the unity of God was always a fundamental tenet of the uncorrupted faith of the more learned Brahmins.

The opinion of this philosopher, that the soul, after death, assumes a body of the purer elements, is not peculiar to the Brahmins. It descended from the Druids of Europe, to the Greeks, and was the same with the ἐιδωλον[a] of Homer. His idea of the manner of the transmigration of the human soul into various bodies, is peculiar to himself. As he holds it as a maxim that a portion of the Great Soul or God, animates every living thing; he thinks it no ways inconsistent, that the same portion that gave life to man, should afterwards pass into the body of any other animal. This transmigration does not, in his opinion, debase the quality of the soul: for when it extricates itself from the fetters of the flesh, it reassumes its original nature.

The followers of the Bedang Shaster do not allow that any physical evil exists. They maintain that God created all things perfectly good, but that man, being a free agent, may be guilty of moral evil: which, however, only respects himself and society, but is of no detriment to the general system of nature. God, say they, has no passion but benevolence: and being possessed of no wrath, he never punishes the wicked, but by the pain and affliction which are the natural consequences of evil actions. The more learned Brahmins therefore affirm, that the hell which is mentioned in the Bedang, was only intended as a mere bugbear to the vulgar, to inforce upon their minds, the duties of morality: for that hell is no other than a consciousness of evil, and those bad consequences which invariably follow wicked deeds.

Before we shall proceed to the doctrine of the Neadirsen Shaster, it may not be improper to give a translation of the first chapter of the Dirm Shaster,[b] which throws a clear light upon the religious tenets, common to both the grand sects of the Hindoos.

[a] Form.
[b] Presumably *Dharma Shastra*. It is not possible to identify the text from which Dow is quoting.

It is a dialogue between Brimha, or the wisdom of God; and Narud, or human reason.

NARUD: O thou first of God![1] Who is the greatest of all Beings?

BRIMHA: Brimh; who is infinite and almighty.

NARUD: Is he exempted from death?

BRIMHA: He is: being eternal and incorporeal.

NARUD: Who created the world?

BRIMHA: God, by his power.

NARUD: Who is the giver of bliss?

BRIMHA: Krishen: and whosoever worshippeth him, shall enjoy heaven.[2]

NARUD: What is his likeness?

BRIMHA: He hath no likeness: but to stamp some idea of him upon the minds of men, who cannot believe in an immaterial being, he is represented under various symbolical forms.

NARUD: What image shall we conceive of him?

BRIMHA: If your imagination cannot rise to devotion without an image; suppose with yourself, that his eyes are like the Lotos, his complexion like a cloud, his cloathing of the lightning of heaven, and that he hath four hands.

NARUD: Why should we think of the almighty in this form?

BRIMHA: His eyes may be compared to the Lotos, to show that they are always open, like that flower which the greatest depth of water cannot surmount. His complexion being like that of a cloud, is an emblem of that darkness with which he veils himself from mortal eyes. His cloathing is of lightning, to express that awful majesty which surrounds him: and his four hands are symbols of his strength and almighty power.

NARUD: What things are proper to be offered unto him?

BRIMHA: Those things which are clean, and offered with a grateful heart. But all things which by the law are reckoned impure, or have been defiled by the touch of a woman in her times; things which have been coveted by your own soul, seized by oppression, or obtained by deceit, or that have any natural blemish, are offerings unworthy of God.

NARUD: We are commanded then to make offerings to God of such things as are pure and without blemish, by which it would appear that God eateth and drinketh, like mortal man, or if he doth not, for what purpose are our offerings?

---

[1] Brimha, as we have already observed, is the genitive case of Brimh; as Wisdom is, by the Bramhins, reckoned the chief attribute of God.

[2] Krishen is derived from *Krish* giving, and *Ana* joy. It is one of the thousand names of God.

Alexander Dow

BRIMHA: God neither eats nor drinks like mortal men. But if you love not God, your offerings will be unworthy of him; for as all men covet the good things of this world, God requires a free offering of their substance, as the strongest testimony of their gratitude and inclinations towards him.

NARUD: How is God to be worshipped?

BRIMHA: With no selfish view; but for love of his beauties, gratitude for his favours, and for admiration of his greatness.

NARUD: How can the human mind fix itself upon God, being, that it is in its nature changeable, and perpetually running from one object to another?

BRIMHA: True: the mind is stronger than an elephant, whom men have found means to subdue, though they have never been able entirely to subdue their own inclinations. But the ankush[1] of the mind is true wisdom, which sees into the vanity of all worldly things.

NARUD: Where shall we find true wisdom?

BRIMHA: In the society of good and wise men.

NARUD: But the mind, in spite of restraint, covets riches, women, and all worldly pleasures. How are these appetites to be subdued?

BRIMHA: If they cannot be overcome by reason, let them be mortified by penance. For this purpose it will be necessary to make a public and solemn vow, lest your resolution should be shaken by the pain which attends it.

NARUD: We see that all men are mortal, what state is there after death?

BRIMHA: The souls of such good men as retain a small degree of worldly inclinations, will enjoy Surg[2] for a time; but the souls of those who are holy, shall be absorbed into God, never more to reanimate flesh. The wicked shall be punished in Nirick[3] for a certain space, and afterwards their souls are permitted to wander in search of new habitations of flesh.

NARUD: Thou, O father, dost mention God as one; yet we are told, that Râm, whom we are taught to call God, was born in the house of Jessarit: that Kishen, whom we call God, was born in the house of Basdeo, and many others in the same manner. In what light are we to take this mystery?

BRIMHA: You are to look upon these as particular manifestations of the providence of God, for certain great ends, as in the case of the sixteen hundred women, called Gopi, when all the men of Sirendiep[4] were

---

[1] Ankush is an iron instrument used for driving elephants.

[2] Heaven. [3] Hell.

[4] The island of Ceylon.[a]

[a] According to the *Oxford English Dictionary*, Horace Walpole invented the word 'serendipity' in 1754 after reading a fairy story called *The Three Princes of Serendip*.

destroyed in war. The women prayed for husbands, and they had all their desires gratified in one night, and became with child. But you are not to suppose, that God, who is in this case introduced as the actor, is liable to human passions or frailties, being in himself, pure and incorporeal. At the same time he may appear in a thousand places, by a thousand names, and in a thousand forms; yet continue the same unchangeable, in his divine nature.

Without making any reflections upon this chapter of the Dirm Shaster, it appears evident, that the religion of the Hindoos has hitherto been very much misrepresented in Europe. The followers of the Neadirsen Shaster, differ greatly in their philosophy, from the sect of the Bedang, though both agree about the unity of the supreme being. To give some idea of the Neadirsen philosophy, we shall, in this place, give some extracts from that Shaster.

Neadirsen is a compound from Nea, signifying right, and Dirsen, to teach or explain; so that the word may be translated an *exhibition of truth*. Though it is not reckoned so antient as the Bedang, yet it is said to have been written by a philosopher called Goutam, near four thousand years ago.[a] The philosophy contained in this Shaster, is very abstruse and metaphysical; and therefore it is but justice to Goutam to confess, that the author of the dissertation, notwithstanding the great pains he took to have proper definitions of the terms, is by no means certain, whether he has fully attained his end. In this state of uncertainty he chose to adhere to the literal meaning of words, rather than by a free translation, to deviate perhaps from the sense of his author.

The generality of the Hindoos of Bengal, and all the northern provinces of Hindostan, esteem the Neadirsen a sacred Shaster;[b] but those of the Decan, Coromandel, and Malabar, totally reject it. It consists of seven volumes. The first only came to the hands of the author of the dissertation, and he has, since his arrival in

---

[a] Akshapada Gautama, the reputed founder of the *Nyaya* philosophical school, who probably lived at about the era of Christ.

[b] The *Nyaya* system seems to have been strongly entrenched in Bengal at the end of the eighteenth century. William Ward, the Baptist missionary, wrote that 'almost every town in Bengal contains some Nyayayiku schools...Indeed, the Nyayu has obtained so decided a preeminence over all the durshunus now studied in these parts, that it is read by nine students in ten, while the other durshunus are scarcely read at all' (*A View of the History, Literature, and Religion of the Hindoos*, 3rd ed. (1820), IV, 226).

England, deposited it in the British Museum.*ᵃ* He can say nothing
for certain, concerning the contents of the subsequent volumes;
only that they contain a compleat system of the theology and
philosophy of the Brahmins of the Neadirsen sect.*ᵇ*

Goutam does not begin to reason, *a priori*, like the writer of
the Bedang. He considers the present state of nature, and the
intellectual faculties, as far as they can be investigated by human
reason; and from thence he draws all his conclusions. He reduces
all things under six principal heads; substance, quality, motion,
species, assimulation and construction.[1] In substance, besides
time, space, life, and spirit, he comprehends earth, water, fire,
air, and akash. The four grosser elements, he says, come under
the immediate comprehension of our bodily senses; and akash,
time, space, soul and spirit, come under mental perception.

He maintains, that all objects of perception are equally real, as
we cannot comprehend the nature of a solid cubit, any more than
the same extent of space. He affirms, that distance in point of time
and space, are equally incomprehensible; so that if we shall admit, that space is a real existence, time must be so too. That the
soul, or vital principle, is a subtile element, which pervades all
things; for that intellect, which, according to experience in animals, cannot proceed from organization and vital motion only,
must be a principle totally distinct from them.

'The author of the Bedang,'[2] says Goutam, 'finding the impossibility of forming an idea of substance, asserts, that all
nature is a mere delusion. But as imagination must be acted upon
by some real existence, as we cannot conceive that it can act upon
itself, we must conclude, that there is something real, otherwise
philosophy is at an end.'

[1] These are in the original Shanscrita, Dirba, Goon, Kirmo, Summania,
Bishesh, Sammabae.

[2] A system of sceptical philosophy, to which many of the Brahmins adhere.

ᵃ Add. MS 4830 is inscribed 'Neadirsen Shaster. Alex. Dow', but it in fact consists of a number of detached pieces, none of which are related to Dow's translation
(C. Bendall, *Catalogue of the Sanskrit Manuscripts in the British Museum* (1902),
p. 147). I am grateful for Dr G. E. Marrison's assistance in locating this manuscript.

ᵇ What follows appears to be a fairly conventional exposition of the principles of
the *Nyaya*. There is a full commentary on the *Nyaya* with explanations of many of
the terms quoted by Dow in S. Das Gupta, *A History of Indian Philosophy* (reprinted
Cambridge, 1963), i, 274–366.

He then proceeds to explain what he means by his second principle, or Goon, which, says he, comprehends twenty-four things; form, taste, smell, touch, sound, number, quantity, gravity, solidity, fluidity, elasticity, conjunction, separation, priority, posteriority, divisibility, indivisibility, accident, perception, ease, pain, desire, aversion, and power.[1] Kirmo or motion is, according to him, of two kinds, direct and crooked. Sammania, or species, which is his third principle, includes all animals and natural productions. Bishesh he defines to be a tendency in matter towards productions; and Sammabae, or the last principle, is the artificial construction or formation of things, as a statue from a block of marble, a house from stones, or cloth from cotton.

Under these six heads, as we have already observed, Goutam comprehends all things which fall under our comprehension; and after having reasoned about their nature and origin, in a very philosophical manner, he concludes with asserting, that five things must of necessity be eternal. The first of these is Pirrum Attima, or the Great Soul, who, says he, is immaterial, one, invisible, eternal, and indivisible, possessing omniscience, rest, will, and power.[2]

The second eternal principle is the Jive Attima, or the vital soul, which he supposes is material, by giving it the following properties; number, quantity, motion, contraction, extension, divisibility, perception, pleasure, pain, desire, aversion, accident, and power. His reasons for maintaining, that the *vital soul* is different from the *great soul*, are very numerous, and it is upon this head that the followers of the Bedang and Neadirsen are principally divided. The first affirm that there is no soul in the universe but God, and the second strenuously hold that there is, as they cannot conceive, that God can be subject to such affections and passions as they feel in their own minds; or that he can possibly have a propensity to evil. Evil, according to the author of the Neadirsen Shaster, proceeds entirely from Jive Attima, or the vital soul. It is a selfish craving principle, never to be satis-

---

[1] The twenty-four things are, in the Shanscrita, in order these; Rup, Ris, Gund, Supursa, Shubardo, Sirika, Purriman, Gurritte, Dirbitte, Sinniha, Shanskan, Sangoog, Bibag, Pirrible, Particca, Apporticta, Addaristo, Bud, Suc, Duc, Itcha, Desh, Jotna.

[2] These properties of the divinity, are the following in order; Nidekaar, Akitta, Oderisa, Nitte, Apparticta, Budsirba, Suck, Itcha, Jotna.

fied; whereas God remains in eternal rest, without any desire but benevolence.

Goutam's third eternal principle is time or duration, which, says he, must of necessity have existed, while any thing did exist; and is therefore infinite. The fourth principle is space or extension, without which nothing could have been; and as it comprehends all quantity, or rather is infinite, he maintains, that it is indivisible and eternal. The fifth eternal principle is Akash, a subtile and pure element, which fills up the vacuum of space, and is compounded of purmans or quantities, infinitely small, indivisible and perpetual. 'God,' says he, 'can neither make nor annihilate these atoms, on account of the love which he bears to them, and the necessity of their existence; but they are, in other respects, totally subservient to his pleasure.'

'God,' says Goutam,

at a certain season, endued these atoms, as we may call them, with Bishesh or plasticity, by virtue of which they arranged themselves into four gross elements, fire, air, water, and earth. These atoms being, from the beginning, formed by God into the *seeds* of all productions, Jive Attima, or the vital soul, associated with them, so that animals, and plants of various kinds, were produced upon the face of the earth.

'The same vital soul,' continues Goutam, 'which before associated with the Purman of an animal, may afterwards associate with the Purman of a man.' This transmigration is distinguished by three names, Mirt, Mirren, and Pirra-purra-purvesh, which last literally signifies *the change of abode*. The superiority of man, according to the philosophy of the Neadirsen, consists only in the finer organization of his parts, from which proceed reason, reflexion, and memory, which the brutes only possess in an inferior degree, on account of their less refined organs.

Goutam supposes, with the author of the Bedang, that the soul after death, assumes a body of fire, air, and akash, unless in the carnal body, it has been so purified by piety and virtue, that it retains no selfish inclinations. In that case it is absorbed into the Great Soul of Nature, never more to reanimate flesh. Such, says the philosopher, shall be the reward of all those who worship God from pure love and admiration, without any selfish views. Those that shall worship God from motives of future happiness, shall be indulged with their desires in heaven, for a certain time. But they must also expiate their crimes, by suffering adequate punishments; and afterwards their souls will return to the earth, and wander about for new habitations. Upon their return to the earth, they shall casually associate with the first organized Purman they shall meet. They shall not retain any consciousness of their former state, unless it is revealed to them by God. But those favoured persons are very few, and are distinguished by the names of Jates Summon.[1]

The author of the Neadirsen teaches, for the purposes of morality, that the sins of the parents will descend to their posterity; and that, on the other hand, the virtues of the children will mitigate the punishments of the parents in Nirick, and hasten their return to the earth. Of all sins he holds ingratitude[2] to be the greatest. Souls guilty of that black crime, says he, will remain in hell, while the sun remains in heaven, or to the general dissolution of all things.

Intellect, says Goutam, is formed by the combined action of the senses. He reckons six senses: five external,[3] and one internal. The last he calls Manus, by which he seems to mean conscience. In the latter he comprehends reason, perception[4] and memory: and he concludes, that by their means only, mankind may possibly acquire knowledge. He then proceeds to explain the manner by which these senses act.

Sight, says he, arises from the Shanskar or repulsive qualities of bodies, by which the particles of light which fall upon them, are reflected back upon the eyes from all parts of their surfaces. Thus the object is painted in a perfect manner upon the organ of seeing, whither the soul repairs to receive the image. He affirms, that, unless the soul fixes its attention upon the figure in the eye, nothing can be perceived by the mind; for a man in a profound reverie, though his eyes are open to the light, perceives nothing. Colours, says Goutam, are particular feelings in the eye, which are proportioned to the quantity of light reflected from any solid body.

Goutam defines hearing in the same manner with the European

---

[1] The acquainted with their former state.
[2] Mitterdro.　　　[3] Chakous, Shraban, Rasan, Granap, Tawass.
[4] Onnuman, reason. Upimen, perception.

philosophers, with this difference only, that he supposes, that the sound which affects the ear, is conveyed through the purer element of akash, and not by the air; an error which is not very surprizing, in a speculative philosopher. Taste, he defines to be a sensation of the tongue and palate, occasioned by the particular form of those particles which compose food. Smell, says he, proceeds from the effluvia which arise from bodies to the nostrils. The feeling, which arises from touching, is occasioned by the contact of dense bodies with the skin, which, as well as the whole body, excepting the bones, the hair and the nails, is the organ of that sense. There runs, says he, from all parts of the skin, very small nerves to a great nerve, which he distinguishes by the name of Medda. This nerve is composed of two different coats, the one sensitive, and the other insensitive. It extends from the crown of the head, down the right side of the vertebrae to the right foot.[1] When the body becomes languid, the soul, fatigued with action, retires within the insensible coat, which checks the operation of the senses, and occasions sound sleep. But should there remain in the soul, a small inclination to action, it starts into the sensitive part of the nerve, and dreams immediately arise before it. These dreams, says he, invariably relate to something perceived before by the senses, though the mind may combine the ideas together at pleasure.

Manus, or conscience, is the internal feeling of the mind, when it is in no way affected by external objects. Onnuman, or reason, says Goutam, is that faculty of the soul which enables us to conclude that things and circumstances exist, from an analogy to things, which had before fallen under the conception of our bodily senses: for instance, when we see smoak, we conclude that it proceeds from a fire; when we see one end of a rope, we are persuaded that it must have another.

By reason, continues Goutam, men perceive the existence of God; which the Boad[a] or atheists deny, because his existence does not come within the comprehension of the senses. These atheists, says he, maintain, that there is no God but the universe;

[1] To save the credit of Goutam, in this place, it is necessary to observe, that anatomy is not at all known among the Hindoos, being strictly prohibited from touching a dead body, by the severest ties of religion.

[a] Buddhists.

that there is neither good nor evil in the world; that there is no such thing as a soul; that all animals exist, by a mere mechanism of the organs, or by a fermentation of the elements; and that all natural productions are but the fortuitous concourse of things.

The philosopher refutes these atheistical opinions, by a long train of arguments, such as have been often urged by European divines. Though superstition and custom may biass reason to different ends, in various countries, we find a surprising similarity in the arguments used by all nations, against the Boad, those common enemies of every system of religion.

'Another sect of the Boad', says Goutam, 'are of opinion that all things were produced by chance.'[1] This doctrine he thus refutes. Chance is so far from being the origin of all things, that it has but a momentary existence of its own; being alternately created and annihilated, at periods infinitely small, as it depends entirely on the action of real essences. This action is not accidental, for it must inevitably proceed from some natural cause. Let the dice be rattled eternally in the box, they are determined in their motion, by certain invariable laws. What therefore we call chance, is but an effect proceeding from causes which we do not perceive.

'Perception,' continues Goutam, 'is that faculty by which we instantaneously know things without the help of reason. This is perceived by means of relation, or some distinguishing property in things, such as high and low, long and short, great and small, hard and soft, cold and hot, black and white.'

Memory, according to Goutam, is the elasticity of the mind, and is employed in three different ways; on things present as to time, but absent as to place; on things past, and on things to come. It would appear from the latter part of the distinction, that the philosopher comprehends imagination in memory. He then proceeds to define all the original properties of matter, and all the passions and faculties of the mind. He then descants on the nature of generation.

'Generation,' says he,

may be divided into two kinds; jonidge, or generation by copulation; and adjonidge, generation without copulation. All animals are produced by the first, and all plants by the latter. The purman or seed of things, was formed

[1] Addaristo.

from the beginning, with all its parts. When it happens to be deposited in a matrix suitable to its nature, a soul associates with it; and, by assimulating more matter, it gradually becomes a creature or plant; for plants, as well as animals, are possessed of a portion of the *vital soul* of the world.

Goutam, in another place, treats diffusely of providence and free will. He divides the action of man under three heads: the will of God, the power of man, and casual or accidental events. In explaining the first, he maintains a particular providence; in the second, the freedom of will in man; and in the third, the common course of things, according to the general laws of nature. With respect to providence, though he cannot deny the possibility of its existence, without divesting God of his omnipotence, he supposes that the deity never exerts that power, but that he remains in eternal rest, taking no concern, neither in human affairs, nor in the course of the operations of nature.

The author of the Neadirsen maintains, that the world is subject to successive dissolutions and renovations at certain stated periods. He divides these dissolutions into the lesser and the greater. The lesser dissolution will happen at the end of a revolution of the Jugs. The world will be then consumed by fire, and the elements shall be jumbled together, and after a certain space of time, they will again resume their former order. When a thousand of those smaller dissolutions shall have happened, a Mahperley or great dissolution will take place. All the elements will then be reduced to their original Purmans or atoms, in which state they shall long remain. God will then, from his mere goodness and pleasure, restore Bishesh or plasticity. A new creation will arise; and thus things have revolved in succession, from the beginning, and will continue to do so to eternity.

These repeated dissolutions and renovations have furnished an ample field for the inventions of the Brahmins. Many allegorical systems of creation are upon that account contained in the Shasters. It was for this reason, that so many different accounts of the cosmogony of the Hindoos have been promulgated in Europe; some travellers adopting one system, and some another. Without deviating from the good manners due to those writers, we may venture to affirm, that their tales, upon this subject, are extreamly puerile, if not absurd. They took their accounts from any common

Brahmin, with whom they chanced to meet, and never had the curiosity or industry to go to the fountain head.

In some of the renovations of the world, Brimha, or the wisdom of God, is represented in the form of an infant with his toe in his mouth, floating on a comala or water flower, or sometimes upon a leaf of that plant, upon the watery abyss. The Brahmins mean no more by this allegory, than that at that time, the wisdom and designs of God will appear, as in their infant state. Brimha floating upon a leaf, shews the instability of things at that period. The toe which he sucks in his mouth, implies that infinite wisdom subsists of itself; and the position of Brimha's body is an emblem of the endless circle of eternity.

We see Brimha sometimes creeping forth from a winding shell. This is an emblem of the untraceable way by which divine wisdom issues forth from the infinite ocean of God. He, at other times, blows up the world with a pipe, which implies, that the earth is but a bubble of vanity, which the breath of his mouth can destroy. Brimha, in one of the renovations, is represented in the form of a snake, one end of which, is upon a tortoise which floats upon the vast abyss, and upon the other, he supports the world. The snake is the emblem of wisdom, the tortoise is a symbol of security, which figuratively signifies providence, and the vast abyss is the eternity and infinitude of God.

What has been already said has, it is hoped, thrown a new light on the opinions of the Hindoos, upon the subject of religion and philosophical inquiry. We find that the Brahmins, contrary to the ideas formed of them in the west, invariably believe in the unity, eternity, omniscience and omnipotence of God: that the polytheism of which they have been accused, is no more than a symbolical worship of the divine attributes, which they divide into three principal classes. Under the name of Brimha, they worship the wisdom and creative power of God; under the appellation of Bishen, his providential and preserving quality; and under that of Shibah, that attribute which tends to destroy.

This system of worship, say the Brahmins, arises from two opinions. The first is, that as God is immaterial, and consequently invisible, it is impossible to raise a proper idea of him, by any image in the human mind. The second is, that it is necessary to strike the gross ideas of man, with some emblems of God's attributes, otherwise, that all sense of religion will naturally vanish from the mind. They, for this purpose, have made symbolical representations of the three classes of the divine attributes; but they aver, that they do not believe them to be separate intelligences. Brimh, or the supreme divinity, has a thousand names; but the Hindoos would think it the grossest impiety to represent him under any form. 'The human mind,' say they, 'may form some conception of his attributes separately, but who can grasp the whole, within the circle of finite ideas?'

That in any age or country, human reason was ever so depraved as to worship the work of hands, for the creator of the universe, we believe to be an absolute deception, which arose from the vanity of the abettors of particular systems of religion. To attentive inquirers into the human mind, it will appear, that common sense, upon the affairs of religion, is pretty equally divided among all nations. Revelation and philosophy have, it is confessed, lopped off some of those superstitious excrescences and absurdities that naturally arise in weak minds, upon a subject so mysterious: but it is much to be doubted, whether the want of those necessary purifiers of religion, ever involved any nation in gross idolatry, as many ignorant zealots have pretended.

In India, as well as in many other countries, there are two religious sects; the one look up to the divinity, through the medium of reason and philosophy; while the others receive, as an article of their belief, every holy legend and allegory which have been transmitted down from antiquity. From a fundamental article in the Hindoo faith, that God is *the soul of the world*, and is consequently diffused through all nature, the vulgar revere all the elements, and consequently every great natural object, as containing a portion of God; nor is the infinity of the supreme being, easily comprehended by weak minds, without falling into this error. This veneration for different objects, has, no doubt, given rise among the common Indians, to an idea of subaltern intelligences; but the learned Brahmins, with one voice, deny the existence of inferior divinities; and, indeed, all their religious books of any antiquity, confirm that assertion.

3

Nathaniel Brassey Halhed, 'The Translator's Preface' to *A Code of Gentoo Laws*

Letter from Warren Hastings, Esq.

Governor-General of Fort-William, in Bengal, to the Court of Directors of the United Company of Merchants of England, Trading to the East-Indies

Honourable Sirs,

I have now the satisfaction to transmit to you a complete and corrected copy of a Translation of the Gentoo Code, executed with great ability, diligence and fidelity, by Mr. Halhed, from a Persian version of the original Shanscrit, which was undertaken under the immediate inspection of the Pundits or compilers of this work.

I have not time to offer any observations upon these productions; indeed they will best speak for themselves: I could have wished to have obtained an omission or amendment of some passages, to have rendered them more fit for the public eye; but the Pundits, when desired to revise them, could not be prevailed upon to make any alterations, as they declared, they had the sanction of their Shaster, and were therefore incapable of amendment; possibly these may be considered as essential parts of the work, since they mark the principles on which many of the Laws were formed, and bear the stamp of a very remote antiquity, in which the refinements of society were less known, and the manners more influenced by the natural impulse of the passions.

I have the honour to be, with the greatest respect,

Honourable Sirs,
Your most obedient,
And most faithful humble Servant,
Warren Hastings

Fort-William,
27th March, 1775

Nathaniel Brassey Halhed

Letter

To the Chairman of the Court of Directors of the
United East-India Company, dated at Calcutta, 6th August, 1775.

Sir,

I have too long served under Mr. Hastings not to be convinced, that he would never have suffered the accompanying address to go home in his enclosure; reduced therefore to the necessity of eluding his knowledge, I have taken the liberty, by this only possible method, to express my gratitude for his favours: and the peculiar circumstances of the case will, I hope, apologize to you, Sir, for the abruptness of this intrusion. I humbly request, that when the *Code of Gentoo Laws, Preliminary Treatise, &c.* shall come to be printed, you will also be pleased to permit the publication of this address.

I am, with the greatest respect,

Sir,

Your most obedient humble Servant,
Nathaniel Brassey Halhed

To the Hon*ble* Warren Hastings, Esq.

Governor-General of the British Settlements in the East-Indies, &c. &c.

Honourable Sir,

By the publication of the collection of Gentoo Laws, made under your immediate authority, I find myself involuntarily held forth to the public as an author, almost as soon as I have commenced to be a man.[a]

It is therefore with some propriety that I claim to this work the continuation of your patronage, which as it at first selected me from a number of more worthy competitors to undertake the task, so it has by constant assistance and encouragement been the entire instrument of its completion. Indeed, if all the lights, which at different periods have been thrown upon this subject, by your happy suggestions, had been with-held, there would have remained for my share of the performance nothing but a mass of obscurity and confusion; so that in your own right, the whole result of the execution is yours, as well as the entire merit of the original plan.

It is my earnest wish that you may long be the prime administrator of an establishment, to which you have so excellently paved the way; as I am sure your extensive general knowledge, joined to your particular experience in the affairs of India, give you advantages which can scarcely fall to the share of any other subject of the British Empire.

I am, with the greatest respect and gratitude,

Honourable Sir,

Your most obliged,

And most obedient Servant,
Nathaniel Brassey Halhed

[a] Halhed was twenty-six.

141

The Translator's Preface

The importance of the commerce of India, and the advantages of a territorial establishment in Bengal, have at length awakened the attention of the British Legislature to every circumstance that may conciliate the affections of the natives, or ensure stability to the acquisition. Nothing can so favourably conduce to these two points as a well-timed toleration in matters of religion, and an adoption of such original institutes of the country, as do not immediately clash with the laws or interests of the conquerors.

To a steady pursuance of this great maxim, much of the success of the Romans may be attributed, who not only allowed to their foreign subjects the free exercise of their own religion, and the administration of their own civil jurisdiction, but sometimes by a policy still more flattering, even naturalized such parts of the mythology of the conquered, as were in any respect compatible with their own system.

With a view to the same political advantages, and in observance of so striking an example, the following compilation was set on foot; which must be considered as the only work of the kind, wherein the genuine principles of the Gentoo jurisprudence are made public, with the sanction of their most respectable Pundits (or lawyers) and which offers a complete confutation of the belief too common in Europe, that the Hindoos have no written laws whatever, but such as relate to the ceremonious peculiarities of their superstition.[a]

The professors of the ordinances here collected still speak the original language in which they were composed, and which is entirely unknown to the bulk of the people, who have settled upon those professors several great endowments and benefactions in all parts of Hindostan, and pay them besides a degree of personal respect little short of idolatry, in return for the advantages supposed to be derived from their studies. A set of the most experi-

[a] Whether Asian societies were or were not 'despotic', that is whether their rulers were restrained by written laws and the established rights of the subject, was a matter of controversy in Europe. Montesquieu was the most notable exponent of the theory of Asiatic despotism. More recently, Alexander Dow, in a Dissertation attached to the third volume of his *History of Hindostan*, p. xxxv, had argued that Hindu government was 'despotic'.

enced of these lawyers was selected from every part of Bengal for the purpose of compiling the present work,[a] which they picked out sentence by sentence from various originals in the Shanscrit language, neither adding to nor diminishing any part of the ancient text. The articles thus collected were next translated literally into Persian, under the inspection of one of their own body; and from that translation were rendered into English with an equal attention to the closeness and fidelity of the version. Less studious of elegance than of accuracy, the translator thought it more excusable to tire the reader with the flatness of a literal interpretation, than to mislead him by a vague and devious paraphrase; so that the entire order of the book, and several divisions of its contents, and the whole turn of the phrase, is in every part the immediate product of the Bramins. The English dialect in which it is here offered to the public, and that only, is not the performance of a Gentoo. From hence therefore may be formed a precise idea of the customs and manners of these people, which, to their great injury, have long been misrepresented in the Western world. From hence also materials may be collected towards the legal accomplishment of a new system of government in Bengal, wherein the British laws may, in some degree, be softened and tempered by a moderate attention to the peculiar and national prejudices of the Hindoo; some of whose institutes, however fanciful and injudicious, may perhaps be preferable to any which could be substituted in their room. They are interwoven with the religion of the country, and are therefore revered as of the highest authority: they are the conditions by which they hold their rank in society. Long usage has persuaded them of their equity, and they will always gladly embrace the permission to obey them; to be obliged to renounce their obedience would probably be esteemed among them as real hardship.

The attention which the translator was forced to bestow upon so uncommon a subject, the number of enquiries necessary for the elucidation of almost every sentence, and the many opportunities of most decisive information, which the course of the work presented, give him in some measure a right to claim the conviction

---

[a] Eleven *pandits* were listed as responsible for compiling the Code (*Code of Gentoo Laws*, p. 6).

of the world upon many dubious points, which have long eluded the nicest investigation. He is very far from wishing to establish his own doctrines upon the ruins of those which he found already erected; and when he opposes popular opinion, or contradicts any ill-grounded assertion, it is with the utmost distrust of his own abilities, and merely in submission to the authority of that truth which the candid will ever be glad to support, even in prejudice to a system of their own formation.

In a tract so untrodden as this, many paths must be attempted before we can hit upon the right. We owe much to every person, who in so troublesome a road hath removed a single obstacle, or opened the smallest channel for discovery; and the more difficult the completion of the adventure, the greater is the merit of each attempt. The present work however is the only one of this nature ever undertaken by authority; the only instance, in which the Bramins have ever been persuaded to give up a part of their own consequence for the general benefit of the whole community: and the pen of the translator must be considered as entirely the passive instrument, by which the laws of this singular nation are ushered into the world from those Bramins themselves.

In this preliminary treatise it is proposed, after a few general and introductory observations, to attempt a short account of the Shanscrit language, and an explanation of such passages in the body of the Code, as may appear by their peculiarity or repugnance to our sentiments to lie most open to objection.

Many conjectural doctrines have been circulated by the learned and ingenious of Europe upon the mythology of the Gentoos; and they have unanimously endeavoured to construe the extravagant fables with which it abounds into sublime and mystical symbols of the most refined morality. This mode of reasoning, however common, is not quite candid or equitable, because it sets out with supposing in those people a deficiency of faith with respect to the authenticity of their own Scriptures, which, although our better information may convince us to be altogether false and erroneous, yet are by them literally esteemed as the immediate revelations of the Almighty; and the same confidential reliance, which we put in the Divine Text upon the authority of its Divine Inspirer himself, is by their mistaken prejudices implicitly transferred to the

Beids of the Shaster. Hence we are not justified in grounding the standard and criterion of our examination of the Hindoo religion upon the known and infallible truth of our own, because the opposite party would either deny the first principles of our argument, or insist upon an equal right on their side to suppose the veracity of their own scriptures uncontrovertible.

It may possibly be owing to this vanity of reconciling every other mode of worship to some kind of conformity with our own, that allegorical constructions, and forced allusions to a mystic morality, have been constantly foisted in upon the plain and literal context of every pagan mythology. But we should consider, that the institution of a religion has been in every country the first step towards an emersion from savage barbarism, and the establishment of civil society; that the human mind at that period, when reason is just beginning to dawn, and science is yet below the horizon, has by no means acquired that facility of invention, and those profound habits of thinking, which are necessary to strike out, to arrange, and to complete a connected, consistent chain of abstruse allegory. The vulgar and illiterate have always understood the mythology of their country in its most simple and literal sense; and there was a time to every nation, when the highest rank in it was equally vulgar and illiterate with the lowest. Surely then, we have no right to suspect in them a greater propensity to, or capability of the composition of such subtle mysteries in those ages of ignorance, than we find to exist in their legitimate successors, the modern vulgar and illiterate at this day.

We have seen frequent and unsuccessful attempts among ourselves to sublimate into allusive and symbolical meanings the Mosaic account of the Creation: such erratic systems have risen but to be exploded; and their mutual disagreement with each other, in these fanciful interpretations, is to us an additional argument for the literal veracity of the inspired penman. The faith of a Gentoo (misguided as it is, and groundless as it may be) is equally implicit with that of a Christian, and his allegiance to his own supposed revelations of the Divine Will altogether as firm. He therefore esteems the astonishing miracles attributed to a Brihmā, a Raām, or a Kishen, as facts of the most indubitable authenticity, and the relation of them as most strictly historical.

But not to interfere with such parts of the Hindoo mythology as have not been revealed or explained to him, the translator can positively affirm, that the doctrine of the Creation, as set forth in the prefatory discourse to this Code, is there delivered as simple and plain matter of fact, and as a fundamental article in every pious Gentoo's creed; that it was so meant and understood by the compilers of this work unanimously, who bore the first characters in Bengal, both for their natural and acquired abilities; and that their accounts have been corroborated by the information of many other learned Bramins in the course of a wide and laborious enquiry; nor can it be otherwise, unless the progress of science, instead of being slow and gradual, were quick and instantaneous; unless men could start up at once into divines and philosophers from the very cradle of civilization, or could defer the profession of any religion at all, until progressive centuries had ripened them into a fitness for the most abstracted speculations.

Yet it may fairly be presumed, that when the manners of a people become polished, and their ideas enlightened, attempts will be made to revise and refit their religious creed into a conformity with the rest of their improvements; and that those doctrines, which the ignorant ancestor received with reverence and conviction, as the literal exposition of undoubted fact, the philosophic descendant will strive to gloss over by *a posteriori* constructions of his own; and, in the fury of symbol and allegory, obscure and distort that text which the simplicity of its author never suspected as liable to the possibility of such mutilation. These innovations however have always been screened, with the most scrupulous attention, from the general view of mankind; and, if a hardy sage hath at any time ventured to remove the veil, his opinions have usually been received with detestation, and his person hath frequently paid the forfeit of his temerity.

The real intention and subject of the Eleusinian Mysteries are now well known;[a] but it cannot, with much plausibility, be pretended, that those mysteries were coeval with the mythology to whose disproval they owed their establishment: probably, the

---

[a] William Warburton (see above, p. 63) had put forward the theory that the Eleusinian mysteries were intended to discredit polytheism by instilling a belief in the unity of God and the immortality of the soul.

institution was formed at a more advanced period of science, when the minds of the learned were eager to pierce through the obscurity of superstition, and when the vanity of superior penetration made them ashamed literally to believe those tenets, which popular prejudice would not suffer them utterly to renounce.

Instances in support of this argument might perhaps, without a strain, be drawn even from some parts of the Holy Scriptures: and here the account of the scape-goat, in the Laws of Moses, offers itself for that purpose with the greater propriety, as it is not altogether dissimilar to a particular institute of the Gentoos. The inspired author, after describing the preliminary ceremonies of this sacrifice, proceeds thus:

And Aaron shall lay both his hands upon the head of the scape-goat, and confess over him all the iniquities of the Children of Israel, and all their transgressions in all their sins, putting them upon the head of the goat, and shall send him away by the hand of a fit man into the wilderness: and the goat shall bear upon him all their iniquities unto a land not inhabited; and he shall let go the goat in the wilderness.[a]

The Jews, at the period when this ceremony was ordained, were very little removed from a state of barbarism: gross in their conceptions, illiterate in their education, and uncultivated in their manners; they were by no means fit subjects for the comprehension of a mystery; and doubtless, at that time, believed that their crimes were thus really and *bona fide* laid upon the head of the victim: yet the more wise, in succeeding ages, might well start from such a prejudice, and rightly conceive it to be a typical representation of the doctrine of absolution.

Hence it may be understood, that what has been herein advanced does not mean to set aside the improvements of philosophy, or to deny the occasional employment of allegory, but merely to establish one plain position, that religion in general, at its origin, is believed literally as it is professed, and that it is afterwards rather refined by the learned than debased by the ignorant.

The Gentoo ceremony, which was hinted at as bearing a remote likeness to the sacrifice of the scape-goat, is the Ashummeed Jugg, of which a most absurd and fabulous explanation may be found in the body of the Code: yet, unnatural as the account there stands,

[a] Lev. xvi, 21-2.

it is seriously credited by the Hindoos of all denominations, except perhaps a few individuals, who, by the variety and contradictions of their several allegorical interpretations, have mutually precluded each other from all pretentions to infallibity.

That the curious may form some idea of this Gentoo sacrifice when reduced to a symbol, as well as from the subsequent plain account given of it in a chapter of the Code, an explanation of it is here inserted from Dārul Shekûh's famous Persian translation of some commentaries upon the four Beids, or original scriptures of Hindostan: the work itself is extremely scarce, and perhaps of dubious authenticity; and it was by mere accident that this little specimen was procured.[a]

EXPLANATION OF THE ASHUMMEED JUGG

The Ashummeed Jugg does not merely consist in the performance of that ceremony which is open to the inspection of the world, namely, in bringing a horse and sacrificing him; but Ashummeed is to be taken in a mystic signification, as implying, that the sacrificer must look upon himself to be typified in that horse, such as he shall be described, because the religious duty of the Ashummeed Jugg comprehends all those other religious duties, to the performance of which all the wise and holy direct all their actions, and by which all the sincere professors of every different faith aim at perfection: the mystic signification thereof is as follows: the head of that unblemished horse is the symbol of the morning; his eyes are the sun; his breath the wind; his wide-opening mouth is the Bishwāner, or that innate warmth which invigorates all the world; his body typifies one entire year; his back paradise; his belly the plains; his hoof this earth; his sides the four quarters of the heavens; the bones thereof the intermediate spaces between the four quarters; the rest of his limbs represent all distinct matter; the places where those limbs meet, or his joints, imply the months and halves of the months, which are called Pĕchĕ (or fortnights); his feet signify night and day; and night and day are of four kinds: 1st. the night and day of Brihmā; 2d. the night and day of angels; 3d. the night and day of the world of the spirits of deceased ancestors; 4th. the night and day of mortals: these four kinds are typified in his four feet. The rest of his bones are the constellations of the fixed stars, which are the twenty-eight stages of the moon's course, called

[a] Dara Shukoh (1615–59), the eldest son of the Emperor Shah Jahan translated fifty-two *Upanishads* into Persian in his *Sirr-i Akbar* of 1657. Halhed later obtained a full version of the *Sirr-i Akbar* (B. M. Add. MS 5616) and made an English translation from it in 1787, which he evidently intended for publication (B. M. Add. MS 5658).

the lunar year; his flesh is the clouds; his food the sand; his tendons the rivers; his spleen and liver the mountains; the hair of his body the vegetables, and his long hair the trees; the forepart of his body typifies the first half of the day, and the hinder part the latter half; his yawning is the flash of the lightning, and his turning himself is the thunder of the cloud; his urine represents the rain; and his mental reflection is his only speech. The golden vessels which are prepared before the horse is let loose are the light of the day, and the place where those vessels are kept is a type of the ocean of the East; the silver vessels which are prepared after the horse is let loose are the light of the night, and the place where those vessels are kept is a type of the ocean of the West: these two sorts of vessels are always before and after the horse.—The Arabian Horse, which on account of his swiftness is called Hy, is the performer of the journies of angels; the Tājee, which is of the race of Persian Horses, is the performer of the journies of the Kundherps (or good spirits); the Wāzbā, which is of the race of the deformed Tāzee Horses, is the performer of the journies of the Jins (or Demons); and the Ashoo, which is of the race of Turkish Horses, is the performer of the journies of mankind: this one horse, which performs these several services, on account of his four different sorts of riders, obtains the four different appellations: the place where this horse remains is the great ocean, which signifies the great spirit of Perm-Atmā, or the universal soul, which proceeds also from that Perm-Atmā, and is comprehended in the same Perm-Atmā. The intent of this sacrifice is, that a man should consider himself to be in the place of that horse, and look upon all these articles as typified in himself; and, conceiving the Atmā (or divine Soul) to be an ocean, should let all thought of self be absorbed in that Atmā.[a]

This is the very acme and enthusiasm of allegory, and wonderfully displays the picturesque powers of fancy in an Asiatic genius. But it would not have been inserted at length in this place, if the circumstance of letting loose the horse had not seemed to bear a great resemblance to the ceremonies of the scape-goat; and perhaps the known intention of this latter may plead for the like hidden meaning in the former. But to quit this digression. The real appellations of the country and of the inhabitants of Hindostan, by which they are constantly denominated in the ancient writings of the natives, seem hitherto to have escaped the notice of the Western world.

Hindostan is a Persian word, equally unknown to the old and modern Shanscrit, compounded of Stān, a region, and the word Hind, or Hindoo: probably Colonel Dow's elegant translation

[a] This is the opening of the *Brihad Aranyaka Upanishad.*

of Ferishteh's History gives us the true derivation, in that author's conjecture, that it is taken from Hind, a supposed son of Ham, the son of Noah;[a] and, whatever antiquity the Indians may assert for themselves (of which some notice will subsequently be taken) the Persians, we believe, will rest contented to allow, that the first intercourse between the two nations commenced in the third descent from the deluge. But, if this definition were rejected, the common opinion, that India was so named by foreigners after the river Indus, is by no means repugnant to probability: in the Shanscrit however, Hindostan is constantly denominated Bhertekhunt, or Jumboodeep (as it is hereafter called in the present work, from Jumboo, or Jumbook, a jackall, an animal remarkably abundant in this country, and Deep, any large portion of land surrounded by the sea).[b] Khunt signifies a continent, or wide tract of land, and Bhĕrrut is the name of one of the first Indian Rajahs, whose name was adopted for that of the kingdom: Hindoo therefore is not the term by which the inhabitants originally stiled themselves, but, according to the idiom of their language, Jumboodeepee, or Bhĕrtekhuntee; and it is only since the æra of the Tartar government that they have assumed the name of Hindoos, to distinguish themselves from their conquerors, the Mussulmen. The word Gentoo has been, and is still, equally mistaken to signify, in the proper sense of the term, the professors of the Braminical religion, whereas Gent, or Gentoo, means animal in general, and in its more confined sense, mankind; but is never, in the Shanscrit dialect, nor even in the modern jargon of Bengal, appropriated particularly to such as follow the doctrines of Brihmā. The four great tribes have each their own separate appellation; but they have no common or collective term that comprehends the whole nation under the idea affixed by Europeans to the word Gentoo. Possibly the Portuguese on their first arrival in India, hearing the word frequently in the mouths of the natives as applied to mankind in general, might adopt it for the domestic appellation of the Indians themselves; perhaps also their bigotry might force from the word Gentoo a fanciful allusion to gentile, a pagan.

[a] *History of Hindostan*, 1, 9.
[b] The actual explanation of the name is given by Jones, see below, p. 250.

Nathaniel Brassey Halhed

The Shanscrit language is very copious and nervous, but the style of the best authors wonderfully concise. It far exceeds the Greek and Arabick in the regularity of its etymology, and like them has a prodigious number of derivatives from each primary root. The grammatical rules also are numerous and difficult, though there are not many anomalies. As one instance of the truth of this assertion, it may be observed, that there are seven declensions of nouns, all used in the singular, the dual, and the plural number, and all of them differently formed, according as they terminate with a consonant, with a long or a short vowel; and again different also as they are of different genders: not a nominative case can be formed to any one of these nouns, without the application of at least four rules, which differ likewise with each particular difference of the nouns as above stated: add to this, that every word in the language may be used through all the seven declensions, and there needs no farther proof of the difficulty of the idiom.

The Shanscrit grammars are called Beeākĕrun, of which there are many composed by different authors; some too abstruse even for the comprehension of most Bramins, and others too prolix to be ever used but as references. One of the shortest, named the Sărăsootee, contains between two and three hundred pages, and was compiled by Anŏŏbhōōtēē Seroopĕnām Achārige with a conciseness that can scarcely be parallelled in any other language.[a]

The Shanscrit alphabet contains fifty letters, and it is one boast of the Bramins that it exceeds all other alphabets in this respect: but when we consider that of their thirty-four consonants near half carry combined sounds, and that six of their vowels are merely the correspondent long ones to as many which are short, the advantage seems to be little more than fanciful.

The Shanscrit character, used in Upper Hindostan, is said to be the same original letter that was first delivered to the people by Brihmā, and is now called Diewnāgur, or the language of angels; whereas the character used by the Bramins of Bengal is by no means so ancient, and though somewhat different is evidently a corruption of the former.

[a] Halhed possessed a copy of the grammar called *Sarasvati Sutra* with commentary by Anubhutis Varupacharya, which is now in the British Museum, Add. MS 5584.

To rank rĕĕ and lĕĕ among the vowels may perhaps be cen-
sured as unnatural; we can only say, that being liquids, they par-
take in some small measure of the vowel, and that to an European
ear it seems equally extraordinary to find the Persian and Arabic
ع ain to be a consonant. It will also be observed in the preceding
alphabets, that the vowels have different forms when combined
with consonants from those they bear when unconnected.

In the four Beids (the original and sacred text of the great Hindoo creator and legislator Brihmā) the length of the vowels is
determined and pointed out by a musical note or sign, called
Mātrāng (implying one whole tone) which is placed over every
word; and in reading the Beids these distinctions of tone and time
must be nicely observed; the account of this modulation as given
in the Shanscrit grammar, called Sărăsootee,[a] is here translated.

The vowels are of three sorts, short, long, and continued (or to use a more
musical term, holding). The Chāsh (a small bird peculiar to Hindostan)
utters one Mātrāng, the crow two Mātrāngs, and the peacock three
Mātrāngs; the mouse half a Mātrāng. One Mātrāng is the short vowel,
two Mātrāngs the long vowel, and three Mātrāngs the continued: a consonant without a vowel has the half Mātrāng. These vowels are again to be
distinguished by a high note for the one Mātrāng, a low note for the two
Mātrāngs, and an intermediate or tenor for the three Mātrāngs, either with
nasals or gutturals. ēē, ēī, ō, ōū, are dipthongs, and cannot be short; but
these four, together with the other five, ĕ, ĕĕ, ŏŏ, rĕĕ, lĕĕ, are to be taken
as vowels.

It has been mentioned that these distinctions are all marked in
the Beids, and must be modulated accordingly, so that they produce all the effect of a laboured recitative; but by an attention to
the music of the chant, the sense of the passage recited equally
escapes the reader and the audience. It is remarkable, that the
Jews in their synagogues chant the Pentateuch in the same kind
of melody, and it is supposed that this usage has descended to
them from the remotest ages.

To give some faint idea of these arbitrary notes, a line is here
inserted with the several Mātrāngs.

Tĕsĕ mŏŏndĕĕ Krēēlĕ bĕdĕrōō bĕdĕrōō bĕdĕrōō.

[a] *Sarasvati Sutra*, see above, p. 151.

The last syllable of the word bĕdĕrōō with three Mātrāṅgs is held for near a minute, gradually sinking, and then swelling out with a fresh rinforza to mark each Mātrāng.

The Shanscrit poetry comprehends a very great variety of different metres, of which the most common are these:

The Munnee hurreneh Chhund, or line of twelve or nineteen syllables, which is scanned by three syllables in a foot, and the most approved foot is the anapæst.

The Cābee Chhund, or line of eleven syllables.

The Anûshtose Chhund, or line of eight syllables.

The poems are generally composed in stanzas of four lines, called Ashlogues, which are regular or irregular.

The most common Ashlogue is that of the Anûshtose Chhund, or regular stanza of eight syllables in each line. In this measure greatest part of the Māhābāret is composed.[a] The rhyme in this kind of stanza should be alternate; but the poets do not seem to be very nice in the observance of a strict correspondence in the sounds of the terminating syllables, provided the feet of the verse are accurately kept.

This short Anûshtose Ashlogue is generally written by two verses in one line, with a pause between, so that the whole then assumes the form of a long distich.

The irregular stanza is constantly called Aryāchhund, of whatever kind of irregularity it may happen to consist. It is most commonly compounded of the long line Cābee Chhund, and the short Anûshtose Chhund alternately; in which form it bears some resemblance to the most common lyric measure of the English.

It will in this place be pardonable to quote a few stanzas of Shanscrit poetry, as examples of the short account here given of its prosody. The specimens give us no despicable idea of the old Hindoo bards. The images are in general lively and pleasing, the diction elegant and concise, and the metre not inharmonious.

[a] Halhed possessed a Sanskrit copy of the *Mahabharata* in eight volumes transcribed at Benares in 1776 (B. M. Add. MSS 5569–76).

An Ashlogue Anûshtose Chhund, or regular, of eight Syllables in each Line

A father in debt is an enemy (to his son.)
A mother of scandalous behaviour is an enemy (to her son.)
A wife of a beautiful figure is an enemy (to her husband.)
A son of no learning is an enemy (to his parents.)

These verses are regular dimeter iambicks.

An Ashlogue Munnee hurreneh Chhund, or of nineteen Syllables

From the insatiable desire of riches, I have digged beneath the earth; I have sought by chymistry to transmute the metals of the mountains.
I have traversed the queen of the oceans; I have toiled incessant for the gratification of monarchs.
I have renounced the world, to give up my whole heart to the study of incantations; I have passed whole nights on the places where the dead are burnt.
I have not gained one cowry. Begone, O avarice, thy business is over.

An Ashlogue Munnee hurreneh Chhund, or of twelve Syllables

The night is for the moon, and the moon is for the night:
When the moon and the night are together, it is the glory of the heavens.
The lotus, or water-lilly, is for the stream, and the stream is for the water-lilly:
When the stream and the water-lilly meet, it is the glory of the canal.

This species of composition is called Kŏŏndĕlēē Chhund, from Kŏŏndĕlēē, a circle, and answers nearly to the word rondeau, which sort of verse it exactly imitates.

Almost every foot in this beautiful stanza is a pure anapæst.

Three Ashlogues Aryāchhund, or irregular, from a Collection of Poems

1.

A good man goes not upon enmity,
But is well inclined towards another, even while he is ill-treated by him:
So, even while the Sandal-tree is felling,
It imparts to the edge of the axe its aromatic flavour.

Nathaniel Brassey Halhed

2.

So long as there is no danger,
The ass will eat a stranger's vine;
So, not conscious of receiving any hurt,
The Dragon[1] still attempts to devour the Moon.[2]

3.

The good man's heart is like butter,
The poets say, but herein they are mistaken:
Upon beholding another's life exposed to calamities,
The good man melts;[3] but it is not so with butter.

The four Beids are not in verse, as has been hitherto erroneously imagined, but in a kind of measured prose, called Pungtee
Chhund: the translator is therefore obliged to observe, that an
author of much merit has, by wrong information, been induced
to offer four stanzas as specimens of the several Beids, which have
not the least affinity or similitude to those books:[a] his first stanza
is very faulty, and without an interpretation: but, as a proof that
it cannot belong to the Beids, it has already been quoted in the
specimen of the Ashlogue Aryāchhund, together with the stanzas
immediately preceding and following, which are taken from a
work called Kāyāprĕkāsh (or a Collection of Poems) said to have
been composed by one Kiyăt, in the third age of the world.[b]

From the many obsolete terms used in the Beids, from the
conciseness and obscurity of their dialect, and from the particularity of the modulation in which they must be recited, they are
now hardly intelligible: very few of the most learned Pundits, and
those only who have employed many years of painful study upon
this one task, pretend to have the smallest knowledge of the originals, which are now also become extremely scarce and difficult to
be found; but comments have been written on them from the

[1] Alluding to the Gentoos' ideas of an eclipse.
[2] This stanza has been quoted in a former publication as a specimen of the
Reig Beid.
[3] That is, the simile is not just, because it does not express the powers of sympathy, which are the characteristic part of the good man's disposition.
[a] Dow had printed four stanzas, including the one quoted by Halhed, as 'A
Specimen of the Measure of the Bedas' (*History of Hindostan*, I, p. xxx).
[b] The *Kavyaprakasha* is generally attributed to Mammata, who was active at the
end of the eleventh century A.D. Halhed owned a copy of the *Kavyaprakasha* (B. M.
Add. MS 5582).

earliest periods; whereof one of the most ancient and most orthodox was composed by Bisesht^a Mahāmoonee, or the most wise,
a great writer and prophet, who is said to have lived in the Suttee
Jogue, or first age of the world, and from whom Beäss, the celebrated author of the heroic poem Mahābāret, boasted his descent.

The style of this writer is clear, but very concise; a specimen
of it is here offered, in his explanation of the first chapter of the
Reig Beid, which contains a description of the wisdom and powers
of the Almighty.

COMMENTARY OF BISESHT MAHĀMOONEE
UPON THE FIRST CHAPTER OF THE REIG BEID

Glory be to Goneish.[1] That which is exempt from all desires of the senses,
the same is the mighty Lord. He is single, and than him there is nothing
greater. Brehm (the Spirit of God) is absorbed in self-contemplation: the
same is the mighty Lord, who is present in every part of space, whose
omniscience, as expressed in the Reig Beid, I shall now explain. Brehm is
one, and to him there is no second; such is truly Brehm. His omniscience is
self-inspired (or self-intelligent) and its comprehension includes every
possible species. To illustrate this as far as I am able. The most comprehensive of all comprehensive faculties is omniscience; and being self-inspired,
it is subject to no accident of mortality or passion;[2] of vice;[3] to it the three
distinctions of time[4] are not; to it the three modes of being[5] are not; it is
separated from the universe, and independent of all. This omniscience is
named Brehm. By this omniscient spirit, the operations of God are enlivened;
by this spirit also, the twenty-four powers of nature[6] are animated. How is
this? As the eye by the sun, as the pot by the fire, as iron by the magnet, as
variety of imitations by the mimic, as fire by the fuel, as the shadow by the

[1] An invocation never omitted by a pious Gentoo upon the commencement of
any business whatsoever.
[2] Of which they reckon five, conception, birth, growth, decay and death.
[3] In number six, called Opādhee, viz. lust, anger, avarice, folly, drunkenness
and pride.
[4] The past, present and future.
[5] To be awake, to sleep and to be absorbed in a state of unconsciousness—a kind
of trance.
[6] Viz. The five elements (for the Hindoos add to the four a subtile æther, which
they call Akāsh, and suppose to be the medium of sound).
The five members of action, hand, foot, tongue, anus and yard.
The five members of perception, ear, eye, nose, mouth and skin.
The five senses.
The three dispositions of the mind, desire, passion and tranquillity.
Consciousness, or self-perception.
[a] Vasishta.

man, as dust by the wind, as the arrow by the spring of the bow, and as the shade by the tree; so by this spirit the world is endued with the powers of intellect, the powers of the will, and the powers of action; so that, if it emanates from the heart by the channel of the ear, it causes the perception of sounds; if it emanates from the heart by the channel of the skin, it causes the perception of the touch; if it emanates from the heart by the channel of the eye, it causes the perception of visible objects; if it emanates from the heart by the channel of the tongue, it causes the perception of taste; if it emanates from the heart by the channel of the nose, it causes the perception of smell. This also invigorating the five members of action, and invigorating the five members of perception, and invigorating the five elements, and invigorating the five senses, and invigorating the three dispositions of the mind, &c. causes the creation or the annihilation of the universe; while itself beholds every thing as an indifferent spectator. Wherefore that omniscience thus centred in Brehm is called Serwaesher (or the Lord of all); and this Lord, as a player doth, is perpetually shifting his modes of operation, by a variety of gradations, as the dancer shifts his steps. Thus far the doctrine of the Reig Beid.[a]

The translator is conscious, that this short account of the Shanscrit is very defective and insufficient; but he must plead in his own defence, that very lately only, and that altogether by accident, he was enabled to procure even this slender information; that the Pundits who compiled the Code were to a man resolute in rejecting all his solicitations for instruction in this dialect, and that the persuasion and influence of the Governor-General were in vain exerted to the same purpose. However, since the completion of his former task, he has been happy enough to become acquainted with a Bramin of more liberal sentiments, and of a more communicative disposition, joined to an extensive knowledge acquired both by study and travel: he eagerly embraced the opportunity of profiting by the help of so able a master, and means to exert all his diligence upon so curious and uncommon a subject.[b]

The Hindoos as well as the Chinese have ever laid claim to an antiquity infinitely more remote than is authorized by the belief of the rest of mankind. It is certain however, that these two nations have been acquainted with letters from the very earliest

[a] This is a quotation from the *Dvadashamahavakyavivarana*, 'Explanation of twelve great sentences', attributed to the *Vedanta* philosopher Shankaracharya. It is not clear how the name of Vasishta became attached to it. Halhed possessed a copy of the work (B.M. Add. MS 5583). I owe this identification to the kindness of Dr Rosane Rocher.

[b] Halhed made less progress than he hoped, see above, p. 10.

period, and that their annals have never been disturbed or destroyed by any known revolution; and though we may come to the perusal of their records, armed with every argument, and fortified even to prejudice against the admission of their pretensions, at the same time placing the most implicit reliance upon the Mosaic chronology as generally received, yet their plausible accounts of those remote ages, and their undeviating confidence in their own assertions, never can fail to make some impression upon us, in proportion as we gain a clearer insight to them. Suspicions of a like nature are not totally without foundation even in the Western world; and the conscientious scruples of the historiographer of Mount Ætna (as mentioned in a late publication)[1] will always be of some weight in the scale of philosophy.[a]

The Hindoos then reckon the duration of the world by four Jogues, or distinct ages.

1. The Suttee Jogue (or age of purity) is said to have lasted 3,200,000 years; and they hold that the life of man was in that age extended to 100,000 years, and that his stature was 21 cubits.

2. The Tirtāh Jogue (or age in which one third of mankind were reprobate) they suppose to have consisted of 2,400,000 years, and that men then lived to the age of 10,000 years.

3. The Dwāpāār Jogue (in which half of the human race became depraved) endured 1,600,000 years, and mens' lives were reduced to 1000 years.

4. The Collee Jogue (in which all mankind are corrupted; or rather lessened, for that is the true meaning of Collee) is the present æra, which they suppose ordained to subsist for 400,000 years, of which near 5000 are already past, and man's life in this period is limited to 100 years.[b]

Computation is lost, and conjecture overwhelmed in the at-

[1] Brydone's Letters.

[a] Patrick Brydone (1741?–1818) in his *Tour through Sicily and Malta in a series of Letters to William Beckford, Esq.* (1773), I, 130–2, described a conversation with the Sicilian geologist, Guiseppe Recupero (1720–78), about the age of the lava strata round Mount Etna. Recupero believed the lowest strata to be at least 14,000 years old, but he found that 'Moses hangs like a dead weight upon him'. His bishop told him 'not to pretend to be a better natural historian than Moses'.

[b] Cf. the accounts of Holwell and Dow (see above, pp. 105, 124), and Jones (see below, p. 263).

tempt to adjust such astonishing spaces of time to our own confined notions of the world's epoch: to such antiquity the Mosaic Creation is but as yesterday; and to such ages the life of Methuselah is no more than a span! Absurd as this Gentoo doctrine may seem, mere human reason, upon consideration of the present contracted measure of mortality, can no more reconcile to itself the idea of Patriarchal than of Braminical longevity; and when the line of implicit faith is once extended, we can never ascertain the precise limits beyond which it must not pass. One circumstance must not be omitted, that the ages allotted to mankind in the several Jogues by the Bramins tally very exactly with those mentioned by Moses, as far as the chronology of the latter reaches. For the last part of the Dwāpāār Jogue, in which men are said to have attained to one thousand years of life, corresponds with the Mosaic æra of the Antediluvians: and in the commencement of the Collee Jogue, which comes very near to the period of the Deluge,[a] the portion of human existence was contracted to one hundred years, and is seldom supposed even to go so far.

We are not much advanced in our inquiries, by allowing with some excellent authors, that most of the Gentoo Shasters (or Scriptures) were composed about the beginning of the Collee Jogue; for then we at once come to the immediate æra of the Flood, which calamity is never once mentioned in those Shasters, and which yet we must think infinitely too remarkable to have been even but slightly spoken of, much less to have been totally omitted, had it even been known in that part of the world. The Bramins indeed remove this objection by two assertions; one, that all their scriptures were written before the time by us allotted to Noah; the other, that the Deluge really never took place in Hindostan.

But to wave these vague and indefinite disquisitions, it will not here be superfluous to quote a passage or two from some of the most classical and authentic Shasters, which expressly determine and fix the dates of their respective æras to the earliest Jogues.

The first specimen here inserted is from the Book of Munnoo,

---

[a] If the *Kali Yuga* had lasted for some 5,000 years by 1775, as Halhed suggests (see above, p. 158), it would have begun in approximately 3225 B.C., well before the orthodox dating of the Deluge in 2348 B.C. But the Deluge can be put back by another 900 years by using Septuagint chronology.

which the reader will observe stands foremost in the list of those which furnished the subsequent Code,[a] and though the second quotation is not so authoritative, as being the production of a later author (whose name we do not recollect) in testimony of the date of another, yet Jage-Bulk[b] is mentioned among the first legislators, and his books are valued for their antiquity as well as their excellence.

An Ashlogue Munnee hurreneh Chhund, or of Nineteen Syllables, from Munnoo

When ten thousand and ten years of the Suttee Jogue were past, on the night of the full moon, in the month Bhàdun, I Munnoo, at the command of Brehmā, finished this Shaster, that speaks of mens' duty, of justice, and of religion, ever instructive.[c]

This treatise, called Munnoo Smistee, will enlighten the world like a torch.

Two Ashlogues Anûshtose Chhund, or of eight Syllables, upon Jage-Bulk

In the Tirtāh Jogue, the author Jage-Bulk, when ninety-five years were past, in the month of Sāwun, on the moon's increase, on the Wednesday (or literally on the day of Mercury)[1] finished the treatise, called Jage-Bulk, which sets forth the offices of religion, and also informs men of the duties of the magistrate.[d]

[1] It is very remarkable, that the days of the week are named in the Shanscrit language from the same planets to which they were assigned by the Greeks and Romans.[e]

Audĕĕtyĕ Wār ⎱ Solis Dies.	Audĕĕtyĕ ⎱ the Sun.
Rēbēē Wār ⎰	Rēbēē ⎰
Sōmĕ Wār Lunae Dies.	Sōmĕ the Moon.
Mungĕl Wār Martis Dies.	Mungĕlĕ Mars.
Bŏŏdhĕ Wār Mercurii Dies.	Bŏŏdhĕ Mercury.
Brĕĕhĕspĕt Wār Jovis Dies.	Brĕĕhĕspĕt Jupiter.
Shŏŏkrĕ Wār Veneris Dies.	Shŏŏkrĕ Venus.
Shĕnīschĕr Wār Saturni Dies.	Shĕnīschĕr Saturn.

[a] Halhed printed a list of the sources used by the *pandits* in compiling the Code (*Code of Gentoo Laws*, pp. 26–8).   [b] Yajnavalkya.

[c] These lines are not an authentic part of the text of the *Laws of Manu*, which are thought to have been compiled in the second or third century A.D.

[d] The source of these lines has not been identified. The *Yajnavalkya Smriti*, second on the list of the *pandits'* sources after the *Laws of Manu*, is thought to have been compiled about A.D. 400.

[e] The Sanskrit names are now generally thought to have been derived from the Greek and Roman system (A. L. Basham, *The Wonder that was India* (1954), p. 493).

What periods shall we possibly assign to these writers, if we disallow the authorities here quoted? If they are false, there must have been a time when the imposition would have been too palpable to have passed upon mankind, and when the concurrent testimony of the whole world would have risen up in judgment against it; for if we grant Munnoo's works to have been published during his own life-time, it is impossible that he should have ventured to utter so monstrous a forgery; and if they were concealed till after his death, could the memory of his late existence be so shortly obliterated through the whole country? But supposing so much of the book as relates to the date to have been foisted in by another, and afterwards produced as a part of the original text, which till that time had lain undiscovered, nobody surely would have believed him in opposition to the universal faith! For so miraculous a fiction could never gain credit but upon the support of some principle of religious opinion, and every religion has established a chronology of its own: besides, can it be possible, that none of Munnoo's cotemporaries, none of the succeeding writers should have recorded so striking a circumstance? For if the whole Indian world had till that time believed with us in a chronology nearly answering to that of Moses, so astonishing a change in their sentiments upon the introduction of the doctrine of the Jogues would have furnished ample matter for a thousand volumes; but on the contrary, all the parts of every Shaster (however different from each other on religious subjects) are yet uniform and consistent throughout upon this; the same mode of computing their annals has always obtained, and the same belief of the remoteness of antiquity that now prevails may be proved to have been universally acknowledged, even at the time in which some pretend to fix the first appearance of letters in Hindostan.

Rajah Prichutt,[a] who though ranked as a modern on the records of India, is yet known to have lived in the earliest ages of the Collee Jogue, was no less anxious than modern philosophers are to pierce through the obscurity of time, and to trace the progress of the world from its infancy; at his instigation a work was composed by Shŭkeh Diew,[b] a learned Bramin (son of Beäss, the

---

[a] Parikshit. [b] Shukadeva.

famous author of the Mahābāret) containing the history of India through the three preceding Jogues, with the succession of the several Rajahs, and the duration of their reigns. This curious history, called Shree Bhagbut, still subsists, divided into twelve Ascund or books (literally branches) and three thousand and twenty chapters.[a] What shall we say to a work composed four thousand years ago, and from thence tracing mankind upwards through several millions of years? Must we answer, that the earth was at that time an uninhabited marsh, still slowly emerging from an universal inundation?

Great surely and inexplicable must be the doubts of mere human reason upon such a dilemma when unassisted and uninformed by divine revelation; but while we admit the former in our argument, we profess a most unshaken reliance upon the latter, before which every suspicion must subside, and scepticism be absorbed in conviction: yet from the premises already established, this conclusion at least may fairly be deduced, that the world does not now contain annals of more indisputable antiquity than those delivered down by the ancient Bramins.

Collateral proofs of this antiquity may be drawn from every page of the present Code of Laws, in its wonderful correspondence with many parts of the Institutes of Moses, one of the first of known legislators; from whom we cannot possibly find grounds to suppose the Hindoos received the smallest article of their religion or jurisprudence, though it is not utterly impossible, that the doctrines of Hindostan might have been early transplanted into Egypt, and thus have become familiar to Moses.

The Gentoos have in all ages believed in the transmigration of souls, which they denominate Kāyāprĕwâêsh and Kāyāpĕlût: this latter literally answers to the word metempsychosis. An ancient Shaster, called the Gēētā, written by Adhâê Doom, has a beautiful stanza upon this system of the transmigration, which he compares to a change of dress.

---

[a] The *Bhagavat Purana* (see above, p. 120). Halhed was later to make an English translation from a Persian version of its tenth *skanda*. The *Bhagavat Purana* is thought to have attained written form about A.D. 950 (M. Singer ed., *Krishna: Myths, Rites and Attitudes* (Honolulu, 1966), pp. 4, 16).

Nathaniel Brassey Halhed

An Ashlogue Cābee Chhund, or of Eleven Syllables in Each Line

On the Transmigration of Souls

As throwing aside his old habits,
A man puts on others that are new,
So, our lives quitting the old,
Go to other newer animals.[a]

An ingenious author of our own[1] has well explained their ideas upon the subject of a future state, though he laments at the same time, that his materials were too imperfect to afford complete information.

Their creed then is, that those souls which have attained to a certain degree of purity, either by the innocence of their manners, or the severity of their mortifications, are removed to regions of happiness, proportioned to their respective merits: but that those who cannot so far surmount the prevalence of bad example, and the forcible degeneracy of the times, as to deserve such a promotion, are condemned to undergo continual punishment in the animation of successive animal forms, until at the stated period another renovation of the four Jogues shall commence upon the dissolution of the present.

They suppose that there are fourteen Bhoobuns or spheres, seven below and six above the earth; the seven inferior worlds are said to be altogether inhabited by an infinite variety of serpents, described in every monstrous figure that the imagination can suggest; hence the reason why such particular mention is made of serpents in the account of the creation prefixed to this Code. The Earth is called Bhoor, and mankind who inhabit it Bhoor-logue; an instance of which may be seen in the stanza quoted from Munnoo: the spheres gradually ascending from thence are,

1st. Bōbur, whose inhabitants are called the Bōbur-logue. 2d. The Swergeh-logue. 3d. The Mahurr-logue. 4th. The Junneh-logue. 5th. The Tuppeh-logue. 6th. The Suttee-logue.

The Bōbur is the immediate vault of the visible heavens, in which the sun, moon, and stars are placed. The Swergeh is the

---

[1] Mr. Holwell.

[a] *Bhagavad Gita*, ii, 22. Halhed possessed a Sanskrit copy of the *Gita* (B.M. Add. MS 5579).

first paradise and general receptacle for those who merit a removal from the lower earth. The Mahurr-logue are the Fakeers, and such persons as by dint of prayer have acquired an extraordinary degree of sanctity. The Junneh-logue are also the souls of pious and moral men; and beyond this sphere they are not supposed to pass without some uncommon merits and qualifications. The sphere of Tuppeh is the reward of those who have all their lives performed some wonderful act of penance and mortification, or who have died martyrs for their religion. The Suttee or highest sphere is the residence of Brihmā and his particular favourites, whence they are also called Brihmā-logue: this is the placc of destination for those men who have never uttered a falsehood during their whole lives, and for those women who have voluntarily burned themselves with their husbands. How shall we reconcile so splendid and exalted a benediction pronounced upon this spontaneous martyrdom, with the assertion of an author, that the custom for the wives to burn themselves with their husbands' bodies was never reckoned a religious duty in India?[a] This circumstance will again present itself in the remarks on the chapter of women.

But it is now time to draw this essay towards a conclusion, by confining ourselves to the more immediate explanation of such parts of the Code as may not seem entirely consistent with European opinions, or European justice.

The work opens with a short preliminary Discourse, written by the Bramins themselves,[b] as well to set forth the motives and uses of the compilation, as to gratify the honest vanity of every sensible mind, in giving some account of itself and of its labours. Nothing can be more remote from a superstitious adherence to their own domestic prejudices, or more truly elevated above the mean and selfish principles of priestcraft, than the genuine dignity of sentiment that breathes through this little performance. Few Christians, with all the advantages of enlightened understandings, would have expressed themselves with a more becoming reverence for the grand and impartial designs of providence in all its works, or with a more extensive charity towards all their fellow

[a] Halhed is referring to Dow, see above, p. 116.
[b] See below, pp. 182–3.

creatures of every profession. It is indeed an article of faith among the Bramins, that God's all merciful power would not have permitted such a number of different religions, if he had not found a pleasure in beholding their varieties.

The first section of the Preface contains an account of the creation, literally as the Gentoos believe it to have been performed: the four great and original tribes are there said to have proceeded from the four different members of Brihmā, the supposed immediate agent of the creation under the spirit of the Almighty. The Hindoos do not suppose that these several parts of the creator, assigned for their production, are a symbolical token or description of the respective duties of their stations; but that the several qualifications of each cast, and the enjoined exercise of those qualifications, are the natural and unavoidable result of the presiding function in each of the members of their first parent.

The Bramin from the mouth—(wisdom) to pray, to read, to instruct.
The Chehteree from the arms—(strength) to draw the bow, to fight, to govern.
The Bice from the belly or thighs—(nourishment) to provide the necessaries of life by agriculture and traffic.
The Sooder from the feet—(subjection) to labour, to serve, to travel.

These four great tribes comprehend the first grand divisions of a well-regulated state. The mechanic, or petty dealer, as a branch of less importance, and administering rather to the luxuries than to the necessities of life, is furnished from a fifth adventitious tribe, called Burrun Sunker, which is again subdivided into almost as many separate casts as there are trades or occupations to be exercised by its members. The same principle of government, though under a different modification, is said to prevail in China, where every man is enjoined by law to follow the business of his father, and forbidden to thrust himself into any other profession.

But while we commend the policy of the ancient Hindoos, we must lament their most deplorable ignorance in some of the practical sciences, particularly geography, to which they must give up all pretentions after their extravagant description of the seven Deeps, which they suppose to be so many continents separated from each other by an almost infinite ocean, but yet all belonging to the same world which themselves inhabit.

The other division of the Preface contains the requisite qualifications for a magistrate and the duties of his station; most of the
rules there laid down are very pertinent, and display an accurate
knowledge of the human heart. But as the necessary limits of an
essay like this do not give room or opportunity for a general and
diffusive criticism, it is here intended only to speak of such particular parts and passages of the work as contain something
peculiar, local, or characteristic.

Among the qualities required for the proper execution of publick business, mention is made, 'that a man must be able to keep
in subjection his lust, his anger, his avarice, his *folly*, and his
pride.' These vices are sometimes denominated in the Shanscrit
under the general term Opadhee, a word which occurs in the
quoted specimen of the comment upon the Reig Beid. The *folly*
there specified is not to be understood in the usual sense of the
word in an European idiom, as a negative quality, or the mere
want of sense, but as a kind of obstinately stupid lethargy, or
perverse absence of mind, in which the will is not altogether
passive: it seems to be a weakness peculiar to Asia, for we cannot
find a term by which to express the precise idea in the European
languages; it operates somewhat like the violent impulse of fear,
under which men will utter falsehoods totally incompatible with
each other, and utterly contrary to their own opinion, knowledge,
and conviction; and it may be added also, their inclination and
intention. A very remarkable instance of this temporary frenzy
happened lately in the Supreme Court of Judicature at Calcutta,
where a man (not an idiot) swore upon a trial, that he was no
kind of relation to his own brother who was then in Court, and
who had constantly supported him from his infancy; and that he
lived in a house by himself, for which he paid the rent from his
own pocket, when it was proved that he was not worth a Rupee,
and when the person in whose house he had always resided stood
at the bar close to him.

Whenever the word *folly* included among the vices above-
mentioned occurs in this Code, it must always be understood to
carry the meaning here described. Another conjecture, and that
exceedingly acute and ingenious, has been started upon this *folly*,
that it may mean the deception which a man permits to be im-

posed on his judgment by his passions, as acts of rapacity and avarice are often committed by men who ascribe them to prudence and a just assertion of their own right; malice and rancour pass for justice, and brutality for spirit. This opinion, when thoroughly examined, will very nearly tally with the former; for all the passions, as well as fear, have an equal efficacy to disturb and distort the mind: but to account for the *folly* here spoken of, as being the offspring of the passions, instead of drawing a parallel between it and the impulses of those passions, we must suppose the impulse to act with infinitely more violence upon an Asiatic mind than we can ever have seen exemplified in Europe. It is however something like the madness so inimitably delineated in the hero of Cervantes, sensible enough upon some occasions, and at the same time completely wild, and unconscious of itself upon others; and that too originally produced by an effort of the will, though in the end overpowering and superseding its functions.

It will no doubt strike the reader with wonder, to find a prohibition of fire-arms in records of such unfathomable antiquity; and he will probably from hence renew the suspicion which has long been deemed absurd, that Alexander the Great did absolutely meet with some weapons of that kind in India, as a passage in Quintus Curtius seems to ascertain.[a] Gunpowder has been known in China, as well as in Hindostan, far beyond all periods of investigation. The word fire-arms is literally Shanscrit Agnee-aster, a weapon of fire; they describe the first species of it to have been a kind of dart or arrow tipt with fire, and discharged upon the enemy from a bamboo. Among several extraordinary properties of this weapon, one was, that after it had taken its flight, it divided into several separate darts or streams of flame, each of which took effect, and which, when once kindled, could not be extinguished;[1] but this kind of Agnee-aster is now lost. Cannon in the Shanscrit idiom is called Shĕt-Aghnee, or the weapon that kills a hundred men at once, from (Shĕtĕ) a hundred, and ghĕnĕh to

---

[1] It seems exactly to agree with the Feu Gregeois of the Crusades.[b]

[a] Halhed may be referring to the term 'tormenta' applied by Quintus Curtius Rufus (see above, p. 52) to weapons used by the Scythians (*Historiae Alexandri*, book VIII, chap. IX).

[b] 'Greek fire' was a device for projecting liquid fire used in the defence of Constantinople in the seventh century.

kill, and the Pooran Shasters, or Histories, ascribe the invention of these destructive engines to Bĕĕshŏŏkermā, the artist,[a] who is related to have forged all the weapons for the war which was maintained in the Suttee Jogue between Dewtā and Ossoor (or the good and bad spirits) for the space of one hundred years. Was it chance or inspiration that furnished our admirable Milton with exactly the same idea, which had never before occurred to an European imagination?[b]

The battles which are described in this section, ridiculous as they may appear, when compared with the modern art and improvement of war, are the very counterparts of Homer; for, in the early ages of mankind, a battle appears to have been little more than a set of distinct duels between man and man; in which case, every circumstance pointed out in this part of the magistrate's duty might naturally be expected to occur: and this is a forcible argument to prove, that the compilers have not foisted into the Code any novel opinions of their own, when in this place hardly one of the principles of war, as stated by them, is applicable to the present system and situation of mankind.

There is a particular charge to the magistrate to forbid all fires in the month Cheyt, or part of March and April; this is an institution most wisely and usefully calculated for the climate of Hindostan, where, for above four months before that time, there falls no rain, and where the wind always blows hard in that month, and is very dry and parching, so that every thing is in the most combustible situation, and the accidental burning of a handful of straw may spread a conflagration through a whole city. It is observable in India to this day, that fires are more frequent and more dangerous in the month Cheyt than in all the rest of the year.

Upon the whole, the scope and matter of this section is excellent; and, divested of the peculiar tinct it has received from the religious tenets of its authors, is not unworthy the pen of the most celebrated politicians, or philosophers of ancient Greece.

Chapter I. The Code begins with regulations for that which is one of the first cements of civil society, the mutuation of prop-

---

[a] Vishvakarman.
[b] The 'engins' of the rebel angels, *Paradise Lost*, vi, 572 ff.

erty; which, though equally necessary and advantageous to the public, must be confined within certain limits, and conducted upon the faith of known laws, to render it safe, confidential, and equitable. The favourable distinctions marked towards some tribes, and apparent severity with respect to others, in this chapter, though perhaps not reconcileable to our ideas of social compact, must be supposed perfectly consonant to the maxims of the Gentoos, and familiar to their comprehensions, as it may be observed, that the compilers have been scrupulously exact, in pointing out all such cases as have received different decisions in the different originals from whence the abstract is selected. Indeed, the Bramins, indisputably persuaded that their origin is from the mouth, or superior member, of their Creator, and consequently that the superiority of their tribe is interwoven with the very essence of their nature, esteem that to be a full and satisfactory plea for every advantage settled upon them, above the rest of the people, by the laws of their country; nor are the other casts discontented with the lot to which they have been accustomed from their earliest infancy; if they blame any thing, it is that original turn of chance which gave them rather to spring from the belly or the feet of Brihmā, than from his arms or head.

The different rate of interest, established in this chapter to be paid for the use of different articles, is perhaps an institute peculiar to Hindostan; but it reflects a strong light upon the simplicity of ancient manners, before money was universally current as the medium of barter for all commodities, and is at the same time a weighty proof of the great antiquity of these laws, which seem calculated for the crude conceptions of an almost illiterate people upon their first civilization.

Chapter II. The rights of inheritance, in the second chapter, are laid down with the utmost precision, and with the strictest attention to the natural claim of the inheritor, in the several degrees of affinity. A man is herein considered but as tenant for life in his own property; and, as all opportunity of distributing his effects by will, after his death, is precluded, hardly any mention is made of such kind of bequest. By these ordinances also, he is hindered from dispossessing his children of his property in favour of aliens, and from making a blind and partial allotment in behalf of a favourite child, to the prejudice of the rest; by which the weakness of parental affection, or of a misguided mind in its dotage, is admirably remedied. These laws also strongly elucidate the story of the Prodigal Son in the Scriptures; since it appears from hence to have been an immemorial custom in the east, for sons to demand their portion of inheritance during their fathers' life-time, and that the parent, however aware of the dissipated inclinations of his child, could not legally refuse to comply with the application.

Though polygamy has been constantly practised and universally allowed under all the religions that have obtained in Asia, we meet with very few instances of permitted polyandry, or a plurality of husbands, such as mentioned in the fourteenth section of this chapter: but a gentleman, who has lately visited the Kingdoms of Boutān and Thibet, has observed, that the same custom is almost general to this day in those countries; where one wife frequently serves all the males of a whole family, without being the cause of any uncommon jealousy or disunion among them.[a]

The characteristic enthusiasm of the Gentoos is strongly marked in several parts of this chapter, where it appears, that the property of a Bramin is considered as too sacred to fall into profane hands, even those of the magistrate; which proves also that the magistrates are not Bramins. At the same time, we cannot help noticing many striking instances of moderation and self-denial in the members of this tribe, who, being at once the priests and legislators of the country, have yet resigned all the secular and executive power into the hands of another cast; for it appears, that no Bramin has been properly capable of the magistracy since the time of the Suttee Jogue. They have also in one place ordained, that, 'if a widow should give all her property and estate to the Bramins for religious purposes, the gift indeed is valid'; that is, it comes within the letter of the law: 'But the act is improper, and the woman blameable.' Such a censure, though not amounting to an absolute prohibition, is surely a sufficient warning to those whose weak bigotry might thus lead them to error, and an argument that

---

[a] This was reported by George Bogle (1746–81), who was sent to Tibet by Warren Hastings in 1774 (*Narratives of the Mission of George Bogle to Tibet and of the Journey of Thomas Manning to Lhasa*, ed. C. R. Markham (1876), pp. 122–3).

these lawgivers were free from all the narrow principles of self-interested avidity. The only privilege of importance, which they seem to have appropriated to themselves in any part of this compilation, is an exemption from all capital punishment: they may be degraded, branded, imprisoned for life, or sent into perpetual exile; but it is every where expressly ordained, that a Bramin shall not be put to death upon any account whatsoever.[a]

Chapter III. The chapter of justice, in its general tendency, seems to be one of the best in the whole Code. The necessary qualifications for the arbitrator, the rules for the examination of witnesses, and the requisites for propriety of evidence, are stated with as much accuracy and depth of judgment as the generality of those in our own courts. In this chapter mention is made of the Purrekeh, or trial by ordeal, which is one of the most ancient institutes for the distinguishing criterion of guilt and innocence that hath been handed down to us by sacred or profane history: fire or water were the usual resources upon these occasions, and they were constantly prepared and sanctified by the solemnities of a religious ceremonial. The modes of this ordeal are various in India, according to the choice of the parties or the nature of the offence; but the infallibility of the result is to this day as implicitly believed as it could have been in the darkest ages of antiquity.

We find a particular injunction and description of a certain water ordeal among the first laws dictated to Moses by God himself; it is contained in the fifth chapter of Numbers, from the twelfth to the thirtieth verse, and is for the satisfaction of jealous husbands, in the immediate detection or acquittal of their wives.

Chapters IV, V and VI. In the two succeeding chapters no unusual matter occurs, but such as good sense and a freedom from prejudice will easily develope: but, in the second section of the sixth chapter, a passage appears, which, upon a slight examination, might give the reader a very indifferent opinion of the Gentoo system of government, viz. 'A law to regulate the shares of robbers.' This ordinance by no means respects the domestic disturbers of the tranquility of their own countrymen, or violators of the first principles of society, but only such bold and hardy

---

[a] In August 1775 the Brahmin Maharaja Nandakumar was to be executed after being convicted of forgery by the Supreme Court at Calcutta.

adventurers as sally forth to levy contributions in a foreign province. Unjust as this behaviour may appear in the eye of equity, it bears the most genuine stamp of antiquity, and corresponds entirely with the manners of the early Grecians, at or before the period of the Trojan war, and of the Western nations, before their emersion from barbarism; a practice still kept up among the pyratic States of Barbary to its fullest extent by sea, and probably among many herds of Tartars and Arabian banditti by land. However, the known existence and originality of this savage system will justify the Gentoo magistrate of those ancient periods in assisting the freebooters with his advice, and participating in their plunder, when, at that time, such expeditions were esteemed both legal and honourable.

It is not necessary, in an essay like this, to attempt an investigation of every local anomaly, or national peculiarity, that may arise in the course of this work; but merely to speak of such as seem to contradict the general opinions of mankind, and to round off those harsher features of the picture which appear unnatural or distorted, as well as uncommon.

Chapters VII and VIII. Omitting therefore the modes of gift in the seventh chapter, and the particular ordinances respecting slaves in the eighth, let us proceed to the second section of the ninth chapter, 'Of the wages of dancing women or prostitutes.'

Chapter IX. From the most distant ages the Asiatic world has observed the custom of employing women trained up, and hired for the purpose to sing and dance at the public festivals and religious ceremonies. We find that, 'When David was returned from the slaughter of the Philistines, the women came out of all the cities of Israel singing and dancing to meet King Saul, with tabrets, with joy, and with instruments of music.'[a]

It is still an universal practice among the Gentoos, to entertain a number of such women for the celebration of their solemn festivals; and in many parts of the Deccan, a band of them is kept in every village at the public charge, and they are frequently dispatched to meet any person passing in a public character, exactly conformable to the reception of Saul by the women of Israel. Probably their being exposed to general view and to a free conver-

---

[a] 1 Sam. xviii, 6.

sation with men (so contrary to the reserve and privacy of the rest of their sex in Asia) first betrayed them into prostitution: and in former ages, a prostitute seems to have been by no means so despicable a character as at present, since one of the first acts of King Solomon's government that was thought worthy to be recorded was a decision from the throne, upon the suit of two harlots.[a] Many states, even among the moderns, have found the necessity as well as utility of tolerated prostitution; they have discovered it to be one of the most effectual methods for preserving the peace of families and the health of individuals; and publick stews have accordingly been licensed under every regulation that could be devised to obviate their probable ill effects, and to secure all their advantages; so, in Asia, the profession of singing and dancing by distinct sets or companies naturally formed these women into a kind of community. And as the policy of a good government will always look with an eye of regard upon every branch of society, it was but just and proper to enact laws for the security and protection of this publick body, as well as of the rest of the state, particularly as the sex and employment of those who composed it rendered them more than usually liable to insult and ill usage.

It can be no objection to the rules laid down in this place, that the language in which they are delivered is plain even to grossness; it is well known that the ancients, even in their most refined ages, admitted a freedom of speech utterly incompatible with the delicacy of modern conversation, and that we are on that account frequently much embarrassed in translating even the most classical authors of Greece and Rome. Indecency too seems to be a word unknown to the law, which ever insists upon a simple definition of fact. The English courts, upon trials for rape or adultery, are full as little modest and equivocal in their language as any part of this or some of the succeeding chapters; neither rank nor sex, nor innocence can protect a woman who is unfortunate enough to be called in as a witness, even upon the most trivial points of such a cause, from being obliged to hear, and even to utter the most indecent and shocking expressions, which are necessarily urged upon her, so far as to authenticate every

[a] 1 Kings iii, 16–28.

circumstance in question, without the least disguise of circumlocution or reserve in favour of modesty: yet trials of this nature are published at length among us, and read with eagerness, as much perhaps to the scandal of the law as to the corruption of our imaginations, and the debasement of our manners.

But a work upon so diffusive a plan as that of this Code is calculated for the perusal of the judge and of the philosopher, and is far above the cavil of narrow understandings and selfish prejudices. These indeed will sometimes feel, or pretend to feel, a greater shock at the mention of certain crimes, than it is to be suspected they would undergo in the commission of them; but for the warning of the subject, and for the guidance of the magistrate, no delineation of offences can be too minute, and no discrimination too particular.

Chapter XVI. From hence, in conformity to the intention of this treatise, we shall at once proceed to the sixteenth chapter of assault, and of preparation to assault; which seems entirely founded upon the peculiar tenderness of a Gentoo's conscience, with respect to the purity of his cast. Here we see almost every uncleanness that can be practised accurately specified, and strongly prohibited; and the penalty is constantly enhanced in proportion to the rank or circumstances of the parties. The same notions of defilement from contact with any unclean article appear to have been diligently inculcated into the Jews by their inspired legislator; and the nineteenth chapter of Numbers bears an evident relation to the spirit and meaning of the chapter here, though it differs in the statement of the several objects from whence the defilement is supposed to proceed. The regulations before us were entirely necessary for a people, whose very degree and place in society were conditionally dependant upon a scrupulous avoidance of all uncleanness. Hence even the preparation or attempt to assault was forbidden, as well as the act itself; and the tautological enumeration of every possible mode of this assault, by the most minute gradations, needs no other plea to reconcile it to our ideas.

Chapter XVII. The chapter upon theft contains a complete answer to every objection that might be brought against a former expression in the Code, 'Of the magistrates sharing in the plunder of robbers,' as almost every possible species of fraud or robbery is in this place impartially condemned. Among other punishments, those of 'cutting off the hair, shaving with the urine of an ass, &c.' are several times mentioned. These are like the stocks and pillory among ourselves, intended to operate upon the feelings of the mind, rather than those of the body, and, by awakening the sense of shame and disgrace, to obviate the necessity of corporal chastisement. They are constantly considered among the Hindoos as the most complete degradation they can undergo, next to the absolute loss of cast. And some imagine, though without foundation, that they are by this punishment really expelled from their tribe; that however is not the case, they are meant merely as temporary humiliations, and as a kind of warning, that upon the next offence the sword of justice will be aimed at the head itself.

The fines or penalties enjoined for concealed theft, in the third section of this chapter, comprehend most of the modes of capital punishment prescribed by ancient or modern tribunals. Hanging and crucifixion seem to have been the usual kinds of death inflicted by the Jews; but their laws were also no strangers to the practice of burning, as we find by the twenty-first chapter of Leviticus, 'The daughter of any priest, if she profane herself by playing the whore, she profaneth her father, she shall be burned with fire.'

The crime of men-stealing, mentioned in this part of the Code, however repugnant to every principle of humanity, is not by any means peculiar to the Gentoos, for it is likewise forbidden, under pain of death, in Deuteronomy, chapter twenty-fourth: 'If a man be found stealing any of his brethren of the children of Israel, and maketh merchandize of him, then that thief shall die, and thou shalt put away evil from among you.'

This part of the compilation exhibits a variety of crimes punishable by various modes of capital retribution, contrary to the general opinion adopted in Europe, that the Gentoo administration was wonderfully mild, and averse to the deprivation of life. One cause for this opinion might be, that, since the Tartar empire became absolute in India, the Hindoos (like the Jews in the Captivity) though in some respects permitted to live by their own rules and laws, have for reasons of government been in most cases prohibited from dying by them. This chapter however displays instances of what might seem unjustifiable severity, did not the Jewish dispensation afford us a number of examples to the same purpose. The ordinance in Moses for stoning a rebellious son,[a] or a girl found not to be a virgin.[b] Samuel's hewing Agag to pieces before the Lord in Gilgal:[c] whole nations cut off at once by unlimitted proscription: David's harrassing his enemies with harrows of iron;[d] and a thousand other passages of the same tendency, prove that the laws of most nations of antiquity were written in letters of blood; and if in England (as it is said) we have near eighty kinds of felonies, all liable to capital punishment, the Gentoos need not think their own legislature uncommonly fertile in employments for the executioner.

The latter part of this section is particularly set apart to treat of thefts committed by the Bramin tribe; and the many dreadful penalties there enjoined leave the delinquents but a slender satisfaction in their exemption from capital punishment: add too, that from these circumstances it may be collected, that this exemption is really founded upon a reverential regard to the sanctity of their function and character, rather than upon the unjust preference of self-interested partiality.

Chapter XIX. The nineteenth and twentieth chapters present us a lively picture of Asiatic manners, and in them a strong proof of their own originality.[e] To men of liberal and candid sentiments, neither the grossness of the portrait nor the harshness of the colouring will seem improper or indecent, while they are convinced of the truth of the resemblance; and if this compilation does not exhibit mankind as they might have been, or as they ought to have been, the answer is plain, 'Because it paints them as they were.' Vices, as well as fashions, have their spring and their fall, not with individuals only, but in whole nations, where one reigning foible for awhile swallows up the rest, and then retires in its turn to make room for the epidemic influence of a newer passion. Wherefore, if any opinions not reconcileable to our modes of thinking, or any crimes not practised, and so not pro-

---

[a] Deut. xxi, 20–1.   [b] *Ibid*. xxii, 20–1.   [c] 1 Sam. xv, 33.
[d] 2 Sam. xii, 31; 1 Chron. xx, 3.
[e] Chapters 'of adultery' and 'of what concerns women'.

hibited among us, should occur in these chapters, they must be imputed to the different effects produced on the human mind by a difference of climates, customs and manners, which will constantly give a particular turn and bias to the national vices. Hence it would be a weak and frivolous argument for censuring the fifth section of this nineteenth chapter,[a] to object that it was levelled at an offence absurd in itself, not likely to be frequent, or supposing it frequent, still to be deemed of trivial consequence; and to make this objection merely in consideration that the offence may not be usual among us, and has certainly never been forbidden by our legislature, such cavils would betray a great ignorance of the general system of human nature, as well as of the common principles of legislation, for penal laws (except for the most ordinary crimes) are not enacted until particular instances of offence have pointed out their absolute necessity; for which reason parricide was not specified among the original institutes of the celebrated lawgiver of Sparta.[b] Hence we may with safety conclude, that the several prohibitions and penalties of this fifth section were subsequent to and in consequence of the commission of every species of enormity therein described.

In Asia, the indubitable virginity of the bride has ever been a requisite and most necessary condition of a marriage; and indeed the warmth of constitution in either sex, and the universal jealousy of the men in those climates, give great propriety to the caution; for in women the first breach of chastity was always esteemed decisive; and Moses considered the offence in at least as serious a light as the Gentoos have done, since he ordained, that, if the tokens of virginity were not found upon a girl at her marriage, she should be stoned.[c] A hard fate surely, if we reflect to how many accidents so frail an article is liable, without any intention or fault of its possessor! And if a Hindoo's conscience is equally nice with a Jew's, upon this point it cannot be judged extraordinary, that a particular section of this Code should be appropriated to the condemnation of such practices as may violate virginity, and destroy its tokens, even without actual copulation, since the disgrace and other unhappy consequences to the woman

---

[a] 'Of thrusting a finger into the pudenda of an unmarried girl'.
[b] Lycurgus.   [c] Deut. xxii, 20–1.

are equally inevitable, to what cause soever it be owing that the proofs of her chastity are deficient.

The best security for female virtue is the total absence of temptation, and consequently, to endeavour to remove the one is a prudent caution for the preservation of the other. We find therefore the several modes and gradations of Asiatic gallantry separately forbidden at the beginning of this chapter, which, by slightly punishing the first preparatives and leading steps to an offence, shews a tender concern for the offender's welfare, to whom it thus gives a monitory check at the very commencement of his design, and before the execution of it has subjected him to the extreme rigour of the law.

Chapter XX. It may not be improper to mention upon this chapter, that the Bramins who compiled the Code were men far advanced in years, as one of them above eighty, and only one under thirty-five, by way of apology for the observations they have selected, and the censures they have passed upon the conduct and merits of the fair sex.[a] Solomon however, who probably had as much experience in women as any Pundit in any of the four Jogues, was nearly of the same sentiments, as we may collect from numerous passages in his Proverbs, one of which, in the thirtieth chapter, so exactly corresponds with a sentence in this part of the Code, that the one almost seems a literal transcript from the other. 'There are,' says Solomon, 'three things that are never satisfied; yea, four things say not, it is enough: the grave and the barren womb; the earth that is filled not with water, and the fire that saith not, it is enough.'

The passage in the Code will speak for itself; so striking a resemblance needs neither quotation nor comment: yet neither the royal author of the Proverbs, nor the composers of the Shasters, are by any means so censorious or so unjust as to deny the possibility of excellence in the female sex, though they allow the instances to be somewhat scarce, and that wives of this quality are only to be obtained by many and great acts of piety, or, as Solomon expresses it, 'A prudent wife is from the Lord.'[b]

[a] Chapter xx began with a warning that 'if a wife have her own free will, notwithstanding she be sprung from a superior cast, she will behave amiss'.
[b] Prov. xix, 14.

The many rules laid down in this chapter, for the preservation of domestic authority to the husband, are relicks of that characteristic discipline of Asia, which sacred and profane writers testify to have existed from all antiquity; where women have ever been the subjects, not the partners of their *Lords*, confined within the walls of a Haram, or busied without doors in drudgeries little becoming their delicacy. The Trojan Princesses were employed in washing linen; and Rebecca was first discovered by Abraham's servant with a pitcher upon her shoulder to water camels. 'Two women shall be grinding at the mill,'[a] says the Prophet; but the notoriety of this fact obviates the necessity of quotations: it may just be observed, that Solomon in praising a good wife mentions, that 'She rises while it is yet night,'[b] which we must suppose to be before her husband; and we find this to be one of the qualifications for a good Gentoo wife also.

The latter part of this chapter relates to the extraordinary circumstance of women burning themselves with their deceased husbands: the terms of the injunction as there set forth are plain, moderate and conditional: 'It is proper for a woman to burn with her husband's corps'; and a proportionate reward is offered in compensation for her sufferings. Notwithstanding the ordinance is not in the absolute style of a command, it is surely sufficiently direct to stand for a religious duty; the only proof that it is not positive is the proposal of inviolable chastity as an alternative, though it is not to be taken for an equivalent. The Bramins seem to look upon this sacrifice as one of the first principles of their religion, the cause of which it would hardly be orthodox to investigate. There are however several restrictions with respect to it, as that a woman must not burn herself if she is with child, nor if her husband died at a distance from her, unless she can procure his turban and girdle to put on at the pile, with other exceptions of the same nature, which they closely conceal from the eyes of the world, among the other mysteries of their faith: but we are convinced equally by information and experience, that the custom has not for the most part fallen into desuetude in India, as a celebrated writer has supposed.[c]

Chapter XXI. The twenty-first chapter comprehends a number

---

[a] Matt. xxiv, 41.   [b] Prov. xxxi, 15.   [c] Dow, see above, p. 116.

of unconnected articles, of which the last section is a kind of peroration to the whole work. But of such parts of these ordinances as relate merely to the religious opinions of the Hindoos we certainly are not authorized to judge; they were instituted in conformity to *their* prejudices; and the consciences of the people, as well as the penalties of the law, enforce their obedience. Hence little observation need be made upon the accountable prohibitions of the second section, but that the commission of such ridiculous crimes, for which no possible temptation can be pleaded, may be severely punished, without much danger to the generality of mankind.[a]

The article of the third section is of a more serious nature, and contains an injunction not unnecessary for the general peace and good order of every community.[b] The vulgar in all nations are tied down to the continual exercise of bodily labour for their own immediate subsistence; and their employments are as incompatible with the leisure requisite for religious speculations, as their ideas are too gross for the comprehension of their subtilty; add to this, that illiterate minds are usually so apt to kindle at the least touch of enthusiastic zeal, as to make their headstrong superstition the most dangerous of all weapons in the hands of a designing partizan; like the *Agnee-aster*, it rages with unquenchable violence, and separating into a thousand flames, all equally destructive, subsides not but with the exaltation of a Cromwell, or a Massacre of Saint Bartholomew. Moses observed a like severity with this Code, in prohibiting the rest of the people from any interference with the profession of the priesthood; the ordinance is issued from the mouth of God himself: 'Thou shalt appoint Aaron and his sons, and they shall wait on their priest's office, and the stranger that cometh nigh shall be put to death.'[c]

Indeed the whole office, as well as the sacred preeminence of the Braminical tribe, is almost an exact counterpart of that of the Levitical: the Levites were particularly forbidden wine; so are the Bramins: the Levites were more than others enjoined to avoid the contact of all uncleanness; so are the Bramins: the Levites were to assist the magistrate's judgment in difficult cases; so are

---

[a] Halhed seems to be referring to the section 'of serving unclean victuals'.
[b] 'Of the punishment to be inflicted on a Sooder for reading the Beids'.
[c] Num. xviii, 7.

the Bramins: and, in every other respect, the resemblance might well authorize a suspicion, that they had originally some remote affinity to each other, though conjecture cannot possibly trace the source of the connexion.

The patience of the publick has now been sufficiently exercised and trespassed upon in this essay, which was but designed to obviate some of the most plausible objections, which are likely to be stated against so uncommon a compilation. We have every where produced instances of a similitude between the Mosaical and the Hindoo Dispensation, though without attempting to insert the hundredth part of what occurred upon so fruitful a subject.

But it is not only to the Laws of Moses that this Code bears a striking likeness; many other parts of the Holy Scriptures may from hence be elucidated or confirmed: thus in the book of Genesis we find Laban excusing himself for having substituted Leah in the place of Rachel to Jacob, in these words: 'It must not be so done in our country, to give the youngest (daughter) before the first-born':[a] this was long before Moses was born. So in this compilation it is made criminal for a man to give his younger daughter in marriage before the elder, or for a younger son to marry while his elder brother remains unmarried.

Comparisons of this nature will illustrate many doubtful passages, and explain many obsolete customs and usages alluded to throughout the Bible; so that should no part of these laws be thought worthy of adoption into the system of a British government in Asia, they will yet well deserve the consideration of the politician, the judge, the divine, and the philosopher, as they contain the genuine sentiments of a great and flourishing people, at a time when it was impossible for them to have any connexion or communication with the European world, upon subjects in which all mankind have a common interest; as they abound with maxims of general policy and justice, which no particularity of manners, or diversity of religious opinions can alter; as they may become useful references for a number of national and local distinctions in our own sacred writings, and as the several powers of the mind, in the gradual progress of civilization, may by judicious comparisons from hence be investigated almost to their first principles.

[a] Gen. xxix, 26.

Preliminary Discourse

From men of enlightened understandings and sound judgment, who, in their researches after truth, have swept from their hearts the dust of malice and opposition, it is not concealed, that the contrarieties of religion, and diversities of belief, which are causes of envy, and of enmity to the ignorant, are in fact a manifest demonstration of the power of the Supreme Being: for it is evident, that a painter, by sketching a multiplicity of figures, and by arranging a variety of colours, procures a reputation among men; and a gardener, for planting a diversity of shrubs, and for producing a number of different flowers, gains credit and commendation; wherefore it is absurdity and ignorance to view, in an inferior light, Him who created both the painter and the gardener. The truly intelligent well know, that the differences and varieties of created things are a ray of His glorious essence, and that the contrarieties of constitutions are a type of His wonderful attributes; whose complete power formed all creatures of the animal, vegetable and material world, from the four elements of fire, water, air and earth, to be an ornament to the magazine of creation; and whose comprehensive benevolence selected man, the center of knowledge, to have the dominion and authority over the rest; and, having bestowed, upon this favourite object, judgment and understanding, gave him supremacy over the corners of the world; and, when He had put into his hand the free control and arbitrary disposal of all affairs, He appointed to each tribe its own faith, and to every sect its own religion; and having introduced a numerous variety of casts, and a multiplicity of different customs, He views in each particular place the mode of worship respectively appointed to it; sometimes He is employed with the attendants upon the mosque, in counting the sacred beads; sometimes He is in the temple, at the adoration of idols; the intimate of the Mussulman, and the friend of the Hindoo; the companion of the Christian, and the confidant of the Jew. Wherefore men of exalted notions, not being bent upon hatred and opposition, but considering the collected body of creatures as an object of the power of the Almighty, by investigating the contrarieties of sect, and the different customs of religion, have stamped to themselves a lasting reputation upon the page of the world; particularly in the extensive empire of Hindostan, which is a most delightful country, and wherein are collected great numbers of Turks, of Persians, of Tartars, of Scythians, of Europeans, of Armenians, and of Abyssinians. And whereas, this kingdom was the long residence of Hindoos, and was governed by many powerful Roys and Rajahs, the Gentoo religion became catholick and universal here; but when it was afterwards ravaged, in several parts, by the armies of Mahomedanism, a change of religion took place, and a contrariety of customs arose, and all affairs were transacted, according to the principles of faith in the conquering party, upon which perpetual oppositions were engendered, and continual differences in the decrees of justice; so that in every place the immediate magistrate decided all causes according to his own religion; and the Laws of Mahomed were the standard of judgment for the Hindoos. Hence terror and confusion found a way to all the people, and justice was not impartially administered; wherefore a thought suggested itself to the Governor General, the Honourable Warren Hastings, to investigate the principles of the Gentoo religion, and to explore the customs of the Hindoos, and to procure a translation of them in the Persian language, that they might become universally known by the perspicuity of that idiom, and that a book might be compiled to preclude all such contradictory decrees in future, and that, by a proper attention to each religion, justice might take place impartially, according to the tenets of every sect. Wherefore Bramins, learned in the Shaster (whose names are here subjoined) were invited from all parts of the kingdom to Fort William, in Calcutta, which is the capital of Bengal and Bahar, and the most authentick books, both ancient and modern, were collected, and the original text, delivered in the Hindoo language, was faithfully translated by the interpreters into the Persian idiom. They began their work in May, 1773, answering to the month *Jeyt*, 1180 (Bengal style) and finished it by the end of February, 1775, answering to the month *Phaùgoon*, 1182 (Bengal style).

4

Warren Hastings, 'Letter to Nathaniel Smith', from *The Bhăgvăt-Gēētā*

Advertisement

The following work is published under the authority of the Court of Directors of the East India Company, by the particular desire and recommendation of the Governor General of India; whose letter to the Chairman of the Company will sufficiently explain the motives for its publication, and furnish the best testimony of the fidelity, accuracy, and merit of the translator.

The antiquity of the original, and the veneration in which it hath been held for so many ages, by a very considerable portion of the human race, must render it one of the greatest curiosities ever presented to the literary world.

To Nathaniel Smith, Esquire[a]

Banaris, 4th October 1784

Sir,

To you, as to the first member of the first commercial body, not only of the present age, but of all the known generations of mankind, I presume to offer, and to recommend through you, for an offering to the public, a very curious specimen of the literature, the mythology, and morality of the ancient Hindoos. It is an episodical extract from the 'Mắhābhārắt', a most voluminous poem, affirmed to have been written upwards of four thousand years ago, by Krĕĕshnắ Dwypayen Veiâs, a learned Bramin; to whom is also attributed the compilation of 'The Four Vêdes, or Bêdes', the only existing

---

[a] Nathaniel Smith (1730–94), Chairman of the East India Company

184

original scriptures of the religion of Brahmâ; and the composition of all the Poorâns, which are to this day taught in their schools, and venerated as poems of divine inspiration. Among these, and of superior estimation to the rest, is ranked the Măhābhărăt. But if the several books here enumerated be really the productions of their reputed author, which is greatly to be doubted, many arguments may be adduced to ascribe to the same source the invention of the religion itself, as well as its promulgation: and he must, at all events, claim the merit of having first reduced the gross and scattered tenets of their former faith into a scientific and allegorical system.

The Măhābhărăt contains the genealogy and general history of the house of Bhaurut, so called from Bhurrut its founder; the epithet Mahâ, or Great, being prefixed in token of distinction: but its more particular object is to relate the dissentions and wars of the two great collateral branches of it, called Kooroos and Pandoos; both lineally descended in the second degree from Veĕcheĕtrăveĕrya, their common ancestor, by their respective fathers Dreetrarashtra and Pandoo.

The Kooroos, which indeed is sometimes used as a term comprehending the whole family, but most frequently applied as the patronymic of the elder branch alone, are said to have been one hundred in number, of whom Dooryŏdun was esteemed the head and representative even during the life of his father, who was incapacitated by blindness. The sons of Pandoo were five; Yoodhishteer, Bheem, Arjŏŏn, Nĕkool, and Sehădĕo; who, through the artifices of Dooryŏdun, were banished, by their uncle and guardian Dreetrarashtra, from Hastenapoor, at that time the seat of government of Hindostan.

The exiles, after a series of adventures, worked up with a wonderful fertility of genius and pomp of language into a thousand sublime descriptions, returned with a powerful army to avenge their wrongs, and assert their pretentions to the empire in right of their father; by whom, though the younger brother, it had been held while he lived, on account of the disqualification already mentioned of Dreetrarashtra.

In this state the episode opens, and is called 'The Gēētā of Bhăgvăt', which is one of the names of Krĕĕshnă. Arjŏŏn is represented as the favorite and pupil of Krĕĕshnă, here taken for God himself, in his last Ootâr, or descent to earth in a mortal form.

The Preface of the translator will render any further explanation of the work unnecessary. Yet something it may be allowable for me to add respecting my own judgment of a work which I have thus informally obtruded on your attention, as it is the only ground on which I can defend the liberty which I have taken.

Might I, an unlettered man, venture to prescribe bounds to the latitude of criticism, I should exclude, in estimating the merit of such a production, all rules drawn from the ancient or modern literature of Europe, all references to such sentiments or manners as are become the standards of propriety for opinion and action in our own modes of life, and equally all appeals to our revealed tenets of religion, and moral duty. I should exclude them, as by no means applicable to the language, sentiments, manners, or morality appertaining to a system of society with which we have been for ages unconnected, and of an antiquity preceding even the first efforts of civilization in our own quarter of the globe, which, in respect to the general diffusion and common participation of arts and sciences, may be now considered as one community.

I would exact from every reader the allowance of obscurity, absurdity, barbarous habits, and a perverted morality. Where the reverse appears, I would have him receive it (to use a familiar phrase) as so much clear gain, and allow it a merit proportioned to the disappointment of a different expectation.

In effect, without bespeaking this kind of indulgence, I could hardly venture to persist in my recommendation of this production for public notice.

Many passages will be found obscure, many will seem redundant; others will be found cloathed with ornaments of fancy unsuited to our taste, and some elevated to a track of sublimity into which our habits of judgment will find it difficult to pursue them; but few which will shock either our religious faith or moral sentiments. Something too must be allowed to the subject itself, which is highly metaphysical, to the extreme difficulty of rendering abstract terms by others exactly corresponding with them in another language, to the arbitrary combination of ideas, in words expressing unsubstantial qualities, and more, to the errors of interpretation. The modesty of the translator would induce him to defend the credit of his work, by laying all its apparent defects to his own charge, under the article last enumerated; but neither does his accuracy merit, nor the work itself require that concession.

It is also to be observed, in illustration of what I have premised, that the Brāhmăns are enjoined to perform a kind of spiritual discipline, not, I believe, unknown to some of the religious orders of Christians in the Romish Church. This consists in devoting a certain period of time to the contemplation of the Deity, his attributes, and the moral duties of this life. It is required of those who practise this exercise, not only that they divest their minds of all sensual desire, but that their attention be abstracted from every external object, and absorbed, with every sense, in the prescribed subject of their meditation. I myself was once a witness of a man employed in this species of devotion, at the principal temple of Banaris. His right hand and arm were enclosed in a loose sleeve or bag of red cloth, within which he passed the beads of his rosary, one after another, through his fingers, repeating with the touch of each (as I was informed) one of the names of God, while his mind laboured to catch and dwell on the idea of the quality which appertained to it, and shewed the violence of its exertion to attain this purpose by the convulsive movements of all his features, his eyes being at the same time closed, doubtless to assist the abstraction. The importance of this duty cannot be better illustrated, nor stronger marked, than by the last sentence with which Krĕĕshnă closes his instruction to Arjŏŏn, and which is properly the conclusion of the Gĕĕtā: 'Hath what I have been speaking, O Arjŏŏn, been heard *with thy mind fixed to one point?* Is the *distraction* of thought, which arose from thy ignorance, removed?'

To those who have never been accustomed to this separation of the mind from the notices of the senses, it may not be easy to conceive by what means such a power is to be attained; since even the most studious men of our hemisphere will find it difficult so to restrain their attention but that it will wander to some object of present sense or recollection; and even the buzzing of a fly will sometimes have the power to disturb it. But if we are told that there have been men who were successively, for ages past, in the daily habit of abstracted contemplation, begun in the earliest period of youth, and continued in many to the maturity of age, each adding some portion of knowledge to the store accumulated by his predecessors; it is not assuming too much to conclude, that, as the mind ever gathers strength, like the body, by exercise, so in such an exercise it may in each have acquired the faculty to which they aspired, and that their collective studies may have led them to the discovery of new tracks and combinations of sentiment, totally different from the doctrines with which the learned of other nations are acquainted: doctrines, which however speculative and subtle, still, as they possess the advantage of being derived from a source so free from every adventitious mixture, may be equally founded in truth with the most simple of our own. But as they must differ, yet more than the most abstruse of ours, from the common modes of thinking, so they will require consonant modes of expression, which it may be impossible to render by any of the known terms of science in our language, or even to make them intelligible by definition. This is probably the case with some of the English phrases, as those of 'action,' 'application,' 'practice,' &c. which occur in Mr. Wilkins's translation; and others, for the reasons which I have recited, he has left with the same sounds in which he found them. When the text is rendered obscure from such causes, candor requires that credit be given to it for some accurate meaning, though we may not be able to discover it; and that we ascribe their obscurity to the incompetency of our own perceptions, on so novel an application of them, rather than to the less probable want of perspicuity in the original composition.

With the deductions, or rather qualifications, which I have thus premised, I hesitate not to pronounce the Gĕĕtā a performance of great originality; of a sublimity of conception, reasoning, and diction, almost unequalled; and a single exception, among all the known religions of mankind, of a theology accurately corresponding with that of the Christian dispensation, and most powerfully illustrating its fundamental doctrines.

It will not be fair to try its relative worth by a comparison with the original text of the first standards of European composition; but let these be taken even in the most esteemed of their prose translations; and in that equal scale let their merits be weighed. I should not fear to place, in opposition to the best French versions of the most admired passages of the Iliad or Odyssey, or of the 1st and 6th Books of our own Milton, highly as I venerate the latter, the English translation of the Măhābhārăt.

One blemish will be found in it, which will scarcely fail to make its own impression on every correct mind; and which for that reason I anticipate. I mean, the attempt to describe spiritual existences by terms and images which appertain to corporeal forms. Yet even in this respect it will appear less faulty than other works with which I have placed it in competition; and, defective as it may at first appear, I know not whether a doctrine so elevated above common perception did not require to be introduced by such ideas as were familiar to the mind, to lead it by a gradual advance to the pure and abstract comprehension of the subject. This will seem to have been, whether intentionally or accidentally, the order which is followed by the author of the Gēētā; and so far at least he soars far beyond all competitors in this species of composition. Even the frequent recurrence of the same sentiment, in a variety of dress, may have been owing to the same consideration of the extreme intricacy of the subject, and the consequent necessity of trying different kinds of exemplification and argument, to impress it with due conviction on the understanding. Yet I believe it will appear, to an attentive reader, neither deficient in method, nor in perspicuity. On the contrary, I thought it at the first reading, and more so at the second, clear beyond what I could have reasonably expected, in a discussion of points so far removed beyond the reach of the senses, and explained through so foreign a medium.

It now remains to say something of the translator, Mr Charles Wilkins. This gentleman, to whose ingenuity, unaided by models for imitation, and by artists for his direction, your government is indebted for its printing-office, and for many official purposes to which it has been profitably applied, with an extent unknown in Europe, has united to an early and successful attainment of the Persian and Bengal languages, the study of the Sănskrĕĕt. To this he devoted himself with a perseverance of which there are few examples, and with a success which encouraged him to undertake the translation of the Măhābhārăt. This book is said to consist of more than one hundred thousand metrical stanzas, of which he has at this time translated more than a third; and, if I may trust to the imperfect tests by which I myself have tried a very small portion of it, through the medium of another language, he has rendered it with great accuracy and fidelity. Of its elegance, and the skill with which he has familiarized (if I may so express it) his own native language to so foreign an original, I may not speak, as from the specimen herewith presented, whoever reads it, will judge for himself.

Mr Wilkins's health having suffered a decline from the fatigues of business, from which his gratuitous labors allowed him no relaxation, he was advised to try a change of air for his recovery. I myself recommended that of Banaris, for the sake of the additional advantage which he might derive from a residence in a place which is considered as the first seminary of Hindoo learning; and I promoted his application to the Board, for their permission to repair thither, without forfeiting his official appointments during the term of his absence.

I have always regarded the encouragement of every species of useful diligence, in the servants of the Company, as a duty appertaining to my office; and have severely regretted that I have possessed such scanty means of exercising it, especially to such as required an exemption from official attendance; there being few emoluments in this service but such as are annexed to official employment, and few offices without employment. Yet I believe I may take it upon me to pronounce, that the service has at no period more abounded with men of cultivated talents, of capacity for business, and liberal knowledge; qualities which reflect the greater lustre on their possessors, by having been the fruit of long and laboured application, at a season of life, and with a licence of conduct, more apt to produce dissipation than excite the desire of improvement.

Such studies, independently of their utility, tend, especially when the pursuit of them is general, to diffuse a generosity of sentiment, and a disdain of the meaner occupations of such minds as are left nearer to the state of uncultivated nature; and you, Sir, will believe me, when I assure you, that it is on the virtue, not the ability of their servants, that the Company must rely for the permanency of their dominion.

Nor is the cultivation of language and science, for such are the studies to which I allude, useful only in forming the moral character and habits of the service. Every accumulation of knowledge, and especially such as is obtained by social communication with people over whom we exercise a dominion founded on the right of conquest, is useful to the state: it is the gain of humanity: in the specific instance which I have stated, it attracts and conciliates distant affections; it lessens the weight of the chain by which the natives are held in subjection; and it imprints on the hearts of our own countrymen the sense and obligation of benevolence. Even in England, this effect of it is greatly wanting. It is not very long since the inhabitants of India were considered by many, as creatures scarce elevated above the degree of savage life; nor, I fear, is that prejudice yet wholly eradicated, though surely abated. Every instance which brings their real character home to observation will impress us with a more generous sense of feeling for their natural rights, and teach us to estimate them by the measure of our own. But such instances can only be obtained in their writings: and these will survive when the British dominion in India shall have long ceased to exist, and when the sources which it once yielded of wealth and power are lost to remembrance.

If you, Sir, on the perusal of Mr. Wilkins's performance, shall judge it worthy of so honorable a patronage, may I take the further liberty to request that you will be pleased to present it to the Court of Directors, for publication by their authority, and to use your interest to obtain it? Its public reception will be the test of its real merit, and determine Mr. Wilkins in the prosecution or cessation of his present laborious studies. It may, in the first event, clear the way to a wide and unexplored field of fruitful knowledge; and suggest, to the generosity of his honorable employers, a desire to encourage the first persevering adventurer in a service in which his example will have few followers, and most probably none, if it is to be performed with the gratuitous labor of years lost to the provision of future subsistence: for the study of the Sănskrĕĕt cannot, like the Persian language, be applied to official profit, and improved with the official exercise of it. It can only derive its reward, beyond the breath of fame, in a fixed endowment. Such has been the fate of his predecessor, Mr. Halhed, whose labors and incomparable genius, in two useful productions,[a] have been crowned with every success that the public estimation could give them; nor will it detract from the no less original merit of Mr. Wilkins, that I ascribe to another the title of having led the way, when I add, that this example held out to him no incitement to emulate it, but the prospect of barren applause. To say more, would be disrespect; and I believe that I address myself to a gentleman who possesses talents congenial with those which I am so anxious to encourage, and a mind too liberal to confine its beneficence to such arts alone as contribute to the immediate and substantial advantages of the state.[b]

I think it proper to assure you, that the subject of this address, and its design, were equally unknown to the person who is the object of it; from whom I originally obtained the translation for another purpose, which on a second revisal of the work I changed, from a belief that it merited a better destination.

A mind rendered susceptible by the daily experience of unmerited reproach, may be excused if it anticipates even unreasonable or improbable objections. This must be my plea for any apparent futility in the following observation. I have seen an extract from a foreign work of great literary credit, in which my name is mentioned, with very undeserved applause, for an attempt to introduce the knowledge of Hindoo literature into the European world, by forcing or corrupting the religious consciences of the Pundits, or professors of their sacred doctrines. This reflexion was produced by the publication of Mr. Halhed's translation of the Poottee, or code of Hindoo laws; and is totally devoid of foundation.[c] For myself I can declare truly, that if the acquisition could not have been obtained but by

[a] The Code and the *Grammar of the Bengal Language*.

[b] Smith presented the *Gita* to the Court of Directors of the East India Company on 9 June 1785. The Directors ordered that it be published 'under the patronage of this Court, on condition however than an expence not exceeding £200 shall be incurred by the Company in the publication' (India Office Records, Court Minutes, B/101, pp. 118–19).

[c] The translator of the French edition of the Code, thought to be Jean-Baptiste-René Robinet (1735–1820), had written that Hastings had needed 'toute l'adresse et toute la fermeté...pour obliger enfin les Brames à révéler ces grands secrets... Il a été réduit à corrompre les uns, à combattre, par la raison, les opinions superstitieuses des autres' (*Code des Loix des Gentoux* (Paris, 1778), pp. i–ii).

such means as have been supposed, I should never have sought it. It was contributed both cheerfully and gratuitously, by men of the most respectable characters for sanctity and learning in Bengal, who refused to accept more than the moderate daily subsistence of one rupee each, during the term that they were employed on the compilation; nor will it much redound to my credit, when I add, that they have yet received no other reward for their meritorious labors. Very natural causes may be ascribed for their reluctance to communicate the mysteries of their learning to strangers, as those to whom they have been for some centuries in subjection, never enquired into them, but to turn their religion into derision, or deduce from them arguments to support the intolerant principles of their own. From our nation they have received a different treatment, and are no less eager to impart their knowledge than we are to receive it. I could say much more in proof of this fact, but that it might look too much like self-commendation.

I have the honor to be, with respect,

Sir,

Your most obedient, and
Most humble Servant,
Warren Hastings

Calcutta, 3d Dec. 1784

P.S. Since the above was written, Mr. Wilkins has transmitted to me a corrected copy of his Translation, with the Preface and Notes much enlarged and improved. In the former, I meet with some complimentary passages, which are certainly improper for a work published at my own solicitation. But he is at too great a distance to allow of their being sent back to him for correction, without losing the opportunity, which I am unwilling to lose, of the present dispatch; nor could they be omitted, if I thought myself at liberty to expunge them, without requiring considerable alterations in the context. They must therefore stand; and I hope that this explanation will be admitted as a valid excuse for me in passing them.   W.H.

5

Charles Wilkins, 'The Translator's Preface', from *The Bhăgvăt-Gēētā*

To the Honourable Warren Hastings, Esq.
Governor General, &c. &c.

Honourable Sir,

Unconscious of the liberal purpose for which you intended the *Gēētā*, when, at your request, I had the honor to present you with a copy of the manuscript, I was the less solicitous about its imperfections, because I knew that your extensive acquaintance with the customs and religious tenets of the Hindoos would elucidate every passage that was obscure, and I had so often experienced approbation from your partiality, and correction from your pen: it was the theme of a pupil to his preceptor and patron. But since I received your commands to prepare it for the public view, I feel all that anxiety which must be inseparable from one who, for the first time, is about to appear before that awful tribunal; and I should dread the event, were I not convinced that the liberal sentiments expressed in the letter you have done me the honor to write, in recommendation of the work, to the Chairman of the Direction, if permitted to accompany it to the press, would screen me, under its own intrinsic merit, from all censure.

The world, Sir, is so well acquainted with your boundless patronage in general, and of the personal encouragement you have constantly given to my fellow-servants in particular, to render themselves more capable of performing their duty in the various branches of commerce, revenue, and policy, by the study of the languages, with the laws and customs of the natives, that it must deem the first fruit of every genius you have raised a tribute justly due to the source from which it sprang. As that personal encouragement alone first excited emulation in my breast, and urged me to prosecute my particular studies, even beyond the line of pecuniary reward, I humbly request you will permit me, in token of my gratitude, to lay the *Gēētā* publicly at your feet.

I have the honor to subscribe myself, with great respect,

Honorable Sir,

Your most obedient, and

Most humble Servant,

Banaris,

19th November, 1784   Chas Wilkins

Charles Wilkins

The Translator's Preface

The following work, forming part of the *Măhābhārăt*, an ancient
Hindoo poem, is a dialogue supposed to have passed between
Krĕĕshnă, an incarnation of the Deity, and his pupil and favorite
Arjŏŏn, one of the five sons of *Pāndŏŏ*, who is said to have
reigned about five thousand years ago, just before the commencement of a famous battle fought on the plains of *Kŏŏrŏŏkshētră*, near
Dehly, at the beginning of the *Kălĕĕ-Yoog*, or fourth and present
age of the world, for the empire of *Bhārăt-vērsh*, which, at that
time, included all the countries that, in the present division of the
globe, are called India, extending from the borders of Persia to
the extremity of China; and from the snowy mountains to the
southern promontory.

The *Brāhmăns* esteem this work to contain all the grand mysteries of their religion; and so careful are they to conceal it from
the knowledge of those of a different persuasion, and even the vulgar of their own, that the translator might have sought in vain for
assistance, had not the liberal treatment they have of late years
experienced from the mildness of our government, the tolerating
principles of our faith, and, above all, the personal attention paid
to the learned men of their order by him under whose auspicious
administration they have so long enjoyed, in the midst of sur-
rounding troubles, the blessings of internal peace, and his exemp-
lary encouragement, at length happily created in their breasts a
confidence in his countrymen sufficient to remove almost every
jealous prejudice from their minds.

It seems as if the principal design of these dialogues was to
unite all the prevailing modes of worship of those days; and, by
setting up the doctrine of the unity of the Godhead, in opposition
to idolatrous sacrifices, and the worship of images, to undermine
the tenets inculcated by the *Vēds*; for although the author dared
not make a direct attack, either upon the prevailing prejudices of
the people, or the divine authority of those ancient books; yet, by
offering eternal happiness to such as worship *Brăhm*, the Almighty, whilst he declares the reward of such as follow other Gods
shall be but a temporary enjoyment of an inferior heaven, for a

period measured by the extent of their virtues, his design was to bring about the downfall of polytheism; or, at least, to induce men to believe *God* present in every image before which they bent, and the object of all their ceremonies and sacrifices.

The most learned *Brāhmăns* of the present times are Unitarians according to the doctrines of *Krĕĕshnă*; but, at the same time that they believe but in one God, an universal spirit, they so far comply with the prejudices of the vulgar, as outwardly to perform all the ceremonies inculcated by the *Vēds*, such as sacrifices, ablutions, &c. They do this, probably, more for the support of their own consequence, which could only arise from the great ignorance of the people, than in compliance with the dictates of *Krĕĕshnă*: indeed, this ignorance, and these ceremonies, are as much the bread of the *Brāhmăns*, as the superstition of the vulgar is the support of the priesthood in many other countries.

The reader will have the liberality to excuse the obscurity of many passages, and the confusion of sentiments which runs through the whole, in its present form. It was the translator's business to remove as much of this obscurity and confusion as his knowledge and abilities would permit. This he hath attempted in his Notes; but as he is conscious they are still insufficient to remove the veil of mystery, he begs leave to remark, in his own justification, that the text is but imperfectly understood by the most learned *Brāhmăns* of the present times; and that, small as the work may appear, it has had more comments than the Revelations. These have not been totally disregarded; but, as they were frequently found more obscure than the original they were intended to elucidate, it was thought better to leave many of the most difficult passages for the exercise of the reader's own judgment, than to mislead him by such wild opinions as no one syllable of the text could authorize.

Some apology is also due for a few original words and proper names that are left untranslated, and unexplained. The translator was frequently too diffident of his own abilities to hazard a term that did but nearly approach the sense of the original, and too ignorant, at present, of the mythology of this ancient people, to venture any very particular account, in his Notes, of such deities, saints, and heroes, whose names are but barely mentioned in the text. But should the same genius, whose approbation first kindled emulation in his breast, and who alone hath urged him to undertake, and supported him through the execution of far more laborious tasks than this, find no cause to withdraw his countenance, the translator may be encouraged to prosecute the study of the theology and mythology of the *Hindoos*, for the future entertainment of the curious.

It is worthy to be noted, that *Krēēshnă*, throughout the whole, mentions only three of the four books of the *Vēds*, the most ancient scriptures of the *Hindoos*, and those the three first, according to the present order. This is a very curious circumstance, as it is the present belief that the whole four were promulgated by *Brăhmā* at the creation. The proof then of there having been but three before his time, is more than presumptive, and that so many actually existed before his appearance; and as the fourth mentions the name of *Krēēshnă*,[a] it is equally proved that it is a posterior work. This observation has escaped all the commentators, and was received with great astonishment by the *Păndĕĕt*, who was consulted in the translation.

The translator has not as yet had leisure to read any part of those ancient scriptures. He is told, that a very few of the original number of chapters are now to be found, and that the study of these is so difficult, that there are but few men in *Banaris* who understand any part of them. If we may believe the *Măhābhārăt*, they were almost lost five thousand years ago; when *Vyās*, so named from having superintended the compilation of them, collected the scattered leaves, and, by the assistance of his disciples, collated and preserved them in four books.

[a] It is not clear where Wilkins derived his information about the *Vedas*. 'Krishna' in fact occurs as a name in the *Rig Veda*, but without any of its later significance (A. A. MacDonell, A. B. Keith, *Vedic Index of Names and Subjects* (1911), I, 184).

6

William Jones, 'On the Gods of Greece, Italy, and India'

We cannot justly conclude, by arguments preceding the proof of facts, that one idolatrous people must have borrowed their deities, rites, and tenets from another; since Gods of all shapes and dimensions may be framed by the boundless powers of imagination, or by the frauds and follies of men, in countries never connected; but, when features of resemblance, too strong to have been accidental, are observable in different systems of polytheism, without fancy or prejudice to colour them and improve the likeness, we can scarce help believing, that some connection has immemorially subsisted between the several nations, who have adopted them: it is my design in this essay, to point out such a resemblance between the popular worship of the old Greeks and Italians and that of the Hindus; nor can there be room to doubt of a great similarity between their strange religions and that of Egypt, China, Persia, Phrygia, Phœnice, Syria; to which, perhaps, we may safely add some of the southern kingdoms and even islands of America; while the Gothick system, which prevailed in the northern regions of Europe, was not merely similar to those of Greece and Italy, but almost the same in another dress with an embroidery of images apparently Asiatick. From all this, if it be satisfactorily proved, we may infer a general union or affinity between the most distinguished inhabitants of the primitive world, at the time when they deviated, as they did too early deviate, from the rational adoration of the only true God.

There seem to have been four principal sources of all mythology. I. Historical, or natural, truth has been perverted into fable by ignorance, imagination, flattery, or stupidity; as a king of Crete, whose tomb had been discovered in that island, was con-

ceived to have been the God of Olympus;[a] and Minos, a legislator
of that country, to have been his son, and to hold a supreme
appellate jurisdiction over departed souls; hence too probably
flowed the tale of Cadmus, as Bochart learnedly traces it;[b] hence
beacons or volcanos became one-eyed giants and monsters vomit-
ing flames; and two rocks, from their appearance to mariners in
certain positions, were supposed to crush all vessels attempting
to pass between them; of which idle fictions many other instances
might be collected from the *Odyssey* and the various Argonautick
poems. The less we say of Julian stars,[c] deifications of princes or
warriours, altars raised, with those of Apollo, to the basest of
men, and divine titles bestowed on such wretches as Cajus
Octavianus,[d] the less we shall expose the infamy of grave
senators and fine poets, or the brutal folly of the low multitude:
but we may be assured, that the mad apotheosis of truly great
men, or of little men falsely called great, has been the origin of
gross idolatrous errors in every part of the pagan world. II. The
next source of them appears to have been a wild admiration of the
heavenly bodies, and, after a time, the systems and calculations of
astronomers: hence came a considerable portion of Egyptian and
Grecian fable; the Sabian worship in Arabia;[e] the Persian types
and emblems of Mihr or the sun, and the far extended adoration
of the elements and the powers of nature; and hence perhaps, all
the artificial chronology of the Chinese and Indians, with the invention of demigods and heroes to fill the vacant niches in their
extravagant and imaginary periods. III. Numberless divinities
have been created solely by the magick of poetry; whose essential
business it is, to personify the most abstract notions, and to place
a nymph or a genius in every grove and almost in every flower:

[a] The Cretans believed that Zeus had died in Crete and was buried there.

[b] The French Protestant theologian Samuel Bochart (1559–1667) traced the
legend of Cadmus to events in Phoenician history in his *Geographia sacra, seu
Phaleg et Chanaan* (*Samuelis Bocharti Omnia Opera* (Leyden, 1712), I, 447–54).

[c] The comet which appeared at Rome in July 44 B.C. was regarded as the
apotheosis of the recently murdered Julius Caesar.

[d] The Emperor Augustus.

[e] In the eighteenth century the term 'Sabian' was applied to the Harranian
community of Syria. Their star worship was thought to be founded on Chaldean
astronomy (E. Gibbon, *The Decline and Fall of the Roman Empire*. ed. J. B. Bury
(1896–1900), V, 331).

hence Hygieia and Jaso, health and remedy, are the poetical daughters of Æsculapius, who was either a distinguished physician, or medical skill personified; and hence Chloris, or verdure, is married to the Zephyr. IV. The metaphors and allegories of moralists and metaphysicians have been also very fertile in Deities; of which a thousand examples might be adduced from Plato, Cicero, and the inventive commentators on Homer in their pedigrees of the Gods, and their fabulous lessons of morality: the richest and noblest stream from this abundant fountain is the charming philosophical tale of Psyche, or the *Progress of the Soul*;[a] than which, to my taste, a more beautiful, sublime, and well supported allegory was never produced by the wisdom and ingenuity of man. Hence also the Indian *Maya*, or, as the word is explained by some Hindu scholars, 'the first inclination of the Godhead to diversify himself (such is their phrase) by creating worlds,' is feigned to be the mother of universal nature, and of all the inferiour Gods; as a Cashmirian[b] informed me, when I asked him, why Cama, or Love, was represented as her son; but the word *Maya*, or delusion, has a more subtile and recondite sense in the *Vedanta* philosophy, where it signifies the system of perceptions, whether of secondary or of primary qualities, which the Deity was believed by Epicharmus,[c] Plato, and many truly pious men, to raise by his omnipresent spirit in the minds of his creatures, but which had not, in their opinion, any existence independent of mind.

In drawing a parallel between the Gods of the Indian and European heathens, from whatever source they were derived, I shall remember, that nothing is less favourable to inquiries after truth than a systematical spirit, and shall call to mind the saying of a Hindu writer, 'that whoever obstinately adheres to any set of opinions, may bring himself to believe that the freshest sandalwood is a flame of fire': this will effectually prevent me from insisting, that such a God of India was the Jupiter of Greece; such, the Apollo; such, the Mercury: in fact, since all the causes of polytheism contributed largely to the assemblage of Grecian

[a] In books IV to VI of the *Metamorphoses* or 'the Golden Ass' of Apuleius, written in the second century A.D.
[b] Presumably Goverdhana, see below, p. 270.
[c] A Sicilian poet of the fifth and sixth centuries B.C.

divinities, (though Bacon reduces them all to refined allegories,[a] and Newton to a poetical disguise of true history),[b] we find many Joves, many Apollos, many Mercuries, with distinct attributes and capacities; nor shall I presume to suggest more, than that, in one capacity or another, there exists a striking similitude between the chief objects of worship in ancient Greece or Italy and in the very interesting country, which we now inhabit.

The comparison, which I proceed to lay before you, must needs be very superficial, partly from my short residence in Hindustan, partly from my want of complete leisure for literary amusements, but principally because I have no European book, to refresh my memory of old fables, except the conceited, though not unlearned, work of Pomey, entitled the *Pantheon*, and that so miserably translated, that it can hardly be read with patience.[c] A thousand more strokes of resemblance might, I am sure, be collected by any, who should with that view peruse Hesiod,[d] Hyginus,[e] Cornutus,[f] and the other mythologists; or, which would be a shorter and a pleasanter, way, should be satisfied with the very elegant *Syntagmata* of Lilius Giraldus.[g]

Disquisitions concerning the manners and conduct of our species in early times, or indeed at any time, are always curious at least and amusing; but they are highly interesting to such, as can say of themselves with Chremes in the play, 'We are men, and take an interest in all that relates to mankind':[h] they may even be of solid importance in an age, when some intelligent and virtuous persons are inclined to doubt the authenticity of the accounts, delivered by Moses, concerning the primitive world;

[a] In *De Sapientia Veterum* (1609), and in parts of *De Augmentis Scientiarum* (1623).

[b] In his posthumously published *The Chronology of Ancient Kingdoms Amended* (1728).

[c] The *Pantheum Mythicum; seu fabulosa Deorum historia* of François-Antoine Pomey (1619–73) was first published in 1659. A translation by Andrew Tooke (1673–1732) was frequently reprinted.

[d] A Greek poet of uncertain date, to whom the *Theogony*, a history of the gods was attributed.

[e] The otherwise unknown author of the *Genealogiae*, or *Fabulae*, a mythology written in the second century A.D.

[f] Lucius Annaeus Cornutus, who wrote a summary of mythology in Greek in the first century A.D. (see below, p. 214).

[g] *De Deis Gentium Libri sive Syntagmata XVII* (Ferrara, 1515), by Lilio Gregario Giraldi (1479–1552).

[h] Terence, *Heauton Timorumenos*, I, i, 25.

since no modes or sources of reasoning can be unimportant, which have a tendency to remove such doubts. Either the first eleven chapters of *Genesis*, all due allowances being made for a figurative Eastern style, are true, or the whole fabrick of our national religion is false; a conclusion, which none of us, I trust, would wish to be drawn. I, who cannot help believing the divinity of the Messiah, from the undisputed antiquity and manifest completion of many prophecies, especially those of Isaiah, in the only person recorded by history, to whom they are applicable, am obliged of course to believe the sanctity of the venerable books, to which that sacred person refers as genuine; but it is not the truth of our national religion, as such, that I have at heart: it is truth itself; and, if any cool unbiassed reasoner will clearly convince me, that Moses drew his narrative through Egyptian conduits from the primeval fountains of Indian literature,[a] I shall esteem him as a friend for having weeded my mind from a capital error, and promise to stand among the foremost in assisting to circulate the truth, which he has ascertained. After such a declaration, I cannot but persuade myself, that no candid man will be displeased, if, in the course of my work, I make as free with any arguments, that he may have advanced, as I should really desire him to do with any of mine, that he may be disposed to controvert. Having no system of my own to maintain, I shall not pursue a very regular method, but shall take all the Gods, of whom I discourse, as they happen to present themselves; beginning, however, like the Romans and the Hindus, with Janus or Ganesa.

The titles and attributes of this old Italian deity are fully comprized in two choriambick verses of Sulpitius; and a farther account of him from Ovid would here be superfluous:[b]

> *Jane* pater, *Jane* tuens, dive biceps, biformis,
> O cate rerum sator, O principium deorum!

'Father Janus, all-beholding Janus, thou divinity with two heads, and with two forms; O sagacious planter of all things, and leader of deities!'[c]

[a] Halhed had suggested this possibility (see above, p. 162).

[b] Janus is discussed in the first book of the *Fasti*.

[c] These lines are now attributed to Septimius Serenus, a lyric poet who wrote in the age of Hadrian (W. Morel, *Fragmenta Poetarum Latinorum epicorum et lyricorum* (Leipzig, 1927), p. 148).

He was the God, we see, of Wisdom; whence he is represented on coins with two, and, on the Hetruscan image found at Falisci, with four, faces;[a] emblems of prudence and circumspection: thus is Ganesa, the God of Wisdom in Hindustan, painted with an elephant's head, the symbol of sagacious discernment, and attended by a favorite rat, which the Indians consider as a wise and

[a] For the statue of Janus Quadrifrons said to have been found at Falerii (Falisci), see L. R. Taylor, *Local Cults in Etruria* (Rome, 1923), p. 76.

provident animal. His next great character (the plentiful source of many superstitious usages) was that, from which he is emphatically styled the father, and which the second verse before-cited more fully expresses, the origin and founder of all things: whence this notion arose, unless from a tradition that he first built shrines, raised altars, and instituted sacrifices, it is not easy to conjecture; hence it came however, that his name was invoked before any other God; that, in the old sacred rites, corn and wine, and, in later times, incense also, were first offered to Janus; that the doors or entrances to private houses were called *Januæ*, and any pervious passage or thorough-fare, in the plural number, *Jani*, or with two beginnings; that he was represented holding a rod, as guardian of ways, and a key, as opening, not gates only, but all important works and affairs of mankind; that he was thought to preside over the morning, or beginning of day; that, although the Roman year began regularly with March, yet the eleventh month, named Januarius, was considered as first of the twelve, whence the whole year was supposed to be under his guidance, and opened with great solemnity by the consuls inaugurated in his fane, where his statue was decorated on that occasion with fresh laurel; and, for the same reason, a solemn denunciation of war, than which there can hardly be a more momentous national act, was made by the military consul's opening the gates of his temple with all the pomp of his magistracy. The twelve altars and twelve chapels of Janus might either denote, according to the general opinion, that he leads and governs twelve months, or that, as he says of himself in Ovid,[a] all entrance and access must be made through him to the principal Gods, who were, to a proverb, of the same number. We may add, that Janus was imagined to preside over infants at their birth, or the beginning of life.

The Indian divinity has precisely the same character: all sacrifices and religious ceremonies, all addresses even to superiour Gods, all serious compositions in writing, and all worldly affairs of moment, are begun by pious Hindus with an invocation of Ganesa; a word composed of *isa*, the governor or leader, and *gana*, or a company of deities, nine of which companies are enumerated

[a] *Fasti*, I, 222–3.

in the *Amarcosh.*[a] Instances of opening business auspiciously by an ejaculation to the Janus of India (if the lines of resemblance here traced will justify me in so calling him) might be multiplied with ease. Few books are begun without the words salutation to Ganes, and he is first invoked by the Brahmans, who conduct the trial by ordeal, or perform the ceremony of the *homa*, or sacrifice to fire: M. Sonnerat represents him as highly revered on the Coast of Coromandel;

where the Indians, he says, would not on any account build a house, without having placed on the ground an image of this deity, which they sprinkle with oil and adorn every day with flowers; they set up his figure in all their temples, in the streets, in the high roads, and in open plains at the foot of some tree; so that persons of all ranks may invoke him, before they under-take any business, and travellers worship him, before they proceed on their journey.[b]

To this I may add, from my own observation, that in the commodious and useful town, which now rises at Dharmaranya or Gaya,[c] under the auspices of the active and benevolent Thomas Law, Esq. collector of Rotas,[d] every new-built house, agreeably to an immemorial usage of the Hindus, has the name of Ganesa superscribed on its door; and, in the old town, his image is placed over the gates of the temples.

We come now to Saturn, the oldest of the pagan Gods, of whose office and actions much is recorded. The jargon of his being the son of Earth and of Heaven, who was the son of the Sky and the Day, is purely a confession of ignorance, who were his parents or who his predecessors; and there appears more sense in the tradition said to be mentioned by the inquisitive and well informed Plato, 'that both Saturn or time, and his consort Cybele, or the Earth, together with their attendants, were the children of Ocean and Thetis, or, in less poetical language, sprang from the waters of the great deep.'[e] Ceres, the goddess of harvests,

---

[a] The *Amarakosha*, the famous Sanskrit glossary probably written in the seventh century A.D. Three versions belonging to Jones were subsequently presented to the Royal Society (Wilkins, *A Catalogue of Manuscripts*, p. 12).

[b] *Voyage aux Indes Orientales et à la Chine* (Paris, 1782), I, 182, by Pierre Sonnerat (1749–1814).

[c] The new town at Gaya in Bihar, now called Sahibganj, was once named Ilahabad after its founder (L. S. S. O'Malley, *Bengal District Gazetteers, Gaya* (Calcutta, 1906), pp. 212–13).   [d] Thomas Law (1759–1834).

[e] This seems to be a paraphrase of the *Timaeus*, 40.

was, it seems, their daughter; and Virgil describes 'the mother and nurse of all as crowned with turrets, in a car drawn by lions, and exulting in her hundred grand-sons, all divine, all inhabiting splendid celestial mansions.'[a] As the God of Time, or rather as time itself personified, Saturn was usually painted by the heathens holding a scythe in one hand, and, in the other, a snake with its tail in its mouth, the symbol of perpetual cycles and revolutions of ages: he was often represented in the act of devouring years, in the form of children, and, sometimes, encircled by the seasons appearing like boys and girls. By the Latins he was named Satunnus; and the most ingenious etymology of that word is given by Festus the grammarian; who traces it, by a learned analogy to many similar names, *à satu*, from planting, because, when he reigned in Italy, he introduced and improved agriculture:[b] but his distinguishing character, which explains, indeed, all his other titles and functions, was expressed allegorically by the stern of a ship or galley on the reverse of his ancient coins; for which Ovid assigns a very unsatisfactory reason, 'because the divine stranger arrived in a ship on the Italian coast';[c] as if he could have been expected on horse-back or hovering through the air.

The account, quoted by Pomey from Alexander Polyhistor,[d] casts a clearer light, if it really came from genuine antiquity, on the whole tale of Saturn; 'that he predicted an extraordinary fall of rain, and ordered the construction of a vessel, in which it was necessary to secure men, beasts, birds, and reptiles from a general inundation.'[e]

Now it seems not easy to take a cool review of all these testimonies concerning the birth, kindred, offspring, character, occupations, and entire life of Saturn, without assenting to the opinion of Bochart, or admitting it at least to be highly probable, that the fable was raised on the true history of Noah:[f] from whose flood a new period of time was computed, and a new series of ages may be said to have sprung; who rose fresh, and, as it were, newly

---

[a] *Aeneid*, VI, 784–8.
[b] See a note to the entry 'Saturno' in book XVII of *De Verborum Significatione* abridged by Sextus Pompeius Festus, who wrote in the second century A.D.
[c] *Fasti*, I, 227–8.
[d] A prolific writer on a wide range of subjects who lived in the first century B.C.
[e] *The Pantheon*, trans. Tooke, 2nd ed. (1717), p. 163.
[f] Bochart, *Omnia Opera*, I, 1.

born from the waves; whose wife was in fact the universal mother, and, that the earth might soon be repeopled, was early blessed with numerous and flourishing descendants: if we produce, therefore, an Indian king of divine birth, eminent for his piety and beneficence, whose story seems evidently to be that of Noah disguised by Asiatick fiction, we may safely offer a conjecture, that he was also the same personage with Saturn. This was Menu, or Satyavrata, whose patronymick name was Vaivaswata, or Child of the Sun; and whom the Indians believe to have reigned over the whole world in the earliest age of their chronology, but to have resided in the country of Dravira, on the coast of the eastern Indian peninsula: the following narrative of the principal event in his life I have literally translated from the *Bhagavat*;[a] and it is the subject of the first *Purana*, entitled that of the *Matsya*, or Fish.

Desiring the preservation of herds, and of Brahmans, of genii and virtuous men, of the *Vedas*, of law, and of precious things, the lord of the universe assumes many bodily shapes; but, though he pervades, like the air, a variety of beings, yet he is himself unvaried since he has no quality subject to change. At the close of the last *Calpa*, there was a general destruction occasioned by the sleep of Brahma; whence his creatures in different worlds were drowned in a vast ocean. Brahma, being inclined to slumber, desiring repose after a lapse of ages, the strong demon Hayagriva came near him, and stole the *Vedas*, which had flowed from his lips. When Heri, the preserver of the universe, discovered this deed of the Prince of *Danavas*, he took the shape of a minute fish, called *saphari*. A holy king, named Satyavrata, then reigned; a servant of the spirit, which moved on the waves, and so devout, that water was his only sustenance. He was the child of the sun, and, in the present *Calpa*, is invested by Narayan in the office of Menu, by the name of Sraddhadeva, or the God of Obsequies. One day, as he was making a libation in the river Critamala, and held water in the palm of his hand, he perceived a small fish moving in it. The king of Dravira immediately dropped the fish into the river together with the water, which he had taken from it; when the *saphari* thus pathetically addressed the benevolent monarch: 'How canst thou, O king, who showest affection to the oppressed, leave me in this river-water, where I am too weak to resist the monsters of the stream, who fill me with dread?' He, not knowing who had assumed the form of a fish,

[a] Jones had read a Persian translation of the *Bhagavat Purana* (see above, p. 120) shortly after his arrival in India. He found it 'by far the most entertaining book, on account of its novelty and wildness, that I ever read' (Lord Teignmouth, *Memoirs of the Life and Writings and Correspondence of Sir William Jones*, 2nd ed. (1807), p. 305).

applied his mind to the preservation of the *saphari*, both from good nature and from regard to his own soul; and, having heard its very suppliant address, he kindly placed it under his protection in a small vase full of water; but, in a single night, its bulk was so increased, that it could not be contained in the jar, and thus again addressed the illustrious prince: 'I am not pleased with living miserably in this little vase; make me a large mansion, where I may dwell in comfort.' The king, removing it thence, placed it in the water of a cistern; but it grew three cubits in less than fifty minutes, and said: 'O king, it pleases me not to stay vainly in this narrow cistern: since thou hast granted me an asylum, give me a spacious habitation.' He then removed it, and placed it in a pool, where, having ample space around its body, it became a fish of considerable size. 'This abode, O king, is not convenient for me, who must swim at large in the waters: exert thyself for my safety; and remove me to a deep lake': thus addressed, the pious monarch threw the suppliant into a lake, and, when it grew of equal bulk with that piece of water, he cast the vast fish into the sea. When the fish was thrown into the waves, he thus again spoke to Satyavrata: 'Here the horned sharks, and other monsters of great strength will devour me; thou shouldst not, O valiant man, leave me in this ocean.' Thus repeatedly deluded by the fish, who had addressed him with gentle words, the king said: 'Who art thou, that beguilest me in that assumed shape? Never before have I seen or heard of so prodigious an inhabitant of the waters, who, like thee, hast filled up, in a single day, a lake an hundred leagues in circumference. Surely, thou art Bhagavat, who appearest before me; the great Heri, whose dwelling was on the waves; and who now, in compassion to thy servants, bearest the form of the natives of the deep. Salutation and praise to thee, O first male, the lord of creation, of preservation, of destruction! Thou art the highest object, O supreme ruler, of us thy adorers, who piously seek thee. All thy delusive descents in this world give existence to various beings: yet I am anxious to know, for what cause that shape has been assumed by thee. Let me not, O lotus-eyed, approach in vain the feet of a deity, whose perfect benevolence has been extended to all; when thou hast shown us to our amazement the appearance of other bodies, not in reality existing, but successively exhibited.' The lord of the universe, loving the pious man, who thus implored him, and intending to preserve him from the sea of destruction, caused by the depravity of the age, thus told him how he was to act. 'In seven days from the present time, O thou tamer of enemies, the three worlds will be plunged in an ocean of death; but, in the midst of the destroying waves, a large vessel, sent by me for thy use, shall stand before thee. Then shalt thou take all medicinal herbs, all the variety of seeds; and, accompanied by seven saints, encircled by pairs of all brute animals, thou shalt enter the spacious ark and continue in it, secure from the flood on one immense ocean without light, except the radiance of thy holy companions. When the ship shall be agitated by an impetuous wind, thou shalt fasten it with a large sea-serpent on my horn; for I will be near thee: drawing the vessel, with thee and thy attendants, I will

remain on the ocean, O chief of men, until a night of Brahma shall be completely ended. Thou shalt then know my true greatness, rightly named the
supreme Godhead; by my favour, all thy questions shall be answered, and
thy mind abundantly instructed.' Heri, having thus directed the monarch,
disappeared; and Satyavrata humbly waited for the time, which the ruler of
our senses had appointed. The pious king, having scattered toward the East
the pointed blades of the grass *darbha*, and turning his face toward the
North, sate meditating on the feet of the God, who had borne the form of a
fish. The sea, overwhelming its shores, deluged the whole earth; and it was
soon perceived to be augmented by showers from immense clouds. He, still
meditating on the command of Bhagavat, saw the vessel advancing, and
entered it with the chiefs of Brahmans, having carried into it the medicinal
creepers and conformed to the directions of Heri. The saints thus addressed
him: 'O king, meditate on Cesava; who will, surely, deliver us from this
danger, and grant us prosperity.' The God, being invoked by the monarch,
appeared again distinctly on the vast ocean in the form of a fish, blazing like
gold, extending a million of leagues, with one stupendous horn; on which
the king, as he had before been commanded by Heri, tied the ship with a
cable made of a vast serpent, and, happy in his preservation, stood praising
the destroyer of Madhu. When the monarch had finished his hymn, the
primeval male, Bhagavat, who watched for his safety on the great expanse
of water, spoke aloud to his own divine essence, pronouncing a sacred
Purana, which contained the rules of the *Sanchya* philosophy: but it was an
infinite mystery to be concealed within the breast of Satyavrata; who,
sitting in the vessel with the saints, heard the principle of the soul, the
Eternal Being, proclaimed by the preserving power. Then Heri, rising
together with Brahma, from the destructive deluge, which was abated, slew
the demon Hayagriva, and recovered the sacred books. Satyavrata, instructed in all divine and human knowledge, was appointed in the present *Calpa*,
by the favour of Vishnu, the seventh Menu, surnamed Vaivaswata: but the
appearance of a horned fish to the religious monarch was *Maya*, or delusion;
and he, who shall devoutly hear this important allegorical narrative, will
be delivered from the bondage of sin.

This epitome of the first Indian history, that is now extant,
appears to me very curious and very important; for the story,
though whimsically dressed up in the form of an allegory, seems
to prove a primeval tradition in this country of the universal
deluge described by Moses, and fixes consequently the time,
when the genuine Hindu chronology actually begins. We find, it
is true, in the *Puran*, from which the narrative is extracted,
another deluge which happened towards the close of the third
age, when Yudhisthir was labouring under the persecution of his
inveterate foe Duryodhan, and when Crishna, who had recently

become incarnate for the purpose of succouring the pious and of destroying the wicked, was performing wonders in the country of Mathura; but the second flood was merely local and intended only to affect the people of Vraja: they, it seems, had offended Indra, the God of the firmament, by their enthusiastick adoration of the wonderful child, 'who lifted up the mountain Goverdhena, as if it had been a flower, and, by sheltering all the herdsmen and shepherdesses from the storm, convinced Indra of his supremacy.' That the *Satya*, or (if we may venture so to call it) the Saturnian, age was in truth the age of the general flood, will appear from a close examination of the ten *Avatars*, or descents, of the deity in his capacity of preserver; since of the four, which are declared to have happened in the *Satya yug*, the three first apparently relate to some stupendous convulsion of our globe from the fountains of the deep, and the fourth exhibits the miraculous punishment of pride and impiety: first, as we have shown, there was, in the opinion of the Hindus, an interposition of Providence to preserve a devout person and his family (for all the Pandits agree, that his wife, though not named, must be understood to have been saved with him) from an inundation, by which all the wicked were destroyed; next, the power of the deity descends in the form of a boar, the symbol of strength, to draw up and support on his tusks the whole earth, which had been sunk beneath the ocean; thirdly, the same power is represented as a tortoise sustaining the globe, which had been convulsed by the violent assaults of demons, while the Gods churned the sea with the mountain Mandar, and forced it to disgorge the sacred things and animals, together with the water of life, which it had swallowed: these three stories relate, I think, to the same event, shadowed by a moral, a metaphysical, and an astronomical, allegory; and all three seem connected with the hieroglyphical sculptures of the old Egyptians. The fourth *Avatar* was a lion issuing from a bursting column of marble to devour a blaspheming monarch, who would otherwise have slain his religious son; and of the remaining six, not one has the least relation to a deluge: the three, which are ascribed to the *Tretayug*, when tyranny and irreligion are said to have been introduced, were ordained for the overthrow of tyrants, or, their natural types, giants with a thousand arms formed for the most extensive oppression; and, in the *Dwaparyug*, the incarnation of Crishna was partly for a similar purpose, and partly with a view to thin the world of unjust and impious men, who had multiplied in that age, and began to swarm on the approach of the *Caliyug*, or the age of contention and baseness. As to Buddha, he seems to have been a reformer of the doctrines contained in the *Vedas*; and, though his good nature led him to censure those ancient books, because they enjoined sacrifices of cattle, yet he is admitted as the ninth *Avatar* even by the Brahmans of Casi, and his praises are sung by the poet Jayadeva:[a] his character is in many respects very extraordinary; but, as an account of it belongs rather to history than to mythology, it is reserved for another dissertation. The tenth *Avatar*, we are told, is yet to come, and is expected to appear mounted (like the crowned conqueror in the *Apocalyps*) on a white horse, with a cimeter blazing like a comet to mow down all incorrigible and impenitent offenders, who shall then be on earth.

These four *Yugs* have so apparent an affinity with the Grecian and Roman ages, that one origin may be naturally assigned to both systems: the first in both is distinguished as abounding in gold, though *Satya* means truth and probity, which were found, if ever, in the times immediately following so tremendous an exertion of the divine power as the destruction of mankind by a general deluge; the next is characterized by silver, and the third, by copper; though their usual names allude to proportions imagined in each between vice and virtue: the present, or earthen, age seems more properly discriminated than by iron, as in ancient Europe; since that metal is not baser or less useful, though more common in our times and consequently less precious, than copper; while mere earth conveys an idea of the lowest degradation. We may here observe, that the true history of the world seems obviously divisible into four ages or periods; which may be called, first, the Diluvian, or purest age; namely, the times preceding the deluge, and those succeeding it till the mad introduction of idolatry at Babel; next, the Patriarchal, or pure, age; in which, indeed, there were mighty hunters of beasts and of men, from

---

[a] The twelfth-century poet of Bengal, part of whose *Gita Govinda* Jones was later to translate (*The Works of Sir William Jones* (1799), I, 463–84). Jones quoted Jayadeva's verse on Buddha in his essay on Chronology, see below, p. 269.

the rise of patriarchs in the family of Sem to the simultaneous establishment of great empires by the descendants of his brother Ham; thirdly, the Mosaick, or less pure, age; from the legation of Moses, and during the time, when his ordinances were comparatively well-observed and uncorrupted; lastly, the Prophetical, or impure, age, beginning with the vehement warnings given by the Prophets to apostate kings and degenerate nations, but still subsisting and to subsist, until all genuine prophecies shall be fully accomplished. The duration of the historical ages must needs be very unequal and disproportionate; while that of the Indian *Yugs* is disposed so regularly and artificially, that it cannot be admitted as natural or probable: men do not become reprobate in a geometrical progression or at the termination of regular periods; yet so well-proportioned are the *Yugs*, that even the length of human life is diminished, as they advance, from an hundred thousand years in a subdecuple ratio; and, as the number of principal *Avatars* in each decreases arithmetically from four, so the number of years in each decreases geometrically, and all together constitute the extravagant sum of four million three hundred and twenty thousand years, which aggregate, multiplied by seventy-one, is the period, in which every Menu is believed to preside over the world. Such a period, one might conceive, would have satisfied Archytas, the measurer of sea and earth and the numberer of their sands,[a] or Archimedes, who invented a notation, that was capable of expressing the number of them; but the comprehensive mind of an Indian chronologist has no limits; and the reigns of fourteen Menus are only a single day of Brahma, fifty of which days have elapsed, according to the Hindus, from the time of the Creation: that all this puerility, as it seems at first view, may be only an astronomical riddle, and allude to the apparent revolution of the fixed stars, of which the Brahmans made a mystery, I readily admit, and am even inclined to believe; but so technical an arrangement excludes all idea of serious history. I am sensible, how much these remarks will offend the warm advocates for Indian antiquity; but we must not sacrifice truth to a base fear of giving offence: that the *Vedas* were

[a] A Pythagorean philosopher who lived at Tarentum in the fourth century B.C. Jones is quoting from Horace, *Carmina*, I, xxviii, 1–2.

actually written before the flood, I shall never believe; nor can we infer from the preceding story, that the learned Hindus believe it; for the allegorical slumber of Brahma and the theft of the sacred books mean only, in simpler language, that the human race was become corrupt; but that the *Vedas* are very ancient, and far older than other Sanscrit compositions, I will venture to assert from my own examination of them,[a] and a comparison of their style with that of the *Purans* and the *Dherma Sastra*. A similar comparison justifies me in pronouncing, that the excellent law-book ascribed to Swayambhuva Menu, though not even pretended to have been written by him,[b] is more ancient than the *Bhagavat*; but that it was composed in the first age of the world, the Brahmans would find it hard to persuade me; and the date, which has been assigned to it, does not appear in either of the two copies, which I possess, or in any other, that has been collated for me: in fact the supposed date is comprized in a verse, which flatly contradicts the work itself;[c] for it was not Menu who composed the system of law, by the command of his father Brahma, but a holy personage or demigod, named Bhrigu, who revealed to men what Menu had delivered at the request of him and other saints or patriarchs. In the *Manava Sastra*, to conclude this digression, the measure is so uniform and melodious, and the style so perfectly Sanscrit, or polished, that the book must be more modern than the scriptures of Moses, in which the simplicity, or rather nakedness, of the Hebrew dialect, metre, and style, must convince every unbiassed man of their superior antiquity.

I leave etymologists, who decide every thing, to decide whether the word Menu, or, in the nominative case, Menus, has any connexion with Minos, the Lawgiver, and supposed son of Jove: the Cretans, according to Diodorus of Sicily, used to feign,

---

[a] Jones had been shown the copy of the *Vedas* acquired by Colonel Antoine-Louis-Henri Polier (1741–95), the first full version ever to have been obtained by a European, before he took it to London to present to the British Museum (Polier to Banks, 20 May 1789, B.M. Add. MS 5346, f. 3). But when Jones attempted to write a 'Dissertation on the Primitive Religion of the Hindus' he seems to have relied on the texts of the *Vedas* in Dara Shukoh's Persian *Upanishads* (see above, p. 148) and on a 'paraphrase' of them by his *pandit* Radhakanta (*Jones Works*, VI, 415–27).

[b] *The Laws of Manu*, to be translated by Jones in 1794 as *Institutes of Hindi Law, or the Ordinances of Menu*.

[c] This verse was reproduced by Halhed, see above, p. 160.

that most of the great men, who had been deified in return for the benefits, which they had conferred on mankind, were born in their island;[a] and hence a doubt may be raised, whether Minos was really a Cretan. The Indian legislator was the first, not the seventh, Menu, or Satyavrata, whom I suppose to be the Saturn of Italy: part of Saturn's character, indeed, was that of a great lawgiver,

Qui genus indocile ac dispersum montibus altis
Composuit, legesque dedit,[b]

and, we may suspect, that all the fourteen Menus are reducible to one, who was called Nuh by the Arabs, and probably by the Hebrews, though we have disguised his name by an improper pronunciation of it. Some near relation between the seventh Menu and the Grecian Minos may be inferred from the singular character of the Hindu God, Yama, who was also a child of the Sun, and thence named Vaivaswata: he had too the same title with his brother, Sraddhadeva; another of his titles was Dhermaraja, or King of Justice; and a third, Pitripeti, or Lord of the Patriarchs; but he is chiefly distinguished as judge of departed souls; for the Hindus believe, that, when a soul leaves its body, it immediately repairs to Yamapur, or the city of Yama, where it receives a just sentence from him, and either ascends to Swerga, or the first heaven, or is driven down to Narac, the region of serpents, or assumes on earth the form of some animal, unless its offence had been such, that it ought to be condemned to a vegetable, or even to a mineral, prison. Another of his names is very remarkable: I mean that of Cala, or time, the idea of which is intimately blended with the characters of Saturn and of Noah; for the name Cronos[c] has a manifest affinity with the word *chronos*, and a learned follower of Zeratusht[d] assures me, that, in the books, which the *Behdins*[e] hold sacred, mention is made of an universal inundation, there named the deluge of Time.[f]

[a] See the opening paragraph of book v, chap. IV of the 'World History' of Diodorus Siculus of Agyrium, written in the first century B.C.
[b] Virgil, *Aeneid*, VIII, 321–2.
[c] In Roman mythology Kronos was often identified with Saturnus.
[d] Zoroaster.   [e] The Parsi laity.
[f] See the account of the Deluge in the *Bundahis* (*Pahlavi Texts*, trans. E. W. West, I, *Sacred Books of the East*, v (1880), pp. 25–8).

Jones on the Gods

It having been occasionally observed, that Ceres was the poetical daughter of Saturn, we cannot close this head without adding, that the Hindus also have their Goddess of Abundance, whom they usually call Lacshmi, and whom they consider as the daughter (not of Menu, but) of Bhrigu, by whom the first code of sacred ordinances was promulgated: she is also named Pedma and Camala from the sacred Lotos or *Nymphœa*; but her most remarkable name is Sri, or, in the first case, Sris, which has a resemblance to the Latin, and means fortune or prosperity. It may be contended, that, although Lacshmi may be figuratively called the Ceres of Hindustan, yet any two or more idolatrous nations, who subsisted by agriculture, might naturally conceive a deity to preside over their labours, without having the least intercourse with each other; but no reason appears, why two nations should concur in supposing that deity to be a female: one at least of them would be more likely to imagine, that the Earth was a goddess, and that the god of abundance rendered her fertile. Besides, in very ancient temples near Gaya, we see images of Lacshmi, with full breasts and a cord twisted under her arm like a horn of plenty, which look very much like the old Grecian and Roman figures of Ceres.

The fable of Saturn having been thus analysed, let us proceed to his descendents; and begin, as the poet advises, with Jupiter, whose supremacy, thunder, and libertinism every boy learns from Ovid; while his great offices of Creator, Preserver, and Destroyer, are not generally considered in the systems of European mythology. The Romans had, as we have before observed, many Jupiters, one of whom was only the Firmament personified, as Ennius clearly expresses it:

Aspice hoc sublime candens, quem invocant omnes *Jovem*.[a]

This Jupiter or Diespiter is the Indian God of the visible heavens, called Indra, or the King, and Divespetir, or Lord of the Sky, who has also the character of the Roman Genius, or chief of the good spirits; but most of his epithets in Sanscrit are the same with those of the Ennian Jove. His consort is named Sachi; his celestial city, Amaravati; his palace, Vaijayanta; his garden, Nandana; his chief elephant, Airavat; his charioteer, Matali; and his weapon,

[a] *Melanippa*, 351, by Quintus Ennius (239–169 B.C.), 'father' of Roman poetry.

Vajra, or the thunderbolt: he is the regent of winds and showers, and, though the East is peculiarly under his care, yet his Olympus is Meru, or the north pole allegorically represented as a mountain of gold and gems. With all his power he is considered as a subordinate deity, and far inferior to the Indian Triad, Brahma, Vishnu, and Mahadeva or Siva, who are three forms of one and the same Godhead: thus the principal divinity of the Greeks and Latians, whom they called Zeus and Jupiter with irregular inflexions Dios and Jovis, was not merely *Fulminator*, the Thunderer, but, like the destroying power of India, *Magnus Divus*, *Ultor*, *Genitor*; like the preserving power, *Conservator*, *Soter*, *Opitulus*, *Altor*, *Ruminus*, and, like the creating power, the Giver of Life; an attribute, which I mention here on authority of Cornutus, a consummate master of mythological learning.[a] We are advised by Plato himself to search for the roots of Greek words in some barbarous, that is, foreign, soil;[b] but, since I look upon etymological conjectures as a weak basis for historical inquiries, I hardly dare suggest, that Zev, Siv, and Jov, are the same syllable differently pronounced: it must, however be admitted, that the Greeks having no palatial sigma, like that of the Indians, might have expressed it by their *zeta*, and that the initial letters of *zugon* and *jugum*[c] are (as the instance proves) easily interchangeable.

Let us now descend, from these general and introductory remarks, to some particular observations on the resemblance of Zeus or Jupiter to the triple divinity Vishnu, Siva, Brahma; for that is the order, in which they are expressed by the letters A, U, and M, which coalesce and form the mystical word OM; a word, which never escapes the lips of a pious Hindu, who meditates on it in silence: whether the Egyptian ON, which is commonly supposed to mean the sun,[d] be the Sanscrit monosyllable, I leave others to determine. It must always be remembered, that the learned Indians, as they are instructed by their own books, in truth acknowledge only one Supreme Being, whom they call

[a] *De Natura Deorum Gentilium Commentarius* (printed Basle, 1543), p. 186.
[b] *Cratylus*, 425.
[c] Latin and Greek words for a yoke.
[d] The city of On, called Heliopolis by the Greeks, was the centre for the worship of the sun god Re.

Brahme, or the Great One in the neuter gender: they believe his essence to be infinitely removed from the comprehension of any mind but his own; and they suppose him to manifest his power by the operation of his divine spirit, whom they name Vishnu, the Pervader, and Narayan, or moving on the waters, both in the masculine gender, whence he is often denominated the first male; and by this power they believe, that the whole order of nature is preserved and supported; but the *Vedantis*, unable to form a distinct idea of brute matter independent of mind, or to conceive that the work of Supreme Goodness was left a moment to itself, imagine that the deity is ever present to his work, and constantly supports a series of perceptions, which, in one sense, they call illusory, though they cannot but admit the reality of all created forms, as far as the happiness of creatures can be affected by them. When they consider the divine power exerted in creating, or in giving existence to that which existed not before, they call the deity Brahma in the masculine gender also; and, when they view him in the light of Destroyer, or rather changer of forms, they give him a thousand names, of which Siva, Isa or Iswara, Rudra, Hara, Sambhu, and Mahadeva or Mahesa, are the most common. The first operations of these three powers are variously described in the different *Puranas* by a number of allegories, and from them we may deduce the Ionian philosophy of primeval water,[a] the doctrine of the Mundane Egg,[b] and the veneration paid to the *Nymphœa*, or Lotos, which was anciently revered in Egypt, as it is at present in Hindustan, Tibet, and Nepal: the Tibetians are said to embellish their temples and altars with it, and a native of Nepal made prostrations before it on entering my study, where the fine plant and beautiful flowers lay for examination. Mr. Holwell, in explaining his first plate, supposes Brahma to be floating on a leaf of betel in the midst of the abyss; but it was manifestly intended by a bad painter for a lotos-leaf or for that of the Indian fig-tree; nor is the species of pepper, known in Bengal by the name of *Tambula*, and on the Coast of Malabar by that of betel, held sacred, as he asserts, by the Hindus, or necessarily cultivated

---

[a] The Ionians were Greek colonists on the west coast of Asia Minor. The doctrine of primeval water is particularly associated with Thales of Miletus, who lived about 600 B.C.

[b] A concept of Orphic cosmogony.

under the inspection of Brahmans;[a] though, as the vines are tender, all the plantations of them are carefully secured, and ought to be cultivated by a particular tribe of *Sudras*, who are thence called *Tambulis*.

That water was the primitive element and first work of the Creative Power, is the uniform opinion of the Indian philosophers; but, as they give so particular an account of the general deluge and of the Creation, it can never be admitted, that their whole system arose from traditions concerning the flood only, and must appear indubitable, that their doctrine is in part borrowed from the opening of *Birasit* or *Genesis*, than which a sublimer passage, from the first word to the last, never flowed or will flow from any human pen: ' In the beginning God created the heavens and the earth. And the earth was void and waste, and darkness was on the face of the deep, and the Spirit of God moved upon the face of the waters; and God said: Let Light be—and Light was.' The sublimity of this passage is considerably diminished by the Indian paraphrase of it, with which Menu, the son of Brahma, begins his address to the sages, who consulted him on the formation of the universe:

This world, says he, was all darkness, undiscernible, undistinguishable, altogether as in a profound sleep; till the self-existent invisible God, making it manifest with five elements and other glorious forms, perfectly dispelled the gloom. He, desiring to raise up various creatures by an emanation from his own glory, first created the waters, and impressed them with a power of motion: by that power was produced a golden egg, blazing like a thousand suns, in which was born Brahma, self-existing, the great parent of all rational beings. The waters are called *nara*, since they are the offspring of Nera (or Iswara); and thence was Narayana named, because his first *ayana*, or moving, was on them.

That Which Is, the invisible cause, eternal, self-existing, but unperceived, becoming masculine from neuter, is celebrated among all creatures by the name of Brahma. That God, having dwelled in the egg, through revolving years, Himself meditating on Himself, divided it into two equal parts; and from those halves formed the heavens and the earth, placing in the midst the subtil ether, the eight points of the world, and the permanent receptacle of waters.[b]

To this curious description, with which the *Manava Sastra* begins, I cannot refrain from subjoining the four verses, which

[a] See above, p. 102. [b] *Laws of Manu*, i, 3–13, *Jones Works*, iii, 66–7.

216

are the text of the *Bhagavat,* and are believed to have been pronounced by the Supreme Being to Brahma: the following version
is most scrupulously literal.

Even I was even at first, not any other thing; that, which exists, unperceived;
supreme: afterwards I am That Which Is; and he, who must remain, am I.

Except the First Cause, whatever may appear, and may not appear, in
the mind, know that to be the mind's *Maya,* (or Delusion) as light, as
darkness.

As the great elements are in various beings, entering, yet not entering,
(that is, pervading, not destroying) thus am I in them, yet not in them.

Even thus far may inquiry be made by him, who seeks to know the principle of mind, in union and separation, which must be Everywhere Always.

Wild and obscure as these ancient verses must appear in a
naked verbal translation, it will perhaps be thought by many, that
the poetry or mythology of Greece or Italy afford no conceptions
more awfully magnificient: yet the brevity and simplicity of the
Mosaick diction are unequalled.

As to the creation of the world, in the opinion of the Romans,
Ovid, who might naturally have been expected to describe it with
learning and elegance, leaves us wholly in the dark, which of the
Gods was the actor in it: other mythologists are more explicit;
and we may rely on the authority of Cornutus, that the old European heathens considered Jove (not the son of Saturn, but of the
Ether, that is of an unknown parent) as the great life-giver, and
father of Gods and men;[a] to which may be added the Orphean
doctrine, preserved by Proclus, that 'the abyss and empyreum,
the earth and sea, the Gods and Goddesses, were produced by
Zeus or Jupiter.'[b] In this character he corresponds with Brahma;
and, perhaps, with that God of the Babylonians, (if we can rely
on the accounts of their ancient religion) who, like Brahma, reduced the universe to order, and, like Brahma, lost his head, with
the blood of which new animals were instantly formed:[c] I allude
to the common story, the meaning of which I cannot discover,

[a] *De Natura Deorum Gentilium,* 1543 ed., pp. 9 ff.
[b] *The Commentaries of Proclus on the Timaeus of Plato,* trans. T. Taylor (1820),
pp. 263–4. This work by the Neoplatonist Proclus Diodochus (A.D. 412–85) was
thought to contain 'the greatest part of the fragments' of Orpheus (T. Taylor,
The Philosophical and Mathematical Commentaries of Proclus (1788–9), I, 35).
[c] Jones seems to be referring to Belus, who ordered another deity to decapitate
him (I. P. Cory, *The Ancient Fragments* (1828), p. 28).

that Brahma had five heads till one of them was cut off by Narayan.

That, in another capacity, Jove was the helper and supporter of all, we may collect from his old Latin epithets, and from Cicero, who informs us, that his usual name is a contraction of *Juvans Pater*;[a] an etymology, which shows the idea entertained of his character, though we may have some doubt of its accuracy. Callimachus, we know, addresses him as the bestower of all good, and of security from grief; and, since neither wealth without virtue, nor virtue without wealth, give complete happiness, he prays, like a wise poet, for both.[b] An Indian prayer for riches would be directed to Lacshmi, the wife of Vishnu, since the Hindu goddesses are believed to be the powers of their respective lords: as to Cuvera, the Indian Plutus, one of whose names is Paulastya, he is revered, indeed, as a magnificent deity, residing in the palace of Alaca, or borne through the sky in a splendid car named Pushpaca, but is manifestly subordinate, like the other seven Genii, to the three principal Gods, or rather to the principal God considered in three capacities. As the soul of the world, or the pervading mind, so finely described by Virgil,[c] we see Jove represented by several Roman poets; and with great sublimity by Lucan in the known speech of Cato concerning the Ammonian oracle, 'Jupiter is, wherever we look, wherever we move.'[d] This is precisely the Indian idea of Vishnu, according to the four verses above exhibited, not that the Brahmans imagine their male Divinity to be the divine essence of the great one, which they declare to be wholly incomprehensible; but, since the power of preserving created things by a superintending providence, belongs eminently to the Godhead, they hold that power to exist transcendently in the preserving member of the Triad, whom they suppose to be Every Where, Always, not in substance, but in spirit and energy: here, however, I speak of the *Vaishnavas*; for the *Saivas* ascribe a sort of pre-eminence to Siva, whose attributes are now to be concisely examined.

[a] *De Natura Deorum*, book II, chap. xxv.
[b] See the first of the 'Hymns' of Callimachus, the Alexandrian poet of the third century B.C., 'to Zeus'.
[c] Presumably *Aeneid*, VI, 724 ff.
[d] *De Bello Civile*, IX, 580.

Jones on the Gods

It was in the capacity of Avenger and Destroyer, that Jove encountered and overthrew the Titans and Giants, whom Typhon, Briareus, Tityus, and the rest of their fraternity, led against the God of Olympus; to whom an eagle brought lightning and thunderbolts during the warfare: thus, in a similar contest between Siva and the Daityas, or children of Diti, who frequently rebelled against heaven, Brahma is believed to have presented the God of Destruction with fiery shafts. One of the many poems, entitled *Ramayan*, the last book of which has been translated into Italian,[a] contains an extraordinary dialogue between the crow Bhushunda, and a rational eagle, named Garuda, who is often painted with the face of a beautiful youth, and the body of an imaginary bird; and one of the eighteen *Puranas* bears his name and comprizes his whole history. M. Sonnerat informs us, that Vishnu is represented in some places riding on the Garuda,[b] which he supposes to be the Pondicheri eagle of Brisson,[c] especially as the Brahmans of the Coast highly venerate that bird, and provide food for numbers of them at stated hours: I rather conceive the Garuda to be a fabulous bird, but agree with him, that the Hindu god, who rides on it, resembles the ancient Jupiter. In the old temples at Gaya, Vishnu is either mounted on this poetical bird or attended by it together with a little page; but, lest an etymologist should find Ganymed in Garud, I must observe that the Sanscrit word is pronounced *Garura*; though I admit, that the Grecian and Indian stories of the celestial bird and the page appear to have some resemblance. As the Olympian Jupiter fixed his court and held his councils on a lofty and brilliant mountain, so the appropriated seat of Mahadeva, whom the *Saivas* consider as the chief of the deities, was mount Cailasa, every splinter of whose rocks was an inestimable gem: his terrestrial haunts are the snowy hills of Himalaya, or that branch of them to the east of the Brahmaputra, which has the name of Chandrasichara, or

---

[a] Marco della Tomba (d. 1803), an Italian Capuchin missionary who was stationed for some years at Bettiah in Bengal, translated into Italian sections of a *Ramayana* used by followers of Kabir. Part of this translation, called 'Il Libro di Lanka', is printed in *Gli Scritti del Padre Marco della Tomba*, ed. A. de Gubernatis (Florence, 1878), pp. 132–63.   [b] *Voyage aux Indes*, I, 172.
[c] A species of eagle identified by Mathurin-Jacques Brisson (1723–1806), *Ornithologia sive Synopsis methodica* (Paris, 1760), I, 450–1, plate xxxv.

the Mountain of the Moon. When, after all these circumstances, we learn that Siva is believed to have three eyes, whence he is named also Trilochan, and know from Pausanias, not only that *Triophthalmos* was an epithet of Zeus, but that a statue of him had been found, so early as the taking of Troy, with a third eye in his forehead,[a] as we see him represented by the Hindus, we must conclude, that the identity of the two Gods falls little short of being demonstrated.

In the character of Destroyer also we may look upon this Indian deity as corresponding with the Stygian Jove, or Pluto; especially since Cali, or Time in the feminine gender, is a name of his consort, who will appear hereafter to be Proserpine: indeed, if we can rely on a Persian translation of the *Bhagavat*, (for the original is not yet in my possession) the sovereign of Patala, or the Infernal Regions, is the King of Serpents, named Seshanaga; for Crishna is there said to have descended with his favourite Arjun to the seat of that formidable divinity, from whom he instantly obtained the favour, which he requested, that the souls of a Brahman's six sons, who had been slain in battle, might reanimate their respective bodies; and Seshanaga is thus described:

He had a gorgeous appearance, with a thousand heads, and, on each of them, a crown set with resplendent gems, one of which was larger and brighter than the rest; his eyes gleamed like flaming torches; but his neck, his tongues, and his body were black; the skirts of his habiliment were yellow, and a sparkling jewel hung in every one of his ears; his arms were extended, and adorned with rich bracelets, and his hands bore the holy shell, the radiated weapon, the mace for war, and the lotos.

Thus Pluto was often exhibited in painting and sculpture with a diadem and sceptre; but himself and his equipage were of the blackest shade.

There is yet another attribute of Mahadeva, by which he is too visibly distinguished in the drawings and temples of Bengal. To destroy, according to the *Vedantis* of India, the *Sufis* of Persia, and many philosophers of our European schools, is only to generate and reproduce in another form: hence the God of Destruction is holden in this country to preside over generation; as a symbol

[a] See book II, chap. XXIV of the 'Description of Greece', written by Pausanias in the second century A.D.

of which he rides on a white bull. Can we doubt, that the loves and feats of Jupiter Genitor (not forgetting the white bull of Europa) and his extraordinary title of *Lapis*,[a] for which no satisfactory reason is commonly given, have a connexion with the Indian philosophy and mythology? As to the deity of Lampsacus, he was originally a mere scare-crow, and ought not to have a place in any mythological system;[b] and, in regard to Bacchus, the God of Vintage, (between whose acts and those of Jupiter we find, as Bacon observes, a wonderful affinity)[c] his Ithyphallick images, measures, and ceremonies alluded probably to the supposed relation of love and wine; unless we believe them to have belonged originally to Siva, one of whose names is Vagis or Bagis, and to have been afterwards improperly applied. Though, in an essay on the gods of India, where the Brahmans are positively forbidden to taste fermented liquors, we can have little to do with Bacchus, as God of Wine, who was probably no more than the imaginary president over the vintage in Italy, Greece, and the lower Asia, yet we must not omit Suradevi, the Goddess of Wine, who arose, say the Hindus, from the ocean, when it was churned with the mountain Mandar: and this fable seems to indicate, that the Indians came from a country, in which wine was anciently made and considered as a blessing; though the dangerous effects of intemperance induced their early legislators to prohibit the use of all spirituous liquors; and it were much to be wished, that so wise a law had never been violated.

Here may be introduced the Jupiter *Marinus*, or Neptune, of the Romans, as resembling Mahadeva in his generative character; especially as the Hindu god is the husband of Bhavani, whose relation to the waters is evidently marked by her image being restored to them at the conclusion of her great festival called *Durgotsava*:[d] she is known also to have attributes exactly similar to those of Venus *Marina*, whose birth from the sea-foam and splendid rise from the conch, in which she had been cradled, have

[a] Stone.

[b] Priapus, the fertility god, who was said to have been worshipped first at Lampsacus on the Hellespont.

[c] In *De Augmentis Scientiarum* (*The Philosophical Works of Francis Bacon*, ed., J. M. Robertson (1905), pp. 450–2).

[d] The great autumn festival of Bengal.

afforded so many charming subjects to ancient and modern artists; and it is very remarkable, that the Rembha of Indra's court, who seems to correspond with the popular Venus, or Goddess of Beauty, was produced, according to the Indian fabulists, from the froth of the churned ocean. The identity of the *trisula* and the trident, the weapon of Siva and of Neptune, seems to establish this analogy; and the veneration paid all over India to the large buccinum, especially when it can be found with the spiral line and mouth turned from left to right, brings instantly to our mind the musick of Triton. The genius of water is Varuna; but he, like the rest, is far inferior to Mahesa, and even to Indra, who is the prince of the beneficent genii.

This way of considering the gods as individual substances, but as distinct persons in distinct characters, is common to the European and Indian systems; as well as the custom of giving the highest of them the greatest number of names: hence, not to repeat what has been said of Jupiter, came the triple capacity of Diana; and hence her petition in Callimachus, that she might be *polyonymous* or many-titled.^a The consort of Siva is more eminently marked by these distinctions than those of Brahma or Vishnu: she resembles the Isis *Myrionymos*, to whom an ancient marble, described by Gruter, is dedicated;^b but her leading names and characters are Parvati, Durga, Bhavani.

As the mountain-born goddess, or Parvati, she has many properties of the Olympian Juno: her majestick deportment, high spirit, and general attributes are the same; and we find her both on Mount Cailasa, and at the banquets of the deities, uniformly the companion of her husband. One circumstance in the parallel is extremely singular: she is usually attended by her son Carticeya; who rides on a peacock; and, in some drawings, his own robe seems to be spangled with eyes; to which must be added that, in some of her temples, a peacock, without a rider, stands near her image. Though Carticeya, with his six faces and numerous eyes, bears some resemblance to Argus, whom Juno employed as her principal wardour, yet, as he is a deity of the second class, and the commander of celestial armies, he seems clearly to be the Orus of Egypt and the Mars of Italy: his name Scanda, by which he is celebrated in one of the *Puranas*,^c has a connexion, I am persuaded, with the old Secander of Persia, whom the poets ridiculously confound with the Macedonian.^d

The attributes of Durga, or difficult of access, are also

---

^a In the third of his 'Hymns', 'to Artemis', where she asks her father for more names than Phoebus.

^b See *Inscriptiones antiquae totius orbis Romani* (Amsterdam, 1707), I, lxxxiii, by Jan Gruter (1560–1627).

^c The *Skanda Purana*.

^d The name 'Iskander' or 'al-Iskander' frequently occurs in Arabic and Persian literature. The legends connected with it probably do originate with Alexander.

conspicuous in the festival above-mentioned, which is called by her name, and in this character she resembles Minerva, not the peaceful inventress of the fine and useful arts, but Pallas, armed with a helmet and spear: both represent heroick Virtue, or Valour united with Wisdom; both slew demons and giants with their own hands, and both protected the wise and virtuous, who paid them due adoration. As Pallas, they say, takes her name from vibrating a lance, and usually appears in complete armour, thus Curis, the old Latian word for a spear, was one of Juno's titles; and so, if Giraldus be correct, was Hoplosmia,[a] which at Elis,[b] it seems, meant a female dressed in panoply or complete accoutrements. The unarmed Minerva of the Romans apparently corresponds, as patroness of science and genius, with Sereswati, the wife of Brahma, and the emblem of his principal Creative Power: both goddesses have given their names to celebrated grammatical works; but the *Sareswata* of Sarupacharya[c] is far more concise as well as more useful and agreeable than the *Minerva* of Sanctius.[d] The Minerva of Italy invented the flute, and Sereswati presides over melody: the protectress of Athens was even, on the same account, surnamed Musice.

Many learned mythologists, with Giraldus, at their head,[e] consider the peaceful Minerva as the Isis of Egypt; from whose temple at Sais a wonderful inscription is quoted by Plutarch,[f] which has a resemblance to the four Sanscrit verses above exhibited as the text of the *Bhagavat*: 'I am all, that hath been, and is, and shall be; and my veil no mortal hath ever removed.' For my part I have no doubt, that the Iswara and Isi of the Hindus are the Osiris and Isis of the Egyptians; though a distinct essay in the manner of Plutarch would be requisite in order to demonstrate their identity: they mean, I conceive, the Powers of Nature considered as male and female; and Isis, like the other goddesses, represents the active power of her lord, whose eight forms, under

---

[a] *De Deis Gentium, Libri sive Syntagmata XVII* (Lyons, 1565), p. 114.
[b] A district in the north-western Peloponnese.
[c] The *Sarasvati Sutra*, see above, p. 151.
[d] The *Minerva* was a Latin grammar written by the Spanish scholar Francisco Sanchez (1523–1601). First published in 1587, it was frequently reprinted.
[e] *De Deis Gentium*, p. 290.
[f] *De Iside et Osiride*, chap. ix.

which he becomes visible to man, were thus enumerated by Calidasa near two thousand years ago:

Water was the first work of the Creator; and Fire receives the oblation of clarified butter, as the law ordains; the Sacrifice is performed with solemnity; the two Lights of heaven distinguish time; the subtil Ether, which is the vehicle of sound, pervades the universe; the Earth is the natural parent of all increase; and by Air all things breathing are animated: may Isa, the power propitiously apparent in these eight forms, bless and sustain you![a]

The five elements, therefore, as well as the sun and moon, are considered as Isa or the Ruler, from which word Isi may be regularly formed, though Isani be the usual name of his active power, adored as the Goddess of Nature. I have not yet found in Sanscrit the wild, though poetical, tale of Io;[b] but am persuaded, that, by means of the *Puranas*, we shall in time discover all the learning of the Egyptians without decyphering their hieroglyphicks: the bull of Iswara seems to be Apis, or Ap, as he is more correctly named in the true reading of a passage in Jeremiah;[c] and, if the veneration shown both in Tibet and India to so amiable and useful a quadruped as the cow, together with the regeneration of the Lama himself,[d] have not some affinity with the religion of Egypt and the idolatry of Israel, we must at least allow that circumstances have wonderfully coincided. Bhavani now demands our attention; and in this character I suppose the wife of Mahadeva to be as well the Juno *Cinxia* or Lucina of the Romans (called also by them Diana *Solvizona*, and by the Greeks *Ilithyia*)[e] as Venus herself; not the Italian queen of laughter and jollity, who, with her Nymphs and Graces, was the beautiful child of poetical imagination, and answers to the Indian Rembha with her celestial train of Apsaras, or damsels of paradise; but Venus *Urania*, so luxuriantly painted by Lucretius, and so properly invoked by him

---

[a] This is Jones's version of the Brahmins' benediction in *Sacontala, or the Fatal Ring* (Calcutta, 1789), p. 1.

[b] Io was turned into a heifer by Zeus.

[c] For the reading 'Why has Apis fled?' for Jer. xlvi, 15, see *The Interpreter's Dictionary of the Bible* (New York, 1962), I, 157.

[d] An account by Captain Samuel Turner (*c.* 1749–1802) of an interview granted him in 1783 with the young Panchen Lama, and of the doctrine of each successive Lama as a reincarnation of his predecessor was included in the first volume of *Asiatick Researches*.

[e] The epithets applied to Juno and Diana refer to childbearing. Eileithyia, the Greek goddess of birth, became identified with Juno.

at the opening of a poem on nature;[a] Venus, presiding over generation, and, on that account, exhibited sometimes of both sexes, (an union very common in the Indian sculptures) as in her bearded statue at Rome, in the images perhaps called *Hermathena*,[b] and in those figures of her, which had the form of a conical marble; 'for the reason of which figure we are left', says Tacitus, 'in the dark':[c] the reason appears too clearly in the temples and paintings of Hindustan; where it never seems to have entered the heads of the legislators or people that any thing natural could be offensively obscene; a singularity, which pervades all their writings and conversation, but is no proof of depravity in their morals. Both Plato[d] and Cicero[e] speak of Eros, or the heavenly Cupid, as the son of Venus and Jupiter; which proves, that the monarch of Olympus and the Goddess of Fecundity were connected as Mahadeva and Bhavani: the God Cama, indeed, had Maya and Casyapa, or Uranus, for his parents, at least according to the mythologists of Cashmir; but, in most respects, he seems the twin brother of Cupid with richer and more lively appendages. One of his many epithets is *Dipaca*, the Inflamer, which is erroneously written *Dipuc*; and I am now convinced, that the sort of resemblance, which has been observed between his Latin and Sanscrit names, is accidental: in each name the three first letters are the root, and between them there is no affinity. Whether any mythological connection subsisted between the amaracus, with the fragrant leaves of which Hymen bound his temples, and the *tulasi*[f] of India, must be left undetermined: the botanical relation of the two plants (if amaracus be properly translated marjoram) is extremely near.

One of the most remarkable ceremonies, in the festival of the Indian goddess, is that before-mentioned of casting her image into the river: the Pandits, of whom I inquired concerning its origin and import, answered, 'that it was prescribed by the *Veda*, they knew not why'; but this custom has, I conceive, a relation to the doctrine, that water is a form of Iswara, and consequently

[a] See the opening of *De Rerum Natura*.
[b] Double-headed male and female figures.
[c] *Historiae*, book II, chap. III.
[d] In the *Phaedrus*, 242.
[e] In *De Natura Deorum*, book III, chap. XXIII.   [f] The sacred basil.

of Isani, who is even represented by some as the patroness of that element, to which her figure is restored, after having received all due honours on earth, which is considered as another form of the God of Nature, though subsequent, in the order of creation, to the primeval fluid. There seems no decisive proof of one original system among idolatrous nations in the worship of river-gods and river-goddesses, nor in the homage paid to their streams, and the ideas of purification annexed to them; since Greeks, Italians, Egyptians, and Hindus might (without any communication with each other) have adored the several divinities of their great rivers, from which they derived pleasure, health, and abundance. The notion of Doctor Musgrave, that large rivers were supposed, from their strength and rapidity, to be conducted by Gods, while rivulets only were protected by female deities, is, like most other notions of grammarians on the genders of nouns, overthrown by facts.[a]   Most of the great Indian rivers are feminine; and the three goddesses of the waters, whom the Hindus chiefly venerate, are Ganga, who sprang, like armed Pallas, from the head of the Indian Jove; Yamuna, daughter of the Sun, and Sereswati: all three meet at Prayaga thence called *Triveni*, or the three plaited locks;[b] but Sereswati, according to the popular belief, sinks under ground, and rises at another Triveni near Hugli, where she rejoins her beloved Ganga. The Brahmaputra is, indeed, a male river; and, as his name signifies the son of Brahma, I thence took occasion to feign that he was married to Ganga, though I have not yet seen any mention of him, as a god, in the Sanscrit books.

Two incarnate deities of the first rank, Rama and Crishna, must now be introduced, and their several attributes distinctly explained. The first of them, I believe, was the Dionysos of the Greeks, whom they named *Bromius*, without knowing why, and *Bugenes*, when they represented him horned, as well as *Lyaios* and *Eleutherios*, the Deliverer, and *Triambos* or *Dithyrambos*, the triumphant: most of those titles were adopted by the Romans, by whom he was called *Bruma, Tauriformis, Liber, Triumphus*;

---

[a] See *Two Dissertations* (1783), p. 22, by Samuel Musgrave (1732–80), physician and classical scholar.
[b] Now called Allahabad.

and both nations had records or traditionary accounts of his giving laws to men and deciding their contests, of his improving navigation and commerce, and, what may appear yet more observable, of his conquering India and other countries with an army of Satyrs, commanded by no less a personage than Pan; whom Lilius Giraldus, on what authority I know not, asserts to have resided in Iberia, 'when he had returned', says the learned mythologist, 'from the Indian war, in which he accompanied Bacchus.'[a]

[a] This reference, presumably from *De Deis Gentium*, has not been located.

Jones on the Gods

It were superfluous in a mere essay, to run any length in the parallel between this European god and the sovereign of Ayodhya, whom the Hindus believe to have been an appearance on earth of the Preserving Power; to have been a conqueror of the highest renown, and the deliverer of nations from tyrants, as well as of his consort Sita from the giant Ravan, king of Lanca, and to have commanded in chief a numerous and intrepid race of those large monkeys, which our naturalists, or some of them, have denominated Indian Satyrs: his general, the Prince of Satyrs, was named Hanumat, or with high cheek-bones; and, with workmen of such agility, he soon raised a bridge of rocks over the sea, part of which, say the Hindus, yet remains; and it is, probably, the series of rocks, to which the Muselmans or the Portuguese have given the foolish name of Adam's (it should be called Rama's) bridge. Might not this army of Satyrs have been only a race of mountaineers, whom Rama, if such a monarch ever existed, had civilized? However that may be, the large breed of Indian apes is at this moment held in high veneration by the Hindus, and fed with devotion by the Brahmans, who seem, in two or three places on the banks of the Ganges, to have a regular endowment for the support of them: they live in tribes of three or four hundred, are wonderfully gentle, (I speak as an eye-witness) and appear to have some kind of order and subordination in their little sylvan polity. We must not omit, that the father of Hanumat was the God of Wind, named Pavan, one of the eight Genii; and, as Pan improved the pipe by adding six reeds, and 'played exquisitely on the cithern a few moments after his birth,' so one of the four systems of Indian musick bears the name of Hanumat, or Hanuman in the nominative, as its inventor, and is now in general estimation.

The war of Lanca is dramatically represented at the festival of Rama on the ninth day of the new moon of *Chaitra*;[a] and the drama concludes (says Holwell, who had often seen it)[b] with an exhibition of the fire-ordeal, by which the victor's wife Sita gave proof of her connubial fidelity: 'the dialogue', he adds, 'is taken from one of the Eighteen holy books,' meaning, I suppose, the

[a] *Chaitra* extends from March to April.
[b] *Interesting Historical Events*, ii, 145–6.

Puranas; but the Hindus have a great number of regular dramas at least two thousand years old, and among them are several very fine ones, on the story of Rama. The first poet of the Hindus was the great Valmic,[a] and his *Ramayan* is an epick poem on the same subject, which, in unity of action, magnificence of imagery, and elegance of style, far surpasses the learned and elaborate work of Nonnus,[b] entitled *Dionysiaca*, half of which, or twenty-four books, I perused with great eagerness, when I was very young, and should have travelled to the conclusion of it, if other pursuits had not engaged me: I shall never have leisure to compare the *Dionysiacks* with the *Ramayan*, but am confident, that an accurate comparison of the two poems would prove Dionysos and Rama to have been the same person; and I incline to think, that he was Rama, the son of Cush,[c] who might have established the first regular government in this part of Asia. I had almost forgotten, that Meros is said by the Greeks to have been a mountain of India, on which their Dionysos was born, and that Meru, though it generally means the north pole in the Indian geography, is also a mountain near the city of Naishada or Nysa, called by the Grecian geographers Dionysopolis,[d] and universally celebrated in the Sanscrit poems; though the birth place of Rama is supposed to have been Ayodhya or Audh. That ancient city extended, if we believe the Brahmans, over a line of ten *Yojans*, or about forty miles, and the present city of Lachnau, pronounced Lucnow, was only a lodge for one of its gates, called *Lacshmanadwara*, or the gate of Lacshman, a brother of Rama: M. Sonnerat supposes Ayodhya to have been Siam; a most erroneous and unfounded supposition, which would have been of little consequence, if he had not grounded an argument on it, that Rama was the same person with Buddha, who must have appeared many centuries after the conquest of Lanca.[e]

The second great divinity, Crishna, passed a life, according to the Indians, of a most extraordinary and incomprehensible nature.

---

[a] The legendary Valmiki.

[b] A Greek poet of the fifth century A.D.   [c] Gen. x, 7.

[d] Mount Meros and Nysa are mentioned by Strabo, the name Dionysopolis by Ptolemy (J. W. McCrindle, *Ancient India as described in Classical Literature* (1901), pp. 12–13; *Ancient India as described by Ptolemy* (1885), pp. 112–13).

[e] *Voyage aux Indes*, I, 163.

He was the son of Devaci by Vasudeva; but his birth was concealed through fear of the tyrant Cansa, to whom it had been predicted, that a child born at that time in that family would destroy him: he was fostered, therefore, in Mathura by an honest herdsman, surnamed Ananda, or Happy, and his amiable wife Yasoda, who, like another Pales,[a] was constantly occupied in her pastures and her dairy. In their family were a multitude of young *Gopas* or cowherds, and beautiful *Gopis*, or milkmaids, who were his playfellows during his infancy; and, in his early youth, he selected nine damsels as his favourites,with whom he passed his gay hours in dancing, sporting, and playing on his flute. For the remarkable number of his *Gopis* I have no authority but a whimsical picture, where nine girls are grouped in the form of an elephant, on which he sits and pipes; and, unfortunately, the word *nava* signifies both nine and new or young; so that, in the following stanza, it may admit of two interpretations:

> *taranijapuline navaballavi*
> *perisada saha celicutuhalat*
> *drutavilamwitacharuviharinam*
> *herimaham hridayena sada vahe.*

'I bear in my bosom continually that god, who, for sportive recreation with a train of nine (young) dairy-maids, dances gracefully, now quick now slow, on the sands just left by the Daughter of the Sun.'[b]

Both he and the three Ramas are described as youths of perfect beauty; but the princesses of Hindustan, as well as the damsels of Nanda's farm, were passionately in love with Crishna, who continues to this hour the darling god of the Indian women. The sect of Hindus, who adore him with enthusiastick and almost exclusive, devotion, have broached a doctrine, which they maintain with eagerness, and which seems general in these provinces; that he was distinct from all the *Avatars*, who had only an *ansa*, or portion, of his divinity; while Crishna was the person of Vishnu himself in a human form: hence they consider the third Rama, his elder brother, as the eighth *Avatar* invested with an emanation of his divine radiance; and, in the principal Sanscrit dictionary,[c]

---

[a] Pales was a deity of flocks.
[b] This quotation has not been identified.
[c] The *Amarakosha*, see above, p. 203.

compiled about two thousand years ago, Crishna, Vasadeva, Govinda, and other names of the Shepherd God, are intermixed with epithets of Narayan, or the Divine Spirit. All the *Avatars* are painted with gemmed Ethiopian, or Parthian, coronets; with rays encircling their heads; jewels in their ears; two necklaces, one straight, and one pendent on their bosoms with dropping gems; garlands of well-disposed many-coloured flowers, or collars of pearls, hanging down below their waists; loose mantles of golden tissue or dyed silk, embroidered on their hems with flowers, elegantly thrown over one shoulder, and folded, like ribbands, across the breast; with bracelets too on one arm, and on each wrist; they are naked to the waists, and uniformly with dark azure flesh, in allusion, probably, to the tint of that primordial fluid, on which Narayan moved in the beginning of time; but their skirts are bright yellow, the colour of the curious pericarpium in the centre of the water-lily, where Nature, as Dr. Murray observes, in some degree discloses her secrets,[a] each seed containing, before it germinates, a few perfect leaves: they are sometimes drawn with that flower in one hand; a radiated elliptical ring, used as a missile weapon, in a second; the sacred shell, or left-handed buccinum, in a third; and a mace or battle-ax, in a fourth; but Crishna, when he appears, as he sometimes does appear, among the *Avatars*, is more splendidly decorated than any, and wears a rich garland of sylvan flowers, whence he is named Vanamali, as low as his ankles, which are adorned with strings of pearls. Dark blue, approaching to black, which is the meaning of the word *Crishna*, is believed to have been his complexion; and hence the large bee of that colour is consecrated to him, and is often drawn fluttering over his head: that azure tint, which approaches to blackness, is peculiar, as we have already remarked, to Vishnu; and hence, in the great reservoir or cistern at Catmandu the capital of Nepal, there is placed in a recumbent posture a large well-proportioned image of blue marble, representing Narayan floating on the waters.[b] But let us return to the actions of Crishna; who was not less heroick, than lovely, and, when à

---

[a] This reference has not been identified.

[b] Jones derived this information from 'An account of the Kingdom of Nepal', later to be published in *Asiatick Researches*, II, 313, by the Prefect of the Catholic mission in Nepal, Guiseppe da Rovato (d. 1786).

boy, slew the terrible serpent Caliya with a number of giants and monsters: at a more advanced age, he put to death his cruel enemy Cansa; and, having taken under his protection the king Yudhisht-hir and the other Pandus, who had been grievously oppressed by the Curus, and their tyrannical chief, he kindled the war described in the great epick poem, entitled the *Mahabharat*, at the prosperous conclusion of which he returned to his heavenly seat in Vaicontha, having left the instructions comprized in the *Gita* with his disconsolate friend Arjun, whose grandson became sovereign of India.

In this picture it is impossible not to discover, at the first glance, the features of Apollo, surnamed *Nomios*, or the Pastoral, in Greece, and *Opifer* in Italy; who fed the herds of Admetus, and slew the serpent *Python*; a God amorous, beautiful, and warlike: the word *Govinda* may be literally translated *Nomios*, as *Cesava* is *Crinitus*, or with fine hair; but whether *Gopala*, or the herdsman, has any relation to Apollo, let our etymologists determine. Colonel Vallancey, whose learned inquiries into the ancient literature of Ireland are highly interesting,[a] assures me, that *Crishna* in Irish means the Sun;[b] and we find Apollo and Sol considered by the Roman poets as the same deity: I am inclined, indeed, to believe, that not only Crishna or Vishnu, but even Brahma and Siva, when united, and expressed by the mystical word OM, were designed by the first idolaters to represent the solar fire; but Phoebus or the orb of the sun personified, is adored by the Indians as the god Surya, whence the sect, who pay him particular adoration, are called *Sauras*: their poets and painters describe his car as drawn by seven green horses, preceded by Arun, or the Dawn, who acts as his charioteer, and followed by thousands of genii worshipping him and modulating his praises. He has a multitude of names, and among them twelve epithets or titles, which denote his distinct powers in each of the twelve months: those powers are called Adityas, or sons of Aditi by Casyapa, the Indian Uranus; and one of them has, according to some authorities, the name of Vishnu or Pervader. Surya is believed to have descended frequently from his car in a human shape, and to have left a race on earth, who are equally renowned in the Indian stories with the *Heliadai* of Greece:[c] it is very singular, that his two sons called Aswinau or Aswinicumarau, in the dual, should be considered as twin-brothers, and painted like Castor and Pollux, but they have each the character of Æsculapius among the gods, and are believed to have been born of a nymph, who, in the form of a mare,

[a] Charles Vallancey (1721–1812).
[b] In an *Essay on the Primitive Inhabitants of Great Britain and Ireland. Proving ...that they were Persians or Indoscythae* (Dublin, 1807), Vallancey specifically identified the Indian 'Crishna' with the Irish 'Cris, Crisheen, Creasana-hain'.
[c] The children of Helios, the Greek sun god.

was impregnated with sun-beams. I suspect the whole fable of Casyapa and his progeny to be astronomical; and cannot but imagine, that the Greek name Cassiopeia has a relation to it.[a] Another great Indian family are called the Children of the Moon, or Chandra; who is a male deity, and consequently not to be compared with Artemis or Diana; nor have I yet found a parallel in India for the Goddess of the Chase, who seems to have been the daughter of an European fancy, and very naturally created by the invention of Bucolick and Georgick poets: yet, since the Moon is a form of Iswara, the God of Nature, according to the verse of Calidasa,[b] and since Isani has been shown to be his consort or power, we may consider her, in one of her characters, as Luna; especially as we shall soon be convinced that, in the shades below, she corresponds with the Hecate of Europe.

The worship of solar, or vestal, fire may be ascribed, like that of Osiris and Isis, to the second source of mythology, or an enthusiastick admiration of Nature's wonderful powers; and it seems, as far as I can yet understand the *Vedas*,[c] to be the principal worship recommended in them. We have seen, that Mahadeva himself is personated by fire; but, subordinate to him, is the god Agni, often called Pavaca, or the Purifier, who answers to the Vulcan of Egypt, where he was a deity of high rank; and his wife Swaha resembles the younger Vesta, or Vestia, as the Eolians[d] pronounced the Greek word for a hearth; Bhavani, or Venus, is the consort of the Supreme Destructive and Generative Power; but the Greeks and Romans, whose system is less regular than that of the Indians, married her to their divine artist, whom they also named Hephaistos and Vulcan, and who seems to be the Indian Viswacarman, the forger of arms for the Gods, and inventor of the *agnyastra*, or fiery shaft, in the war between them and the Daityas or Titans. It is not easy here to refrain from observing (and, if the observation give offence in England, it is contrary to my intention) that the newly discovered planet should unquestionably be named Vulcan;[e] since the confusion of analogy

---

[a] The mother of Andromeda, she was turned into a constellation.
[b] Kalidasa, author of *Shakuntala*, see above, p. 225.
[c] See above, p. 211.   [d] A Greek community in Asia Minor.
[e] The planet later called Uranus was first observed by Sir William Herschell (1738–1822) in March 1781.

in the names of the planets is inelegant, unscholarly, and unphilosophical: the name Uranus is appropriated to the firmament; but Vulcan, the slowest of the Gods, and, according to the Egyptian priests, the oldest of them, agrees admirably with an orb, which must perform its revolution in a very long period; and, by giving it this denomination, we shall have seven primary planets with the names of as many Roman deities, Mercury, Venus, Tellus, Mars, Jupiter, Saturn, Vulcan.

It has already been intimated, that the Muses and Nymphs are the Gopya of Mathura, and of Goverdhan, the Parnassus of the Hindus; and the lyrick poems of Jayadcva[a] will fully justify this opinion; but the Nymphs of Musick are the thirty Raginis or female passions, whose various functions and properties are so richly delineated by the Indian painters and so finely described by the poets; but I will not anticipate what will require a separate essay, by enlarging here on the beautiful allegories of the Hindus in their system of musical modes, which they call Ragas, or Passions, and suppose to be genii or demigods.[b] A very distinguished son of Brahma, named Nared, whose actions are the subject of a *Purana*,[c] bears a strong resemblance to Hermes or Mercury: he was a wise legislator, great in arts and in arms, an eloquent messenger of the gods either to one another or to favoured mortals, and a musician of exquisite skill; his invention of the *Vina*, or Indian lute, is thus described in the poem entitled *Magha*: 'Nared sat watching from time to time his large *Vina*, which, by the impulse of the breeze, yielded notes, that pierced successively the regions of his ear, and proceeded by musical intervals.'[d] The law tract, supposed to have been revealed by Nared,[e] is at this hour cited by the Pandits; and we cannot, therefore, believe him to have been the patron of thieves; though an innocent theft of Crishna's cattle, by way of putting his divinity to a proof, be strangely imputed, in the *Bhagavat*, to his father Brahma.

[a] See above, p. 209.
[b] Jones published an essay 'On the Musical Modes of the Hindus' (*Asiatick Researches*, iii, 55–87).
[c] The *Naradiya Purana*.
[d] Magha is the name of a poet, probably of the seventh century A.D. Jones is quoting from his *Shishupalavadha*, i, 10.   [e] The *Naradiya-dharma-shastra*.

The last of the Greek or Italian divinities, for whom we find a parallel in the Pantheon of India, is the Stygian or Taurick Diana, otherwise named Hecate, and often confounded with Proserpine; and there can be no doubt of her identity with Cali, or the wife of Siva in his character of the Stygian Jove. To this black goddess with a collar of golden skulls, as we see her exhibited in all her principal temples, human sacrifices were anciently offered, as the *Vedas* enjoined; but, in the present age, they are absolutely prohibited, as are also the sacrifices of bulls and horses: kids are still offered to her; and, to palliate the cruelty of the slaughter, which gave such offence to Buddha, the Brahmans inculcate a belief, that the poor victims rise in the heaven of Indra, where they become the musicians of his band. Instead of the obsolete, and now illegal, sacrifices of a man, a bull, and a horse, called *Neramedha*, *Gomedha*, and *Aswamedha*, the powers of nature are thought to be propitiated by the less bloody ceremonies at the end of autumn, when the festivals of Cali and Lacshmi are solemnized nearly at the same time: now, if it be asked, how the Goddess of Death came to be united with the mild patroness of Abundance, I must propose another question, 'How came Proserpine to be represented in the European system as the daughter of Ceres?' Perhaps, both questions may be answered by the proposition of natural philosophers, that 'the apparent destruction of a substance is the production of it in a different form.' The wild musick of Cali's priests at one of her festivals brought instantly to my recollection the Scythian measures of Diana's adorers in the splendid opera of Iphigenia in Tauris, which Gluck exhibited at Paris with less genius, indeed, than art, but with every advantage that an orchestra could supply.[a]

That we may not dismiss this assemblage of European and Asiatick divinities with a subject so horrid as the altars of Hecate and Cali, let us conclude with two remarks, which properly, indeed, belong to the Indian philosophy, with which we are not at present concerned. First; Elysium (not the place, but the bliss enjoyed there, in which sense Milton uses the word)[b] cannot but appear, as described by the poets, a very tedious and insipid kind

---

[a] *Iphigénie en Tauride* by Cristoph Willibald Gluck (1714–87) was performed in Paris in May 1779, a year when Jones went to France (G. H. Cannon, *Oriental Jones* (1964), p. 162).   [b] *Comus*, 257.

of enjoyment: it is, however, more exalted than the temporary Elysium in the court of Indra, where the pleasures, as in Muhammed's paradise, are wholly sensual; but the *Mucti*, or Elysian happiness of the *Vedanta* school is far more sublime; for they represent it as a total absorption, though not such as to destroy consciousness, in the divine essence; but, for the reason before suggested, I say no more of this idea of beatitude, and forbear touching on the doctrine of transmigration and the similarity of the *Vedanta* to the Sicilian, Italick, and old Academick schools.

Secondly; in the mystical and elevated character of Pan, as a personification of the Universe, according to the notion of lord Bacon,[a] there arises a sort of similitude between him and Crishna considered as Narayan. The Grecian god plays divinely on his reed, to express, we are told, ethereal harmony; he has his attendant nymphs of the pastures and the dairy; his face is as radiant as the sky, and his head illumined with the horns of a crescent; whilst his lower extremities are deformed and shaggy, as a symbol of the vegetables, which the earth produces, and of the beasts, who roam over the face of it: now we may compare this portrait, partly with the general character of Crishna, the Shepherd God, and partly with the description in the *Bhagavat* of the divine spirit exhibited in the form of this Universal World; to which we may add the following story from the same extraordinary poem. The nymphs had complained to Yasoda, that the child Crishna had been drinking their curds and milk: on being reproved by his foster-mother for this indiscretion, he requested her to examine his mouth; in which, to her just amazement, she beheld the whole universe in all its plenitude of magnificence.

We must not be surprized at finding, on a close examination, that the characters of all the pagan deities, male and female, melt into each other, and at last into one or two; for it seems a well-founded opinion, that the whole crowd of gods and goddesses in ancient Rome, and modern Varanes, mean only the powers of nature, and principally those of the sun, expressed in a variety of ways and by a multitude of fanciful names.

Thus have I attempted to trace, imperfectly at present for want of ampler materials, but with a confidence continually increasing

---

[a] *Philosophical Works*, ed. Robinson, pp. 442–7, 828–32.

as I advanced, a parallel between the gods adored in three very different nations, Greece, Italy, and India; but, which was the original system and which the copy, I will not presume to decide; nor are we likely, I believe, to be soon furnished with sufficient grounds for a decision: the fundamental rule, that natural, and most human, operations proceed from the simple to the compound, will afford no assistance on this point; since neither the Asiatick nor European system has any simplicity in it; and both are so complex, not to say absurd, however intermixed with the beautiful and the sublime, that the honour, such as it is, of the invention cannot be allotted to either with tolerable certainty.

Since Egypt appears to have been the grand source of knowledge for the western, and India for the more eastern, parts of the globe, it may seem a material question, whether the Egyptians communicated their mythology and philosophy to the Hindus, or conversely; but what the learned of Memphis wrote or said concerning India, no mortal knows; and what the learned of Varanes have asserted, if any thing, concerning Egypt, can give us little satisfaction: such circumstantial evidence on this question as I have been able to collect, shall nevertheless be stated; because, unsatisfactory as it is, there may be something in it not wholly unworthy of notice; though after all, whatever colonies may have come from the Nile to the Ganges, we shall, perhaps, agree at last with Mr. Bryant,[a] that Egyptians, Indians, Greeks and Italians, proceeded originally from one central place, and that the same people carried their religion and sciences into China and Japan: may we not add, even to Mexico and Peru?

Every one knows, that the true name of Egypt is *Misr*, spelled with a palatial sibilant both in Hebrew and Arabick: it seems in Hebrew to have been the proper name of the first settler in it; and, when the Arabs use the word for a great city, they probably mean a city like the capital of Egypt. Father Marco,[b] a Roman missionary, who, though not a scholar of the first rate, is incapable, I am persuaded, of deliberate falsehood, lent me the last book of a *Ramayan*, which he had translated through the Hindi

---

[a] Jacob Bryant (1715–1804), author of *A New System, or, an Analysis of Ancient Mythology*, 3 vols (1774–6), a work about which Jones had strong views (see below, pp. 246–8).

[b] Marco della Tomba, see above, p. 219.

into his native language, and with it a short vocabulary of mythological and historical names;[a] which had been explained to him by the Pandits of Betiya,[b] where he had long resided: one of the articles in his little dictionary was, 'Tirut, a town and province, in which the priests from Egypt settled'; and, when I asked him, what name Egypt bore among the Hindus, he said *Misr*, but observed, that they sometimes confounded it with Abyssinia. I perceived, that his memory of what he had written was correct; for *Misr* was another word in his index, 'from which country', he said, 'came the Egyptian priests, who settled in Tirut.' I suspected immediately, that his intelligence flowed from the Muselmans, who call sugar-candy *Misri* or Egyptian; but, when I examined him closely, and earnestly desired him to recollect from whom he had received his information, he repeatedly and positively declared, that 'it had been given him by several Hindus, and particularly by a Brahman, his intimate friend, who was reputed a considerable Pandit, and had lived three years near his house.' We then conceived, that the seat of his Egyptian colony must have been Tirohit, commonly pronounced Tirut, and anciently called Mithila, the principal town of Janacadesa, or north Bahar; but Mahesa Pandit, who was born in that very district, and who submitted patiently to a long examination concerning *Misr*, overset all our conclusions: he denied, that the Brahmans of his country were generally surnamed *Misr*, as we had been informed; and said, that the addition of Misra to the name of Vachespeti,[c] and other learned authors, was a title formerly conferred on the writers of miscellanies, or compilers of various tracts on religion or science, the word being derived from a root signifying to mix. Being asked, where the country of *Misr* was, 'There are two', he answered, 'of that name; one of them in the west under the dominion of Muselmans, and another, which all the *Sastras* and *Puranas* mention, in a mountainous region to the north of Ayodhya': it is evident, that by the first he meant Egypt, but what he meant by the second, it is not easy to ascertain. A country, called Tiruhut by our geographers, appears in the maps between

[a] This vocabulary was not included in della Tomba's published *Scritti*, see above, p. 219.

[b] There had been a mission at Bettiah since 1740.

[c] Vachaspati Misra, the ninth-century *Vedanta* philosopher.

the north-eastern frontier of Audh and the mountains of Nepal;[a] but whether that was the Tirut mentioned to father Marco by his friend of Betiya, I cannot decide. This only I know with certainty, that *Misra* is an epithet of two Brahmans in the drama of *Sacontala*,[b] which was written near a century before the birth of Christ; that some of the greatest lawyers, and two of the finest dramatick poets, of India[c] have the same title; that we hear it frequently in court added to the names of Hindu parties; and that none of the Pandits, whom I have since consulted, pretend to know the true meaning of the word, as a proper name, or to give any other explanation of it than that it is a surname of Brahmans in the west. On the account given to Colonel Kyd by the old Raja of Crishnanagar, 'concerning traditions among the Hindus' that some Egyptians had settled in this country, I cannot rely; because I am credibly informed by some of the Raja's own family, that he was not a man of solid learning, though he possessed curious books, and had been attentive to the conversation of learned men: besides, I know that his son and most of his kinsmen have been dabblers in Persian literature, and believe them very likely, by confounding one source of information with another, to puzzle themselves and mislead those, with whom they converse.[d] The word *Misr*, spelled also in Sanscrit with a palatial sibilant, is very remarkable; and, as far as etymology can help us, we may safely derive *Nilus* from the Sanscrit word *nila*, or blue; since Dionysius expressly calls the waters of that river 'an azure stream';[e] and, if we can depend on Marco's Italian version of the *Ramayan*, the name of Nila is given to a lofty and sacred mountain with a summit of pure gold, from which flowed a river of clear, sweet, and

[a] See James Rennell's map of 'Bengal and Bahar' (1779).

[b] *Sacontala*, p. 88.

[c] Perhaps Damodara Misra, author of one of the recensions of the *Hanumannataka*, probably composed in the ninth century, and Krishnamisra, author of the allegorical play *Prabodhachandrodaya*, probably of the eleventh century.

[d] The account given to Colonel Robert Kyd (d. 1793) by Krishna Chandra, Raja of Nadia (d. 1782), has not been located. But Halhed in the Preface to his *Grammar of the Bengal Language* (Hooghli, 1778), p. v, called Krishna Chandra 'by much the most learned and able antiquary which Bengal has produced within this century' and reported that the Raja had 'in his own possession Shanscrit books which give an account of a communication formerly subsisting between India and Egypt'.

[e] The 'Survey of the World', 220 ff. by Dionysius 'Periegetes', a Greek geographer of the second century A.D.

fresh water. M. Sonnerat refers to a dissertation by Mr. Schmit, which gained a prize at the Academy of Inscriptions, 'On an Egyptian Colony established in India': it would be worth while to examine his authorities, and either to overturn or verify them by such higher authorities, as are now accessible in these provinces.[a] I strongly incline to think him right, and to believe that Egyptian priests have actually come from the Nile to the Ganga and Yamuna, which the Brahmans most assuredly would never have left: they might indeed, have come either to be instructed or to instruct; but it seems more probable, that they visited the Sarmans[b] of India, as the sages of Greece visited them, rather to acquire than to impart knowledge; nor is it likely, that the self-sufficient Brahmans would have received them as their preceptors.

Be all this as it may, I am persuaded, that a connexion subsisted between the old idolatrous nations of Egypt, India, Greece, and Italy, long before they migrated to their several settlements, and consequently before the birth of Moses; but the proof of this proposition will in no degree affect the truth and sanctity of the Mosaick history, which, if confirmation were necessary, it would rather tend to confirm. The Divine Legate, educated by the daughter of a king, and in all respects highly accomplished, could not but know the mythological system of Egypt; but he must have condemned the superstitions of that people, and despised the speculative absurdities of their priests; though some of their traditions concerning the creation and the flood were grounded on truth. Who was better acquainted with the mythology of Athens than Socrates? Who more accurately versed in the Rabbinical doctrines than Paul? Who possessed clearer ideas of all ancient astronomical systems than Newton, or of scholastick metaphysics than Locke? In whom could the Romish Church have had a more formidable opponent than in Chillingworth,[c] whose deep

---

[a] *Dissertation sur une colonie Egyptienne établie aux Indes* (Berne, 1759), by the Swiss scholar Friedrich Samuel Schmidt (1737–96), was submitted for the Easter prize for 1758 offered by the Académie royale des Inscriptions et Belles Lettres. It relied on the usual Greek sources, etymological speculation and the apparent similarity of customs.

[b] A term used by Megasthenes as repeated by Strabo (McCrindle, *Ancient India in Classical Literature*, p. 65).

[c] William Chillingworth (1602–44), the Anglican theologian who had at one time been admitted into the Catholic Church.

knowledge of its tenets rendered him so competent to dispute them? In a word, who more exactly knew the abominable rites and shocking idolatry of Canaan than Moses himself? Yet the learning of those great men only incited them to seek other sources of truth, piety, and virtue, than those in which they had long been immersed. There is no shadow then of a foundation for an opinion, that Moses borrowed the first nine or ten chapters of *Genesis* from the literature of Egypt: still less can the adamantine pillars of our Christian faith be moved by the result of any debates on the comparative antiquity of the Hindus and Egyptians, or of any inquiries into the Indian theology. Very respectable natives have assured me, that one or two missionaries have been absurd enough, in their zeal for the conversion of the Gentiles, to urge, 'that the Hindus were even now almost Christians, because their Brahma, Vishnu, and Mahesa, were no other than the Christian Trinity'; a sentence, in which we can only doubt, whether folly, ignorance, or impiety predominates. The three powers, Creative, Preservative, and Destructive, which the Hindus express by the triliteral word OM, were grossly ascribed by the first idolaters to the heat, light, and flame of their mistaken divinity, the sun; and their wiser successors in the East, who perceived that the sun was only a created thing, applied those powers to its creator; but the Indian Triad, and that of Plato, which he calls the Supreme Good, the Reason, and the Soul, are infinitely removed from the holiness and sublimity of the doctrine, which pious Christians have deduced from texts in the Gospel, though other Christians, as pious, openly profess their dissent from them. Each sect must be justified by its own faith and good intentions: this only I mean to inculcate, that the tenet of our Church cannot without profaneness be compared with that of the Hindus, which has only an apparent resemblance to it, but a very different meaning. One singular fact, however, must not be suffered to pass unnoticed. That the name of Crishna, and the general outline of his story, were long anterior to the birth of our Saviour, and probably to the time of Homer, we know very certainly; yet, the celebrated poem, entitled *Bhagavat*, which contains a prolix account of his life, is filled with narratives of a most extraordinary kind, but strangely variegated and intermixed with poetical decorations:

the incarnate deity of the Sanscrit romance was cradled, as it informs us, among herdsmen, but it adds, that he was educated among them, and passed his youth in playing with a party of milkmaids; a tyrant, at the time of his birth, ordered all new-born males to be slain, yet this wonderful babe was preserved by biting the breast, instead of sucking the poisoned nipple, of a nurse commissioned to kill him; he performed amazing, but ridiculous, miracles in his infancy, and, at the age of seven years, held up a mountain on the tip of his little finger: he saved multitudes partly by his arms and partly by his miraculous powers; he raised the dead by descending for that purpose to the lowest regions; he was the meekest and best-tempered of beings, washed the feet of the Brahmans, and preached very nobly, indeed, and sublimely, but always in their favour; he was pure and chaste in reality, but exhibited an appearance of excessive libertinism, and had wives or mistresses too numerous to be counted; lastly, he was benevolent and tender, yet fomented and conducted a terrible war. This motley story must induce an opinion that the spurious Gospels, which abounded in the first age of Christianity, had been brought to India, and the wildest part of them repeated to the Hindus, who ingrafted them on the old fable of Cesava, the Apollo of Greece.

As to the general extension of our pure faith in Hindustan, there are at present many sad obstacles to it. The Muselmans are already a sort of heterodox Christians: they are Christians, if Locke reasons justly,[a] because they firmly believe the immaculate conception, divine character, and miracles of the Messiah; but they are heterodox, in denying vehemently his character of Son, and his equality, as God, with the Father, of whose unity and attributes they entertain and express the most awful ideas; while they consider our doctrine as perfect blasphemy, and insist, that our copies of the Scriptures have been corrupted both by Jews and Christians. It will be inexpressibly difficult to undeceive them, and scarce possible to diminish their veneration for Mohammed and Ali, who were both very extraordinary men, and the second,

---

[a] In *The Reasonableness of Christianity as delivered in the Scriptures* Locke argued that belief in Christ as the Messiah and in his resurrection were alone required for salvation. He himself rejected the accusation that this was 'no other than what Turks believe' (*A Second Vindication of the Reasonableness of Christianity, Works of John Locke*, 12th ed. (1824), VI, 282).

a man of unexceptionable morals: the *Koran* shines, indeed, with a borrowed light, since most of its beauties are taken from our Scriptures; but it has great beauties, and the Muselmans will not be convinced that they were borrowed. The Hindus on the other hand would readily admit the truth of the Gospel; but they contend, that it is perfectly consistent with their *Sastras*: the deity, they say, has appeared innumerable times, in many parts of this world and of all worlds, for the salvation of his creatures; and though we adore him in one appearance, and they in others, yet we adore, they say, the same God, to whom our several worships, though different in form, are equally acceptable, if they be sincere in substance. We may assure ourselves, that neither Muselmans nor Hindus will ever be converted by any mission from the Church of Rome, or from any other church; and the only human mode, perhaps, of causing so great a revolution will be to translate into Sanscrit and Persian such chapters of the Prophets, particularly of Isaiah, as are indisputably Evangelical, together with one of the Gospels, and a plain prefatory discourse containing full evidence of the very distant ages, in which the predictions themselves, and the history of the divine person predicted, were severally made publick; and then quietly to disperse the work among the well-educated natives; with whom if in due time it failed of producing very salutary fruit by its natural influence, we could only lament more than ever the strength of prejudice and the weakness of unassisted reason.

7

William Jones, 'On the Hindus'

In the former discourses, which I had the honour of addressing to you, Gentlemen, on the institution and objects of our Society, I confined myself purposely to general topicks; giving in the first a distant prospect of the vast career, on which we were entering, and, in the second, exhibiting a more diffuse, but still superficial, sketch of the various discoveries in history, science, and art, which we might justly expect from our inquiries into the literature of Asia. I now propose to fill up that outline so comprehensively as to omit nothing essential, yet so concisely as to avoid being tedious; and, if the state of my health shall suffer me to continue long enough in this climate, it is my design, with your permission, to prepare for our annual meetings a series of short dissertations, unconnected in their titles and subjects, but all tending to a common point of no small importance in the pursuit of interesting truths.

Of all the works, which have been published in our own age, or, perhaps, in any other, on the history of the ancient world, and the first population of this habitable globe, that of Mr Jacob Bryant, whom I name with reverence and affection, has the best claim to the praise of deep erudition ingeniously applied, and new theories happily illustrated by an assemblage of numberless converging rays from a most extensive circumference:[a] it falls, nevertheless, as every human work must fall, short of perfection; and the least satisfactory part of it seems to be that, which relates to the derivation of words from Asiatick languages.[b] Etymology has,

[a] *A New System of Ancient Mythology* by Jacob Bryant, see above, p. 239.
[b] Bryant had tried to trace the migration of ancient peoples by apparent similarities in place names. Since he professed himself to be ignorant of all Asian languages except Hebrew and therefore relied on modern transcriptions, this part of his work was very vulnerable to criticism. It was 'whispered' at Oxford that Jones had already helped one of Bryant's fiercest critics, the Persian scholar John Richardson (1741–1811?), in his polemics against the *New System* (T. Maurice, *Memoirs of the Author of Indian Antiquities* (1819–22), II, 41).

no doubt, some use in historical researches; but it is a medium of proof so very fallacious, that, where it elucidates one fact, it obscures a thousand, and more frequently borders on the ridiculous, than leads to any solid conclusion: it rarely carries with it any internal power of conviction from a resemblance of sounds or similarity of letters; yet often, where it is wholly unassisted by those advantages, it may be indisputably proved by extrinsick evidence. We know *a posteriori*, that both *fitz* and *hijo*, by the nature of two several dialects, are derived from *filius*;[a] that *uncle* comes from *avus*, and *stranger* from *extra*; that *jour* is deducible, through the Italian, from *dies*; and *rossignol* from *luscinia*,[b] or the singer in groves; that *sciuro*, *écureuil*, and *squirrel* are compounded of two Greek words descriptive of the animal; which etymologies, though they could not have been demonstrated *a priori*, might serve to confirm, if any such confirmation were necessary, the proofs of a connection between the members of one great empire; but, when we derive our *hanger*, or short pendent sword, from the Persian, because ignorant travellers thus mis-spell the word *khanjar*, which in truth means a different weapon, or sandal-wood from the Greek, because we suppose, that sandals were sometimes made of it, we gain no ground in proving the affinity of nations, and only weaken arguments, which might otherwise be firmly supported. That Cus then, or, as it certainly is written in one ancient dialect, Cut, and in others, probably, Cas, enters into the composition of many proper names, we may very reasonably believe;[c] and that Algeziras takes its name from the Arabick word for an island, cannot be doubted; but, when we are told from Europe, that places and provinces in India were clearly denominated from those words, we cannot but observe, in the first instance, that the town, in which we now are assembled, is properly written and pronounced *Calicata*; that both *Cata* and *Cut* unquestionably mean places of strength, or, in general, any inclosures; and that Gujarat is at least as remote from Jezirah in sound, as it is in situation.[d]

---

[a] Norman French, Spanish and Latin words for a son.

[b] French and Latin names for a nightingale.

[c] Bryant believed that all places with names of this kind had once been inhabited by the descendants of Cush the son of Ham. He appears even to have thought that this was the origin of the name Calcutta (*New System*, iii, 199).

[d] Bryant deduced the name Gujarat 'from its situation, Giezerette, or the island' (*New System*, iii, 194).

Another exception (and a third could hardly be discovered by any candid criticism) to the *Analysis of Ancient Mythology*, is, that the method of reasoning and arrangement of topicks adopted in that learned work are not quite agreeable to the title, but almost wholly synthetical; and, though synthesis may be the better mode in pure science, where the principles are undeniable, yet it seems less calculated to give complete satisfaction in historical disquisitions, where every postulatum will perhaps be refused, and every definition controverted: this may seem a slight objection, but the subject is in itself so interesting, and the full conviction of all reasonable men so desirable, that it may not be lost labour to discuss the same or a similar theory in a method purely analytical, and, after beginning with facts of general notoriety or undisputed evidence, to investigate such truths, as are at first unknown or very imperfectly discerned.

The five principal nations, who have in different ages divided among themselves, as a kind of inheritance, the vast continent of Asia, with the many islands depending on it, are the Indians, the Chinese, the Tartars, the Arabs, and the Persians: who they severally were, whence, and when they came, where they now are settled, and what advantage a more perfect knowledge of them all may bring to our European world, will be shown, I trust, in five distinct essays; the last of which will demonstrate the connexion or diversity between them, and solve the great problem, whether they had any common origin, and whether that origin was the same, which we generally ascribe to them.

I begin with India, not because I find reason to believe it the true centre of population or of knowledge, but, because it is the country, which we now inhabit, and from which we may best survey the regions around us; as, in popular language, we speak of the rising sun, and of his progress through the Zodiack, although it had long ago been imagined, and is now demonstrated, that he is himself the centre of our planetary system. Let me here premise, that, in all these inquiries concerning the history of India, I shall confine my researches downwards to the Mohammedan conquests at the beginning of the eleventh century, but extend them upwards, as high as possible, to the earliest authentick records of the human species.

India then, on its most enlarged scale, in which the ancients appear to have understood it, comprises an area of near forty degrees on each side, including a space almost as large as all Europe; being divided on the west from Persia by the Arachosian[a] mountains, limited on the east by the Chinese part of the farther peninsula, confined on the north by the wilds of Tartary, and extending to the south as far as the isles of Java. This trapezium, therefore, comprehends the stupendous hills of Potyid, or Tibet,[b] the beautiful valley of Cashmir, and all the domains of the old Indoscythians, the countries of Nepal and Butant, Camrup[c] or Asam, together with Siam, Ava,[d] Racan,[e] and the bordering kingdoms, as far as the China of the Hindus or *Sin* of the Arabian geographers; not to mention the whole western peninsula with the celebrated island of Sinhala, or Lion-like men, at its southern extremity.[f] By India, in short, I mean that whole extent of country, in which the primitive religion and languages of the Hindus prevail at this day with more or less of their ancient purity, and in which the *Nagari* letters are still used with more or less deviation from their original form.

The Hindus themselves believe their own country, to which they give the vain epithets of *Medhyama* or Central, and *Punyab-humi*, or the Land of Virtues, to have been the portion of Bharat, one of nine brothers, whose father had the dominion of the whole earth; and they represent the mountains of Himalaya as lying to the north, and, to the west, those of Vindhya, called also Vindian by the Greeks; beyond which the Sindhu[g] runs in several branches to the sea, and meets it nearly opposite to the point of Dwaraca, the celebrated seat of their Shepherd God:[h] in the south-east they place the great river Saravatya; by which they probably mean that of Ava, called also Airavati[i] in part of its course, and giving perhaps its ancient name to the gulf of Sabara.[j] This domain of

---

[a] In southern Afghanistan.

[b] According to Augustino Antonio Giorgi (1711–97), who achieved the remarkable feat of compiling a guide to the Tibetan language without understanding a word of it, the Tibetans called their country 'Potjid' (*Alphabetum Tibetanum, Missionum Apostolicarum commodo editum* (Rome, 1762), pp. 14–15).

[c] Kamarupa.   [d] Burma.   [e] Arakan.

[f] Ceylon.   [g] The Indus.   [h] Dvaraka, the town of Krishna.

[i] Presumably the Irrawaddy.

[j] Ptolemy refers to the Gulf of Martaban as 'sinus Sabaracus'.

Bharat they consider as the middle of the *Jambudwipa*, which the Tibetians also call the Land of *Zambu*; and the appellation is extremely remarkable; for *Jambu* is the Sanscrit name of a delicate fruit called *Jaman* by the Muselmans, and by us rose-apple;[a] but the largest and richest sort is named *Amrita*, or Immortal; and the mythologists of Tibet apply the same word to a celestial tree bearing ambrosial fruit, and adjoining to four vast rocks, from which as many sacred rivers derive their several streams.[b]

The inhabitants of this extensive tract are described by Mr. Lord with great exactness, and with a picturesque elegance peculiar to our ancient language: 'A people', says he, 'presented themselves to mine eyes, clothed in linen garments somewhat low descending, of a gesture and garb, as I may say, maidenly and well nigh effeminate, of a countenance shy and somewhat estranged, yet smiling out a glozed and bashful familiarity.'[c] Mr. Orme, the historian of India, who unites an exquisite taste for every fine art with an accurate knowledge of Asiatick manners, observes, in his elegant preliminary Dissertation, that this 'country has been inhabited from the earliest antiquity by a people, who have no resemblance, either in their figure or manners, with any of the nations contiguous to them,' and that, 'although conquerors have established themselves at different times in different parts of India, yet the original inhabitants have lost very little of their original character.'[d] The ancients, in fact, give a description of them, which our early travellers confirmed, and our own personal knowledge of them nearly verifies; as you will perceive from a passage in the Geographical Poem of Dionysius,[e] which the analyst of ancient mythology has translated with great spirit:

> To th' east a lovely country wide extends,
> India, whose borders the wide ocean bounds;
> On this the sun, new rising from the main,

[a] Cf. Halhed's version, see above, p. 150.

[b] Giorgi, *Alphabetum Tibetanum*, p. 186.

[c] Jones is quoting from the first section, 'The Sect of the Banians', of *A Display of Two Forraigne Sects in the East Indies* (1630), by Henry Lord, English chaplain at Surat.

[d] *A History of the Military Transactions of the British Nation in Indostan* (1763–78), I, 2, by Robert Orme (1728–1801).

[e] See above, p. 241.

Smiles pleas'd, and sheds his early orient beam.
Th' inhabitants are swart, and in their locks
Betray the tints of the dark hyacinth.
Various their functions; some the rock explore,
And from the mine extract the latent gold;
Some labour at the woof with cunning skill,
And manufacture linen; others shape
And polish iv'ry with the nicest care:
Many retire to river's shoal, and plunge
To seek the beryl flaming in its bed,
Or glitt'ring diamond. Oft the jasper's found
Green, but diaphanous; the topaz too
Of ray serene and pleasing; last of all
The lovely amethyst, in which combine
All the mild shades of purple. The rich soil,
Wash'd by a thousand rivers, from all sides
Pours on the natives wealth without control.[a]

Their sources of wealth are still abundant even after so many revolutions and conquests; in their manufactures of cotton they still surpass all the world; and their features have, most probably, remained unaltered since the time of Dionysius; nor can we reasonably doubt, how degenerate and abased so ever the Hindus may now appear, that in some early age they were splendid in arts and arms, happy in government, wise in legislation, and eminent in various knowledge: but, since their civil history beyond the middle of the nineteenth century from the present time, is involved in a cloud of fables, we seem to possess only four general media of satisfying our curiosity concerning it; namely, first, their languages and letters; secondly, their philosophy and religion; thirdly, the actual remains of their old sculpture and architecture; and fourthly, the written memorials of their sciences and arts.

I. It is much to be lamented, that neither the Greeks, who attended Alexander into India, nor those who were long connected with it under the Bactrian princes, have left us any means of knowing with accuracy, what vernacular languages they found on their arrival in this Empire. The Mohammedans, we know, heard the people of proper Hindustan, or India on a limited scale, speaking a *Bhasha,* or living tongue, of a very singular

[a] *New System,* III, 227-8.

construction, the purest dialect of which was current in the districts round|Agra, and chiefly on the poetical ground of Mathura; and this is commonly called the idiom of *Vraja.*[a] Five words in six, perhaps, of this language were derived from the Sanscrit, in which books of religion and science were composed, and which appears to have been formed by an exquisite grammatical arrangement, as the name itself implies, from some unpolished idiom; but the basis of the Hindustani, particularly the inflexions and regimen of verbs, differed as widely from both those tongues, as Arabick differs from Persian, or German from Greek. Now the general effect of conquest is to leave the current language of the conquered people unchanged, or very little altered, in its ground-work, but to blend with it a considerable number of exotick names both for things and for actions; as it has happened in every country, that I can recollect, where the conquerors have not preserved their own tongue unmixed with that of the natives, like the Turks in Greece, and the Saxons in Britain; and this analogy might induce us to believe, that the pure Hindi, whether of Tartarian or Chaldean origin, was primeval in Upper India, into which the Sanscrit was introduced by conquerors from other kingdoms in some very remote age; for we cannot doubt that the language of the *Vedas* was used in the great extent of country, which has before been delineated, as long as the religion of Brahma has prevailed in it.

The Sanscrit language, whatever be its antiquity, is of a wonderful structure; more perfect than the Greek, more copious than the Latin, and more exquisitely refined than either, yet bearing to both of them a stronger affinity, both in the roots of verbs and in the forms of grammar, than could possibly have been produced by accident; so strong indeed, that no philologer could examine them all three, without believing them to have sprung from some common source, which, perhaps, no longer exists: there is a similar reason, though not quite so forcible, for supposing that both the Gothick and the Celtick,[b] though blended with a very

[a] One of the earliest forms of Hindi was the dialect spoken around Mathura (Muttra) and known as *Braj-Bhasha*. The Braj country, the area round Mathura, was the scene of Krishna's boyhood. Jones's Muslim source has not been identified.

[b] Eighteenth-century philologists believed that the modern German, English, Dutch and Scandinavian languages were derived from a single 'Gothic' parent language, while languages such as Welsh, Irish or Cornish were derived from a

different idiom, had the same origin with the Sanscrit; and the old Persian might be added to the same family, if this were the place for discussing any question concerning the antiquities of Persia.[a]

The characters, in which the languages of India were originally written, are called *Nagari*, from *Nagara*, a city, with the word *Deva* sometimes prefixed, because they are believed to have been taught by the Divinity himself, who prescribed the artificial order of them in a voice from heaven. These letters, with no greater variation in their form by the change of straight lines to curves, or conversely, than the Cufick[b] alphabet has received in its way to India, are still adopted in more than twenty kingdoms and states, from the borders of Cashgar and Khoten, to Rama's bridge, and from the Sindhu to the river of Siam; nor can I help believing, although the polished and elegant *Devanagari* may not be so ancient as the monumental characters in the caverns of Jarasandha,[c] that the square, Chaldaick letters[d] in which most Hebrew books are copied, were originally the same, or derived from the same prototype, both with the Indian and Arabian characters: that the Phenician, from which the Greek and Roman alphabets were formed by various changes and inversions, had a similar origin, there can be little doubt; and the inscriptions at Canarah, of which you now possess a most accurate copy, seem to be compounded of *Nagari* and Ethiopick[e] letters, which bear a close relation to each other, both in the mode of writing from the left hand, and in the singular manner of connecting the vowels with

'Celtic' parent. What were thought to be the earliest examples of both were printed in Thomas Percy's translator's preface to *Northern Antiquities: or a Description of the Manners, Customs, Religion and Laws of the Ancient Danes* (1770), pp. xx–xxvii.

[a] In his essay 'On the Persians' delivered in 1789 Jones was to argue that strong similarities existed between 'Parsi' and (on the evidence of a 'zend glossary' in Duperron's *Zend-Avesta*) Avestan and Sanskrit (*Jones Works*, I, 79–87).

[b] Kufik, or angular script, was thought in the eighteenth century to be the origin of all Arabic scripts.

[c] Jarasandha was a king of Magadha mentioned in the *Mahabharata*. Jones is probably referring to inscriptions in the caves at Rajagriha, the ancient capital of Magadha (M. M. H. Kuraishi, *Ancient Monuments...in the Province of Bihar and Orissa* (*Archaeological Survey of India*, new series, LI) (Calcutta, 1931), pp. 120–9).

[d] The development of 'square' Hebrew characters was thought in the eighteenth century to have been a consequence of the Jewish captivity in Babylon.

[e] Presumably Coptic.

the consonants.[a] These remarks may favour an opinion entertained by many, that all the symbols of sound, which at first, probably, were only rude outlines of the different organs of speech, had a common origin; the symbols of ideas, now used in China and Japan, and formerly, perhaps, in Egypt and Mexico, are quite of a distinct nature; but it is very remarkable, that the order of sounds in the Chinese grammars corresponds nearly with that observed in Tibet, and hardly differs from that, which the Hindus consider as the invention of their Gods.

II. Of the Indian religion and philosophy, I shall here say but little; because a full account of each would require a separate volume: it will be sufficient in this dissertation to assume, what might be proved beyond controversy, that we now live among the adorers of those very deities, who were worshipped under different names in old Greece and Italy, and among the professors of those philosophical tenets, which the Ionick and Attick writers illustrated with all the beauties of their melodious language. On one hand we see the trident of Neptune, the eagle of Jupiter, the satyrs of Bacchus, the bow of Cupid, and the chariot of the Sun; on another we hear the cymbals of Rhea, the songs of the Muses, and the pastoral tales of Apollo Nomius. In more retired scenes, in groves, and in seminaries of learning, we may perceive the Brahmans and the Sarmanes, mentioned by Clemens,[b] disputing in the forms of logick, or discoursing on the vanity of human enjoyments, on the immortality of the soul, her emanation from the eternal mind, her debasement, wanderings, and final union with her source. The six philosophical schools, whose principles are explained in the *Dersana Sastra*, comprise all the metaphysicks of the old Academy, the Stoa, the Lyceum; nor is it possible to read the *Vedanta*, or the many fine compositions in illustration of it, without believing, that Pythagoras and Plato derived their sublime theories from the same fountain with the sages of India. The

---

[a] The cave temples at Kanheri, on the island of Salsette near Bombay, had been frequently described by Europeans. Copies of inscriptions from Kanheri had recently been reproduced in R. Gough, *A Comparative View of the Antient Monuments of India, particularly those in the island of Salset* (1785), and in *Archaeologia: or Miscellaneous Tracts relating to Antiquity*, vii (1785).

[b] Clemens Alexandrinus, who wrote early in the third century A.D., mentioned both Brahmins and 'Sarmans' in his *Stromata* (McCrindle, *Ancient India in Classical Literature*, pp. 183–4).

Jones on the Hindus

Scythian and Hyperborean doctrines and mythology may also be traced in every part of these eastern regions; nor can we doubt, that Wod or Oden, whose religion, as the northern historians admit, was introduced into Scandinavia by a foreign race,[a] was the same with Buddh, whose rites were probably imported into India nearly at the same time, though received much later by the Chinese, who soften his name into Fo.[b]

This may be a proper place to ascertain an important point in the chronology of the Hindus; for the priests of Buddha left in Tibet and China the precise epoch of his appearance, real or imagined, in this empire; and their information, which had been preserved in writing, was compared by the Christian missionaries and scholars with our own era. Couplet,[c] De Guignes,[d] Giorgi,[e] and Bailly,[f] differ a little in their accounts of this epoch, but that of Couplet seems the most correct: on taking, however, the medium of the four several dates, we may fix the time of Buddha, or the ninth great incarnation of Vishnu, in the year one thousand and fourteen before the birth of Christ, or two thousand seven hundred and ninety-nine years ago. Now the Cashmirians, who boast of his descent in their kingdom, assert that he appeared on earth about two centuries after Crishna the Indian Apollo, who took so decided a part in the war of the *Mahabharat*; and, if an etymologist were to suppose, that the Athenians had embellished their poetical history of Pandion's expulsion and the restoration of Ægeus[g] with the Asiatick tale of the Pandus and Yudhishtir,[h] neither of which words they could have articulated, I should not hastily deride his conjecture: certain it is, that Pandumandel is called by the Greeks the country of Pandion.[i] We have, therefore, determined another interesting epoch, by fixing the age of

---

[a] The name Odin was attached both to a historical figure and to a god. Both were thought to have come to Scandinavia 'from some country of Scythia, or from the borders of Persia' (*Northern Antiquities*, p. 69).

[b] Jones was later to abandon this identification (see below, p. 273).

[c] See below, p. 273.   [d] See below, p. 273.

[e] See above, p. 249.   [f] See below, p. 264.

[g] Pandion was a legendary king of Athens who was expelled from his kingdom but was succeeded by his son Ægeus.

[h] In the *Mahabharata* king Pandu who dies in exile is later succeeded by his son Yudhishthira.

[i] For Greek references to a south Indian ruler called Pandion, see McCrindle, *Ancient India in Classical Literature*, pp. 9, 112.

Crishna near the three thousandth year from the present time; and, as the three first *Avatars*, or descents of Vishnu, relate no less clearly to an universal deluge, in which eight persons only were saved,[a] than the fourth and fifth do to the punishment of impiety and the humiliation of the proud,[b] we may for the present assume, that the second, or silver, age of the Hindus was subsequent to the dispersion from Babel; so that we have only a dark interval of about a thousand years, which were employed in the settlement of nations, the foundation of states or empires, and the cultivation of civil society. The great incarnate Gods of this intermediate age are both named Rama but with different epithets; one of whom bears a wonderful resemblance to the Indian Bacchus, and his wars are the subject of several heroick poems.[c] He is represented as a descendent from Surya, or the sun, as the husband of Sita, and the son of a princess named Causelya: it is very remarkable, that the Peruvians, whose Incas boasted of the same descent, styled their greatest festival Ramasitoa;[d] whence we may suppose, that South America was peopled by the same race, who imported into the farthest parts of Asia the rites and fabulous history of Rama. These rites and this history are extremely curious; and, although I cannot believe with Newton, that ancient mythology was nothing but historical truth in a poetical dress,[e] nor, with Bacon, that it consisted solely of moral and metaphysical allegories,[f] nor with Bryant, that all the heathen divinities are only different attributes and representations of the sun or of deceased progenitors, but conceive that the whole system of religious fables rose, like the Nile, from several distinct sources, yet I cannot but agree, that one great spring and fountain of all idolatry in the four quarters of the globe was the veneration paid by men to the vast body of fire, which 'looks from his sole dominion like the God of this world'; and another, the immoderate respect shown to the memory of powerful or virtuous ancestors, especially the founders of kingdoms, legislators, and

[a] The 'fish', the 'tortoise' and the 'boar' incarnations (see below, p. 269).
[b] The 'man-lion' and the 'dwarf' incarnations (see below, p. 269).
[c] For Jones's identification of Rama and Bacchus, see above, p. 230.
[d] This appears to be a conflation of two separate Inca festivals, *Raymi* and *Situa*. Jones appears to be perpetrating the sort of etymological wishful thinking which he so severely castigates in Bryant.
[e] See above, p. 199.   [f] See above, p. 199.

warriors, of whom the sun or the moon were wildly supposed to be the parents.

III. The remains of architecture and sculpture in India, which I mention here as mere monuments of antiquity, not as specimens of ancient art, seem to prove an early connection between this country and Africa: the pyramids of Egypt, the colossal statues described by Pausanias[a] and others, the sphinx, and the Hermes *Canis*[b], which last bears a great resemblance to the *Varahavatar*, or the incarnation of Vishnu in the form of a Boar, indicate the style and mythology of the same indefatigable workmen, who formed the vast excavations of Canarah,[c] the various temples and images of Buddha, and the idols, which are continually dug up at Gaya, or in its vicinity. The letters on many of those monuments appear, as I have before intimated, partly of Indian, and partly of Abyssinian or Ethiopick, origin; and all these indubitable facts may induce no ill-grounded opinion, that Ethiopia and Hindustan were peopled or colonized by the same extraordinary race; in confirmation of which, it may be added, that the mountaineers of Bengal and Bahar can hardly be distinguished in some of their features, particularly their lips and noses, from the modern Abyssinians, whom the Arabs call the children of Cush: and the ancient Hindus, according to Strabo, differed in nothing from the Africans, but in the straitness and smoothness of their hair, while that of the others was crisp or woolly;[d] a difference proceeding chiefly, if not entirely, from the respective humidity or dryness of their atmospheres; hence the people who received the first light of the rising sun, according to the limited knowledge of the ancients, are said by Apuleius to be the *Aru* and Ethiopians,[e] by which he clearly meant certain nations of India; where we frequently see figures of Buddha with curled hair apparently designed for a representation of it in its natural state.

IV. It is unfortunate, that the *Silpi Sastra*,[f] or collection of

[a] Pausanias's 'Description of Greece' (see above, p. 220), book II, chap. XLI.

[b] Greek interpretations of the Egyptian god Hermanubis assumed a connexion with Hermes. The god was often represented with a jackal's head (J. Hastings ed., *The Encyclopaedia of Religion and Ethics* (Edinburgh, 1908–26), VI, 380).

[c] Kanheri, see above, p. 254.

[d] McCrindle, *Ancient India in Classical Literature*, pp. 29–30.

[e] *Florida*, VI of Lucius Apuleius, see above, p. 198.

[f] A term applied to any technical treatise.

treatises on arts and manufactures, which must have contained a treasure of useful information on dying, painting, and metallurgy, has been so long neglected, that few, if any, traces of it are to be found; but the labours of the Indian loom and needle have been universally celebrated; and fine linen is not improbably supposed to have been called Sindon, from the name of the river near which it was wrought in the highest perfection:[a] the people of Colchis[b] were also famed for this manufacture, and the Egyptians yet more, as we learn from several passages in scripture, and particularly from a beautiful chapter in Ezekiel containing the most authentick delineation of ancient commerce, of which Tyre had been the principal mart.[c] Silk was fabricated immemorially by the Indians, though commonly ascribed to the people of Serica or Tancut,[d] among whom probably the word *Ser*, which the Greeks applied to the silk-worm, signified gold; a sense, which it now bears in Tibet. That the Hindus were in early ages a commercial people, we have many reasons to believe; and in the first of their sacred law-tracts, which they suppose to have been revealed by Menu many millions of years ago, we find a curious passage on the legal interest of money, and the limited rate of it in different cases, with an exception in regard to adventures at sea;[e] an exception, which the sense of mankind approves, and which commerce absolutely requires, though it was not before the reign of Charles I that our own jurisprudence fully admitted it in respect of maritime contracts.

We are told by the Grecian writers, that the Indians were the wisest of nations; and in moral wisdom, they were certainly eminent: their *Niti Sastra*, or System of Ethicks, is yet preserved, and the fables of Vishnuserman, whom we ridiculously call *Pilpay*, are the most beautiful, if not the most ancient, collection of apologues in the world: they were first translated from the Sanscrit, in the sixth century, by the order of Buzerchumihr, or

[a] The Indus.　　　　　　　　　　[b] An area in what is now western Georgia.

[c] Ezek. xxvii.

[d] Serica was a name used by ancient geographers for an area north of India and west of China (McCrindle, *Ancient India as described by Ptolemy*, pp. 297–305). 'Tangut' was defined as 'a kingdom of Chinese Tartary, in Asia, having China on the east and Ava on the south' (*A Compendious Geographical Dictionary*, 2nd ed., (1795)).

[e] *Laws of Manu*, viii, 157; *Jones Works*, iii, 297.

Bright as the Sun, the chief physician and afterwards Vezir of the great Anushirevan, and are extant under various names in more than twenty languages; but their original title is *Hitopadesa*, or Amicable Instruction;[a] and, as the very existence of Esop, whom the Arabs believe to have been an Abyssinian, appears rather doubtful, I am not disinclined to suppose, that the first moral fables, which appeared in Europe, were of Indian or Ethiopian origin.

The Hindus are said to have boasted of three inventions, all of which, indeed, are admirable, the method of instructing by apologues, the decimal scale adopted now by all civilized nations, and the game of chess, on which they have some curious treatises;[b] but, if their numerous works on grammar, logick, rhetorick, musick, all which are extant and accessible, were explained in some language generally known, it would be found, that they had yet higher pretentions to the praise of a fertile and inventive genius. Their lighter poems are lively and elegant; their epick, magnificent and sublime in the highest degree; their *Puranas* comprise a series of mythological histories in blank verse from the Creation to the supposed incarnation of Buddha; and their *Vedas*, as far as we can judge from that compendium of them, which is called *Upanishat*,[c] abound with noble speculations in metaphysicks, and fine discourses on the being and attributes of God. Their most ancient medical book, entitled *Chereca*,[d] is believed to be the work of Siva; for each of the divinities in their Triad has at least one sacred composition ascribed to him; but, as to mere human works on history and geography, though they are said to be extant in Cashmir, it has not been yet in my power

[a] The *Hitopadesha* narrated by Vishnusharma contained material from an earlier collection, the *Panchatantra*, which had reached Europe through Persian and Arabic translations and was known in English as 'The Fables of Pilpay' (apparently a corruption of 'Vidyapati', the name of one of its characters). Jones made a translation from the *Hitopadesha* which was to be published after his death (*Jones Works*, VI, 1–176). Buzurgmihr was the legendary minister of the sixth-century Persian king Anusharwan.

[b] Jones later published an essay 'On the Indian game of chess' (*Jones Works*, I, 521–7).

[c] Jones's knowledge of the *Upanishads* seems to have been confined to Daru Sukoh's Persian translation (see above, p. 148).

[d] A treatise named after the semi-legendary Charaka, probably a court physician of the second century A.D.

to procure them. What their astronomical and mathematical writings contain, will not, I trust, remain long a secret: they are easily procured, and their importance cannot be doubted. The philosopher, whose works are said to include a system of the universe founded on the principle of attraction and the central position of the sun, is named Yavan Acharya, because he had travelled, we are told, into Ionia: if this be true, he might have been one of those, who conversed with Pythagoras; this at least is undeniable, that a book on astronomy in Sanscrit bears the title of *Yavana Jatica*, which may signify the Ionick Sect;[a] nor is it improbable, that the names of the planets and Zodiacal stars, which the Arabs borrowed from the Greeks, but which we find in the oldest Indian records, were originally devised by the same ingenious and enterprizing race, from whom both Greece and India were peopled;[b] the race, who, as Dionysius describes them,

> first assayed the deep,
> And wafted merchandize to coasts unknown,
> Those, who digested first the starry choir,
> Their motions mark'd, and call'd them by their names.[c]

Of these cursory observations on the Hindus, which it would require volumes to expand and illustrate, this is the result: that they had an immemorial affinity with the old Persians, Ethiopians, and Egyptians, the Phenicians, Greeks, and Tuscans, the Scythians or Goths, and Celts, the Chinese, Japanese, and Peruvians; whence, as no reason appears for believing, that they were a colony from any one of those nations, or any of those nations from them, we may fairly conclude that they all proceeded from some central country, to investigate which will be the object of

[a] It seems to be generally accepted that Indian astronomy owed much to the Greeks. *Yavanacharya* means 'Greek teacher' and the treatise *Yavan-Jataka* was probably of Greek origin.

[b] It had long been known in Europe that Indian astronomers used signs of the zodiac similar to those of the Greeks. But the publication in 1772 of a sketch of the signs on a south Indian *chaultri* (*Philosophical Transactions of the Royal Society*, LXVII (1772), pp. 352 ff.) set off controversy as to which was the oldest. In a 'Discourse on the Antiquity of the Indian Zodiac' Jones elaborated on his view that the Indian version could not have been borrowed from the Greeks (as is now believed to have been the case), but that both Indians and Greeks must have 'received it from an older nation' (*Jones Works*, I, 334).

[c] Cf. Bryant, *A New System*, III, 230.

my future Discourses; and I have a sanguine hope, that your collections during the present year will bring to light many useful discoveries; although the departure for Europe of a very ingenious member,[a] who first opened the inestimable mine of Sanscrit literature, will often deprive us of accurate and solid information concerning the languages and antiquities of India.

[a] Charles Wilkins.

8

William Jones, 'On the Chronology of the Hindus'

The great antiquity of the Hindus is believed so firmly by themselves, and has been the subject of so much conversation among Europeans, that a short view of their chronological system, which has not yet been exhibited from certain authorities, may be acceptable to those, who seek truth without partiality to received opinions, and without regarding any consequences, that may result from their inquiries: the consequences, indeed, of truth cannot but be desirable, and no reasonable man will apprehend any danger to society from a general diffusion of its light; but we must not suffer ourselves to be dazzled by a false glare, nor mistake enigmas and allegories for historical verity. Attached to no system, and as much disposed to reject the Mosaick history, if it be proved erroneous, as to believe it, if it be confirmed by sound reasoning from indubitable evidence, I propose to lay before you a concise account of Indian chronology extracted from Sanscrit books, or collected from conversations with Pandits, and to subjoin a few remarks on their system, without attempting to decide a question, which I shall venture to start, 'whether it is not in fact the same with our own, but embellished and obscured by the fancy of their poets and the riddles of their astronomers.'

One of the most curious books in Sanscrit, and one of the oldest after the *Vedas*, is a tract on religious and civil duties, taken, as it is believed, from the oral instructions of Menu, son of Brahma, to the first inhabitants of the earth: a well-collated copy of this interesting law-tract is now before me; and I begin my dissertation with a few couplets from the first chapter of it:

The sun causes the division of day and night, which are of two sorts, those of men and those of the Gods; the day, for the labour of all creatures in their several employments; the night, for their slumber. A month is a day and night of the Patriarchs; and it is divided into two parts; the bright half is their day for laborious exertions; the dark half, their night for sleep. A year is a day and night of the Gods; and that is also divided into two halves; the day is, when the sun moves toward the north; the night, when it moves toward the south. Learn now the duration of a night and day of Brahma, with that of the ages respectively and in order. Four thousand years of the Gods they call the *Crita*, (or *Satya*) age; and its limits at the beginning and at the end are, in like manner, as many hundreds. In the three successive ages, together with their limits at the beginning and end of them, are thousands and hundreds diminished by one. This aggregate of four ages, amounting to twelve thousand divine years, is called an age of the Gods; and a thousand such divine ages added together must be considered as a day of Brahma: his night has also the same duration. The before mentioned age of the Gods, or twelve thousand of their years, multiplied by seventy-one, form what is named here below a *Manwantara*. There are alternate creations and destructions of worlds through innumerable *Manwantaras*: the Being Supremely Desirable performs all this again and again.[a]

Such is the arrangement of infinite time, which the Hindus believe to have been revealed from heaven, and which they generally understand in a literal sense: it seems to have intrinsick marks of being purely astronomical; but I will not appropriate the observations of others, not anticipate those in particular which have been made by two or three of our members, and which they will, I hope, communicate to the Society.[b] A conjecture, however, of Mr. Paterson[c] has so much ingenuity in it, that I cannot forbear mentioning it here, especially as it seems to be confirmed by one of the couplets just-cited: he supposes, that, as a month of mortals is a day and night of the Patriarchs from the analogy of its bright and dark halves, so, by the same analogy, a day and night of mortals might have been considered by the ancient Hindus as a month of the lower world; and then a year of such months will consist only of twelve days and nights, and thirty such years will compose a lunar year of mortals; whence he surmises, that the four million three hundred and twenty thousand years, of which the four Indian ages are supposed to

[a] *Laws of Manu*, 1, 65–72; *Jones Works*, 111, 74–6.
[b] A long paper on the 'Astronomical Computations of the Hindus' by Samuel Davis (1760–1819) was also included in vol. 11 of *Asiatick Researches*.
[c] John David Paterson (d. 1809) of the Company's civil service. His paper does not appear to have been published.

consist, mean only years of twelve days; and, in fact, that sum, divided by thirty, is reduced to an hundred and forty-four thousand: now a thousand four hundred and forty years are one *pada*, a period in the Hindu astronomy, and that sum, multiplied by eighteen, amounts precisely to twenty-five thousand nine hundred and twenty, the number of years in which the fixed stars appear to perform their long revolution eastward. The last mentioned sum is the product also of an hundred and forty-four, which, according to M. Bailly, was an old Indian cycle, into an hundred and eighty, or the Tartarian period, called *Van*,[a] and of two thousand eight hundred and eighty into nine, which is not only one of the lunar cycles, but considered by the Hindus as a mysterious number and an emblem of divinity, because, if it be multiplied by any other whole number, the sum of the figures in the different products remains always nine, as the deity, who appears in many forms, continues one immutable essence. The important period of twenty-five thousand nine hundred and twenty years is well known to arise from the multiplication of three hundred and sixty into seventy-two; the number of years in which a fixed star seems to move through a degree of a great circle; and, although M. Le Gentil assures us, that the modern Hindus believe a complete revolution of the stars to be made in twenty-four thousand years, or fifty-four seconds of a degree to be passed in one year,[b] yet we may have reason to think, that the old Indian astronomers had made a more accurate calculation, but concealed their knowledge from the people under the veil of fourteen *Menwantaras*, seventy-one divine ages, compound cycles, and years of different sorts, from those of Brahma to those of *Patala*, or the infernal regions.

If we follow the analogy suggested by Menu, and suppose only a day and night to be called a year, we may divide the number of years in a divine age by three hundred and sixty, and the quotient will be twelve thousand, or the number of his divine years in one age: but, conjecture apart, we need only compare the two periods 4,320,000 and 25,920, and we shall find, that among their com-

[a] *Histoire de l'Astronomie ancienne* (Paris, 1775), pp. 76–7, 342, by Jean-Sylvain Bailly (1736–93).

[b] 'Suite du premier mémoire sur l'Inde', *Mémoires de l'Académie royale des sciences* (1772), pt. II, p. 191, by Guillaume-Joseph-Hyacinthe Le Gentil de La Galaisière (1725–92).

mon divisors, arc 6, 9, 12 &c. 18, 36, 72, 144, &c. which numbers with their several multiples, especially in a decuple progression, constitute some of the most celebrated periods of the Chaldeans, Greeks, Tartars, and even of the Indians. We cannot fail to observe, that the number 432, which appears to be the basis of the Indian system, is a 60th part of 25,920, and, by continuing the comparison, we might probably solve the whole enigma. In the preface to a Varanes Almanack I find the following wild stanza: 'A thousand Great Ages are a day of Brahma; a thousand such days are an Indian hour of Vishnu; six hundred thousand such hours make a period of Rudra; and a million of Rudras (or two quadrillions five hundred and ninety-two thousand trillions of lunar years), are but a second to the Supreme Being.' The Hindu theologians deny the conclusion of the stanza to be orthodox: 'Time', they say, 'exists not at all with God'; and they advise the astronomers to mind their own business without meddling with theology. The astronomical verse, however, will answer our present purpose; for it shows, in the first place, that cyphers are added at pleasure to swell the periods; and, if we take ten cyphers from a Rudra, or divide by ten thousand millions, we shall have a period of 259,200,000 years, which, divided by 60 (the usual divisor of time among the Hindus) will give 4,320,000, or a Great Age, which we find subdivided in the proportion of 4, 3, 2, 1, from the notion of virtue decreasing arithmetically in the golden, silver, copper, and earthen, ages. But, should it be thought improbable, that the Indian astronomers in very early times had made more accurate observations than those of Alexandria, Bagdad, or Maraghah,[a] and still more improbable that they should have relapsed without apparent cause into error, we may suppose, that they formed their divine age by an arbitrary multiplication of 24,000 by 180 according to M. Le Gentil,[b] or of 21,600 by 200, according to the comment on the *Surya Siddhanta*.[c] Now, as it is hardly possible, that such coincidences should be

[a] A Persian town, site of the observatory of Nasir-ud-din.
[b] See above, p. 264.
[c] A treatise on astronomy containing material dating back to A.D. 400. Its existence had been known to Europeans for some time, but no adequate translation was made before that completed by Samuel Davis at Calcutta in 1791 (*Transactions of the Royal Asiatic Society of Great Britain and Ireland*, III (1835), p. 19).

accidental, we may hold it nearly demonstrated, that the period of a divine age was at first merely astronomical, and may consequently reject it from our present inquiry into the historical or civil chronology of India. Let us, however, proceed to the avowed opinions of the Hindus, and see, when we have ascertained their system, whether we can reconcile it to the course of nature and the common sense of mankind.

The aggregate of their four ages they call a divine age, and believe that, in every thousand such ages, or in every day of Brahma, fourteen Menus are successively invested by him with the sovereignty of the earth: each Menu, they suppose, transmits his empire to his sons and grandsons during a period of seventy-one divine ages; and such a period they name a *Manwantara*; but, since fourteen multiplied by seventy-one are not quite a thousand, we must conclude, that six divine ages are allowed for intervals between the *Manwantaras*, or for the twilight of Brahma's day. Thirty such days, or *Calpas*, constitute, in their opinion, a month of Brahma; twelve such months, one of his years; and an hundred such years, his age; of which age they assert, that fifty years have elapsed. We are now then, according to the Hindus, in the first day or *Calpa* of the first month of the fifty-first year of Brahma's age, and in the twenty-eighth divine age of the seventh *Manwantara*, of which divine age the three first human ages have passed, and four thousand eight hundred and eighty-eight of the fourth.

In the present day of Brahma the first Menu was surnamed Swayambhuva, or Son of the Self-existent; and it is he, by whom the *Institutes of Religious and Civil Duties* are supposed to have been delivered: in his time the Deity descended at a sacrifice, and, by his wife Satarupa, he had two distinguished sons, and three daughters. This pair was created, for the multiplication of the human species, after that new creation of the world, which the Brahmans call *Padmacalpiya*, or the Lotos-creation.

If it were worth while to calculate the age of Menu's Institutes, according to the Brahmans, we must multiply four million three hundred and twenty thousand by six times seventy-one, and add to the product the number of years already past in the seventh *Manwantara*. Of the five Menus, who succeeded him, I have seen little more than the names; but the Hindu writings are very diffuse on the life and posterity of the seventh Menu, surnamed Vaivaswata, or Child of the Sun: he is supposed to have had ten sons, of whom the eldest was Icshwacu; and to have been accompanied by seven *Rishis*, or holy persons, whose names were, Casyapa, Atri, Vasishtha, Viswamitra, Gautama, Jamadagni, and Bharadwaja; an account, which explains the opening of the fourth chapter of the *Gita*: 'This immutable system of devotion', says Crishna, 'I revealed to Vivaswat, or the Sun; Vivaswat declared it to his son Menu; Menu explained it to Icshwacu: thus the chief *Rishis* know this sublime doctrine delivered from one to another.'[a]

In the reign of this sun-born monarch the Hindus believe the whole earth to have been drowned, and the whole human race destroyed by a flood, except the pious prince himself, the seven *Rishis*, and their several wives; for they suppose his children to have been born after the deluge. This general *pralaya*, or destruction, is the subject of the first *Purana*,[b] or sacred poem, which consists of fourteen thousand stanzas; and the story is concisely, but clearly and elegantly, told in the eighth book of the *Bhagawata*,[c] from which I have extracted the whole, and translated it with great care, but will only present you here with an abridgement of it.

The demon Hayagriva having purloined the *Vedas* from the custody of Brahma, while he was reposing at the close of the sixth *Manwantara*, the whole race of men became corrupt, except the seven *Rishis*, and Satyavrata, who then reigned in Dravira, a maritime region to the south of Carnata: this prince was performing his ablutions in the river Critamala, when Vishnu appeared to him in the shape of a small fish, and, after several augmentations of bulk in different waters, was placed by Satyavrata in the ocean, where he thus addressed his amazed votary: 'In seven days all creatures, who have offended me, shall be destroyed by a deluge, but thou shalt be secured in a capacious vessel miraculously formed: take therefore all kinds of medicinal herbs and esculent grain for food, and, together with the seven holy men, your respective wives, and pairs of all animals, enter the ark without fear; then shalt thou know God face to face, and all thy questions shall be answered.'

Saying this, he disappeared; and, after seven days, the ocean began

[a] *Bhagavad Gita*, IV, 1–2.
[b] Jones called the *Matsya Purana*, the first of the *Shiva Puranas*, the first *Purana* (see above, p. 205).   [c] The *Bhagavat Purana*.

to overflow the coasts, and the earth to be flooded by constant showers, when Satyavrata, meditating on the Deity, saw a large vessel moving on the waters: he entered it, having in all respects conformed to the instructions of Vishnu; who, in the form of a vast fish, suffered the vessel to be tied with a great sea-serpent, as with a cable, to his measureless horn. When the deluge had ceased, Vishnu slew the demon, and recovered the *Vedas*, instructed Satyavrata in divine knowledge, and appointed him the seventh Menu by the name of Vaivaswata.

Let us compare the two Indian accounts of the Creation and the Deluge with those delivered by Moses. It is not made a question in this tract, whether the first chapters of *Genesis* are to be understood in a literal, or merely in an allegorical, sense: the only points before us are, whether the creation described by the first Menu, which the Brahmans call that of the Lotus, be not the same with that recorded in our Scripture, and whether the story of the seventh Menu be not one and the same with that of Noah. I propose the questions, but affirm nothing; leaving others to settle their opinions, whether Adam be derived from *adim*, which in Sanscrit means the first, or Menu from Nuh, the true name of the Patriarch; whether the sacrifice, at which God is believed to have descended, alludes to the offering of Abel;[a] and, on the whole, whether the two Menus can mean any other persons than the great progenitor, and the restorer, of our species.

On a supposition, that Vaivaswata, or Sun-born, was the Noah of Scripture, let us proceed to the Indian account of his posterity, which I extract from the *Puranarthaprecasa*, or *The Puranas Explained*, a work lately composed in Sanscrit by Radhacanta Sarman, a Pandit of extensive learning and great fame among the Hindus of this province.[b] Before we examine the genealogies of kings, which he has collected from the *Puranas*, it will be necessary to give a general idea of the *Avataras*, or descents, of the deity: the Hindus believe innumerable such descents or special interpositions of providence in the affairs of mankind, but they reckon ten principal *Avataras* in the current period of four ages;

---

[a] Gen. iv, 4.

[b] This work was written in 1784 for Warren Hastings. A Sanskrit copy, a Persian translation and an English translation made by Halhed are in the British Museum (MS Or. 1124, Add. MSS 5655, 5657, ff. 163–94). Radhakanta was recommended to Jones by John Shore in 1787 (S. N. Mukherjee, *Sir William Jones* (Cambridge, 1968), p. 102).

and all of them are described, in order as they are supposed to occur, in the following ode of Jayadeva, the great lyrick poet of India.[a]

1. Thou recoverest the *Veda* in the water of the ocean of destruction, placing it joyfully in the bosom of an ark fabricated by thee; O Cesava, assuming the body of a fish: be victorious, O Heri, lord of the Universe!

2. The earth stands firm on thy immensely broad back, which grows larger from the callus occasioned by bearing that vast burden, O Cesava, assuming the body of a tortoise: be victorious, O Heri, lord of the Universe!

3. The earth, placed on the point of thy tusk, remains fixed like the figure of a black antelope on the moon, O Cesava, assuming the form of a boar: be victorious, O Heri, lord of the Universe!

4. The claw with a stupendous point, on the exquisite lotos of thy lion's paw, is the black bee, that stung the body of the embowelled Hiranyacasipu, O Cesava, assuming the form of a man-lion: be victorious, O Heri, lord of the Universe!

5. By thy power thou beguilest Bali, O thou miraculous dwarf, thou purifier of men with the water (of Ganga) springing from thy feet, O Cesava, assuming the form of a dwarf: be victorious, O Heri, lord of the Universe!

6. Thou bathest in pure water, consisting of the blood of *Cshatriyas*, the world, whose offences are removed and who are relieved from the pain of other births, O Cesava, assuming the form of Parasu-Rama: be victorious, O Heri, lord of the Universe!

7. With ease to thyself, with delight to the Genii of the eight regions, thou scatterest on all sides in the plain of combat the demon with ten heads, O Cesava, assuming the form of Rama-Chandra: be victorious, O Heri, lord of the Universe!

8. Thou wearest on thy bright body a mantle shining like a blue cloud, or like the water of Yamuna tripping toward thee through fear of thy furrowing plough share, O Cesava, assuming the form of Bala-Rama: be victorious, O Heri, lord of the Universe!

9. Thou blamest, (oh, wonderful!) the whole *Veda*, when thou seest, O kind-hearted, the slaughter of cattle prescribed for sacrifice, O Cesava, assuming the body of Buddha: be victorious, O Heri, lord of the Universe!

10. For the destruction of all the impure thou drawest thy cimeter like a blazing comet, (how tremendous!) O Cesava, assuming the body of Calci: be victorious, O Heri, lord of the Universe!

These ten *Avataras* are by some arranged according to the thousands of divine years in each of the four ages, or in an arithmetical proportion from four to one; and, if such an arrangement were universally received, we should be able to ascertain a very

[a] The following hymn to Vishnu is part of the *Gita Govinda* of Jayadeva, see above, p. 209.

material point in the Hindu chronology; I mean the birth of Buddha, concerning which the different Pandits, whom I have consulted, and the same Pandits at different times, have expressed a strange diversity of opinion. They all agree, that Calci is yet to come, and that Buddha was the last considerable incarnation of the deity; but the astronomers at Varanes place him in the third age, and Radhacant insists, that he appeared after the thousandth year of the fourth: the learned and accurate author of the *Dabistan*, whose information concerning the Hindus is wonderfully correct, mentions an opinion of the Pandits, with whom he had conversed, that Buddha began his career ten years before the close of the third age;[a] and Goverdhana of Cashmir, who had once informed me, that Crishna descended two centuries before Buddha, assured me lately, that the Cashmirians admitted an interval of twenty-four years (others allow only twelve) between those two divine persons. The best authority, after all, is the *Bhagawat* itself, in the first chapter of which it is expressly declared, that 'Buddha, the son of Jina, would appear at Cicata, for the purpose of confounding the demons, just at the beginning of the *Caliyug*.' I have long been convinced, that, on these subjects, we can only reason satisfactorily from written evidence, and that our forensick rule must be invariably applied, to take the declarations of the Brahmans most strongly against themselves, that is, against their pretensions to antiquity; so that, on the whole, we may safely place Buddha just at the beginning of the present age: but what is the beginning of it? When this question was proposed to Radhacant, he answered: 'Of a period comprising more than four hundred thousand years, the first two or three thousand may reasonably be called the beginning.' On my demanding written evidence, he produced a book of some authority, composed by a learned *Goswami*, and entitled *Bhagawatamrita*, or, the *Nectar* of the *Bhagawat*,[b] on which it is a metrical comment; and the couplet,

[a] The *Dabistan al-Madhahib*, or 'school of religions', is an account of Indian religions written in Persian in the seventeenth century. There is no clear evidence as to who was its author. For the statement referred to by Jones, see *The Dabistan or School for Manners*, trans. D. Shea, A. Troyer (Paris, 1843), II, 24.

[b] Presumably either the *Brihad Bhagavatamrita* or the *Samksepa Bhagavatamrita*, which were written in the sixteenth century by the brothers Sanatana Goswami and Rupa Goswami (S. K. De, *Early History of the Vaisnava Faith and Movement in Bengal* (Calcutta, 1942), pp. 177–92).

which he read from it deserves to be cited: after the just mentioned account of Buddha in the text, the commentator says, 'He became visible, the-thousand-and-second-year-of-the-Cali-age being past; his body of-a-colour-between-white-and-ruddy, with-two-arms, without-hair on his head.'

Cicata, named in the text as the birth place of Buddha, the *Goswami* supposes to have been Dhermaranya, a wood near Gaya, where a colossal image of that ancient deity still remains:[a] it seemed to me of black stone; but, as I saw it by torch-light, I cannot be positive as to its colour, which may, indeed, have been changed by time.

The Brahmans universally speak of the Bauddhas with all the malignity of an intolerant spirit; yet the most orthodox among them consider Buddha himself as an incarnation of Vishnu: this is a contradiction hard to be reconciled; unless we cut the knot, instead of untying it, by supposing with Giorgi, that there were two Buddhas, the younger of whom established the new religion, which gave so great offence in India, and was introduced into China in the first century of our era.[b] The Cashmirian before mentioned asserted this fact, without being led to it by any question that implied it; and we may have reason to suppose, that Buddha is in truth only a general word for a philosopher: the author of a celebrated Sanscrit dictionary, entitled from his name *Amaracosha*, who was himself a Bauddha,[c] and flourished in the first century before Christ, begins his vocabulary with nine words, that signify heaven, and proceeds to those, which mean a deity in general; after which come different classes of gods, demigods, and demons, all by generick names; and they are followed by two very remarkable heads; first, (not the general names of Buddha, but) the names of a Buddha-in-general, of which he gives us eighteen, such as *Muni, Sastri, Munindra, Vinayaca, Samantabhadra, Dhermaraja, Sugata*, and the like; most of them significative of excellence, wisdom, virtue, and sanctity; secondly, the names of a particular-Buddha-*Muni*-who-descended

[a] This may possibly be the great image which is now in the main Hindu temple at Buddh Gaya.

[b] *Alphabetum Tibetanum*, p. 235.

[c] The author of the *Amarakosha* (see above, p. 203) is thought to have been a Buddhist, but the work was probably composed in the seventh century A.D.

-in-the-family-of-Sacya[a] (those are the very words of the original), and his titles are, *Sacyamuni, Sacyasinha, Servarthasiddha, Saudhodani, Gautama, Arcabandhu,* or kinsman of the sun, and *Mayadevisuta,* or child of Maya: thence the author passes to the different epithets of particular Hindu deities. When I pointed out this curious passage to Radhacant, he contended, that the first eighteen names were general epithets, and the following seven, proper names, or patronymicks, of one and the same person; but Ramalochan, my own teacher, who, though not a Brahman, is an excellent scholar and a very sensible unprejudiced man, assured me, that Buddha was a generick word, like *Deva,* and that the learned author, having exhibited the names of a *Devata* in general, proceeded to those of a Buddha in general, before he came to particulars: he added, that Buddha might mean a sage or a philosopher, though Budha was the word commonly used for a mere wise man without supernatural powers. It seems highly probable, on the whole, that the Buddha, whom Jayadeva celebrates in his Hymn,[b] was the *Sacyasinha,* or Lion of Sacya, who, though he forbad the sacrifices of cattle, which the *Vedas* enjoin, was believed to be Vishnu himself in a human form, and that another Buddha, one perhaps of his followers in a later age, assuming his name and character, attempted to overset the whole system of the Brahmans, and was the cause of that persecution, from which the Bauddhas are known to have fled into very distant regions. May we not reconcile the singular difference of opinion among the Hindus as to the time of Buddha's appearance, by supposing that they have confounded the two Buddhas, the first of whom was born a few years before the close of the last age, and the second, when above a thousand years of the present age had elapsed?[c] We know, from better authorities, and with as much certainty as can justly be expected on so doubtful a subject, the real time, compared with our own era, when the ancient Buddha began to distinguish himself; and it is for this reason principally, that I have dwelled with minute anxiety on the subject of the last *Avatar.*

---

[a] The clan of the Buddha's father.   [b] See above, p. 269.
[c] These speculations were without foundation. The historical Buddha appears to have been adopted as an incarnation of Vishnu, and so the two are one and the same.

Jones on Chronology

The Brahmans, who assisted Abu'lfazl in his curious, but superficial, account of his master's empire, informed him, if the figures in the *Ayini Acbari* be correctly written, that a period of 2962 years had elapsed from the birth of Buddha to the 40th year of Acbar's reign,[a] which computation will place his birth in the 1366th year before that of our Saviour; but, when the Chinese government admitted a new religion from India in the first century of our era, they made particular inquiries concerning the age of the old Indian Buddha, whose birth, according to Couplet, they place in the 41st year of their 28th cycle, or 1036 years before Christ, and they call him, says he, Foe the son of Moye or Maya;[b] but M. de Guignes, on the authority of four Chinese historians, asserts, that Fo was born about the year before Christ 1027, in the kingdom of Cashmir:[c] Giorgi, or rather Cassiano, from whose papers his work was compiled, assures us, that, by the calculation of the Tibetians, he appeared only 959 years before the Christian epoch;[d] and M. Bailly, with some hesitation, places him 1031 years before it, but inclines to think him far more ancient, confounding him, as I have done in a former tract,[e] with the first Budha, or Mercury, whom the Goths called Woden,[f] and of whom I shall presently take particular notice. Now, whether we assume the medium of the four last-mentioned dates, or implicitly rely on the authorities quoted by De Guignes, we may conclude, that Buddha was first distinguished in this country about a thousand years before the beginning of our era; and whoever, in so early an age, expects a certain epoch unqualified with about or nearly, will be greatly disappointed. Hence it is clear, that, whether the fourth age of the Hindus began about one thousand years before Christ, according to Goverdhan's account of Buddha's birth, or

[a] *The Ayeen Akbery; or Institutes of the Emperor Akber*, trans. F. Gladwin, 2nd ed. (1800), II, 459. For Abu 'l Fazl, see above, p. 109.

[a] *Tabula Chronologica Monarchiae Sinicae* (Paris, 1686), p. 10, by the Belgian Jesuit Philippe Couplet (1628–92).

[c] 'Recherches historiques sur la religion Indienne', *Mémoires de l'Académie royale des Inscriptions et Belles Lettres*, XL (1773–6), 195, 201, by Joseph de Guignes (1721–1800).

[d] In his *Alphabetum Tibetanum* (see above, p. 249) Giorgi had used the journal of a visit to Tibet in 1740–2 by the Italian Capuchin, Cassiano Beligatti (1708–85), published as *Relazione inedita di un viaggio al Tibet*, ed. A. Magnaghi (Florence, 1902).

[e] See above, p. 255.   [f] *Histoire de l'Astronomie ancienne*, p. 334.

two thousand, according to that of Radhacant, the common opinion, that 4888 years of it are now elapsed, is erroneous; and here for the present we leave Buddha, with an intention of returning to him in due time; observing only, that, if the learned Indians differ so widely in their accounts of the age, when their ninth *Avatar* appeared in their country, we may be assured, that they have no certain chronology before him, and may suspect the certainty of all the relations concerning even his appearance.

The received chronology of the Hindus begins with an absurdity so monstrous, as to overthrow the whole system; for, having established their period of seventy-one divine ages as the reign of each Menu, yet thinking it incongruous to place a holy personage in times of impurity, they insist, that the Menu reigns only in every golden age, and disappears in the three human ages that follow it, continuing to dive and emerge, like a waterfowl, till the close of his *Manwantara*: the learned author of the *Puranarthapracasa*, which I will now follow step by step, mentioned this ridiculous opinion with a serious face; but, as he has not inserted it in his work, we may take his account of the seventh Menu according to its obvious and rational meaning, and suppose, that Vaivaswata, the son of Surya, the son of Casyapa, or Uranus, the son of Marichi, or Light: the son of Brahma, which is clearly an allegorical pedigree, reigned in the last golden age, or, according to the Hindus, three million eight hundred and ninety-two thousand eight hundred and eighty-eight years ago. But they contend, that he actually reigned on earth one million seven hundred and twenty-eight thousand years of mortals, or four thousand eight hundred years of the gods; and this opinion is another monster so repugnant to the course of nature and to human reason, that it must be rejected as wholly fabulous, and taken as a proof, that the Indians know nothing of their sun-born Menu, but his name and the principal event of his life; I mean the universal deluge, of which the three first *Avatars* are merely allegorical representations, with a mixture, especially in the second, of astronomical mythology.

From this Menu the whole race of men is believed to have descended; for the seven *Rishis*, who were preserved with him in the ark, are not mentioned as fathers of human families; but,

since his daughter Ila was married, as the Indians tell us, to the
first Budha, or Mercury, the son of Chandra, or the Moon, a male
deity, whose father was Atri, son of Brahma, (where again we
meet with an allegory purely astronomical or poetical) his posterity are divided into two great branches, called the Children of
the Sun from his own supposed father, and the Children of the
Moon, from the parent of his daughter's husband: the lineal male
descendants in both these families are supposed to have reigned
in the cities of Ayodhya, or Audh, and Pratishthana, or Vitora,*a*
respectively till the thousandth year of the present age, and the
names of all the princes in both lines having been diligently collected by Radhacant from several *Puranas*, I exhibit them in two
columns arranged by myself with great attention.*b*

Second Age

CHILDREN OF THE SUN AND MOON

	SUN	MOON	
	Icshwacu,	Budha,	
	Vicucshi,	*Pururavas,*	
	Cucutstha,	Ayush,	
	Anenas,	Nahusha,	
5	*Prithu,*	*Yayati,*	5
	Viswagandhi,	*Puru,*	
	Chandra,	Janamejaya,	
	Yuvanaswa,	Prachinwat,	
	Srava,	Pravira,	
10	Vrihadaswa,	Menasyu,	10
	Dhundhumara,	Charupada,	
	Dridhaswa,	Sudyu,	
	Heryaswa,	Bahugava,	
	Nicumbha,	Sanyati,	

a Near the modern Allahabad.

b The lists of names which occupy the major part of the rest of the essay are a
full version of the traditional histories preserved in the *Puranas*. Elucidation and
criticism of the lists will be found in the notes to H. H. Wilson's edition of *The
Vishnu Purana* (reprinted Calcutta, 1961); F. E. Pargiter, *The Puranic Texts of the
Dynasties of the Kali Age* (Oxford, 1913) and *Ancient Indian Historical Tradition*
(1922); and R. C. Majumdar ed., *The Vedic Age* (1951), and *The Age of Imperial
Unity* (Bombay, 1951).

CHILDREN OF THE SUN AND MOON

	SUN	MOON	
15	Crisaswa,	Ahanyati,	15
	Senajit,	Raudraswa,	
	Yuvanaswa,	Riteyush,	
	Mandhatri,	Rantinava,	
	Purucutsa,	Sumati,	
20	Trasadasyu,	Aiti,	20
	Anaranya,	*Dushmanta,*	
	Heryaswa,	*Bharata,**	
	Praruna,	(Vitatha,	
	Trivindhana,	Manyu,	
25	Satyavrata,	Vrihatcshetra,	25
	Trisancu,	Hastin,	
	Harischandra,	Ajamidha,	
	Rohita,	Ricsha,	
	Harita,	Samwarana,	
30	Champa,	*Curu,*	30
	Sudeva,	*Jahnu,*	
	Vijaya,	Suratha,	
	Bharuca,	Viduratha,	
	Vrica,	Sarvabhauma,	
35	Bahuca,	Jayatsena,	35
	Sagara,	Radhica,	
	Asamanjas,	Ayutayush,	
	Ansumat,	Acrodhana,	
	Bhagiratha,	Devatithi,	
40	Sruta,	Ricsha,	40
	Nabha,	*Dilipa,*	
	Sindhudwipa,	Pratipa,	
	Ayutayush,	Santanu,	
	Ritaperna,	*Vichitravirya,*	
45	Saudasa,	Pandu,	45
	Asmaca,	*Yudhishthir.*)	
	Mulaca,		
	Dasaratha,		
	Aidabidi,		
50	Viswasaha,		
	Chatwanga,		
	Dirghabahu,		
	Raghu,		
	Aja,		
55	*Dasaratha,*		
	Rama.		

It is agreed among all the *Pandits*, that Rama, their seventh incarnate divinity, appeared as king of Ayodhya in the interval between the silver and the brazen ages; and, if we suppose him to have begun his reign at the very beginning of that interval, still three thousand three hundred years of the gods, or a million one hundred and eighty-eight thousand lunar years of mortals will remain in the silver age, during which the fifty-five princes between Vaivaswata and Rama must have governed the world; but, reckoning thirty years for a generation, which is rather too much for a long succession of eldest sons, as they are said to have been, we cannot, by the course of nature, extend the second age of the Hindus beyond sixteen hundred and fifty solar years: if we suppose them not to have been eldest sons, and even to have lived longer than modern princes in a dissolute age, we shall find only a period of two thousand years; and, if we remove the difficulty by admitting miracles, we must cease to reason, and may as well believe at once whatever the Brahmans chuse to tell us.

In the Lunar pedigree we meet with another absurdity equally fatal to the credit of the Hindu system: as far as the twenty-second degree of descent from Vaivaswata, the synchronism of the two families appears tolerably regular, except that the Children of the Moon were not all eldest sons; for king Yayati appointed the youngest of his five sons to succeed him in India, and allotted inferior kingdoms to the other four, who had offended him; part of the Dacshin or the South, to Yadu, the ancestor of Crishna; the north, to Anu; the east, to Druhya; and the west, to Turvasu, from whom the Pandits believe, or pretend to believe, in compliment to our nation, that we are descended. But of the subsequent degrees in the lunar line they know so little, that, unable to supply a considerable interval between Bharat and Vitatha, whom they call his son and successor, they are under a necessity of asserting, that the great ancestor of Yudhishthir actually reigned seven and twenty thousand years; a fable of the same class with that of his wonderful birth, which is the subject of a beautiful Indian drama: now, if we suppose his life to have lasted no longer than that of other mortals, and admit Vitatha and the rest to have been his regular successors, we shall fall into another absurdity; for then, if the generations in both lines were nearly equal as they would naturally have been, we shall find Yudhishthir, who reigned confessedly at the close of the brazen age, nine generations older than Rama, before whose birth the silver age is allowed to have ended. After the name of Bharat, therefore, I have set an asterisk to denote a considerable chasm in the Indian history, and have inserted between brackets, as out of their places, his twenty-four successors, who reigned, if at all, in the following age immediately before the war of the *Mahabharat*. The fourth *Avatar*, which is placed in the interval between the first and second ages, and the fifth which soon followed it, appear to be moral fables grounded on historical facts: the fourth was the punishment of an impious monarch by the deity himself bursting from a marble column in the shape of a lion; and the fifth was the humiliation of an arrogant prince by so contemptible an agent as a mendicant dwarf. After these, and immediately before Buddha, come three great warriours all named Rama; but it may justly be made a question, whether they are not three representations of one person, or three different ways of relating the same history: the first and second Ramas are said to have been contemporary; but whether all or any of them mean Rama, the son of Cush,[a] I leave others to determine. The mother of the second Rama was named Caushalya, which is a derivative of Cushala, and, though his father be distinguished by the title or epithet of Dasaratha signifying, that his war-chariot bore him to all quarters of the world, yet the name of Cush, as the Cashmirians pronounce it, is preserved entire in that of his son and successor, and shadowed in that of his ancestor Vicucshi; nor can a just objection be made to this opinion from the nasal Arabian vowel in the word Ramah mentioned by Moses, since the very word Arab begins with the same letter, which the Greeks and Indians could not pronounce; and they were obliged, therefore, to express it by the vowel, which most resembled it. On this question, however, I assert nothing; nor on another, which might be proposed: 'whether the fourth and fifth *Avatars* be not allegorical stories of the two presumptuous monarchs, Nimrod and Belus.' The hypothesis, that government was first established, laws enacted, and agriculture

[a] Gen. x, 7.

encouraged in India by Rama about three thousand eight hundred years ago, agrees with the received account of Noah's death, and the previous settlement of his immediate descendents.

Third Age

CHILDREN OF THE SUN AND MOON

	SUN	MOON	
	Cusha,		
	Atithi,		
	Nishadha,		
	Nabhas,		
5	Pundarica,		
	Cshemadhanwas,	Vitatha,	
	Devanica,	Manyu,	
	Ahinagu,	Vrihatcshetra,	
	Paripatra,	Hastin,	
10	Ranachhala,	Ajamidha,	5
	Vajranabha,	Ricsha,	
	Arca,	Samwarana,	
	Sugana,	*Curu,*	
	Vidhriti,	*Jahnu,*	
15	Hiranyanabha,	Suratha,	10
	Pushya,	Viduratha,	
	Dhruvasandhi,	Sarvabhauma,	
	Sudersana,	Jayatsena,	
	Agniverna,	Radhica,	
20	Sighra,	Ayutayush,	15
	Maru, supposed	Acrodhana,	
	to be still alive.		
	Prasusruta,	Devatithi,	
	Sandhi,	Richsa,	
	Amersana,	Dilipa,	
25	Mahaswat,	Pratipa,	20
	Viswabhahu,	Santanu,	
	Prasenajit,	Vichitravirya,	
	Tacshaca,	Pandu,	
	Vrihadbala,	*Yudhishthira,*	
30	Vrihadrana,	*Paricshit.*	
	Y.B.C. 3100.		

Here we have only nine and twenty princes of the solar line between Rama and Vrihadrana exclusively; and their reigns, during
the whole brazen age, are supposed to have lasted near eight hundred and sixty-four thousand years, a supposition evidently
against nature; the uniform course of which allows only a period
of eight hundred and seventy, or, at the very utmost, of a thous-
and, years for twenty-nine generations. Paricshit, the great
nephew and successor of Yudhishthir, who had recovered the
throne from Duryodhan, is allowed without controversy to have
reigned in the interval between the brazen and earthern ages, and
to have died at the setting in of the *Caliyug*; so that, if the *Pandits*
of Cashmir and Varanes have made a right calculation of Buddha's
appearance, the present, or fourth, age must have begun about a
thousand years before the birth of Christ, and consequently the
reign of Icshwacu, could not have been earlier than four thousand
years before that great epoch; and even that date will, perhaps,
appear, when it shall be strictly examined, to be near two thousand years earlier than the truth. I cannot leave the third Indian
age, in which the virtues and vices of mankind are said to have
been equal, without observing, that even the close of it is manifestly fabulous and poetical, with hardly more appearance of
historical truth, than the tale of Troy or of the Argonauts; for
Yudhishthir, it seems, was the son of Dherma, the Genius of
Justice; Bhima of Pavan, or the God of Wind; Arjun of Indra, or
the Firmament; Nacul and Sahedeva, of the two Cumars, the
Castor and Pollux of India; and Bhishma their reputed great
uncle, was the child of Ganga, or the Ganges, by Santanu, whose
brother Devapi is supposed to be still alive in the city of Calapa;
all which fictions may be charming embellishments of an heroick
poem, but are just as absurd in civil history, as the descent of two
royal families from the Sun and the Moon.

Fourth Age

CHILDREN OF THE SUN AND MOON

	SUN	MOON	
	Urucriya,	*Janamejaya,*	
	Vatsavriddha,	*Satanica,*	
	Prativyoma,	Sahasranica,	
	Bhanu,	Aswamedhaja,	
5	Devaca,	Asimacrishna,	5
	Sahadeva,	Nemichacra,	
	Vira,	Upta,	
	Vrihadaswa,	Chiratatha,	
	Bhanumat,	Suchiratha,	
10	Praticaswa,	Dhritimat,	10
	Supratica,	Sushena,	
	Marudeva,	Sunitha,	
	Sunacshatra,	Nrichacshuh,	
	Pushcara,	Suchinala,	
15	Antaricsha,	Pariplava,	15
	Sutapas,	Sunaya,	
	Amitrajit,	Medhavin,	
	Vrihadraja,	Nripanjaya,	
	Barhi,	Derva,	
20	Critanjaya,	Timi,	20
	Rananjaya,	Vrihadratha,	
	Sanjaya,	Sudasa,	
	Slocya,	Satanica,	
	Suddhoda,	Durmadana,	
25	Langalada,	Rahinara,	25
	Prasenajit,	Dandapani,	
	Cshudraca,	Nimi,	
	Sumitra,	Cshemaca.	
	Y.B.C. 2100.		

In both families, we see, thirty generations are reckoned from Yudhishthir and from Vrihadbala his contemporary (who was killed, in the war of Bharat, by Abhimanyu, son of Arjun and father of Paricshit), to the time, when the Solar and Lunar dynasties are believed to have become extinct in the present divine age; and for these generations the Hindus allot a period of one thousand years only, or a hundred years for three generations;

which calculation, though probably too large, is yet moderate enough, compared with their absurd accounts of the preceding ages: but they reckon exactly the same number of years for twenty generations only in the family of Jarasandha, whose son was contemporary with Yudhishthir, and founded a new dynasty of princes in Magadha, or Bahar; and this exact coincidence of the time, in which the three races are supposed to have been extinct, has the appearance of an artificial chronology, formed rather from imagination than from historical evidence; especially as twenty kings, in an age comparatively modern, could not have reigned a thousand years. I, nevertheless, exhibit the list of them as a curiosity; but am far from being convinced, that all of them ever existed: that, if they did exist, they could not have reigned more than seven hundred years, I am fully persuaded by the course of nature and the concurrent opinion of mankind.

KINGS OF MAGADHA

	Sahadeva,	Suchi,	
	Marjari,	Cshema,	
	Srutasravas,	Suvrata,	
	Ayutayush,	Dhermasutra,	
5	Niramitra,	Srama,	15
	Sunacshatra,	Dridhasena,	
	Vrihetsena,	Sumati,	
	Carmajit,	Subala,	
	Srutanjaya,	Sunita,	
10	Vipra,	Satyajit.	20

Puranjaya, son of the twentieth king, was put to death by his minister Sunaca, who placed his own son Pradyota on the throne of his master; and this revolution constitutes an epoch of the highest importance in our present inquiry;[a] first, because it happened according to the *Bhagawatamrita*,[b] two years exactly before Buddha's appearance in the same kingdom; next, because it is believed by the Hindus to have taken place three thousand eight hundred and eighty-eight years ago, or two thousand one

[a] These events are now thought to have happened in Avanti and not in Magadha (Majumdar, *Vedic Age*, pp. 323–4).

[b] See above, p. 270.

hundred years before Christ; and lastly, because a regular chronology, according to the number of years in each dynasty, has been established from the accession of Pradyota to the subversion of the genuine Hindu government; and that chronology I will now lay before you, after observing only, that Radhacant himself says nothing of Buddha in this part of his work, though he particularly mentions the two preceding *Avataras* in their proper places.

KINGS OF MAGADHA

		Y.B.C.
	Pradyota,	2100
	Palaca,	
	Visachayupa,	
	Rajaca,	
	Nandiverdhana,	
	5 reigns = 138 years.	
	Sisunaga,[a]	1962
	Cacaverna,	
	Cshemadherman,	
	Cshetrajnya,	
5	Vidhisara,[b]	
	Ajatasatru,	
	Darbhaca,	
	Ajaya,	
	Nandiverdhana,	
	Mahanandi,	
	10r = 360y.	
	Nanda.	1602

This prince, of whom frequent mention is made in the Sanscrit books, is said to have been murdered, after a reign of a hundred years, by a very learned and ingenious, but passionate and vindictive, Brahman, whose name was Chanacya,[c] and who raised to the throne a man of the Maurya race, named Chandragupta: by the death of Nanda, and his sons, the *Cshatriya* family of Pradyota became extinct.

[a] The order of the Magadha kings is now generally revised to put Sishunaga and Kakavarna later than Ajatashatru.

[b] More commonly known as Bimbisara, generally thought to have been a contemporary of Pradyota of Avanti.

[c] More commonly known as Kautilya, reputed author of the *Arthashastra*.

MAURYA KINGS

		Y.B.C.
	Chandragupta,	1502
	Varisara,	
	Asocaverdhana,	
	Suyasas,	
5	Desaratha,	
	Sangata,	
	Salisuca,	
	Somasarman,	
	Satadhanwas,	
	Vrihadratha,	

$$10r = 137y.$$

On the death of the tenth Maurya king, his place was assumed by his Commander in Chief, Pushpamitra, of the Sunga nation or family.

SUNGA KINGS

		Y.B.C.
	Pushpamitra,	1365
	Agnimitra,	
	Sujyeshtha,	
	Vasumitra,	
5	Abhadraca,	
	Pulinda,	
	Ghosha,	
	Vajramitra,	
	Bhagavata,	
	Devabhuti,	

$$10r = 112y.$$

The last prince was killed by his minister Vasudeva, of the Canna race, who usurped the throne of Magadha.

CANNA KINGS

	Y.B.C.
Vasudeva,	1253
Bhumitra,	
Narayana,	
Susarman,	

$$4r = 345y.$$

284

Jones on Chronology

A *Sudra*, of the Andhra family, having murdered his master Susarman, and seized the government, founded a new dynasty of

ANDHRA KINGS

		Y.B.C.
	Balin,[a]	908
	Crishna,	
	Srisantacarna,	
	Paurnamasa,	
5	Lambodara,	
	Vivilaca,	
	Meghaswata,	
	Vatamana,	
	Talaca,	
10	Sivaswati,	
	Purishabheru,	
	Sunandana,	
	Chacoraca,	
	Bataca,	
15	Gomatin,	
	Purimat,	
	Medasiras,	
	Sirascandha,	
	Yajnyasri,	
20	Vijaya,	
	Chandrabija,	
	$21r = 456y.$	

After the death of Chandrabija, which happened, according to the Hindus, 396 years before Vicramaditya, or 452 B.C.[b], we hear no more of Magadha as an independent kingdom; but Radhacant has exhibited the names of seven dynasties, in which seventy-six princes are said to have reigned one thousand three hundred and ninety-nine years in Avabhriti, a town of the Dacshin, or South, which we commonly call Decan: the names of the seven dynasties, or of the families who established them, are Abhira,[c] Gardabhin,[d]

[a] More commonly known as Simuka.
[b] Jones was clearly aware of the Vikrama era in Hindu dating, beginning in 58 B.C., named after the legendary king Vikramaditya, who, Jones believed, reigned in Avanti and 'gave encouragement to poets, philosophers and mathematicians' (*Sacontala*, p.v.).
[c] The Abhiras were a pastoral tribe, probably from eastern Iran.
[d] A dynasty who reigned in Ujjain (Majumdar, *Age of Imperial Unity*, p. 155).

Canca,[a] Yavana,[b] Turushcara,[c] Bhurunda,[d] Maula,[e] of which the Yavanas are by some, not generally, supposed to have been Ionians, or Greeks, but the Turushcaras and Maulas are universally believed to have been Turcs and Moguls; yet Radhacant adds: 'When the Maula race was extinct, five princes, named Bhunanda, Bangira, Sisunandi, Yasonandi, and Praviraca, reigned an hundred and six years (or till the year 1053) in the city of Cilacila',[f] which, he tells me, he understands to be in the country of the Maharashtras, or Mahratas; and here ends his Indian chronology; for 'after Praviraca', says he, 'this empire was divided among *Mlechhas*, or infidels.' This account of the seven modern dynasties appears very doubtful in itself, and has no relation to our present inquiry; for their dominion seems confined to the Decan, without extending to Magadha; nor have we any reason to believe, that a race of Grecian princes ever established a kingdom in either of those countries: as to the Moguls, their dynasty still subsists, at least nominally; unless that of Chengiz[g] be meant, and his successors could not have reigned in any part of India for the period of three hundred years, which is assigned to the Maulas; nor is it probable, that the word Turc, which an Indian could have easily pronounced and clearly expressed in the *Nagari* letters, should have been corrupted into Turushcara. On the whole we may safely close the most authentick system of Hindu chronology, that I have yet been able to procure, with the death of Chandrabija. Should any farther information be attainable, we shall, perhaps, in due time attain it either from books or inscriptions in the Sanscrit language; but from the materials, with which we are at present supplied, we may establish as indubitable the two following propositions; that the three first ages of the Hindus are chiefly mythological, whether their mythology was founded on the dark enigmas of their astronomers or on the heroick fictions of their poets, and, that the fourth, or historical, age cannot be carried farther back than about two thousand years

[a] Presumably the Shakas, or Scythians.   [b] Bactrian Greeks.
[c] The Kushans, a people of Mongolian origin.
[d] Probably a reference to a tribe of Huns.
[e] Presumably the Malavas of Rajputana.
[f] This seems to be a reference to the Vakataka dynasty, who ruled in Central India from the third to the sixth century A.D.   [g] Changez Khan (c 1155–1227).

before Christ. Even in the history of the present age, the generations of men and the reigns of kings are extended beyond the
course of nature, and beyond the average resulting from the accounts of the Brahmans themselves; for they assign to an hundred
and forty-two modern reigns a period of three thousand one hundred and fifty-three years, or about twenty-two years to a reign
one with another; yet they represent only four Canna princes on
the throne of Magadha for a period of three hundred and forty-
five years; now it is even more improbable, that four successive
kings should have reigned eighty-six years and four months each,
than that Nanda should have been king a hundred years and murdered at last. Neither account can be credited; but, that we may
allow the highest probable antiquity to the Hindu government,
let us grant, that three generations of men were equal on an
average to an hundred years, and that Indian princes have
reigned, one with another, two and twenty: then reckoning thirty
generations from Arjun, the brother of Yudhishthira, to the
extinction of his race, and taking the Chinese account of Buddha's
birth from M. De Guignes, as the most authentick medium
between Abu'lfazl and the Tibetians,[a] we may arrange the
corrected Hindu chronology according to the following table, sup-
plying the word about or nearly (since perfect accuracy cannot be
attained and ought not to be required), before every date.

	Y.B.C.
Abhimanyu, son of	2029
Arjun,	
Pradyota,	1029
Buddha,	1027
Nanda,	699
Balin,	149
Vicramaditya,	56
Devapala, king of	
Gaur.	23[b]

[a] See above, p. 273.

[b] Historians now generally date the events commemorated in the Bharata war at
about 1400 B.C., the reign of Pradyota at about 500 B.C., the death of Buddha at
486 B.C., the Nanda dynasty to 364–324 B.C., the beginning of the Andhra dynasty
at about 30 B.C.; the Vikramaditya era is a fixed point, whatever may be the historical
truth about 'Vikramaditya', and Devapala is thought to have succeeded in Bengal
in about A.D. 810.

British Discovery of Hinduism

If we take the date of Buddha's appearance from Abu'lfazl,[a] we must place Abhimanyu 2368 years before Christ, unless we calculate from the twenty kings of Magadha, and allow seven hundred years, instead of a thousand, between Arjun and Pradyota, which will bring us again very nearly to the date exhibited in the table; and, perhaps, we can hardly approach nearer to the truth. As to Raja Nanda, if he really sat on the throne a whole century, we must bring down the Andhra dynasty to the age of Vicramaditya, who with his feudatories had probably obtained so much power during the reign of those princes, that they had little more than a nominal sovereignty, which ended with Chandrabija in the third or fourth century of the Christian era; having, no doubt, been long reduced to insignificance by the kings of Gaur, descended from Gopala.[b] But, if the author of the *Dabistan* be warranted in fixing the birth of Buddha ten years before the *Caliyug*,[c] we must thus correct the Chronological Table:

	Y.B.C.
Buddha,	1027
Paricshit,	1017
Pradyota,	317
(reckoning 20 or	or 17
30 generations).	
	Y.A.C.
Nanda.	13
	or 313

This correction would bring us to place Vicramaditya before Nanda, to whom, as all the Pandits agree, he was long posterior; and, if this be an historical fact, it seems to confirm the *Bhagawatamrita*, which fixes the beginning of the *Caliyug* about a thousand years before Buddha;[d] besides that Balin would then be brought down at least to the sixth and Chandrabija to the tenth century after Christ, without leaving room for the subsequent dynasties, if they reigned successively.

Thus have we given a sketch of Indian history through the

[a] See above, p. 273.

[b] Gopala I probably founded the Pala dynasty, who ruled Bengal from their capital at Gaur, in approximately A.D. 750. Jones's knowledge of the Palas was presumably based on Wilkins's success in deciphering certain inscriptions of their period (*Asiatick Researches*, I, 123 ff.).

[c] See above, p. 270.

[d] See above, p. 270.

longest period fairly assignable to it, and have traced the foundation of the Indian empire above three thousand eight hundred years from the present time; but, on a subject in itself so obscure, and so much clouded by the fictions of the Brahmans, who, to aggrandize themselves, have designedly raised their antiquity beyond the truth, we must be satisfied with probable conjecture and just reasoning from the best attainable data; nor can we hope for a system of Indian chronology, to which no objection can be made, unless the astronomical books in Sanscrit shall clearly ascertain the places of the colures in some precise years of the historical age, not by loose traditions, like that of a coarse observation by Chiron, who possibly never existed, (for 'he lived', says Newton, 'in the golden age,' which must long have preceded the Argonautick expedition)*a* but by such evidence as our own astronomers and scholars shall allow to be unexceptionable.

a Chiron the Centaur was said to have been the first to delineate the constellations and to have helped the Argonauts to make a sphere by which to navigate. Newton tried to date the Argonauts' expedition by comparing the equinoctual colure on Chiron's constellation with his own observations for 1689 (*The Chronology of Ancient Kingdoms Amended*, pp. 83–95; F. Manuel, *Isaac Newton, Historian* (Cambridge, 1963), pp. 78–88).

A CHRONOLOGICAL TABLE,
according to one of the Hypotheses *intimated in the preceding tract*

CHRISTIAN and MUSELMAN	HINDU	*Years from* 1788 *of our era*
Adam,	Menu I. Age I,	5794
Noah,	Menu II,	4737
Deluge,		4138
Nimrod,	*Hiranyacasipu.* Age II,	4006
Bel,	*Bali,*	3892
Rama,	Rama. Age III,	3817
Noah's death,		3787
	Pradyota	2817
	Buddha. Age IV,	2815
	Nanda,	2487
	Balin,	1937
	Vicramaditya,	1844
	Devapala,	1811
Christ,		1787
	Narayanpala,	1721
	Saca,	1709
Walid,[a]		1080
Mahmud,[b]		786
Chengiz,		548
Taimur,[c]		391
Babur,[d]		276
Nadirshah[e].		49

[a] Presumably Walid I, Caliph of Damascus (d. 715).
[b] Mahmud of Ghazni (d. 1030).
[c] Timur (1336–1404).
[d] The emperor Babur (1483–1530).
[e] Nadir Shah, usurper of the throne of Persia (1687–1747).

Glossary

The glossary is intended to supplement the notes in providing modern transcriptions for attempts made by Holwell, Dow, Halhed, Hastings and Wilkins to reproduce words in Asian languages; Jones's principles of transcription are sufficiently close to those generally in current use to render identification unneoessary. The source of the original version is indicated by the author's initials: JZH for Holwell, AD for Dow, NBH for Halhed, WH for Hastings and CW for Wilkins.

adah (JZH), *adha* — a half
addaristo (AD), *adrishta* — fate, inevitability
adirmo (AD), *adharma* — unrighteousness
adjonidge (AD), *ayonija* — not born of a womb
agnee-astra (NBH), *agneyastra* — weapon of fire
ahankar (AD), *ahamkara* — individuality
aioon (AD), *hayana* — year
akash (AD, NBH), *akasha* — ether
akitta (AD), *akathya* — inexpressible
ankush (AD), *ankusha* — elephant goad
anûshtose (NBH), *anushtubh* — stanza
apparticta (AD),⎫
apporticta (AD),⎬ *aparatva* — nearness
Arjŏŏn (WH, CW), Arjuna — the third of the Pandavas
aryāchhund (NBH), *aryachhanda* — a form of metre
ascund (NBH), *skanda* — stanza, book
ashlogue (AD, NBH), *shloka* — stanza
ashoo (NBH), *ashva* — horse
ashummeed (NBH), *ashvamedha* — horse sacrifice
audĕĕtyĕ (NBH), *aditya* — a celestial being
aughtorrah (JZH), *athara* — eighteen

baiow (AD), *vayu* — wind
Basdeo (AD), Vasudeva — father of Krishna
Bashista (AD), Vasishta — a sage
 also Bisesht
battezaaz (JZH), *bhattacharya* — religious teacher
Beäs (AD),   ⎫
Beäss (NBH), ⎬ Vyasa — legendary arranger of the scriptures
 also Veiâs, Vyās
Beda (AD), *Veda* — the holiest scriptures
 also Bêde, Beid, Vēd, Vêde
Bedang (AD), *Vedanta* — a philosophical school
Bêde (WH), *Veda* — the holiest scriptures
 also Beda, Beid, Vēd, Vêde
beeākĕrun (NBH), *vyakarana* — grammar
Bĕĕshŏŏkermā (NBH), Vishvakarman — the artificer of the gods
Beid (NBH), *Veda* — the holiest scriptures
 also Beda, Bêde, Vēd, Vêde

Glossary

beise (AD), *vaishya* — the third division of castes
   also bice, bise
bhaat (JZH), *bat* — word
bhade (JZH), *vada* — word
Bhadun (NBH), *Bhadon* — a month (August to September)
Bhārăt-vērsh (CW), Bharata-varsha — India
Bhaurut (WH), Bharata — a king in the *Mahabharata*
   also Bhĕrrut, Bhurrut
Bheem (WH), Bhima — the second of the Pandavas
Bhĕrrut (NBH), Bharata — a king in the *Mahabharata*
   also Bhaurut, Bhĕrrut
Bhertekhunt (NBH), Bharatakhanda — India
bhoobun (NBH), *bhuvana* — a world
   also boboon
bhoor (NBH), *bhur* — the earth
   also bu
Bhurrut (WH), Bharata — a king in the *Mahabharata*
   also Bhaurut, Bhĕrrut
bibag (AD), *vibhaga* — division
bice (NBH), *vaishya* — the third division of castes
   also beise, bise
Birga (AD), Bhrigu — a sage
birgalotta (AD), *bija-loka* — vegetation
Birmah (JZH), Brahma — the Creator
   also Brihma, Brimha
bise (AD), *vaishya* — the third division of castes
   also beise, bice
Bisesht (NBH), Vasishta — a sage
   also Bashista
Bishen (AD), Vishnu — the Preserver
   also Bistnoo
bishesh (AD) *vishesha* — particular essence
Bishwaner (NBH), Vaishvanara — a name of Agni, God of Fire
Bistnoo (JZH), Vishnu — the Preserver
   also Bishen
Bittal (AD), *Vitala* — the first infernal region
boboon (JZH), *bhuvana* — a world
   also bhoobun
bōbur (NBH), *bhuvar* — the atmosphere
   also buba
Bŏŏdhĕ (NBH), *Budha* — the planet Mercury
brăhm (CW), *brahman* — the divine essence
   also brehm, brihm
Brĕĕhĕspĕt (NBH), *Brihaspati* — the planet Jupiter
brehm (NBH), } *brahman* — the divine essence
brihm (AD), }
   also brăhm
Brihma (NBH), } Brahma — the Creator
Brimha (AD), }
   also Birmah
bu (AD), *bhur* — the earth
   also bhoor

Glossary

buba (AD), *bhuvar*	the atmosphere
also bōbur	
bud (AD), *buddhi*	wisdom
budsirba (AD), *buddhasarva*	omniscient
bun (AD), *vansa*	race
bur (AD), *vara*	best
burrun sunker (NBH), *varna sankara*	mixed caste
bygon (JZH), *baingan*	egg plant
cābee (NBH), *kavya*	poetry
Cal (AD), Kali	a goddess, also a demon
also Collee, Kalee, Kallee, Kolee	
chakous (AD), *chaksus*	sight
also chowkowna	
chartah (JZH), *chautah*	fourth
chatah (JZH), *chhatha*	sixth
chehteree (NBH), *kshatriya*	the second division of castes
also kittri, koytri, sittri	
Cheyt (NBH), *Chet*	a month (March to April)
chhund (NBH), *chhanda*	poetic metre
chowkowna (AD), *chaksus*	sight
also chakous	
Chunder (JZH, AD), *Chandra*	the moon
Collee (NBH), Kali	a goddess, also a demon
also Cal, Kalee, Kallee, Kolee	
comala (AD), *kamala*	lotus
cutcherry (JZH), *kachahri*	court of justice
debtah (JZH), *devata*	minor deity
also dewta	
debtah nagur (JZH), *devanagari*	North Indian Hindu script
also diewnāgur	
deen (JZH), *din*	day
also dheen, dien	
deep (NBH), *dvipa*	a continent
deo (AD), *danava*	demon
desh (AD), *dvesha*	aversion
dewta (AD, NBH), *devata*	minor deity
also debtah	
dheen (JZH), *din*	day
also deen, dien	
Dico (AD), Daksha	a son of Brahma
dien (AD), *din*	day
also deen, dheen	
diewnāgar (NBH), *devanagari*	North Indian Hindu script
also debtah nagur	
dind (AD), *danda*	a unit of time
dirba (AD), *dravya*	substance
dirbittee (AD), *dravatra*	fluidity
dirm (AD), } *dharma* dirmo (AD), }	justice, law
dirsen (AD), *darshana*	demonstration, proof

Glossary

dooneah (JZH), *dunya* — the world
also dunneah
Dooryōdun (WH), Duryodhana — the leader of the Kauravas
Dreetrarashtra (WH), Dhritarashtra — father of the Kauravas
dua (JZH), *dva* — two
also dwa
duapaar (JZH),
duapur (AD), } *dvapara (yuga)* — the third age
also dupaar, dwapaar
duc (AD), *dukha* — pain
dunneah (JZH), *dunya* — the world
also dooneah
dunneahoudah (JZH), *duyna-i mahawwitah* — the universe
dupaar (JZH), *dvapara (yuga)* — the third age
also duapaar, duapur, dwapaar
dwa (JZH), *dva* — two
also dua
dwapaar (JZH, NBH), *dvapara (yuga)* — the third age
also duapaar, duapur, dupaar
Dwypayen (WH), Dvaipayana — a name of Vyasa

ekhummesha (JZH), *ekamesha* — one lord
ekutter (JZH), *ekhattar* — seventy-one
Endeer (JZH), Indra — God of the Firmament

fouzdar (JZH), *faujdar* — local governor

gent (NBH), *jantu* — living creature
also jount
gheneh (NBH), *-ghna* — to kill
ghoij (JZH), *gao* — cow
goijalbarry (JZH), *goyalabari* — cow-shed
Goneish (NBH), Ganesha — God of Wisdom
also Gunnis
goon (AD), *guna* — quality, attribute
goseyn (JZH), *gosvamin* — *vaishnavite* teacher
granap (AD), *ghrana* — sense of smell
gund (AD), *gandha* — smell
Gunnis (JZH), Ganesha — God of Wisdom
also Goneish
gurree (JZH),
gurry (AD), } *ghari* — hour
gurrittee (AD), *gurutva* — heaviness

Hastenapoor (WH), Hastinapura — capital of the Kauravas
also Histanapore
hazaar (JZH), *hazar* — thousand
Histanapore (AD), Hastinapura — capital of the Kauravas
also Hastenapoor
hy (NBH), *haya* — horse

Indoo (AD), *Indu* — the moon
insoff (JZH), *insaf* — justice

294

Glossary

ish (AD), *isha*	lord
Ishbur (AD), *Ishvara*	God
itcha (AD), *ichachha*	desire
Jage-Bulk (NBH), Yajnavalkya	a sage
Jagga-nat (AD), ⎫ Jagannatha Jaggernaut (JZH), ⎭	a form of Krishna
jate sommon (AD), *jate smarana*	one who is aware of his former life
Jessarit (AD), Dasharatha	father of Rama
Jeyt, (NBH), *Jeth*	a month (May to June)
jhoale (JZH), *jala*	water
also joal	
jin, (NBH), *jinn*	demon
jive attima (AD), *jivatman*	individual soul
joal (AD), *jala*	water
also jhoale	
jogue (JZH), *yuga*	an age
also jug, yogue, yoog	
jonidge (AD), *yonija*	womb-born
jotna (AD), *yatna*	energy, power
jount (AD), *jantu*	living creature
also gent	
Judger Beda (AD), *Yajur Veda*	the second *Veda*
Judishter (AD), Yudhishthira	the eldest Pandava
also Yoodhishteer	
jug (AD), *yuga*	an age
also jogue, yogue, yoog	
jugg (NBH), *yajna*	sacrifice
jumboo (NBH), *jambu*	rose-apple
also jumbook	
Jumboodeep (NBH), *Jambudvipa*	the earth
jumbook (NBH), *jambu*	rose-apple
also jumboo	
Junneh (NBH),⎫ *Janar* Junnoh (AD), ⎭	ₜhe heaven of Brahma's sons
kaal (AD), *kala*	time
kaan (AD), *khan*	a unit of time
Kalee (JZH, CW), Kali	a goddess, also a demon
also Cal, Collee, Kallee, Kolee	
Kalkee (JZH), Kalki	the last incarnation of Vishnu
Kallee (AD), Kali	a goddess, also a demon
also Cal, Collee, Kalee, Kolee	
Kam (AD), Kama	God of Love
Kartic (JZH), Karttikeya	God of War
kāyāpĕlût (NBH), *kayapluta*	transmigration of the soul
kāyāprĕwâêsh (NBH), *kayapravesha*	transmigration of the soul
khorore (JZH), *karor*	ten millions
khunt (NBH), *khanda*	region
Kirku (AD), Kratu	a son of Brahma
kirmo (AD), *karma*	cause and effect

Glossary

kirti (AD), *kriti* — action
Kishen (JZH, NBH), Krishna — an incarnation of Vishnu
  also Krěěshnă, Krishen
kittri (AD), *kshatriya* — the second division of castes
  also chehteree, koytri, sittri
Kolee (JZH), Kali — a goddess, also a demon
  also Cal, Collee, Kalee, Kallee
kŏŏndělēē (NBH), *kundala* — circle
Kŏŏrŏŏkshētră, (WH), Kurukshetra — a plain in northern India
Kooroos (WH), Kauravas — one of the families in the
  Mahabharata

kotah (JZH), *katah* — word
koyt (JZH), *kyastha* — writer caste
koytri (AD), *kshatriya* — the second division of castes
  also chehteree, kittri, sittri
Krěěshnă (CW),⎫ Krishna — an incarnation of Vishnu
Krishen (AD), ⎭
  also Kishen
kundherp (NBH), *gandharva* — a musician of paradise
kurnowa (AD), *karna* — hearing
Kytoo, (JZH), Kaitabha — a demon

lac (JZH), *lakh* — hundred thousand
ligger (JZH), *laghu* — a unit of time
loab (AD), *lobha* — lust
logue (JZH, NBH), *log* — people, a world
Luccon (JZH), Lakshmana — half-brother of Rama
udja (AD), *lajja* — shame

madda (AD), *mada* — female
Māhābāret (NBH),   ⎫ *Mahabharata* — an epic poem
Măhābhārăt (WH, CW),⎭
Mahadebtah (JZH), Mahadevata — a name of Shiva
mahāmoonee (NBH), *mahamuni* — great sage
mahaperley (AD),⎫ *mahapralaya* — destruction of the cosmos
mah-pirly (AD), ⎭
  also maperly
Mahasoor (JZH), Maheshvara — a name of Shiva
  also Moisoor
maha-tit (AD), *mahatattva* — the supreme intellect
Mahurr (NBH), *Mahar* — the heaven of Bhrigu
  also Moha
maiah (AD), *maya* — illusion
manus (AD), *manas* — mind
maperly (AD), *mahapralaya* — destruction of the cosmos
  also mahaperley, mah-pirly
mâsh (AD), *masha* — unit of time
mātrāng (NBH), *matranga* — length of a vowel sound
medda (AD), *majja* — a nerve
mhurd (JZH), *mard* — man
  also mirt
mirren (AD), *marana* — dying

296

Glossary

mirt (AD), *mard*	man
also mhurd	
mitterdro (AD), *mitradrohya*	friendship or enmity
Modoo (JZH), Madhu	a demon
Moha (AD), *Mahar*	the heaven of Bhrigu
also Mahurr	
mohat (AD), *mahat*	the supreme intellect
Moideb (JZH), Mahadeva	a name of Shiva
Moisasoor (JZH), Mahishasura	a demon
Moisoor (JZH), Maheshvara	a name of Shiva
also Mahasoor	
moiyah (JZH), *maiya*	woman
mon (JZH), *man*	mind
also mun	
mucht (AD), ⎰ *mukti*	freedom, release
muchti (AD), ⎱	
mun (JZH, AD), *man*	mind
also mon	
mund (AD), *manda*	evil
Mungĕl (NBH), *Mangala*	the planet Mars
munnee hurreneh (NBH), *malini harini*	a form of metre
Munnoo (JZH, NBH), ⎫	
Munnooah (JZH), ⎬ Manu	a founder of the human race
Munnuah (JZH), ⎭	
munnuntur (JZH), *manvantara*	the lifetime of a Manu
Murichi (AD), Marichi	a son of Brahma
murto (JZH), *martya*	matter
naat (AD), *natha*	'lord'
Narud (AD), Narada	a son of Brahma
nasiga (AD), *nasika*	sense of smell
Neadirsen (AD), *Nyaya darshana*	a philosophical school
Nĕkool (WH), Nakula	fourth of the Pandavas
nemish (AD), *nimesha*	a unit of time
also nimick	
nidakaar (AD),⎱ *nirakara*	formless
nid-akar (AD),⎰	
nimick (JZH), *nimesha*	a unit of time
also nemish	
nir (AD), *nar*	male
nirick (AD), *naraka*	hell
nisht (AD), *nashta*	destroyed
nitte (AD), ⎰ *nitya*	eternal
nitteh (AD),⎱	
obatar (AD), *avatara*	incarnation of a deity
also ootâr	
Obatar Bah Beda (AD), *Atharva Veda*	the fourth *Veda*
oderissa (AD), *adrishya*	invisible
onder (JZH), *andha*	dark
onderah (JZH), *andhera*	darkness
Ongira (AD), Angiras	a son of Brahma

Glossary

onnuman (AD), *anumana*	inference
ootâr (WH), *avatara*	incarnation of a deity
also obatar	
opādhee (NBH), *upadhi*	violent
opposs (AD), *upavasa*	a fast
ossoor (JZH, NBH), *asura*	demon
Ottal (AD), *Atala*	the first infernal region
Otteri (AD), Atri	a son of Brahma
oustmaan (JZH), *asman*	sky
paar (JZH), *pahar*	a unit of time
also par	
packa (AD), *paksha*	half a month
also pĕchĕ	
Pandoo (WH, CW), Pandu	son of Vyasa
Pandoos (WH), Pandavas	one of the families in the *Mahabharata*
pâr (AD), *pahar*	a unit of time
also paar	
particca (AD), *paratva*	distance
pattal (AD), *patala*	the infernal regions
pĕchĕ (NBH), *paksha*	half a month
also packa	
pereeth (JZH), *pitri*	an ancestor of humanity
perm-atmā (NBH), *paramatman*	the supreme soul
also pirrum attima, purmattima	
Phaugoon (NBH), *Phagun*	a month (February to March)
pir (AD), *pra*	first
pir-kirti (AD), *prakriti*	the unresolved substance of the universe
pirra-purra-purvesh (AD), *parapurvapravesha*	incarnation
pirrible (AD), *prithaktva*	difference
pirrim (AD), *parama*	supreme
pirrum attima (AD), *paramatman*	the supreme soul
also perm-atmā, purmattima	
Pooran (NBH, WH), *Purana*	a class of scripture
poottee (WH), *pothi*	compilation
Prichutt (NBH), Parikshit	ruler of Hastinapura
prittavi (AD), *prithivi*	earth
Pulista (AD), Pulastya	a son of Brahma
pull (JZH), *pala*	a unit of time
Pulla (AD), Pulaha	a son of Brahma
pungtee (AD), *pankti*	a metre
purman (AD), *puman*	soul
purmattima (AD), *paramatman*	the supreme soul
also perm-atmā, pirrum attima	
purrekeh (NBH), *parekha*	trial by ordeal
purriman (AD), *parimana*	magnitude
purrus (AD), *purusha*	soul of the universe
Raām (NBH), Rama	an incarnation of Vishnu
also Rhaam	

Glossary

rasan (AD), *rasana*	sense of taste
also rissina	
Rēbēē (NBH), *Ravi*	the sun
redjo-goon (AD), *rajas guna*	the quality of passion
Reig Beid (NBH), *Rig Veda*	the first *Veda*
also Rug Beda	
Rhaabon (JZH), Ravana	a demon
Rhaam (JZH), Rama	an incarnation of Vishnu
also Raām	
rhaanee (JZH), *rani*	female title of honour
rhaat (JZH), *rat*	night
ribbi (AD), *rabi*	season
ris (AD), *rasa*	flavour
Rissatal (AD), *Rasatala*	the sixth infernal region
rissina (AD), *rasana*	sense of taste
also rasan	
roy (NBH), *rai*	a title of honour
Rudder (AD), Rudra	a name of Shiva
Rug Beda (AD), *Rig Veda*	the first *Veda*
also Reig Beid	
rup (AD), *rupa*	form
sammabae (AD), *samavaya*	connexion
sammania (AD), *samanya*	quality held in common
also summania	
sangoog (AD), *samyoga*	connexion
sansah (JZH), *satsang*	unity of truth
satig (AD), *sattva*	goodness
Sawun (NBH), *Savan*	a month (July to August)
Sehādĕo (WH), *Sahadeva*	youngest of the Pandavas
senassey (AD), *sannyasi*	religious mendicant
Serwaesher (NBH), *Sarveshvara*	God
shanskan (AD), shanskar (AD), } *samskara*	mental impression
shastah (JZH), shaster (AD, NBH), } *shastra*	treatise
Sheham Beda (AD), *Sama Veda*	the third *Veda*
Shĕnīschĕr (NBH), *Shanishvara*	the planet Saturn
shĕtĕ (NBH), *sata*	hundred
Shibah (AD), Shiva	the Destroyer
also Sieb	
Shŏŏkrĕ (NBH), *Shukra*	the planet Venus
shraban (AD), *shravana*	hearing
shubardo (AD), *shabda*	sound
Shŭkeh Diew (NBH), Shukadeva	a sage
Sieb (JZH), Shiva	the Destroyer
also Shibah	
sinniha (AD), *sneha*	oiliness
Sinnoc (AD), Sanaka	a son of Brahma
Sinnunda (AD), Sananda	a son of Brahma
sirba-stirrup (AD), *sarvasarupa*	having all forms
sirika (AD), *samkhya*	number

Glossary

sittoh (AD), *satya*	truth
also suttee	
sittohgoon (AD), *sattva guna*	the quality of goodness
sittri (AD), *kshatriya*	the second division of castes
also chehteree, kittri, koytri	
smistee (NBH), *smriti*	inspired writing
Sōmĕ (NBH), *Soma*	the moon
Sonnatin (AD), Sanatana	a son of Brahma
Sonninkunar (AD), Sanatkumara	a son of Brahma
sooder (NBH), *shudra*	the fourth group of castes
also sudder	
subittera-dirsi (AD), *savardarshin*	all-seeing
suc (AD), *sukha*	contentment
also suck	
Succadit (JZH), Shaka	a dynasty of Scythians
suck (AD), *sukha*	contentment
also suc	
sudder (AD), *shudra*	the fourth group of castes
also sooder	
summania (AD), *samanya*	quality held in common
also sammania	
sundass (AD), *sandhyamsha*	evening twilight of Brahma
sundeh (AD), *sandhya*	morning twilight of Brahma
suppursina (AD), *sparshana*	sense of touch
supursa (AD), *sparsha*	touch
sur (AD), *svarga*	heaven
also surg, surgo, swergeh	
Surage (AD), *Surya*	the sun
also Surjee	
surba-birsi (AD), *sarvavarshin*	omnipresent
surg (AD), ⎫ *svarga*	heaven
surgo (AD),⎭	
also sur, swergeh	
Surjee (JZH), *Surya*	the sun
also Surage	
Sursuttee (JZH), Sarasvati	Goddess of Speech and Learning
sutch (JZH), *sach*	truth
Suttal (AD), *Satala*	the third infernal region
suttee (JZH, NBH), *satya*	truth
also sittoh	
Sutteh (AD), *Satya*	the heaven of Brahma
swergeh (NBH), *svarga*	heaven
also sur, surg, surgo	
tagoor (JZH), *thakur*	title of honour
tajee (NBH), *tazi*	Arab horse
also tazee	
Tallattal (AD), *Talatala*	the fourth infernal region
Tapu (AD), *Tapar*	the heaven of Viraj
also Tuppeh	
tarah (JZH), *terah*	thirteen

Glossary

tawass (AD), *tvac*	touch
tazee (NBH), *tazi*	Arab horse
also tajee	
teen (JZH), *tin*	three
tege (AD), *tejas*	light
tetrese (JZH), *tetis*	thirty-three
timmugoon (AD), *tamas guna*	the quality of inertia
tirtah (JZH, NBH),⎫ *treta* (*yuga*) tirteah (AD), ⎭	the second age
tise (JZH), *tis*	thirty
trese (JZH), *teis*	twenty-three
Tuppeh (NBH), *Tapar*	the heaven of Viraj
also Tapu	
upiman (AD),⎫ *upamana* upimen (AD),⎭	knowledge by analogy
Vēd (CW), ⎫ *Veda* Vêde (WH),⎭	the holiest scriptures
also Beda, Bêde, Beid	
Veĕcheĕtrăveĕrya (WH), Vichitravirya	a king in the *Mahabharata*
Veiâs (WH),⎫ Vyasa Vyās (CW), ⎭	legendary arranger of the scriptures
also Beäs, Beäss	
wār (NBH), *vara*	day of the week
yogue (NBH), *yuga*	an age
also jogue, jug, yoog	
Yoodhisteer (WH), Yudhishthira	the eldest Pandava
also Judishter	
yoog (CW), *yuga*	an age
also jogue, jug, yogue	
zinar (AD), *zunnar*	sacred thread

Index

The authors reproduced in this book are identified by their initials: JZH for Holwell, AD for Dow, NBH for Halhed, WH for Hastings, CW for Wilkins, WJ for Jones.

Index

Beligatti, Cassiano, 273
Belus, 217
Bengali language, 150, 151; European knowledge of, 9, 13, 188
Bentham, Jeremy, 11
Bernier, François, 21
Bettiah, 219, 240–1
Bhagavad Gita, 18, 19; cited by NBH, 162–3; cited by WJ, 267; CW's translation, 5, 12, 17, 28, 186–91, 192–5; account of by WH, 185–8; account of by CW, 193–5; account of by WJ, 233–4
Bhagavatamrita, 270, 282, 288
Bhagavat Purana, see Puranas
Bharata, 185, 249, 276, 277, 278; name of country, 150; war, 281, 287
Bhartrihari, 18
Bhavani, *see* Kali
Bhima, 185, 280
Bhrigu, 126, 211, 213
Bimbisara, 283
Blake, William, 12
Bochart, Samuel, *Geographia sacra*, 197, 204
Bogle, George, 170
Bossuet, Jacques-Bénigne, 23
Bouchet, Jean, 24
Boxhorn, Marcus Zuerius, 16
Brahma, 205, 211, 265, 266; compared to Abraham, 24, 33; representation of, 54–5, 102–3, 120, 138, 215; sons of, 125–6, 220, 227, 262, 274, 275; account of by JZH, 28, 54–5, 56–7, 68, 69, 71, 72, 77, 81, 92, 99, 100–3; account of by AD, 111, 112, 114–15, 120–6, 128–30, 138; account of by NBH, 145, 148, 152, 164, 165, 169; account of by WJ, 214, 215, 216, 217–18, 219, 223, 224, 234, 236, 243
Brahmaputra river, 219, 227
Brisson, Mathurin-Jacques, 219
Brothers, Richard, 8, 30
Bruton, William, 20–1
Bryant, Joseph, 256, 260; *New System of Ancient Mythology*, 239, 246–8
Brydone, Patrick, 158
Buddha: as Fo, 79, 255, 273; dating of, 36, 230, 255, 270–4, 280, 282, 283, 287, 288, 290; described by Jayadeva, 204, 269; identified with Odin,

255, 273; images of, 257, 271; account of by WJ, 209, 237, 259, 272; Buddhists as atheists, 135–6, 271
Budha, 160, 275
Burke, Edmund, 7, 11, 39
Buzurgmihr, 258–9

Cadmus, 197
Caesar, Julius, 197
Callimachus, 218, 233
Cassiopeia, 235
Caste: origin of, 59, 165; account of by JZH, 39, 60, 65; account of by AD, 114–15, 116; account of by NBH, 150, 165, 169, 174, 175, 180; account of by WJ, 216
   Brahmins: account of by JZH, 58–9; account of by AD, 109, 114–15, 117; account of by NBH, 170–1, 176, 180–1
Castor and Pollux, 234, 280
Celts, 260; Celtic language, 15, 252–3
Ceres, 203–4, 211–13, 217
Cervantes, Miguel, 167
Ceylon (Lanka, Sinhala), 50, 66, 129 229, 230, 249
Chaldea, *see* Babylonia
Chambers, Sir Robert, 20
Chandra, 101, 114, 235, 275
Chandrabija, 285, 286, 288
Chandragupta, 283, 284
Changez Khan, 286, 290
Charaka, 259
Charnock, Job, 97
Chateaubriand, François-René, Vicomte de, 17
Chillingworth, William, 242
China, 167, 193, 249; antiquity of, 1, 2, 25, 26, 32, 157; Buddhism in, 79, 255, 271–3; chronology of, 36, 197, 255, 273, 287; compared with India, 165, 196, 239, 260; language, 254; *see also* Confucianism
Chiron the Centaur, 32, 289
Chloris, 198
Christianity: Evangelicalism, 41–2, Roman Catholicism, 24, 48, 186, 245; *see also* Hinduism: comparisons with Christianity, Jesuits, Krishna
Cicero, 198; *de Natura Deorum*, 218, 226

303

Index

Index

Goths, 260; language, 15, 252; religion, 196, 273; *see also* Scythia

Goverdhana of Kashmir, 198, 270, 271, 273

Grant, Charles, 42

Greece, 3, 22, 23, 173, 278; Bactrians, 251, 286; Greek accounts of India, 3, 230, 242, 250, 251, 258; Greek astronomy, 160, 260; Greek chronology, 209, 265; Greek customs compared to Hindu, 168, 172; Greek language, 10, 15, 151, 246, 252, 253; Greek philosophy compared to Indian, 215, 243, 254–5; Greek religion, 46, 62–4, 72, 102, 103, 127, 196–245 *passim*, 254; *see also* Alexander the Great, Megasthenes, Plato

Gruter, Jan, 223

Guignes, Joseph de, 4, 36, 255, 273, 287

Guyon, Claude-Marie, 22–3, 47, 48

Halhed, Nathaniel Brassey (Preface, 140–83), 17, 41, 44, 241; career, 8–11, 141, 190; letter to East India Company, 141; letter to WH, 141; linguistic ability, 9–10, 12, 16, 140; on antiquity of Hindus, 15, 26, 30–1, 34, 36, 38, 158–62, 200; reception of, 34, 39–40, 42; religious beliefs, 29–30, 43; sources, 5, 19, 268

Hamilton, Alexander, 21

Hanuman, 229

Hastings, Warren (Letter to Smith, 184–91), 5, 9, 17; letter to East India Company, 140; letter from NBH, 141; letter from CW, 192; Oriental interests, 10, 13, 141, 157, 183, 189–90, 192, 193, 195, 268; verdict on Hinduism, 44, 186–7

Hayagriva, 205–7, 267–8

Hebrew language, 10, 211, 238, 246, 253

Hecate, 235, 237

Helios, 234

Hephaistos, *see* Vulcan

Herder, Johann Gottfried von, 17

Hermes, *see* Mercury

Herschell, Sir William, 235

Hesiod, 199

Hindi language, 239–40, 251–2

'Hindu', origin of name, 114, 149–50

Hinduism:
  brahman, 21, 40; JZH on, 54, 102; AD on, 121, 128, 139; NBH on, 156–7; CW on, 193–4; WJ on, 215
  calendar, 160
  chronology: European views on, 31–5, 37–8; *manvantaras*, 105, 263, 264, 266, 267, 274; *yugas*, 75, 79–82, 84, 105, 124, 137, 156, 158, 178, 193, 209–10, 264–6, 274; account of by JZH, 28–9, 75, 79–82, 84, 89, 104–5; account of by AD, 28, 112, 124; account of by NBH, 30–1, 158–63; account of by WJ, 35–7, 197, 207–10, 256, 262–90 *passim*; account of in *Laws of Manu*, 263
  comparisons with Christianity, 20–4, 25, 33, 38, 43; by JZH, 27, 67; by WH, 187–8; by WJ, 37, 343; *see also* Krishna
  comparisons with *Pentateuch*, 25, 33, 39, 43; by NBH, 147, 159, 161, 162, 172–81; by WJ, 37, 199–200, 242–3, 268
  cosmogony, 182; account of by JZH, 71–89, 98–105; account of by AD, 121–4; account of by NBH, 163–4, 165; account of by WJ, 212, 249; *Nyaya* version of, 131–4, 137; in *Upanishads*, 148–9
  ethical doctrines: European views on, 21–2; account of by JZH, 27, 69–71; account of by AD, 127, 137; account of by WJ, 258
  Ishvara: AD on, 121; NBH on, 157; WJ on, 216, 224–5, 226–7, 235
  marriage customs, 91, 116, 170
  Maya, 41, 207, 217; goddess, 226; mother of Buddha, 272, 273; AD on, 121; WJ on, 198, 215; *see also* *Vedanta*
  moksha: AD on, 123, 129, 133; NBH on, 149; WJ on, 237–8
  monism: European views on, 21, 40–1; AD on, 127, 132, 139; WJ on, 41; *see also* *Vedanta*
  monotheism: Hindus believed to be monotheists, 21, 31, 39; JZH on, 27, 66, 77, 101; AD on, 27, 126–7, 138–9; CW on, 193–4, WJ on, 40, 214–15.

Index

Index

Koran, 117, 119, 245
Krishna, 19, 52, 236, 252; comparisons with Christ, 24, 33, 243–4; dating of, 255–6, 270, 277; account of by JZH, 81, 82; account of by AD, 128, 129; account of by NBH, 145; account of by WH, 185–6; account of by CW, 193–5; account of by WJ, 207–8, 209, 220, 227, 230–4, 238, 243–4, 249
Krishna Chandra, Raja of Nadia, 241
Krishnamisra, *Prabodhachandrodaya*, 241
Kubera, 218
Kurukshetra, battle of, 193
Kushan, dynasty, 286
Kyd, Robert, 241

La Croze, Mathurin, Veyssière de, 61
La Grue, Thomas, 22, 23
Lakshmana, 82, 230
Lakshmi, 213, 218, 237
Lamartine, Alphonse-Marie-Louise de, 17
Lamennais, Hugues-Felicité-Robert de, 17
Langlès, Louis, 33
Lanka, *see* Ceylon
Latin, *see* Rome
Law, Thomas, 203
Le Gentil de La Galaisière, Guillaume-Joseph-Hyacinthe, 4, 32, 264, 265
Leibnitz, Gottfried Wilhelm, Baron von 16, 32
Locke, John 242, 244; *Reasonableness of Christianity*, 244
Lord, Henry, *Display of Two Forraigne Sects*, 21, 250
Lucan, 218
Lucian, 103
Lucretius, 103, 225–6
Lycurgus, 177

Madhu, 99, 100, 101, 207
Magadha, 253, 286; kings of, 282–5, 287
Magha, *Shishupalavadha*, 236
Mahabharata, 11, 68; account of by NBH, 19, 153, 156, 162; account of by WH, 184–5, 188; account of by CW, 193, 195; account of by WJ, 233, 255, 278; *see also Bhagavad Gita*
Mahesha, *Pandit*, 240

Mahishasura, 68, 71, 76, 77, 79, 80, 82, 89
Mahmud, of Ghazni, 290
Maistre, Joseph-Marie, Comte de, 17
Malabar rites, 24
Malava, tribe, 286
Mammata, 155
Manus, 37, 105, 160–1, 216; WJ on, 210, 211, 266–8, 274, 290; Satyavrata (Vaivasvata), 205–7, 211, 267, 274, 277; Svayambhuva, 211, 266, *Laws of Manu*, 16, 19, 264, 266; WJ on, 211; alleged citation by NBH, 159–61; cited by WJ, 216, 258, 262–3
Marathas, 286
Marichi, 125, 274
Mars, 160, 223, 236
Martin, Pierre, 21
Maurice, Rev. Thomas, 37–8, 41
Maurya, dynasty, 283, 284
Megasthenes, 242
Mercury, 160, 198–9, 256, 257, 273, 275
Mexico, 239, 254
Michelet, Jules, 17
Mignot, Etienne, 4, 41, 62
Mill, James, 43
Milton, John, 72, 78, 168, 188, 237
Minerva, 224, 227
Minos, 197, 211–12
Montesquieu, Charles de Secondat, Baron de, 142
Moses, 15, 207; Hindu equivalent, 24; writings influenced by Hinduism, 25, 26, 28, 33, 162, 199–200, 242–3; Mosaic Law, 39, 147, 171, 174, 176, 177, 180, 210; Priestley on, 34, 43; JZH on, 29; NBH on, 145, 158, 159, 161; WJ on, 35–7, 199–200, 211, 217, 242–3, 268, 278
Mugdha-Bodha, 113
Mughal empire, *see* Islam
Muhammad, 238, 244
Munis, 120, 126
Murray, Dr., 232
Musgrave, Samuel, 227

Nadir Shah, 290
Nakula, 185, 280
Nanda, 283, 287, 288, 290
Nandakamur, Maharaja, 171
Narada, 120–4, 126, 128–9, 236; *Naradiya-dharma-shastra*, 236

307

Index

Index

Index